History of Policing, Crime, Disorder, Punishment

Peter Joyce · Wendy Laverick

History of Policing, Crime, Disorder, Punishment

palgrave
macmillan

Peter Joyce
Department of Social and Life Sciences
Wrexham University
Wrexham, UK

Wendy Laverick
School of Criminology, Sociology
and Policing
University of Hull
Hull, UK

ISBN 978-3-031-36891-2 ISBN 978-3-031-36892-9 (eBook)
https://doi.org/10.1007/978-3-031-36892-9

This Palgrave Macmillan imprint is published by the registered company Springer Nature Switzerland AG
The registered company address is: Gewerbestrasse 11, 6330 Cham, Switzerland

To Julie, Emmeline and Eleanor

and

To Benjamin, Charlie, Joseph, Emily, Bethany and Lee

Preface

Both of the authors are criminologists whose impetus for writing this work is to provide students of criminology with a flavour of the social, economic and political background that is relevant to key areas of criminological and penological study and within which the criminal justice system developed. In so doing, it illustrates that criminology draws upon many academic disciplines, in particular asserting how historical issues and events and sociological and political debates weave a tapestry within which crime, criminology, penology and the development of the criminal justice system can be studied.

The scope of the book is ambitious—covering the period 1689–1920. In addition to discussing crime, issues related to crowd behaviour, public order and politically motivated violence are considered to highlight their importance in shaping the way in which state responses to all forms of crime were fashioned.

This book is written as a text book and considerations of length mean that it can do little more than scratch the surface of the large range of issues that it considers. It aims, therefore, to provide students of criminology who may have little or no knowledge of history and politics with a grounding that equips them for more detailed study of the concerns and considerations that form the substance of the book.

In addition to considering crime, the book pays particular attention to public disorder and social unrest. In order to illustrate these issues, a small selection of key events associated with crowd behaviour and disorder from 1689 to 1920 are covered, seeking to provide some introductory knowledge of some of the main issues that helped shape the content and implementation of the state's response to public disorder. This includes the role of the military in civilian affairs and the concept of 'high policing'.

The book is organised into four parts. Parts I and II are organised chronologically, giving coverage to the period 1689–1850. Part III, however, is subject specific, dealing with the development of professional policing in this period. This material is organised as a discrete part of the book as it covers ideas and actions that occurred across the period covered in Parts I and II of this work. Part IV is organised chronologically, dealing with a range of issues, including policing, that relate to the development of criminological and penological thought and to criminal justice policy that took place in the period 1850–1920.

Reforms that occurred to criminal justice policy between 1689 and 1920 took place within the context of broader administrative, economic, political and social changes that in particular affected the role performed by the central state.

Initially the reforms that occurred in the early decades of the nineteenth century resulted in the professionalisation of service delivery within a state that remained highly decentralised. Local government played an important role in service delivery while other public services such as the New Poor Law were delivered by localised machinery subject to central inspection which was designed to ensure that Parliament's wishes were put into effect. The inspection procedure also applied to factories and mines so that dents were made in the doctrine of laissez faire whereby owners and manufacturers could not conduct their businesses totally free from government-imposed restrictions.

Nonetheless, the term 'nightwatchman state' (Townshend, 2000: 15) was applied to the minimal government that arose during this period, which was further justified by accusations of ineffectiveness in the operations of the regulatory regime imposed through the process of inspection (see, for example, Bartrip, 1983: 69 in relation to the immediate impact of the 1833 Factory Act).

However, as the nineteenth century progressed, the central state secured additional powers and this trend was enhanced by developments that took place in the late nineteenth and early years of the twentieth century, inspired by concerns of national decline and the need for national efficiency (which was encouraged by British shortcomings displayed during the Second Boer War, 1899–1902) and by an awareness of social problems such as urban poverty which served to popularise collectivist sentiments (and political organisations that were inspired by such perspectives) at the expense of individualism.

Although the social reforms performed by post-1905 Liberal governments reflected a blend individualism and collectivism (in the sense that although state action became viewed as legitimate to uphold individual rights [especially social rights], the need for the individual to take some responsibility for his or her own circumstances was not entirely abandoned being reflected, for example, in the contributory aspect made by employees in the 1911 National Insurance Act towards costs arising from unemployment and ill health). However, War 1 enhanced the importance of the interventionist, collective state and the period especially witnessed considerable state interventions in economic and social life.

Reference will be made, where appropriate, to criminal justice initiatives that sit within the broader context which has been briefly outlined above. However, the periodisation used in this book does not seek to precisely mirror these broad changes but, rather, aims to illustrate how the development of criminal justice policy was influenced by factors that were unique to crime, disorder and the state's response.

These include discussions as to how changes to what has been referred to as the 'penal temper of society' (Hudson, 2003: 96) influenced the aims and methods of punishment, the importance of public disorder in fashioning the state's physical responses to crowd behaviour and how developments affecting the nature and character of crime influenced the development and responses of key criminal justice agencies such as the police service.

Sociological perspectives on the rationale of punishment (as outlined by Joyce and Laverick, 2023: 364–70) further provide an understanding as to why the aims of punishment and the manner in which those aims were delivered change over historical time periods and the contribution made by key figures that include Emile Durkheim, Max Weber and Michel Foucault are considered within this work.

We would finally like to thank our commissioning editor, Josie Taylor, and our editorial assistant, Sarah Hills, at Palgrave for the help and support they have given us while undertaking this project. Particular thanks is due to the helpful comments of the reviewers who looked at both the proposal and the completed manuscript.

Wrexham, UK
Hull, UK
May 2023

Peter Joyce
Wendy Laverick

References

Bartrip, P. (1983). "State Intervention in Mid-Nineteenth Century Britain: Fact or Fiction?" *Journal of British Studies, 23*(1), 63–83.

Hudson, B. (2003). *Understanding Justice* (2 ed.). Open University Press.

Joyce, P., & Laverick, W. (2023). *Criminal Justice: An Introduction* (4th ed.). Routledge.

Townshend, C. (2000). *The Oxford History of Modern War.* Oxford University Press.

Contents

List of Figures

Part I

Crime and Punishment, 1689–1750

1

Introduction

The 1689 Bill of Rights and the English Legal System

Introduction

This chapter serves as an introduction for a wide range of issues that are the subject of this book. It covers the period from 1689 (the enactment of the Bill of Rights) until around 1750. The 1689 Bill of Rights is an important statement of the rights and liberties of English people and this chapter briefly examines the events that led up to its enactment. It then moves on to consider the operations of the criminal justice system in the period 1689–1750, discussing the way in which breaches of the law were punished and within the context of evaluating the diverse aims that society may wish to accomplish through punishment, evaluates the nature and rationale for the methods of punishment that were deployed in this period to combat crime and disorder.

P. Joyce and W. Laverick, *History of Policing, Crime, Disorder, Punishment*,
https://doi.org/10.1007/978-3-031-36892-9_1

Monmouth's Rebellion and the 1689 Bill of Rights

In February 1685, Prince James, Duke of York, became King of England, Scotland and Ireland on the death of his brother, Charles II. Initially there was no significant opposition to his accession arising from the fear that excluding him could result in a re-run of the civil wars that had engulfed England, Scotland and Ireland between 1639 and 1651. Additionally, at that stage his religion was not universally viewed as a long-term problem since the heir presumptive, his daughter Mary, was a Protestant.

Monmouth's Rebellion and the 'Bloody Assizes'

However, some initial dissent materialised to his rule in the form of Monmouth's rebellion in 1685. Monmouth claimed that as Charles' son, he was the rightful heir to the throne and he had some political support from the Whigs of the Country Party (Granucci, 1969: 853).

Monmouth landed in Lyme Regis on 11 June 1685 and was able to secure recruits to his cause from the local population in the South West which was strongly protestant. Small-scale skirmishes with local militias took place (such as at Bridport on 14 June and Axminster the following day) but Monmouth's army was unable to capture Bristol from where it was planned to march on London. The rebellion finally ended with Monmouth's defeat at the battle of Sedgemoor on 6 July 1685.

Monmouth's ventures in the South West of England were accompanied by a rebellion in Scotland headed by Archibald Campbell, the Earl of Argyll. This enjoyed an initial success with the capture of Ardkinglass castle but disagreements within the ranks of the rebels resulted in the rebellion petering out.

As with the Rye House plot of 1683 (that sought to assassinate King Charles II of England and his brother James, Duke of York), the government's response was brutal. Lord Chief Justice George Jeffreys was despatched to the South West to head a commission of senior judges who would try those involved in the rising in what became known as the 'Bloody Assizes'. This was a series of trials in different West Country venues in which persons alleged to have been involved in the rising and who were tried for treason or for other offences such as spreading false news were mainly executed (around 320) or sentenced to transportation (around 800). Those who were executed were hung, drawn and quartered. Monmouth (who had been the subject of a Bill of Attainder passed by Parliament on 13 June which sentenced him to death as a traitor without the need for any trial to take place) was, following his capture, executed on 15 July 1685 at Tower Hill.

Box 1.1: Judge Jeffreys and the 'Bloody Assizes'

George Jeffreys was born in 1645. In 1668 he began a career in the law and became the Duke of York's Solicitor General in 1676. He was knighted the following year. He subsequently obtained a number of promotions and honours, becoming Lord Chief Justice in 1683.

In 1685, Jeffreys led a team of six judges (the others being Sir William Montague, Sir Robert Wright, Sir Francis Wythens, Sir Creswell Levinz and Sir Henry Pollexfen) to head up a special commission to try around 1400 persons who had been involved in Monmouth's rebellion. These trials were held at various places in the West Country.

Judge Jeffreys embodied the harsh, unforgiving nature of the late seventeenth-century judicial system in which retribution based on the principle of *lex talionis* was emphasised. The manner in which the trials were conducted was designed to extract confessions from the accused, who was perhaps totally unfamiliar with English legal procedures and was thus confused, if not scared. During proceedings, a plea-bargaining agreement was made whereby those who pleaded guilty would not be executed, although this arrangement was not always adhered to subsequently (Granucci, 1969: 854).

The sentences handed out were severe. Most of the accused were condemned to death although only around 300 executions took place. However, as was traditional for those convicted of treason, the condemned men were hung, drawn and quartered, and their heads were taken and displayed on spikes in several towns around South West England. Over 800 others who were found guilty were transported to the West Indies.

However, it has been argued that while Jeffreys 'was harsh in his judgements', it was the case that 'the law of the land demanded the death penalty in all cases of treason and it was the prerogative of the king to grant mercy' (Carradice, 2014: [Online]). Once the jury determined guilt, the trial judge had no discretion in the matter.

In the wake of the Assizes, James II appointed Jeffreys as Chancellor in 1685 and he took the title of Baron Jeffreys of Wem.

Following the crushing of the rebellion, James II sought to consolidate his power. Attempts were made to secure the repeal of the 1678 and 1681 Test Acts (which prevented Catholics from holding public offices) and the Habeas Corpus Act. Catholics were appointed to senior posts within the government and the size of the standing army was raised. However, the refusal of the Scottish and English Parliaments to repeal the Test Acts and unease over the King's appointment of Catholic army officers led James to suspend ('prorogue') Parliament on 20 November 1685. Instead, he governed through the use of the royal prerogative, thus raising the fears of absolutist rule. James, it appeared to his enemies was both a Papist and a would-be tyrant (Deacon, 1980: 79).

Following the legal case of *Godden v. Hales* (1686), the Monarch's ability to exercise prerogative powers to suspend provisions of the Test Acts was confirmed and he then appointed several Catholic Peers to serve in his Privy Council. In April 1687, he issued a Declaration of Indulgence which suspended penal laws against Catholics and also granted religious toleration to some Protestant dissenters. Parliament was dissolved in the Summer of 1687 and the King began to canvass support for the repeal of the Test Acts.

The Declaration of Indulgence was re-issued in 1688 and the King ordered that it be read in every Church. A request by the Archbishop of Canterbury and 6 other Bishops that he reconsider this led to them being locked up in the Tower of London, awaiting trial for seditious libel. This decision led to anti-Catholic riots in England and Scotland and created disaffection among the traditionally loyal Tory-Anglican establishment who had supported James during the 1679–1681 Exclusion crisis on condition that the primacy of the Church of England was upheld and who viewed the trial as a further attack on the position and status of the Church of England.

Two events then exerted a significant erosion of James' power. On 10 June 1688 his son James, Francis Edward Stuart, was born. He replaced Mary as the heir presumptive which raised the prospect of the creation of a Catholic dynasty, and the absolutist features that had been displayed by Louis XIV in France whose 1685 Edict of Fontainebleau ended religious toleration for protestants (and which also led to many French Huguenots fleeing to England). Other examples of Protestant persecution (such as the killing of around 2000 Vaudois Protestants in Savoy in 1686) had raised the spectre of a Catholic counter reformation which now became a realistic possibility in England.

The second blow to the King occurred on 30 June, when all seven bishops were acquitted, leaving James' political authority in tatters (Harris, 2006: 235–236). Additionally, there was a fear that the new Parliament that would be summoned in the Autumn of 1688 would provide the King with sufficient of his supporters to finally repeal the Test Acts.

The 'Glorious Revolution' and the 1689 Bill of Rights

Opposition to the rule of James II formed the background to the 'Glorious Revolution' of 1688 which entailed William, the Protestant stadtholder of Holland (and who had married his cousin, James' daughter Mary in 1677), landing—the word 'invasion' is disputed by historians of this period—at Torbay on 5 November 1688.

William's interests in doing so were in part to prevent a Catholic English monarch cementing a formal alliance with the French which would be contrary to the interests of Holland and instead to harness English resources on his side against them. He was also aware that opposition in England to the rule of James could lead to a rising which carried with it the possibility of the creation of a Republic which was also deemed contrary to Holland's interests. However, he was willing to invade only if invited to do so by leading English statesmen. Such an invitation was sent on 18 June, which cited widespread dissatisfaction with James' rule and especially drew attention to its intrusions on their religion, liberties and properties. It was signed by the 'Immortal Seven', consisting of the Lords Shrewsbury, Devonshire, Danby and Lumley and by Henry Compton, Edward Russell and Henry Sydney.

William had considerable support in England, Scotland and elsewhere in Europe. His initial landing took place at Torbay set off waves of anti-Catholic rioting across England. Military successes (such as the capture of Exeter on 9 November and Plymouth on 18 November) occurred in the South West and elsewhere in England, especially in the North where many nobles declared their allegiance to William. Minor skirmishes occurred but convinced his army was unreliable, James disbanded it. He was captured on 11 December and William entered London on 18 December. James was allowed to leave for France on 23 December. Subsequent attempts by James to regain the throne were repulsed, most notably at the Battle of the Boyne in July 1690.

William assumed control of a provisional government on 23 December that was created by the Peers of the Realm and he convened and assembly consisting of surviving Members of Parliament of Charles II's reign which called for an English Convention Parliament which would determine the succession to the English throne. This was elected on 5 January and convened on 22 January. Following debates as to whether William should be King, or act as regent in James' name or serve as Mary's consort, the situation was resolved on 13 February whereby both William and Mary accepted the throne on the basis of serving as joint Monarchs. In June a similar settlement was made for Scotland.

Before they were crowned on 11 April, William and Mary endorsed the 1689 Bill of Rights which had been drawn up by the Convention Parliament. This listed 12 policies through which it was alleged James had sought to 'subvert and extirpate' the protestant religion and the laws and liberties of the Kingdom and which provided a statement to assert the Nation's 'ancient rights and liberties'. This document confirmed the primacy of Parliament over the Crown through provisions that included the illegality of prerogative suspending and dispensing powers, the prohibition of taxation without parliamentary consent and the need for regular parliaments (which ultimately gave rise to the 1694 Triennial Act and later the 1716 Septennial Act). Following the coronation, in May 1689, Parliament passed the Toleration Act which gave freedom of worship to a number of protestant denominations, but not to Catholics.

The 1689 Bill of Rights is regarded as a cornerstone of the freedoms of English people—a statement of their fundamental rights and liberties. Absolutist monarchy in England was finally laid to rest and in its place was a constitutional monarchy which entailed Parliament playing a major role in the subsequent governing of the country. Key civil rights and political liberties were granted to English people who were now freed from the tyrannical government exercised by the Monarch.

Further reforms in this direction were provided for in the 1701 Act of Settlement. This included.

- Imposing a stipulation to require that the removal of judges had to be instigated by Parliament as opposed to being a unilateral decision of the Monarch, thereby upholding the principle of judicial independence from the Monarch
- Preventing the Monarch from issuing a Royal Pardon in order to save an office holder from being impeached by Parliament.

The rights and liberties provided for by the measures in 1689 and 1701 formed the launch pad for future developments which included the 1998 Human Rights Act. The Bill of Rights also was important to other nations, in particular the American Constitution that was drawn up in 1789.

Box 1.2: The Bill of Rights

The Bill of Rights set out a number of basic entitlements that all 'Englishmen' should be able to exercise and sought to delineate the powers of Parliament in relationship to the Monarch, thereby providing the basis of a constitutional monarchy (Joyce & Wain, 2010: 264). The main provisions of the Bill of Rights were:

1. That the pretended power of suspending of laws, or the execution of laws, by regal authority, without consent of Parliament, is illegal. ['Suspending' laws referred to stopping laws from taking effect in general, while 'dispending' with laws meant not applying them to particular individuals.]
2. That the pretended power of dispensing with laws, or the execution of laws by regal authority, as it hath been assumed and exercised of late, is illegal.
3. That the commission for erecting the late Court of Commissioners for Ecclesiastical causes, and all other commissions and courts of like nature, are illegal and pernicious.
4. That levying money for or to the use of the Crown, by pretence of prerogative, without grant of Parliament, for longer time or in other manner than the same is or shall be granted, is illegal.
5. That it is the right of the subjects to petition the King, and all commitments and prosecutions for such petitioning are illegal.
6. That the raising or keeping a standing army within the kingdom in time of peace, unless it be with consent of Parliament, is against law.
7. That the subjects which are Protestants may have arms for their defence suitable to their conditions, and as allowed by law.
8. That election of members of Parliament ought to be free. That the freedom of speech, and debates or proceedings in Parliament, ought not to be impeached or questioned in any court or place out of Parliament.
9. That excessive bail ought not to be required, nor excessive fines imposed; nor cruel and unusual punishments inflicted.
10. That jurors ought to be duly impanelled and returned, and jurors which pass upon men in trials for high treason ought to be freeholders.
11. That all grants and promises of fines and forfeitures of particular persons before conviction, are illegal and void.
12. And that for redress of all grievances, and for the amending, strengthening, and preserving of laws, Parliaments ought to be held frequently.

(Magnacartaplus, 2000: [Online]).

The provision in the Bill of Rights outlawing 'cruel and unusual punishments' has been the subject of historical debate. It did not apply to methods of punishment that today would be viewed as cruel and inhumane: drawing and quartering, beheading and burning females at the stake persisted long after the Bill was approved. The view that it was directed at the excesses of the 'Bloody Assizes' has been challenged by Granucci (1969: 855–9) who instead argued that it was influenced by the punishments inflicted on the Anglican cleric, Titus Oates. His allegation of a 'Popish Plot' in 1678 involving Jesuits intending to kill King Charles II and place his Catholic brother, the Duke of York, later James II) on the throne led to the executions of over 30 persons alleged to have been involved in it.

Oates' allegations were subsequently adjudged to constitute perjury for which he was punished by a sentence of life imprisonment, a fine, whippings, pilloring and being de-frocked as a clergyman. The issue regarding this, according to Granucci (1969: 859) was that such punishments constituted 'a severe punishment unauthorized by the state and not within the jurisdiction of the court to impose'. This, Granucci argued, was the target of this provision of the Bill of Rights which also embraced a rejection of disproportionate penalties (Granucci, 1969: 860).

The provision that forbade the Monarch from keeping a standing army in peace time without Parliament's consent was of particular relevance to later concerns regarding the creation of a professional police force. This issue will be considered later in this work.

The Punishment of Crime—The Juridical Perspective

Before commencing a discussion of the manner in which seventeenth- and eighteenth-century society punished crime, it is first necessary to see what objectives governed the infliction of punishment on offenders—what did society attempt to achieve through punishment? This section will consider the diverse aims with which punishment can be associated through historical time periods.

Strategies that are based upon what is termed the 'juridical perspective' (Hudson, 2003: 15) are rooted in moral and political philosophy. These are distinct from sociological approaches in that they have a practical application that seeks to link punishment with a desired outcome—what purpose does society wish to achieve through punishment? There are a number of approaches associated with this perspective which are discussed below.

Reductivism

Reductivist theories of punishment draw heavily from utilitarian perspectives on punishment. These derive from the approach towards crime with classicist criminology whose key proponents included Cesare Beccaria and Jeremy

Bentham and whose key belief regarding crime was that individuals were rational beings whose choice to commit crime derived from a calculation as to whether the benefits they would receive outweighed the disadvantages they might suffer if caught. Such ideas would, in the latter decades of the twentieth century, inform routine activities theory (Cohen & Felson, 1979), rational choice theory (Cornish & Clarke, 1987) and underpin situational methods of crime prevention (Clarke, 1992).

A key concern of these political-moral philosophers was how to prevent criminal actions from occurring in society. Their view, as will be considered later in Chapter 5 was to promote a criminal justice system that was predictable in its outcomes so that a potential offender, as a rational being, would know exactly the penalties that would derive from committing crime. They were reductivists in that their outlook was fixed on the future and not the past. Reductivism may be carried out by a wide range of strategies including deterrence and incapacitation (which entails depriving an offender of his or her liberty), or programmes that seek to secure the reform and rehabilitation of offenders.

However, a particular problem with all reductivist strategies is whether behaviour can be altered through punishment (whatever form it takes) since while punishment may temporarily suppress antisocial behaviour, the previous behaviour may return once the punishment is removed (Huesmann & Podolski, 2003: 77). Accordingly, it is also necessary to identify and remove the factors which underpin that behaviour in order to prevent future offending: 'people must "internalise" mechanisms that regulate behaviour so that in the absence of the threat of punishment, they will choose not to act aggressively—not because of the threat of punishment, but because they agree with the behaviour which has been taught' (Huesmann & Podolski, 2003: 78).

Reductivism is associated with several approaches that are considered below.

Deterrence

Deterrence may be individual or general. Individual deterrence seeks to influence the future behaviour of a single convicted offender whereas general deterrence seeks to influence the future actions of the public at large. In common with classicist criminology, deterrence views offenders as rational beings who calculate the costs and benefits of their behaviour, and individual and general deterrence also assume that a consensus exists within society as to what constitutes punishment (Fleisher, 2003: 101). A major problem with deterrence is that it ignores the possibility that crime may be a spontaneous act, propelled by factors that override logical considerations. An alternative view associated with postmodernist criminology suggests that people engage in crime because of its seductive quality, providing them with a thrill it provides that enables them to escape from what is otherwise a humdrum existence (Katz, 1988). It is also unclear whether the certainty of detection or the certainty of punishment is the key factor that deters a criminal act.

Individual deterrence may be delivered in a variety of ways. These include the imposition of severe custodial conditions on an offender which are designed to encourage him or her to refrain from future offending behaviour to avoid a further, and perhaps more severe and/or lengthier, repetition of these unpleasant circumstances.

General deterrence has a broader remit, that of influencing the behaviour of those who might be tempted to commit crime. In addition to severe custodial conditions, this approach may entail severe penalties (which in the period that is discussed in this chapter included the death penalty) based on the assumption that it would be illogical for a person to commit an action attached to dire consequences which contradicted the human impulse to preserve his or her life. However, this approach is based upon the classicist criminological assumption that humans are rational beings and further implies that the behaviour of all members of the general public can be influenced by similar factors and that it is possible to precisely identify what level of punishment will prevent a criminal act from being committed.

Box 1.3: Hanged, Drawn and Quartered

The punishment of being publicly hanged, drawn and quartered was the ultimate manifestation of the purpose of punishment as a deterrent, to dissuade others from undertaking the course of action that led to this sentence being administered.

It was reserved as a penalty for men convicted of high treason. Women convicted of a similar crime were, for reasons of public decency, burned at the stake. The penalty of being hung, drawn and quartered was intermittently practised during the thirteenth century, being inflicted on the Welsh Prince David ap Gruffudd in 1283, and became the statutory penalty for this offence in 1352.

It entailed the victim being hanged almost to the point of death. He was then emasculated (which entailed the penis and testicles being cut off), following which he was beheaded. Ultimately, the body was cut into 4 pieces which were displayed in locations across the country (*'pour encourager les autres*')—a constant reminder of the fate that awaited any who acted in a similar manner.

Michel Foucault (1977: 3–8) provides a graphic account of this penalty in connection with the execution in France of Robert-François Damiens in 1757 for the crime of regicide—an attempt to kill the then King of France, Louis XV.

Foucault was especially concerned with explaining the historic manner in which those in power were able to enforce their will over the population and the execution that he described indicated that they sought to achieve this through what he termed control over the body (Foucault, 1977: 15). Punishments that would now be regarded as barbaric were used to achieve this intention. It was administered in public to make it a spectacle to be viewed by an audience which would serve to reinforce its deterrent nature by terrifying people into being subservient to their rulers.

In England, this penalty (which had been inflicted on Robert the Bruce in 1305 and Guy Fawkes and the other 'Gunpowder Plotters' in 1606) was last used in 1782 in connection with the spying activities alleged to have been committed by David Tyrie. This sentence was also passed in connection with the execution of Colonel Edward Despard and 6 of his fellow co-conspirators in what was known as the Despard Plot in 1802 to assassinate the King and overthrow the government. However, this sentence was commuted to hanging and beheading when it was administered in 1803.

The penalty of disembowelling was ended by the 1814 Treason Act and the sentence of beheading and quartering was officially abolished under the provisions of the Forfeiture Act, 1870.

Incapacitation

Incapacitation is a reductivist strategy in that it removes an offender's ability to engage in future offending behaviour by a range of methods that include physically removing them from society either temporarily or permanently. In the period being discussed in this chapter, this goal was implemented through transportation but was later associated with imprisonment or the use of other methods to restrict a law-breaker's physical ability to reoffend. Its association with a tough approach to crime is associated with retributivist ideas which place the potential victims of crime at the forefront of its concerns by seeking to protect society from the actions of criminals.

Reform and Rehabilitation

Punishment may be inflicted on those convicted of crime with a view to using the period over which the punishment is administered as a means of changing their personal values and habits so that their future behaviour conforms to mainstream social standards. The aim of punishment is thus to take away an offender's desire to reoffend.

As will be discussed in Chapter 5, penal reformers in the late eighteenth and early nineteenth centuries (whether driven by evangelical or utilitarian impulses) viewed prisons as an arena in which bad people could be transformed into good and useful members of society. Reform and rehabilitation may entail programmes directed at tackling the cause of offending behaviour, which in the period being considered were delivered in prison but were subsequently administered in the community (or a combination of both). A difficulty with this approach is the effectiveness of the programmes that are delivered in overcoming other impulses (such as attitudes and beliefs) that may induce a person to commit crime.

Retributivism

The various strategies associated with reductivism focus their concern on future behaviour. Punishment is justified because it may persuade a person or persons not to subsequently indulge in criminal actions. An alternative approach, retributivism, is backward-looking, in that punishment is justified in relation to offending behaviour which has already taken place.

Retributivism insists 'that punishment is justified solely by the offender's desert and blameworthiness in committing the offence' (Lacey, 2003: 176). Expressed simply, criminals are punished because they deserve it. It is based on the Old Testament principle of lex talionis ('an eye for an eye and a tooth for a tooth') which is generally considered as a 'law of retribution' (Granucci, 1969: 844). Although retribution is exacted in an impersonal manner by an agent acting on behalf of the state, this approach to punishment may be viewed (especially by those on the receiving end of it) as akin to vengeance, enabling society to 'get its own back' on those who commit criminal acts. This perception arises if it is felt that the main rationale for inflicting pain on transgressors is for pain's sake which assumes priority over a desire to bring about their rehabilitation (Lacey, 2003: 176).

Retributivism is an approach that is associated with tough responses to crime which include capital punishment which in the period being considered in this chapter could incorporate the offender being hanged, drawn and quartered. A difficulty with this approach is that the deliberate infliction of violence by the state may legitimise the use of violence by its citizens, thus potentially increasing rather than decreasing the overall level of crime. Additionally, the widespread use of such a penalty undermined the classicist belief in the proportionality of punishments which, in part, was also advocated in order to secure their consistent application since the death penalty was not always regularly applied to crimes to which this form of punishment applied.

Denunciation

Retributivist responses to crime may be delivered by strategies that emphasise society views crime as unacceptable. Punishment thus constitutes a public censure or denunciation of this form of behaviour (Duff, 1986). In the words of Lord Denning, 'the ultimate justification of punishment is not that it is a deterrent, but that it is the emphatic denunciation by the community of a crime' (Lord Denning, quoted in Cavadino & Dignan, 1992: 41).

This implies that punishment is justified not because it influences the behaviour of others to refrain from committing similar acts but simply because it expresses society's abhorrence of crime, an approach that is termed 'expressive denunication' (Cavadino & Dignan, 1992: 42). This argument has been presented with specific reference to prisons where it has been contested that 'the separation of prisoners from the rest of society represents a clear statement that physical and social exclusion is the price of nonconformity' (Matthews, 1999: 26).

However, in the period being discussed in this chapter, denunciation also embraced any form of punishment that was delivered in public, including execution and actions such as branding and placing an offender in the stocks or the pillory, methods of punishment which also served to shame and humiliate the offender.

It has also been argued that the role played by punishment in articulating the disapproval of the public towards criminal actions helps to set the boundaries of society—'we collectively define what sort of people we are by denouncing the type of people we are not' (Davies, 1993: 15). It is in this sense that punishment may confirm the core values which hold society together. This argument has been further developed into the view of punishment as an expression of the rational will of citizens who, by entering into a social contract, expect that those who violate the rules of society should be punished (Rawls, 1972).

However, such views imply that a consensus exists within society regarding right and wrong behaviour and that criminals possess alternative values and beliefs which are at variance with those of mainstream society. Although such an opinion is voiced by subcultural theorists such as Albert Cohen (1955), it is challenged by other criminological approaches: see the discussion of arguments in Joyce and Laverick (2023a: 18–20) that relate to techniques of neutralisation (Sykes & Matza, 1957) and subterranean values (Matza & Sykes, 1961) which reject the existence of deviant subcultures.

As denunciation focuses on behaviour that has been committed in the past, it is usually regarded as a means through which a retributive response to crime is delivered. The public nature of executions during the eighteenth and much of the nineteenth century (until ended in 1868) theoretically gave citizens the ability to voice their disapproval of the actions of criminals as they were paraded through the streets—but this reaction was not always guaranteed if the criminal was popular in the public estimation.

Denunciation may also serve other aims, including the reductivist intention of deterrence in which case it maybe argued that denunciation is a hybrid of reductivist and retributivist approaches to the punishment of crime.

Methods Used to Punish Crime in the Eighteenth Century

The distinction between felonies, misdemeanours and summary offences underpinned the manner in which crime was punished in the eighteenth century. These terms refer to the seriousness with which the crimes associated with them were taken by society.

The Death Penalty

The penalty for felonies was invariably that of death and this extended to many crimes that would now be regarded as minor ones. The number of crimes for which people could be executed grew considerably during the eighteenth century, from around 50 in 1688 to 225 by 1815 (McLynn, 1989: ix), the great bulk of which were property crimes (Seal, 2008: 16), thus asserting the function of the law as a guarantor of property (Hay, 2011: 18). Crimes of this nature included arson, burglary and housebreaking and theft and it was observed that 'breaking and entering private property with felonious intent was the most commonly encountered capital crime of the eighteenth century' (McLynn, 1989: 87). Factors that included the expansion of trade and wealth enhanced opportunities to commit crime (Hay, 2011: 20) and with this expansion, the criminal law was augmented with 'more laws to protect particular types of property' from theft and malicious damage (Hay, 2011: 21, 22).

This extent to which capital punishment existed gave rise to a description of the legal system as the 'Bloody Code' and depicted the criminal law as being 'nine-tenths concerned with upholding a radical division of property' and in which the courts were 'a selective instrument of class justice' (Hay, 2011: 26, 35 and 48). The 1723 Waltham Black Act formed an important part of this Code. However, this view of the criminal law as an instrument seeking to subjugate and maintain order among the population has been disputed by arguments that included the law not being used in a consistently oppressive manner by persons of property and that Magistrates before whom property offences were tried often attempted to resolve the matter without the need for a trial to take place (Emsley, 2018: 9–10). The rationale for this was the maintenance of social order based upon the judicious use of mercy. As Hay (2011: 62–3) argued

> Eighteenth century England ... was a society with a bloody penal code, an astute ruling class who manipulated it to their advantage, and a people schooled in the lessons of Justice, Terror and Mercy. The benevolence of rich men to poor, and all the ramifications of patronage, were upheld by the sanction of the gallows and the rhetoric of the death sentence.

This issue will be returned to later in this chapter.

When the death penalty was used, the method of execution was generally that of hanging. For much of the eighteenth century in London this generally took place at Tyburn (close to the present day Marble Arch in London) to where the convict was conveyed from Newgate Prison in an open cart.

Box 1.4: The Hanging Parade

For much of the eighteenth century in London, most executions took place at Tyburn, although some took place at Smithfield and Tower Hill and also at Newgate prison. Between 1571 and 1783 about 1100 men and almost 100 women were hanged at Tyburn (The Proceedings of the Old Bailey, 2018a: [Online]). The majority of these consisted of poor people, it is pointed out that 'workplace theft, begging and vagrancy, prostitution, petty theft, shoplifting, and receiving of stolen goods are all points on the continuum linking poverty and criminality' (Shore, 2003: 144).

What was termed the 'Hanging Parade' reinforced the intention of executions to exercise a deterrent effect and also to bring shame and inflict suffering on an offender. It entailed a prisoner being publicly conveyed from Newgate

Prison to Tyburn in an open cart. This, and the subsequent execution in public, served to provide punishment with the features associated with a spectacle, a form of theatre to be viewed by all those in attendance (Foucault, 1977: 8).

The procession was superintended by the City Marshall and the cart was surrounded by armed guards on horseback to ensure no attempt could be made to free the prisoner (The Proceedings of the Old Bailey, 2018a: [Online]). The procession would customarily halt at public houses along the way where the prisoner would be given a last drink of alcohol (Joyce & Laverick, 2023b: 31–32).

At Tyburn, the prisoner would usually make a last 'Dying Speech' to the crowd (ostensibly to confess their guilt) and a cleric (termed the 'Ordinary' [chaplain] of Newgate Prison) would be present to pray for the condemned person's soul. Then a noose was placed around the neck of the prisoner who would be blindfolded (and sometimes hooded). Finally, the cart was pulled away. This led to death by strangulation (until the sharp drop was introduced in 1783) (The Proceedings of the Old Bailey, 2018b: [Online]), a procedure which could last for up to 45 minutes.

After 1783 (in the wake of the 1780 Gordon Riots in London), fears of public disorder and rioting arising from crowds on the streets resulted in executions taking place inside Newgate Prison (or Horsemonger Lane Gaol in Southwark) rather than at Tyburn (Linebaugh, 2011: 66) although they were still visible to members of the public until 1868.

Public hangings were public holidays in order to encourage people to attend, thus in theory serving the deterrent purposes of the penalty. However, the conveying of prisoners from Newgate to Tyburn could cause disorder so that what was termed the 'Hanging Parade' was ended in 1783 with executions (though still in public) being held near Newgate Prison.

Executions continued to be held in public until 1868 when this practice was ended under the provisions of the Capital Punishment Amendment Act as the authorities believed they failed in their purpose of deterring crime but instead provided for a macabre source of entertainment. Often (as was the case with Jack Shepherd who was executed in 1724) the condemned person was feted and treated as a hero by the assembled crowd.

Ways of death other than 'simple' hanging also existed during the eighteenth century. Men found guilty of treason could be hung, drawn and quartered (a punishment that was last used in 1820 in connection with the Cato Street conspirators). Women who were found guilty of treason, petty treason could be burned at the stake until this penalty was abolished by the 1790 Treason Act and replaced with drawing and hanging. The last woman to suffer the penalty of burning was Catherine Murphy in 1789 (Gattrell, 1996: 36).

From the early fifteenth century, the crime of heresy for males and females was also punishable by burning until finally ended by the 1677 Ecclesiastical Jurisdiction Act (Levy, 1995: 210).

It has been argued that 'the theatre of the gallows in the eighteenth century was seen to be a means whereby ordinary men and women could be made vividly aware of the consequences of criminal behaviour and thereby deterred from committing such acts by the "aweful" consequences displayed before their eyes' (Taylor, 1998: 124). To reinforce this principle of general deterrence, in some instances judges would order the body of a hung convict to be suspended in chains on a gibbet (a harness made of iron hoops and chains designed to hold the head, body and legs in place) near the scene of the crime (which was a penalty often inflicted on highwaymen) where it would be left to rot. The body was often covered with tar to prevent birds from pecking away at the flesh.

The ability to pass the sentence of gibbeting was extended by the 1752 Murder Act.

If not gibbeted, the 1752 Murder Act (officially titled 'An Act for Preventing the Horrid Crime of Murder') made provision for the corpse of a convicted murderer to be available for medical dissection as a 'systematic punishment' (Ward, 2015: 64) to either the Royal College of Physicians or to the Company of Barber-Surgeons. Historically (dating from an Edict of 1540 to the Company of Barber-Surgeons), these two institutions had been enabled to secure access to the bodies of 10 executed felons between them each year (Linebaugh, 2011: 70–1). The intention of the legislation was to intensify the terror associated with the death sentence (Linebaugh, 2011: 76–7), thus enhancing its deterrent effect by instilling dread among the population.

It was, however, a risky strategy since 'the added humiliation of the surgeon's scalpel to the hangman's noose rendered the injustice of the law all the more loathsome' (Linebaugh, 2011: 109). It contributed to disorder at events such as the 'hanging parade' from Newgate to Tyburn that might ultimately threaten to undermine society's existing power relationships whereby mercy was cast aside and substituted by a brutal form of class discipline in which dissection brutalised 'the integrity of the corpse and the respect shown to it' (Linebaugh, 2011: 117). To an extent, however, concerns of this nature were mitigated by restricting the use of dissection as a form of punishment to urban England—London, and in the latter decades of the eighteenth century to places that included Leeds and York (Ward, 2015: [Online]) where traditional methods of social control based on deference secured by the use of discretion to secure clemency in sentencing had no deep roots as was the case in rural England in that period.

What has been described as a private trade in dead bodies (in which these two institutions were in competition with the agents of private surgeons and hospitals for the bodies of executed felons at Tyburn) (Linebaugh, 2011: 72–4) which frequently resulted in unseemly brawls to obtain possession of a corpse in order to secure a financial reward.

This situation was further complicated if the relatives or friends of the dead person sought to get to the body either in the desire underpinned by religious reasons that the body should be buried whole in order to permit a peaceful transition of the soul from this life or simply that the condemned person deserved a proper Christian burial (Linebaugh, 2011: 115) (which was denied to a person who had been dissected) or in the hope that the hangman had not done his work well and the hung person remained alive, temporarily unconscious but not dead, from asphyxia (Linebaugh, 2011: 102–3), constituting a secular form of resurrection.

Such situations led the Royal College of Physicians to cease using this source of anatomical provision by the 1730s, and the Barber-Surgeons (which was renamed the Company of Surgeons in 1745) (Ward, 2015: [Online]) were thus the main beneficiary of the 1752 legislation (with private surgeons relying on securing corpses from their own hospitals or from parish graveyards (Linebaugh, 2011: 78). Bodies were taken to the Barber-Surgeon's Hall, commonly accompanied by a large procession of people. Prior to the procedures of dissection and anatomisation (which limited numbers of people were allowed to view from the building's gallery), the body was placed on public display.

Dissection as a penalty was abolished in 1832 and hanging in chains two years later.

The 1832 Anatomy Act permitted the dead bodies of persons who had been housed in institutions such as workhouses, asylums and prisons—places primarily inhabited by the poor (Ward, 2015: [Online])—to be claimed by anatomists if not claimed by relatives. Following anatomical examination, the remains would be given a Christian burial.

In 1832, the procedure whereby the body of an executed person could be made available for medical dissection ended and in 1834 gibbeting ceased. In this year, the jurisdiction of the Admiralty Sessions (which had commenced in 1536) also ended.

Box 1.5: The Execution of Pirates

Since 1536, persons accused of relevant maritime crimes would be tried by the Admiralty Sessions, part of the High Court of Admiralty, which was convened at the Old Bailey. If found guilty, they would be condemned to death, the execution taking place at Execution Dock.

Execution Dock had been used since the fifteenth century as the place where pirates and those found guilty of other marine offences such as mutiny, murder at sea, and marine insurance fraud were executed.

The method of execution was hanging and in common with other executions of this nature, (until 1783 when the 'new drop'—a trap door—was introduced), the condemned person with a noose around their necks would either climb a ladder which was then pulled away (or in some cases the prisoner was pushed off by the executioner) or be placed on a cart attached to horses which pulled away the support under the felon's feet), having first made a final 'dying' speech.

In many cases involving pirates, a short rope was used which served to prolong the condemned person's misery. They would die of asphyxiation and in their death throes would provide onlookers with the gruesome spectacle of spasms that appeared to onlookers as a kind of airborne dance (which was referred to as the [Admiralty] marshall's dance). It has been described as 'the involuntary thrashing of limbs that occurs during hangings....They swing, their tongues protruding and their eyes bulging—staring but unseeing' (Darby, 2014: [Online]). However, there is some dispute regarding the intentional or consistent use of this means of death for pirates (Ruggeri, 2016: [Online]).

Executions took place at low tide on the Thames foreshore in the area of Wapping known as Execution Dock, although the Dock's precise location is not known.

Following death, the body was either left on the noose or was cut down and chained to a post on the foreshore. In either case it would remain until covered by three Thames' tides. In cases involving more infamous pirates, the body would subsequently be placed in an iron cage known as a gibbet (a harness made of iron hoops and chains designed to hold the head, body and legs in place) and hung somewhere along the Thames where it would remain on public display for the public and seafarers to view. It was customary to cover bodies that had been gibbeted with tar, to stop birds pecking at the flesh.

The last executions for piracy at Execution Dock took place in 1830 when George James Davies and William Watts were executed for the part they had played in a mutiny (and related subsequent events) on the *Cyprus* in 1829.

Selective Use of the Death Penalty

It has been observed that despite the barbaric nature of the 'Bloody Code', the number of executions was low, one estimate suggesting that only one-fifth of death sentences were carried out (The Proceedings of the Old Bailey, 2018b: [Online]) and that 'throughout most of the eighteenth century, approximately 50–60% of convicts sentenced to death were pardoned' (The Proceedings of the Old Bailey, 2018b: [Online]). Despite the increase in felonies that carried the death penalty, the overall number of executions in eighteenth-century England remained stable after 1750 and around half of those who received the death sentence were instead transported or imprisoned (Hay, 2011: 22, 43).

As has been suggested above, this was so for several reasons that included the use of pardons (which could be a free pardon issued by the Monarch on the recommendation of the trial judge or consist of a conditional pardon in which case the judge would pass a lesser sentence such as branding, transportation or hard labour was imposed). In determining whether to use discretion and pardon an offender, great reliance was placed on the use of character witnesses or the advice given to the sentencer by a member of the gentry (Hay, 2011: 42–3).

Additionally, a death sentence could be substituted for service in the army or navy (a sentence most used when Britain was at war being provided for in the 1705 Mutiny Act), the ability of a woman to have a death sentence requited on grounds of pregnancy (which in theory could be carried out after the baby was born but in practice generally resulted in a pardon), the reluctance of judges to pass the death penalty (who may thus discharge a person before the trial had taken place or acquit them following trial) and the ability of those who were well-connected to use their status to their advantage which meant 'a well-connected criminal could, and often did … walk out of the courtroom a free man or woman, even when the evidence was overwhelmingly against them' (Ultimate History Project Staff, undated: [Online]).

There were several reasons to explain this situation. One was that had the death penalty been applied consistently, there was the danger that the impact of this draconian punishment would be diminished (Hay, 2011: 56). It would thus lose its potency to terrify acquiescence to the law as people would come to regard it as part and parcel of everyday life. For this reason, the death penalty had to be used sparingly, but when it was employed it was crucial that its severity produced a shock wave throughout society which explained the usage of public executions and the rituals that preceded them described above (the 'hanging parade' or the procession leading to the execution of a pirate at Execution Dock).

A further explanation for the sparing use of the death penalty was the desire to ensure that public opinion did not regard the law as so brutal that it outraged the public and helped fuel disorder which could lead to revolution, events in France at the end of the century associated with the French Revolution justifying this concern. Accordingly, it was necessary to temper punishment with the practical necessity of maintaining the existing power relationships within society—'to inculcate fear, but not so many as to harden or repel a populace that had to assent … to the rule of property' (Hay, 2011: 57). An important way this was achieved was through the use of discretion.

It has been argued that the use of discretion by both magistrates and judges was designed to serve the interests of the eighteenth-century ruling elite which comprised the gentry and landed aristocracy, whose wealth was founded on the possession of land (Hay, 2011: 61). Explicitly selective enforcement best served the purpose of maintaining those bonds of patronage and deference which were the quintessential features of a persistently aristocratic ruling culture (Hay, 2011: 23–4). This situation was especially suited to securing the allegiance of poorer people to the existing social system, upholding the ability of gentlemen to rule (Hay, 2011: 53).

The law and the punishments it prescribed were harsh but the willingness not to always bring the full force of the law on an offender served to demonstrate a merciful side to persons of property and help to cloak the law and the interests it was designed to protect, with a mantle of popular legitimacy in the form of being seen as an instrument through which justice was secured. Accordingly, the use of pardons was 'part of the tissue of paternalism' (Hay, 2011: 47), a method which contributed to the maintenance of order and deference (Hay, 2011: 58). Discretion extended beyond sentencing decisions—'the mode of prosecution, the manner of trial and the treatment of convicted convicts gave some of the same power to all men of property' (Hay, 2011: 40). This potentially offered a modicum of justice to the poorer and uneducated members of eighteenth-century society who were at a considerable disadvantage from the ways in which trials were conducted and could easily be convicted through ignorance of the law and legal procedures.

However, the consequence of this was an inconsistent British judicial system which, according to classicist criminologists, meant that many criminals were willing to take their chances and commit crime. Sacrificing the full force of punishment was, however, the price the eighteenth-century ruling elite were prepared to pay to preserve the belief in justice (Hay, 2011: 55) and with that, the maintenance of their rule.

Additionally (Brannan, 2021: [Online]) discussed the belief of the legal reformer Charles Romilly that the Code gave too much power to judges who would use their sentencing discretion in a biased manner, so that there arose the strong possibility that poorer people would be treated more harshly than the educated and well-off.

Benefit of Clergy

The use of discretion to temper the operations of the eighteenth-century criminal justice system was augmented by mechanisms provided by the system itself which offset the infliction of severe penalties and which also added to inconsistencies in the operations of the criminal justice system.

One of these was known as 'benefit of clergy', whereby a person found guilty of certain felonies could be spared the death penalty which was substituted for a lesser punishment. The lesser penalty might include a sentence of hard labour in a House of Correction in the early eighteenth century or, following the enactment of the 1718 Transportation Act, removal from the United Kingdom.

The procedure of benefit of clergy dated to the middle ages as a right given to the Church to punish those of its members who had been found guilty by the courts of having committed a crime. It was subsequently extended to other literate persons. Those who claimed benefit of clergy were required to read a passage from the Bible (usually verses from the 51st Psalm in the Old Testament, which was termed the 'neck verse'), but as literacy became more common outside the church, the practice gradually developed of permitting all men convicted of felonies to which benefit of clergy applied to be granted this privilege if they could read the 'neck verse'. This test was flexible, and judges could vary the choice of text and level of literacy required, often depending on whether they wished to impose the death penalty in a specific case, or not. In 1623 women found guilty of the theft of goods less than ten shillings in value were also allowed benefit of clergy, and in 1691 women were granted the privilege on the same terms as men (The Proceedings of the Old Bailey, 2018b: [Online]).

The reading test was abolished in 1706 and benefit of clergy became automatic for any offence (making it rather similar to a conditional discharge) unless it had been specifically excluded as was thus 'non-clergyable'. It could, however, be claimed only once by a convicted criminal and until 1779, those who received it were branded on their thumb.

Concerns in the early eighteenth century regarding the scale of crime, especially in urban England, resulted in a wide range of crimes becoming exempt from benefit of clergy after the 1706 Act had been passed. These included housebreaking, the theft of goods of the value of over 40 shillings from a dwelling house (which was removed in 1713, directed at thefts by domestic workers from their employers), the shop lifting of goods worth more than 5 shillings, sheep and cattle stealing (The Proceedings of the Old Bailey, 2018b: [Online]).

Consequently, these offences carried an automatic sentence of death: however, this was not uniformly administered since juries—through the procedure of a partial verdict, sometimes referred to as 'pious perjury'—would reduce the value of stolen goods thus enabling a lesser penalty (such as transportation) to be applied by the trial judge. This was especially important for women since, before 1691, a female found guilty of stealing goods worth more than ten shillings [50 new pence] was not eligible to receive benefit of clergy and would thus be sentenced to death. To avoid this severe penalty, women would often be convicted on a lesser charge or be acquitted (The Proceedings of the Old Bailey, 2018c: [Online]).

Additionally, those granted benefit of clergy (and also those found guilty of manslaughter rather than murder) were branded ('T' for theft, 'F' for felon or 'M' for murder) to prevent the benefit being claimed more than once (The Proceedings of the Old Bailey, 2018b: [Online]). Branding was applied to the thumb, although between 1699 and 1707 to the cheek. Branding for those receiving benefit of clergy ended in 1779 and was ended in 1829.

Juries in this period also utilised the practice of nullification whereby a person who was guilty was declared to be 'not guilty' because the conscience of the jurors would not permit them to condemn a person to death. They might also enter a plea of mercy when they had found a person guilty of an offence which carried the death penalty (McLynn, 1989: xiii).

The use made of benefit of clergy was reduced following reforms to the penal code in the early nineteenth century (for example, shoplifting ceased to be a capital offence in 1823) and the procedure was completely abolished in 1827 (in which year the threshold for the theft of goods from a dwelling house was raised to 100 shillings).

Other Penalties for Felonies

Transportation

The main rationale of transportation was that of incapacitation—offenders were physically removed from the United Kingdom and placed somewhere else.

Transportation entailed a period of servitude (usually lasting for seven years) which was initially served in the British colonies in North America (mainly Virginia and Maryland). Servitude entailed forced labour in which the convicted person was little better than a slave. It has been observed that 'although it was believed that transportation might lead to the reformation of the offender, the primary motivations behind this punishment were a belief in its deterrent effect, and a desire to simply remove hardened criminals from society' (The Proceedings of the Old Bailey, 2018b: [Online]). Eighteenth-century contemporaries believed that transportation did exert a considerable deterrent effect on crime (McLynn, 1989: 287).

Although criminals had been exported in the seventeenth century (either at their own expense or that of merchants or shipowners), the first Transportation Act was passed in 1718 whereby a felon guilty of offences for which benefit of clergy could be applied could be transported to the American colonies for seven years. From 1720, the state footed the cost of transportation. It has been estimated that between 1718 and 1775, around 50,000 convicts were transported to America: most (around 80%) were male, aged between 15 and 29 and were drawn from the lower social orders (Morgan, 1987: 416).

The American War of Independence (1775–1783) ended transportation to this part of the world and helped promote imprisonment as a penalty for crime. An early innovation in this respect was an Act passed in 1776 which allowed judges to sentence men to hard labour that consisted of dredging the River Thames and who served their sentence on old ships moored on the river, known as hulks. This Act also enabled women to be sentenced to a period of hard labour in a House of Correction. However, transportation was resumed in 1787 with convicts being sent to New South Wales in Australia. It is estimated that 160,000 people suffered this fate (Foxford History, undated: [Online]).

Women and well as men received this penalty. Although this penalty was often used as an alternative to execution, it was a far from humane act—many of those transported died while at sea and others who did survive, died shortly after their arrival.

Custodial Sentences

The 1166 Assize of Clarendon stipulated that every county should possess a prison, although their prime purpose was to house a person who was awaiting trial (May, 2006: 3). Thus for much of the eighteenth century, prisons were primarily places where defendants awaiting trial were detained or where convicts were housed while awaiting punishment. The prison population was low, numbering around 4000 in 1750. They were operated locally by towns and counties but there were no rules concerning how they should be run. Goalers were unpaid and made their money from what they could obtain from prison inmates. Disease, especially typhus or 'goal fever' was rife and claimed the lives of many prisoners each year.

An alternative custodial regime that operated alongside prisons was known as the House of Correction (the first one of which, in London, was known as the 'Bridewell', a term that was subsequently adopted elsewhere). This was created in the sixteenth century which sought to 'provide work for the idle, training for the young, and punishment and reform for petty criminals' (The Proceedings of the Old Bailey, 2018b: [Online]). Offenders were usually committed to Houses of Correction by Magistrates although in London, Beadles also exercised this power (London Lives, 2018: [Online]).

As was considered by Hinkle (2006), the initial objectives of both deterring crime and teaching industrious habits thereby reforming the convicted person made the Bridewell an important step in the evolution of the penitentiary. However, the role and purpose of Bridewells changed during the eighteenth century so that Houses of Correction became primarily perceived as places of punishment where sentences of hard labour (in particular the beating of hemp) were served and the crimes for which a person could be sent to such an institution became extended. An Act of 1720 allowed Houses of Correction to be used solely to detain vagrants and persons charged with small offences (London Lives, 2018: [Online]).

In 1706, legislation permitted a judge to impose a sentence of up to two years' hard labour in a House of Correction on those given benefit of clergy, although in 1718 a further Act resulted in most convicts in this category being sentenced to transportation (The Proceedings of the Old Bailey, 2018b: [Online]).

Most of those committed to the Bridewell were petty offenders who had committed offences that included prostitution, begging, having no visible means of earning a living, abusing the system of poor relief or for having committed 'a host of other types of disorderly conduct, including swearing, drunkenness and assault, pilfering or petty theft or simply "loose, idle and disorderly conduct"' (Shoemaker, 2020: [Online]). A significant number were women and over half of offenders were released within a week and two-thirds within two weeks. By the 1760s and 1770s, prisoners awaiting trial constituted over three-quarters of those committed to the Bridewells at Middlesex and Westminster (London Lives, 2018: [Online]). Following the temporary lapse in transportation in 1776, Houses of Correction became authorised as places to punish felons sentenced to hard labour, a situation reaffirmed by the 1779 Penitentiary Act.

Penalties for Misdemeanours

For lesser crimes (misdemeanours), a number of other penalties could be exacted. These comprised of fines, forms of corporal punishment that included whipping and pillorying and short terms of imprisonment. Transportation was technically possible as a penalty for misdemeanours but was one that was rarely used (Langbein, 1987: 17).

Fines

This method was mainly used to punish misdemeanours in the late seventeenth and early part of the eighteenth century.

Branding

The main purpose of branding was to act as a warning to others not to emulate the behaviour of the person who suffered this form of mutilation. It was designed to humiliate the offender and has been associated (above) with the aim of denunciation.

Branding as a punishment in its own right dates back to the Anglo-Saxon period (usually dated from 410 to 1066) and was subsequently incorporated into legislation in the form of the 1547 Statute of Vagabonds whereby vagabonds and Gypsies would be branded with a large V on the breast and brawlers with an F (standing for 'fraymaker'). Runaway slaves were branded with an S on their cheek or forehead. This law was repealed in 1550 but the use of branding was subsequently associated with the Puritans—a religious sect that emerged from the Church of England and whose views were influenced by the theologian, John Calvin. The Puritan period is dated 1564–1660, but they were especially influential during the 'Commonwealth Period' (1649–1660) when the government of the United Kingdom was headed by Oliver Cromwell.

Branding also became used to identify those who had received benefit of clergy, a process that commenced in the fifteenth century until the practice of benefit of clergy was abolished in 1822. Branding was also used as a punishment for bigamy for much of the eighteenth century. The aim of this form of punishment was to humiliate those who had broken the law.

Technically, branding could be applied to all persons who had committed offences to which this penalty applied but in reality persons of higher social standing were often branded with cold iron, making the punishment symbolic rather than actual.

Its use declined during the eighteenth century. The reasons for its decline included the availability of other punishments, the impact of branding on a person's ability to secure lawful employment (hence aggravating the chance of reoffending) and the fact that the cruelty associated with the punishment was out of touch with the views (and influence) of penal reformers who sought to use humane methods to prevent crime and reform criminals. Branding as a punishment was abolished in 1829 except in cases of desertion from the army. The 1858 Mutiny Act authorised the continuance of this process as a penalty that might be imposed by a court martial, but it was abolished in 1879.

The Stocks and the Pillory

The 1351 Statute of Labourers required every town and village to erect a set of stocks which were to be employed against 'unruly artisans' who had committed offences such as drunkenness and swearing. The stocks were typically positioned in a public place as the intention was to subject the offender to humiliation both by being confined there and also where s/he could be subjected to a range of other abuses from the local population that included being pelted with refuse, having their feet whipped and being tickled.

The pillory was similar to the stocks in which the offender stood rather than sat or squatted. It dates back to Anglo-Saxon times, being known as 'Healsfang' or 'catch-neck' and was directed at a range of crimes that included attempted sodomy, fraud, extortion, seditious words, dishonest trading and perjury that were often of a moral and political nature. As with the stocks, the punishment was delivered in public and the prisoner was subjected to abuses by his or her fellow citizens to add to the humiliation that was being suffered, enabling those in the crowd to express their disapproval for the actions that had taken place. It has been recorded that 'sometimes the offender was drawn to the pillory on a hurdle, accompanied by minstrels and a paper sign hung around his or her head displaying the offence committed' (Wiltshire and Swindon History Centre, 2014: [Online]).

Additionally, 'for political offences, such as libel and sedition, further punishment could be inflicted as one's ears could be nailed to the pillory instead of being locked in by the neck and arms. Afterward the ear was cut off leaving it on the pillory' (Wiltshire and Swindon History Centre,

2014: [Online]. The crime of seditious libel entailed criticising the government and it was sometimes the case that those who had uttered such words received support from the assembled crowd (The Proceedings of the Old Bailey, 2018b: [Online]).

The aim of the pillory (and also stocks) was public humiliation, whereby the criminal suffered denunciation from the abuse and vilification of passers-by and spectators (Shoemaker, 1987: 287). Those termed 'vagabonds and beggars' were a particular target to which this form of punishment was directed. It could be used as a punishment in its own right or used in conjunction with other punishments—for example a person in the pillory could also be branded while restrained in this manner.

In 1816, the use of the pillory became restricted to perjury or subornation (that is, a person seeking to persuade another to commit perjury thus attempting to obstruct justice) and was formally abolished as a means of punishment in 1837. The use of stocks as a means of punishment has never been formally abolished and were intermittently used during the nineteenth century. Their usage died out around 1872.

Flogging

Flogging (or whipping) was widely used as a means of punishment in Tudor and Stewart times for crimes such as refusing to attend church, stealing, and vagrancy. The punishment was administered in public and in the eighteenth century was mainly used as a punishment for theft. It entailed a convicted person being tied to a cart which was pulled through the streets and the convicted person was whipped along the route (the number of strokes to be administered being unspecified for civilians). Flogging could also take place in private (usually in a prison or House of Correction). It continued as a punishment available to the courts until it was abolished in 1948.

Conclusion

This chapter has discussed the background to the 1689 Bill of Rights as providing a key statement of the rights and liberties of English people. It has considered the key ideas associated with social contract theory which was a key underpinning of classicist criminology that emerged during the mid decades of the eighteenth century. The chapter has considered the principle ideas with which this school of criminological thought was associated, in particular in relation to providing for a criminal justice system that was consistent in its operations. It also analysed the operations of the criminal justice system in the late seventeenth and early-mid eighteenth century within the context as to what purposes society desires from the punishment of those who break the law.

The following chapter develops the theme of law-breaking by examining the main manifestations of criminal behaviour in the period 1689–c1750.

? Summary Question

Critically discuss the ways through which that state responded to crime between 1689 and 1750.

References

Brannan, J. (2021). The Waltham Black Act 1723. Available at the link. *Juliabrannan.com.* [Online] https://juliabrannan.com/2021/02/15/the-waltham-black-act-of-1723/. Accessed 31 January 2022.

Carradice, P. (2014). The Death of the Hanging Judge. *BBC*. [Online] https://www.bbc.co.uk/blogs/wales/entries/5bbb0f04-c7fb-34fe-be1e-c57402198e6d. Accessed 7 December 2021.

Cavadino, M., & Dignan, J. (1992). *The Penal System: An Introduction* (1st ed.). Sage.

Clarke, R. (1992). *Situational Crime Prevention: Successful Case Studies*. Harrow & Heston.

Cohen, A. (1955). *Delinquent Boys: The Culture of the Gang*. Chicago Free Press.

Cohen, L., & Felson, M. (1979). Social Change and Crime Rate Trends: A Routine Activity Approach. *American Sociological Review, 44*(4), 588–608.

Cornish, D., & Clarke, R. (1987). Understanding Crime Displacement: An Application of Rational Choice Theory. *Criminology, 25*(4), 933–948.

Darby, N. (2014). The Marshal's Dance: Crime and Punishment at Execution Dock. *Criminal Historian*, [Online] https://criminalhistorian.wordpress.com/category/trials/page/2/ [Accessed 11 June 2021].

Davies, M. (1993). *Punishing Criminals: Developing Community—Based Intermediate Sanctions*. Greenwood Press.

Deacon, R. (1980). *A History of British Secret Service*. Granada Publishing Ltd.

Duff, R. (1986). *Trials and Punishment*. Cambridge University Press.

Emsley, C. (2018). *Crime and Society in England 1750–1900* (5th ed.). Routledge.

Fleisher, M. (2003). Lost Youth and the Futility of Deterrence. In S. McConville (Ed.), *The Use of Punishment*. Willan Publishing.

Foucault, M. (1977). *Discipline and Punish: The Birth of the Prison*. Vintage.

Foxford History (undated). 1700–1900 Crime and Punishment. *Foxford History*. [Online] https://sites.google.com/site/foxfordhistory/home/crime-and-punishment/1700-1900-crime-and-punishment. Accessed 7 October 2020.

Gatrell, V. (1996). *The Hanging Tree: Execution and the English People 1770–1868*. Oxford University Press.

Granucci, A. (1969). Nor Cruel and Unusual Punishment Inflicted: The Original Meaning. *California Law Review, 57*(4), 839–865.

Harris, T. (2006). *Revolution: The Great Crisis of the British Monarchy, 1685–1720*. Allen Lane.

Hay, D. (2011). Property, Authority and the Criminal Law. In D. Hay, P. Linebaugh, J. G. Rule, E. P. Thompson & C. Winslow (Eds.), *Albion's Fatal Tree. Crime and Society in Eighteenth Century England* (Revised ed.). Verso, originally published in 1975.

Hinkle, W. (2006). *A History of Bridewell Prison: 1553–1700*. Edwin Mellen Press.

Hudson, B. (2003). *Understanding Justice* (2nd ed.). Open University Press.

Huesmann, L., & Podolski, C. (2003). Punishment: A Psychological Perspective. In S. McConville (Ed.), *The Use of Punishment*. Willan Publishing.

Joyce, P., & Laverick, W. (2023a). *Criminal Justice: An Introduction* (4th ed.). Routledge.

Joyce, P., & Laverick, W. (2023b). From Newgate Prison to Tyburn Tree: The Old Bailey, London. In A. Lynes, C. Kelly & J. Treadwell (Eds.), *50 Dark Destinations. Crime and Contemporary Tourism*. Policy Press.

Joyce, P., & Wain, N. (2010). *A Dictionary of Criminal Justice*. Routledge.

Katz, J. (1988). *Seductions of Crime: Moral and Sensual Attractions of Doing Evil*. Basic Books.

Lacey, N. (2003). Penal Theory and Penal Practice: A Communitarian Approach. In S. McConville (Ed.), *The Use of Punishment*. Willan Publishing.

Langbein, J. (1987). The English Criminal Trial Jury on the Eve of the French evolution. In A. Schioppa (Ed.), *The Trial Jury in England, France, Germany 1700–1900*. Duncker & Humblot. Law.yale.edu [Online] https://www.law.yale.edu/sites/default/files/documents/pdf/Faculty/langbein_theTrialJury.pdf. Accessed 11 Apr 2022.

Levy, L. (1995). *Blasphemy: Verbal Offense Against the Sacred, from Moses to Salman Rushdie*. UNC Press Books.

Linebaugh, P. (2011). The Tyburn Riot Against the Surgeons. In D. Hay, P. Linebaugh, J. G. Rule, E. P. Thompson & C. Winslow (Eds.), *Albion's Fatal Tree. Crime and Society in Eighteenth Century England* (Revised ed.). Verso.

London Lives. (2018). Houses of Correction. *London Lives 1690–1800*. [Online] https://www.londonlives.org/static/HousesOfCorrection.jsp. Accessed 30 September 2020.

Magnacartaplus. (2000). The 1689 Bill of Rights. *Magnacartaplus.org*. [Online] https://www.magnacartaplus.org/1689-rights/index.htm. Accessed 28 April 2023.

Matthews, R. (1999). *Doing Time: An Introduction to the Sociology of Imprisonment*. Macmillan.

Matza, D., & Sykes, G. (1961). Juvenile Delinquency and Subterranean Values. *American Sociological Review, 26*, 713–719.

May, T. (2006). *Victorian and Edwardian Prisons*. Shire Publications.

McLynn, F. (1989). *Crime and Punishment in Eighteenth Century England*. Oxford University Press.

Morgan, K. (1987). English and American Attitudes towards Convict Transportation 1718–1775. *History, 72*(236), 416–431.

Rawls, J. (1972). *A Theory of Justice*. Oxford University Press.

Ruggeri, A. (2016). The London Gallows Where Pirates were Hanged. *BBC.Com*. [Online] http://www.bbc.com/autos/story/20161216-the-london-gallows-where-pirates-were-hanged. Accessed 13 June 2021.

Seal, L. (2008). Criminalization and the Eighteenth Century's 'Bloody Code.' *Criminal Justice Matters., 74*(1), 16–17.

Shoemaker, R. (1987). The London "Mob" in the Early Eighteenth Century. *Journal of British Studies., 26*(3), 273–304.

Shoemaker, R. (2020). Bridewell House of Correction Prisoners 1740–1795. *Digital Panopticon*. [Online] https://www.digitalpanopticon.org/Bridewell_House_of_Correction_Prisoners_1780-1795. Accessed 30 September 2020.

Shore, H. (2003). Crime, Criminal Networks and the Survival Strategies of the Poor in Early Eighteenth Century London. In S. King & A. Tomkins (Eds.), *The Poor in England 1700–1850. An Economy of Makeshifts*. Manchester University Press.

Sykes, G., & Matza, D. (1957). Techniques of Neutralisation: A Theory of Delinquency. *American Sociological Review, 22*, 664–670.

Taylor, D. (1998). *Crime, Policing and Punishment in England, 1750–1914*. Palgrave/Macmillan.

The Proceedings of the Old Bailey. (2018a). The Journey from Newgate to Tyburn. *Old Bailey Proceedings Online*. [Online] https://www.oldbaileyonline.org/static/JourneyTyburn.jsp. Accessed 12 June 2021.

The Proceedings of the Old Bailey. (2018b). Punishment Sentences at the Old Bailey. *Old Bailey Proceedings Online*. [Online] https://www.oldbaileyonline.org/static/Punishment.jsp#:~:text=It%20is%20alleged%20that%20sometimes,applied%20when%20it%20was%20cold.&text=Branding%20as%20a%20punishment%20for,of%20clergy%20ended%20in%201779. Accessed 27 September 2020.

The Proceedings of the Old Bailey. (2018c). Gender in the Proceedings. *Old Bailey Proceedings Online*. [Online] https://www.oldbaileyonline.org/static/Gender.jsp. Accessed 13 January 2023.

Ultimate History Project Staff. (undated). Crime and Criminals in Eighteenth Century London. *Ultimate History Project*. [Online] http://ultimatehistoryproject.com/crime-and-policing-in-18th-c-london.html. Accessed 26 September 2020.

Ward, R. (2015). The Criminal Corpse, Anatomists, and the Criminal Law: Parliamentary Attempts to Extend the Dissection of Offenders in Late Eighteenth-Century England. *Journal of British Studies, 54*(1), 63–87.
Wiltshire and Swindon History Centre. (2014). The Pillory as Punishment. Wiltshire and Swindon History Centre [Online]). http://www.wshc.eu/blog/item/the-pillory-as-punishment.html. Accessed 27 September 2020.

2

The Character and Nature of Crime in the Early Eighteenth Century

Introduction

This chapter will consider the types of crime that existed in the late seventeenth and early decades of the eighteenth century. These comprised of activities such as highway robbery, poaching and piracy that had existed previously as well as newer forms of crime such as pickpocketing that appeared in the early decades of the eighteenth century, mainly in the expanding towns such as London. These forms of crime are considered within the concept of anomie that was later put forward by Émile Durkheim and the role performed by women in the newer forms of criminality will be assessed. These new types of crime were worrying to people who lived in that period and underpinned police reform that will be examined in Chapter 3.

Traditional Forms of Crime

This section will discuss the key forms of crime which existed during the first half of the eighteenth century. Many of these were not new and constituted long-standing criminal practices which are described as 'traditional forms of crime' in this chapter. These crimes did not die out by 1750 (in some cases developments associated with urbanisation facilitated their further development) although the late seventeenth and first half of the eighteenth century witnessed the heyday of some of the activities that are discussed below.

P. Joyce and W. Laverick, *History of Policing, Crime, Disorder, Punishment*, https://doi.org/10.1007/978-3-031-36892-9_2

Robbery and Highwaymen

Robbery in the early eighteenth century was carried out by two distinct criminal groups. The term 'footpads' is the name given to robbers operating on foot who attacked people who were travelling on foot. Footpads typically operated in gangs whereas highwaymen typically worked alone or in small groups.

Highwaymen were robbers on horseback whose main target consisted of travellers on horseback or in carriages whose occupants were held up at gunpoint and who were made to hand over their money and other possessions. A number of factors aided this crime, including the increase of trade in a period of few banks (which meant there was a lot of cash in transit) and improvements in travel. The construction of turnpikes (main roads whose use required the payment of a toll), 'took off' in the eighteenth century, climaxing with 'turnpike mania' between 1751 and 1752 when turnpike trusts covered 11,500 miles of road in Britain (UK Parliament, 2023: [Online]). This meant that targets (especially in the form of stagecoaches) increased in this period and also made it possible for footpads to go further afield to conduct their criminal activities (McLynn, 1989: 5).

Attacks of this nature often occurred on isolated roads between towns. The streets and roads approaching London were favourite haunts of highwaymen in this period. The use of guns was an important aspect of their effectiveness, since they were frequently robbing persons whose main means of defence was that of a sword. The activities of highwaymen threatened the safety of individuals and also the freedom of travel and commerce (Beattie, 1986: 148).

Highwaymen first appeared in the seventeenth century and initially consisted of supporters of the Royalist cause which had been defeated in the English Civil War. Areas such as Hounslow Heath (on which now stands London Airport) and the Great North Road (which linked London to York) were especially prone to this form of crime. They were immortalised in the career of Dick Turpin (1706–1739) whose career in crime commenced with theft and burglary but who then altered his *modus operandi* to that of a highwayman.

The 1692 Highwayman's Act (reaffirmed by Royal Proclamation in the ensuing years) reflected concerns regarding the fear of highway robbery. The 1692 measure (otherwise known as the 'Blood Money Act') provided around £40,000 in reward money to secure the capture of criminals and offered a reward of £40 for the conviction of a highway robber, which was designed to encourage those who had experienced such a crime to prosecute it (Brain, undated: [Online]).

Subsequently, in 1772, the death penalty was imposed on persons armed and in disguise on the King's highways. The severity of this action indicated that highwaymen - and the fear of crimes committed by them experienced by travellers—was very much viewed as a national problem, the commission of which this penalty sought to deter. However, as is discussed in Chapter 1 in connection with the overall use of the death penalty in the eighteenth century, there was a disinclination to consistently use the death penalty in connection with this offence. Soon after becoming King in 1760, George III agreed that the death sentence for highway robbery should more or less routinely be changed to that of transportation, although this form of discretion was often applied at the last minute, when the condemned person was on their way to the scaffold (Hay, 2011: 52).

The activities of the Bow Street Runners (which are discussed in Chapter 4), whose mounted patrols policed roads approaching London, was an important factor which led to the decline of this form of crime by providing, in the views later expressed by Cohen and Felson's routine activities theory, (1979) a capable guardian that would create an environment that was less conducive to the commission of crime. The continued growth of towns also meant that there were fewer isolated stretches of roads where crime of this nature could take place. Other factors that included the enhanced use of banking (so that individuals were less likely to carry large sums of money around with them) and a legal crackdown that saw licences being withdrawn by Justices of the Peace (JPs) to inns and taverns which were frequented by highwaymen also contributed to the reduction in scale of this form of criminal activity.

The last conviction for highway robbery occurred in 1831.

Piracy

Piracy entails the theft of goods being transported on the water. It was certainly not unique to the eighteenth century and was used against Greek and Roman shipping and still exists today in some parts of the world. However, what is described as 'the golden age' of piracy (Fiske, 1897: 338) embraced the period c 1670–1730 (Simon, 2023: 30) when several thousand pirates were active. The period of pirate activity was not constant, however, and several waves of piracy occurred, the last of which was around 1700–1730, with a peak of activity in the early 1720s.

The period 1713–1715 is an important year in the history of piracy since a series of peace treaties under the overall heading of the Peace of Utrecht ended the hostilities associated with the War of the Spanish Succession (which broke out in 1701) in which the United Kingdom had used privateers (who were effectively state-sponsored pirates with a certificate—known as a 'Letter of Marque'—giving them licence to attack vessels belonging to other countries) in the naval war conducted against the Spanish and French. This resulted in privateers becoming no longer part of British foreign policy. Those involved in privateering thus had to become 'self-employed' and became pirates who operated on a freelance basis, technically the enemies of all established governments.

Box 2.1: Buccaneers

The terms 'buccaneers' and 'privateers' are more or less used in an identical fashion.

The term 'buccaneer' is applied to privateers who were active in the Caribbean and Pacific (West) Coast of America who mainly targeted Spanish ships and Spanish colonies in the second half of the seventeenth century. Buccaneers were willing to hire themselves out to foreign governments and the French, English and Dutch were all willing at various periods to grant licences to those engaged in such activity, thus transforming them into privateers.

Henry Morgan (1635–1688) is an example of an English buccaneer. This form of activity died out around 1680.

Some of the pirates who were active in the final wave of the golden age are well-known historical figures. They include William 'Captain' Kidd (1645–1701), John Rackham (usually known as 'Calico Jack') (1682–1820) and Edward Teach (usually known as Blackbeard) (1680–1718). The pirate regarded as the most successful was Bartholomew Roberts (known to history as 'Black Bart') (1682–1722) who looted more than 400 vessels in his career as a pirate. Piracy was not confined to men and women pirates included Anne Bonney (1698–1782) and Mary Read (1690–1721).

Pirates were active throughout the world, but especially in the Caribbean (in particular Jamaica where the 'turbulent relationship between Spain and England helped fuel piracy) (Simon, 2023: 30), the Atlantic (East) Coast (where the UK Colonies in America were located), the West Coast of Africa, the Indian Ocean (targeting the trade routes from India to the United States via Africa) and the South China Seas. One factor that aided piracy on the Atlantic (East) coast of America was the close relationships between settlers and pirates, the latter obtaining goods that the UK authorities would not allow the settlers to have (Dolin, 2018).

The targets of the pirates were ships conveying goods that included gold, silver, sugar and cocoa back to Europe.

The 'golden age' ended around 1730, mainly because of the scale of crackdowns resulting from international treaties whereby governments used warships and executions to eliminate pirates, many of whom were killed in battle or who were captured and executed. It was estimated that between 1700 and 1726, 4000 pirates were arrested, many of whom were executed (Simon, 2023: 34). One of those who died in battle was 'Black Bart' Williams who was killed on board his ship, the *Royal Fortune* in 1722, following an engagement with *HMS Swallow*, commanded by Captain Ogle, off Cape Lopez, Gabon, Central Africa.

Box 2.2: The Rise and Fall of Piracy

Laverick (2016: 38) argued that piracy has existed since ancient times. Felson and Kalaitzidis (2005: 9), for example, drawing upon the work of De Souza (1999), noted that piracy was the subject of Homeric poems dating around the seventh or eighth centuries BC and has also been implicated in the creation of the Delian League in 478 BC which comprised an alliance of coastal and Aegean city-states directed against Persia.

Academic commentators have viewed piracy as intimately associated with the formation, preservation, undermining and strengthening of state power and empire building. Historical contextualisation has therefore been conceptualised as both an internal and external security issue, entailing both a challenge to states (and the safety of their citizens), and also, historically being used as a tool of statecraft directed against their enemies.

As a tool of statecraft, piracy was utilised to accumulate wealth, and also, as a means of undermining the strength of competitors. The common practice of privateering involved the employment of private sea vessels to assist in attacks against opponents, with states receiving a share of the proceeds from such activities. This officially sanctioned version of piracy was applied towards state enemies and anyone engaging in trading with its enemies (Andreas & Nadelmann, 2006: 22).

Piracy has therefore been linked to state competition for the amassing of wealth, territorial expansion and access and control over trade routes. Piracy followed the trading patterns set by Spain, Britain, and the other colonial powers, and was concentrated around the Caribbean, the Atlantic seaboard of America, the English Channel, and later the coast of West Africa (Vagg, 1995).

According to Andreas and Nadelmann (2006: 22), the expansion of European maritime commerce in the sixteenth century increased the rewards and the incidence of piracy dramatically, with much of it officially or unofficially sponsored by European governments, with colonial governors directed not to interfere with pirates by the French, British and US governments, offering safe harbour in return for a share of their goods (Andreas & Nadelmann, 2006: 22).

Trends in piracy were also associated with conflict resolution. Thus, Gosse (1946) and Rule (1977), cited in Vagg (1995), suggested that the numbers of pirates in the Western world tended to increase following the discharge of superfluous sailors from navies after the resolution of disputes. Able to supply goods at reduced prices, piracy flourished, these authors suggested, receiving widespread support from local magistrates, other officials and local inhabitants who were frequently involved in piracy and wrecking between the sixteenth and eighteenth centuries.

However, while colonial governors and local officials actively supported or turned a blind eye to piratical activities, often lacking the capacity to affect the practice in any significant way, by the end of the seventeenth century the perceived benefits of piracy were called into question as trade and diplomacy increased, and as governments sought to establish stable commercial relations (Felson & Kalaitzidis, 2005: 10).

If prior to the seventeenth century, 'international norms proscribing banditry on the high seas remained limited' (Andreas & Nadelmann, 2006: 23–24), the seventeenth century witnessed increased internal and external state control, strengthened navies and targeted British, American and Dutch action directed towards the eradication of piracy, resulting in a reconceptualisation of such activities as an 'international threat', subject to widespread criminalisation (Felson & Kalaitzidis, 2005: 10). The British Royal Navy was considered pivotal in driving efforts towards the eradication of piracy, seeking to protect their growing empire and introducing norms in both the domestic and international spheres (Williams, 1961, cited in Felson & Kalaitzidis, 2005: 10), resulting in a virtual ban by the mid-eighteenth century.

Furthermore, in accounting for the marked reduction in piracy by the middle of the nineteenth century, in addition to the significance of state control of sea-lanes and officials, Vagg (1995: 67) directed attention to the importance of state infrastructure, particularly highlighting improvements made to roads, which, were recognised as 'decisively' changing 'the transport patterns on which piracy depended', with consequences for the introduction of effective policing.

By the end of the nineteenth century, as noted by Andreas and Nadelmann (2006: 25), 'a once customary form of waging war had been all but eliminated from the face of the earth'. Piracy in European and North Atlantic waters was virtually extinguished coinciding with the advent of the modern nation-state, and attempts to end practices which came to be regarded as official corruption (Vagg, 1995: 65).

Slavery and the Slave Trade

Slavery and the slave trade constitute activities that were not illegal in the seventeenth and early decades of the eighteenth century but which now would be considered as crimes. This example is a useful illustration of definitions of crime altering across history, thus making it difficult to accurately assess trends in crime (and especially to compare the overall volume of crime) over historical time periods.

As documented by Laverick (2016: 292–38), slavery and the slave trade predate the arrival of Europeans on the west coast of Africa (Agozino, 2005: 121) and have existed since antiquity (Felson & Kalaitzidis, 2005: 7). According to these authors, having virtually disappeared from the European continent, slavery re-emerged after 1500 initiated by the conquest of the Americas in the sixteenth century.

The expansion and acceleration of the slave trade has been explained in relation to the development of the plantation economy in the so-called 'New World', which has been viewed as creating a huge market for slaves (Agozino, 2005: 121). Hardt and Negri (2001: 121) suggested that large-scale plantation production with slave labour was initiated in the Caribbean in the mid-seventeenth century by English and French planters who imported African slaves to replace native peoples killed by European weapons and disease. During the seventeenth and eighteenth centuries, the potential areas of supply increased as Europeans established more trading enclaves along the coast (Agozino, 2005: 121) and as European governments acquired a strong interest in developing the transatlantic slave trade, viewing black Africa as a limitless source of labour for the plantations and mines of the Americas (Andreas & Nadelmann, 2006: 27).

Andreas and Nadelmann, drawing upon the work of Craton (1974) and Curtin (1969), noted that, following the signing of the Peace of Utrecht in 1713, British slavers assumed a dominant role in the highly profitable trade, transporting a substantial portion of the estimated 10 million black Africans ultimately imported into the Americas (Andreas & Nadelmann, 2006: 27). By the end of the eighteenth century, the products of slave labour in the Americas have been estimated to constitute one-third of the value of European commerce (Hardt & Negri, 2001: 121).

Most historical accounts of African slavery in the criminological literature chart the criminalisation of the slave trade in 1807 following the signing of an 'Act to Prohibit the Importation of Slaves into any Port or Place Within the Jurisdiction of the United States' by President Jefferson (Deflem, 2011: 79; Nadelmann, 1993: 31–46). Despite the incremental development of a legislative framework, scholars observe the difficulties and challenges of enforcement recognising that 'enforcement was generally lacking' and 'repeatedly violated by entrepreneurs all along the eastern and southern seaboard' (Nadelmann, 1993: 31–33).

While the British Parliament made the slave trade illegal at home in 1807, the suppression of slavery within its colonies occurred much later—in the

British West Indies in 1838 and British India in 1843 (Bassiouni, 1991, cited in Felson & Kalaitzidis, 2005: 8).

Conventional perspectives stress the significance of moral norms presenting the eventual abolition of slavery as evidence of moral progress and modernisation (Pogge, 2008: 2). Associated with this observation is the view that slavery comprised a form of pre-capitalist production, hence the final banning of the Atlantic slave trade during the first two decades of the nineteenth century was regarded as signalling a new 'progressive' approach to tropical Africa (Agozino, 2005: 121), with the capitalist ideology of freedom viewed as a progressive force of enlightenment leading to the replacement of slavery.

However, this perspective has been challenged, with critical scholars calling into question the assumption that slavery comprised a pre-existing form of production and that capitalism was antithetical to slavery. Hardt and Negri (2001: 73) for example, contend that 'Capital's relationship to colonial slavery' is in fact 'much more intimate and complex'. Thus, for Hardt and Negri, the large-scale colonial slave production system, which arose in the Americas between the late seventeenth and mid-nineteenth centuries, should not be viewed as pre-capitalist, but instead, should be understood as part of the complex and contradictory developments of capital. Slave production in the Americas and the African slave trade are therefore reconceptualised as 'a pedestal of super exploitation on which European capitalism stood' (Hardt & Negri, 2001: 122).

Smuggling

Smuggling entails the illegal trading in goods in order to avoid paying customs duties and taxes. It embraced two distinct activities, illegally importing goods without paying the duties on them and illegally exporting goods without paying the duties – the latter crime being known as 'owling' (McLynn, 1989: 173). This originated when, in 1614, the export of wool was made illegal.

Thus although, as with piracy, this form of crime was not unique to the eighteenth century, the period known as the 'golden age' of smuggling reached its climax in the early decades of the nineteenth century during the Napoleonic wars. It frequently involved smuggling goods out of the country, the profits from which were then used to purchase other goods which were smuggled back into Britain: wool in return for tea was an example of this trade in the 1740s (Norton, 2003: [Online]).

The main impetus for smuggling was the introduction of customs duties on a wide range of goods imported and exported goods in the seventeenth century which further increased during the eighteenth century, in part to finance the wars in which Britain was engaged in this period. It has been observed that 'the existence of a customs duty several times the price of a commodity makes smuggling a temptation difficult to resist, particularly when there is little chance of the fraud's detection and a steady demand for the commodity in question' (Barker, 1954: 387).

A further duty, the excise tax—a tax on domestic consumption—augmented customs duties from the late seventeenth century and was levied on an ever-increasing array of goods that included goods such as salt, leather and soap. This was a further spur to the smuggling of imported goods.

High taxes created a market for persons wanting these goods more cheaply and who viewed the smugglers favourably. As with contemporary white-collar crimes, there was a tendency to view smuggling as not constituting a crime, provided no violence was involved (Norton, 2003: [Online]). Additionally, communities in which smugglers operated benefitted from their activities by being able to acquire goods they could not otherwise afford to buy, although quiescence could also be achieved by intimidation (Norton, 2003: [Online]). Pirates were frequently involved in these activities since goods they had looted at sea became the merchandise that was smuggled into the United Kingdom. 'River Pirates' operating on the River Thames also stole goods from ships moored there which formed part of the contraband that was distributed through networks used by smugglers.

The main items smuggled into the country in the eighteenth century were wine, spirits (especially gin and brandy), tea, tobacco and lace, although other goods, such as salt in were also smuggled. The favoured method of smuggling goods into the country was to run them into a remote bay or creek in secluded coastal areas often at night, especially along the south coast of England (Sussex and Kent) and West Wales. Kent's close proximity to France (where many of the smuggled goods could be obtained) and its nearness to London (which provided a market for smuggled goods) made it very much the centre of the smuggling trade.

Smugglers made use of large rowing boats (referred to as 'galleys') which could get across the English Channel in about 5 hours and outrun vessels used by the Customs and Excise officers. These were used in what was termed the 'guinea run' that entailed smuggling gold guinea coins from Britain to France. In Kent, Folkestone cutters were used by smugglers which were met by smaller boats 3–4 miles off the coast which transported the smuggled goods to land (Norton, 2003: [Online]). There was, however, another way of conducting smuggling which involved, with the connivance of the lower ranks of the Customs Service, under-weighing goods brought into the country so that a proportion of the cargo entered the country duty free (Barker, 1954: 388).

As a crime, smuggling became highly organised after the 1740s, and it has been argued that 'by the later eighteenth century, smuggling became an example of organized crime unseen since the days of Jonathan Wild' (Norton, 2003: [Online]). It was at this time that the organisation of smuggling altered so that operations became directed by London merchants and dealers rather than placing a reliance on local people such as innkeepers to distribute the smuggled goods (Norton, 2003: [Online]).

Unlike most forms of crime in this period, smuggling was conducted by large gangs which might number up to 100, whose members carried out specialised tasks and were often funded by investors. The Hawkhurst gang that operated in Kent is an example of this during the 1740s. The highly organised form that smuggling adopted around the 1740s, provided work—and riches—to those involved in it. The numbers involved in the larger smuggling gangs also made it possible for them to fight pitched battles with the Customs officers and the military. Local militias might also be involved in attempts to combat the activities of the smugglers (Norton, 2003: [Online]).

Smuggling was successful in this period in part because of the market that London offered and also because of the deficiency of law enforcement. The Board of Excise was set up in 1643 to collect duties on a number of specified goods. In 1671, Charles II set up the Board of Customs to collect customs duties. The Board was responsible for collecting customs duties and discharged their responsibilities through a number of customs houses that were dotted around ports in coastal areas. customs officers were provided with cutters to patrol the coast to try and apprehend smugglers. Subsequently (in 1690), a number of customs officers were deployed on horseback, termed 'riding officers (Platt, 2007: 112–25). Customs officers were at the forefront of the fight against smugglers. Additionally, the military was often brought in to back up the Customs men.

Legislation was introduced in an attempt to prevent smuggling. The 1718 Hovering Act made it illegal for vessels smaller than 50 tonnes to wait within six miles of the shore, and brandy imported in smaller ships (under 15 tonnes) was also liable to seizure. Vessels involved in these offences were impounded and destroyed (Platt, 2011).

The 1736 Act of Indemnity imposed the death penalty on smugglers who injured an Excise Officer, imposed heavy fines for bribery provided that unarmed smugglers could be transported and provided an indemnity for any smuggler who named his accomplices. The 1745 Offences Against Customs or Excise Act provided for the publication of the names of armed smugglers in the *London Gazette*. A smuggler named in this manner 'Gazetted' had 40 days to turn himself in, and at the end of that period he was declared a convicted felon, subject to the death penalty (Norton, 2003: [Online]) and also had a bounty of £500 placed on his head for any person who 'turned him in' after the 40 day period had lapsed. This was paid one month after the execution had taken place. The death penalty was extended beyond smuggling to include assembling in preparation for a run, and even the harbouring of smugglers. The bodies of smugglers who killed officers were to be hung on gibbets around the coast (Platt, 2011). Legislation of this nature indicates how serious the government took the problem of smuggling in this period. Although as relatively few smugglers were caught, the impact of these sentences was reduced.

There were several reasons to explain the decline of smuggling. The reduction of duties on key goods that were smuggled, making the trade less profitable. The duty on tea was reduced in 1745 and later, the 1784 Commutation Act reduced the duty on tea by over three-quarters. Subsequent reforms affecting duties in the early nineteenth century served to make smuggling less profitable. Additionally, there was an increased willingness by the government to deploy force against them.

In 1809 the Preventive Waterguard was established which provided for enhanced central control and greater coordination of the customs services. In 1816 the Coast Blockade Force (a force consisting of land patrols) was created in Kent together with the Coastguard which operated in areas in which the Coast Blockade Force did not operate. In 1831 the Blockade Force and the Coastguard effectively merged to become the Coastguard Service with responsibility for the entire coastline. Britain's free-trade policy that was introduced during the 1840s led to a major reduction in import duties which made smuggling no longer a viable occupation.

Wrecking

Wrecking is a further aspect of crime associated with coastal locations. It entails taking cargo from a shipwreck which has occurred close to shore. It is viewed as a form of smuggling in that technically all goods washed up on shore should have been declared to the local customs house (Smugglers' Britain, undated: [Online]).

However, wrecking was viewed as a customary right by those living in coastal locations. It was based on a popular understanding of the 1285 Statute of Westminster whereby if a ship wrecked and there was nothing alive on board, it became known as a 'dead wreck'. The practice regarding 'dead wrecks' was that any goods washed ashore could be claimed by the manorial lord exercising control over the land where the ship had foundered. But in practice these goods were shared between him and those who salvaged them (Pearce, 2014: 14).

However, acquiring goods which were taken from wrecked ships had been a criminal offence since the era of Edward I and became subject to additional regulation during the eighteenth century, an important example of which being the 1753 Wreck Act. In line with the sentiments of the Bloody Code which upheld the 'sacredness' of property ownership and passed at the behest of merchants, traders and insurers of the City of London (Pearce, 2014: 6–7), the 1753 measure provided a raft of capital offences in connection with wrecking activities which included plundering, stealing, taking away or destroying goods belonging to a stranded or wrecked ship. Devon and Cornwall and the South East Coast of England were important locations where wrecking occurred.

Poaching

Hunting in the eighteenth century was the preserve of those who owned land worth more than £100 per year. Others who carried out such acts did so illegally and were termed poachers.

One impetus for poaching was the development of capitalist agricultural practices during the eighteenth century that resulted in common land (where previously commoners had grazed a few sheep or killed a few rabbits) being fenced off—a practice known as enclosure. It was henceforth treated as private property by large landowners where more scientific forms of agriculture would be practised. This resulted in commoners and peasants resorting to illegal ways to uphold what they had historically enjoyed freely. Although the underlying causes of poaching were viewed as that of economic necessity it also became a trade, providing a useful form of income to those who engaged in it (Savage, 2018: [Online]).

Poaching was a common crime in the eighteenth century but a novel feature in the early part of the century was that it was frequently conducted not by local poachers looking for food but by gangs who operated on a wide scale. Game—pheasants, partridges, hares, woodcock and deer—was especially a target of these gangs. Attempts by landowners to protect their property by employing numbers of gamekeepers often led to considerable outbreaks of disorder as both sides clashed and people were killed. These clashes also had a destabilising effect on class relationships in the countryside since local people often viewed poachers as allies who were standing up to local landowners and the injustices with which they were associated locally (Savage, 2018: [Online]). This has led to the conclusion that the motives of poachers might correspond to contemporary discussions of illegal hunting which views the activity as political—a 'phenomenon of rural defiance against illegitimate management regimes' (von Hessen et al., 2014: 649).

These poaching gangs were the target of legislation passed in 1723—the Waltham Black Act and was enacted to stop the depredations which were being committed near Waltham, in Hampshire, by persons in disguise or with their faces blacked. It made poaching a capital offence whereas formerly many of the crimes referred to in the Act had been misdemeanours. This measure was titled 'An Act for the more effectual punishing wicked and evil disposed Persons going armed in Disguise, and doing Injuries and Violences to the Persons and Properties of His Majesty's Subjects, and for the more speedy bringing the Offenders to Justice'.

It was observed that the technique of these offenders, who operated in the forests of Waltham, seemed to have been modelled on the criminal activities of the famous band of Roberdsmen, or followers of Robert (or Robin) Hood, who committed great outrages in the reign of Richard the First on the border of England and Scotland (Radzinowicz, 1945: 56).

The Act catered for 'any offender who was armed and with a blacked face, armed and otherwise disguised, merely blacked, merely disguised, accessories after the fact or "any other person or persons"' (Radzinowicz, 1945: 57). Anyone in one of the above categories was found in a forest, chase, down or Royal Park could be executed. The Act also made it an offence to hunt, kill, wound or steal deer in those locations, with the first offence punishable by a fine and the second by transportation. Other criminalised activities included fishing, the hunting of hares, the destruction of fish-ponds, the destruction of trees and the killing of cattle in those locations, the last of which is also punishable by death. An offender could also be executed for setting fire to corn, hay, straw, wood, houses or barns or shooting another person. The same penalties applied to attempting to rescue anyone imprisoned under the Black Act or attempting to solicit other people to participate in crimes that violated it (Radzinowicz, 1945: 58–9, 60–67, 68 and 72).

In total, the Act created over 50 new criminal offences that were punishable by death. Radzinowicz (1945: 57) observed that no other single statute passed during the eighteenth century equalled this measure in severity and that 'none appointed the punishment of death in so many cases'. He added that it constituted 'a rigid system of widely framed and indiscriminately applied laws, the sole purpose of which is to inspire terror' (Radzinowicz, 1945: 73).

The Act provides a useful illustration of approaches compatible with twentieth-century Marxist criminology whereby the state and its institutions are 'primarily concerned with serving the interests of those who owned or controlled the means of production and in particular to ensure that conditions existed for the accumulation of capital which was needed both to buy labour and invest' (Joyce & Laverick, 2023: 26).

This measure remained on the statute books for exactly 100 years when poaching, while remaining illegal, became no longer a capital offence. Poaching remained relatively widely practised for much of the nineteenth century but was on the decline from around the late 1870s onwards.

The Growth of Towns and New Forms of Crime in the Early Eighteenth Century

The growth of towns opened new opportunities for crime. Although it is argued that between 1700 and 1750, the population of England remained relatively stagnant (Wilde, 2020: [Online]), London was an exception: it has been estimated that in the mid-1670 s, its population was around 500,000 and that this figure rose to 630,00 by 1715 and 740,000 by 1760 (The Proceedings of the Old Bailey, 2018a: [Online]). This population increase created new opportunities for crime in the capital, leading to the conclusion that 'in eighteenth century England crime was overwhelmingly a London phenomenon' (McLynn, 1989: 1).

Causes of Early Eighteenth-Century Crime—Anomie Theory

Criminological concerns as to why people committed crime had not been comprehensively developed in the early years of the eighteenth century. However, subsequent criminological examination contains ideas that are of relevance to the commission of crime in the early eighteenth century (and which remain valid for crime conducted later in that century which is discussed in Chapter 4). This section focuses on the theory of anomie: although this was developed in the late nineteenth and twentieth centuries, it has considerable relevance to themes and ideas discussed in this chapter and in Chapter 4 regarding the causes, character and nature of crime throughout the eighteenth century.

Émile Durkheim was a leading figure in late nineteenth-century sociological positivism, in which crime was depicted as the consequence of social upheaval. Durkheim developed the concept of anomie to describe a state of social indiscipline affecting the way in which individuals seek to achieve their personal goals. His theory of crime was devised 'in the context of an overall theory of modernisation' (Vold et al., 1998: 132) whereby societies progressed from feudalism to capitalism (which Durkheim referred to as a transition from a mechanical to an organic society). He asserted that all societies were in the process of transition with none being totally one or the other (Vold et al., 1998: 125).

Durkheim's concept of anomie was initially put forward in 1893 and was subsequently developed in 1897 (Durkheim, 1893, 1897). Anomie occurred in two separate sets of circumstances, the first (which is relevant to this chapter) was in the initial period of transition from one society to another. In this circumstance, the old social order and its methods of enforcing social control broke down but the new social order and rules to regulate the behaviour of its members were not fully developed.

Later in the twentieth century, Durkheim's concept of anomie as an explanation of the causes of crime was developed by social strain theory. This developed from the functionalist perspective that human behaviour was determined by the social structure. Robert Merton was a leading social strain theorist who concentrated on explaining deviancy. His ideas were originally put forward in 1938.

Robert Merton developed Durkheim's concept of anomie. He suggested that there were a number of behavioural patterns which individuals could exhibit in reaction to the culturally approved goals of the society in which they lived and the institutionalised ways of achieving them (Merton, 1938: 676). One of these was by what he termed innovation—an individual prevented from obtaining society's success goals by legitimate means might attempt to achieve them by abandoning the 'rules of the game' and attain them by criminal methods.

Merton thus argued that the state of anomie arose from a mismatch between the culturally induced aspirations to strive for success (which he asserted in Western societies was the pursuit of wealth) and the structurally determined opportunities to achieve it. The 'differential application of opportunity' (Williams, 2001: 345) imposed a strain on an individual's commitment to society's success goals and the approved way of attaining them and resulted in anomie which was characterised by rulebreaking behaviour by those who were socially disadvantaged.

Unlike Durkheim (who believed that an individual set his or her own success goals subject to the constraints imposed by society), Merton contended that these and the means to achieve them were set by society. Merton further asserted that social inequality was the key reason for deviancy. It was not, as Durkheim contended, dependent on social disintegration but was an endemic condition that was particularly associated with the working class. As will be argued in the following section, views of this nature were expressed with regard to early eighteenth-century crime which was especially associated with the poor.

The Nature of Early Eighteenth-Century Crime

It has been remarked that although both at the time and subsequently by crime historians there was and has been a tendency to devote attention to (in)famous criminal such as Jack 'The Lad' Shepherd (executed in 1724), Jonathan Wild (executed in 1725) and to highwaymen such as Dick Turpin (executed in York in 1739), these should be regarded as 'the more extreme examples of London criminality, made even more extreme by literary, and sometimes visual, characterisation' (Shore, 2003: 139). Much urban crime which was brought to the attention of the authorities (which ruled out most crimes such as domestic violence which were committed behind closed doors) was of a more mundane nature. Shore (2003: 139) used Sessions of the Peace records in the early 1720s as evidence of 'the petty and mundane nature of most crimes' with assault cases being the chief form of petty crime in urban areas in the early decades of the eighteenth century (Gray, 2015: 76). Nonetheless, crime of this nature was of considerable concern to the respectable classes of the time.

The early decades of the eighteenth century witnessed what has been described as 'a heightened concern about crime in the metropolis' (Shore, 2003: 147). Much crime was committed locally, within the boundaries of the parish (which was the main social and administrative unit at that time) and thus criminals were part of the local neighbourhood in which they operated (Shore, 2003: 145). It has been asserted that 'the workplace, domestic service [theft by servants], familial connections, sociability and street-life were all points in the lived experience that may have provided opportunities for theft' (Shore, 2003: 140). This made for local reactions designed to limit crime and immorality.

However, urban living also served to extend the opportunities for crime to be committed, especially while shopping, at sporting or social events which attracted rich and poor alike and provided new opportunities for the rich to be victimised through crimes such as pick pocketing in which crowd situations provided the criminal with a degree of anonymity to perform illegal acts. This form of crime was especially attributed to women (sometimes posing as prostitutes) and youths.

There was a tendency to locate the criminal classes (or more accurately, the criminal sub-classes) with the urban poor where it has been argued that crime in urban environments was 'part of the broader makeshift economy of the poor' (Shore, 2003: 141) with workplace theft, prostitution and receiving being key aspects of the 'makeshift economy' (Shore, 2003: 144). It has been argued that 'workplace theft, begging and vagrancy, prostitution, petty theft, shoplifting, and receiving of stolen goods are all points on the continuum linking poverty and criminality' (Shore, 2003: 144) and that what might be seen straight-forwardly as criminal behaviour by the authorities, might by the offender be viewed as solutions to poverty, dearth, crisis, under-and unemployment' (Shore, 2003: 139).

It was concluded that 'many poor Londoners undoubtedly resorted to crime, especially property theft, because it offered them their only chance for earning a living' (Ultimate History Project, undated: [Online]). Accordingly, it was argued that it was hard to distinguish between 'a "criminal" population of London and the poor population as a whole .... we can say of the hanged that they belonged to the poor' (Linebaugh, 2006: xxi). The availability of cheap gin in the early part of the eighteenth century was also seen as a factor in the commission of crime and one which linked the vices of the poor to illegal actions (Ultimate History Project, undated: [Online]).

The perceived relationship between crime and poverty suggests that crime played an important role in 'survival strategies' but it also makes it hard to draw a distinction between 'the poor' and 'the criminal' as 'overlaps of 'deviant' and 'normal' life in the metropolis were much more ambiguous' (Shore, 2003: 141). The extent to which crime was tolerated by poor people within neighbourhoods is one factor that serves to blur the distinction between the criminal classes and the poor in general.

Nonetheless, contemporary commentators did draw such a distinction by attributing urban crime to 'organised gangs of criminals' which thrived comfortably in an inverted world of robbery, gambling, whoring, vice and idleness' (Shore, 2003: 147) and which gave a certain degree of professionalism to crime in that period. It also resulted in certain areas of the city being viewed as 'no go' areas by contemporaries of the period (McLynn, 1989: 3). Such places manifested many of the characteristics that the Chicago School of Human Ecology, building on Durkheim's theory of anomie, would later in the 1930s and 1940s identify as 'social disorganisation' (discussed in Joyce,

2017: 14–15). Specific features of these areas of London in the early eighteenth century included a highly transient population, a high proportion of young and unmarried people (most of whom had migrated from rural Britain), loosened family ties and the inability to apply traditional methods of social control based on deference to control behaviour (Hay, 2011: 55, Linebaugh, 2011: 79–80).

In the 1720s and 1730s fears about crime, especially street crime such as pick pocketing, were especially articulated. Concerns arose from a number of factors which included the activities of Jonathan Wild (which will be considered later) and the demobilisation of troops after the 1713 Treaty of Utrecht (Shore, 2003: 148). The actual extent to which crime actually grew in London in this period is probably incapable of accurate calculation, but there was a moral panic about crime in this period, inflamed by writing of authors such as Daniel Defoe. This concern was especially focused on criminal gangs as opposed to the poor in general.

It has thus been concluded that 'the early eighteenth century was a period of heightened anxiety about crime and order, and consequently one in which the combined forces of media attention, social policy and elite commentary created a vision of the metropolis infested and overrun by organised criminality' (Shore, 2003: 138). This concern extended to numerous forms of criminal activity.

Women and Crime

Beattie's (1975) essay on the criminality of women in seventeenth-and eighteenth-century England examined the judicial records of two south-eastern counties, Surrey and Sussex. Beattie examined cases dealt with in the principal courts of these counties in 63 sample years selected between 1663 and 1802. He argued that

> apart from poaching and forgery, women participated in the same range of crimes as men and that the patterns of male and female crime were similar in the sense that for each, property offences accounted for roughly half of the charges laid and crimes against the person, roughly a third. But the numbers involved were markedly different. Except in some of the less common offences, like counterfeiting, men decisively outnumbered women in all crimes, predominating by more than three to one in the largest categories of property offences and personal violence

He noted, however, that the records of the courts in Surrey revealed that 80 per cent of those charged with felonies were men and that 'A strikingly lower level of criminality of women is clearly apparent' (Beattie, 1975: 80). However, he also concluded that.

> Women's crime ... was very much more extensive in the city than in the rural parishes and market towns of the rest of the county of Surrey or in the essentially rural county of Sussex. And women not only committed a larger number of offences in these urban parishes, but also accounted for a much higher proportion of the total crime in the city than in the countryside" (Beattie, 1975: 81).

This led him to suggest that.

> The contrasting urban and rural crime patterns ... derive from and are evidence of differences in the nature of women's lives and work in these different settings, in the range of their social contacts and in their economic opportunities and difficulties (Beattie, 1975: 81).

Records of cases tried at London's Old Bailey also revealed that the scale and nature of female criminality was different to that conducted by males, although women accounted for around 40% of the defendants from the 1690s to the 1740s (and over half the defendants in the first decade of the eighteenth century (The Proceedings of the Old Bailey, 2018b: [Online]). This situation may have arisen as the consequence of migration into London which led to women facing significant economic hardships.

> New immigrants to the metropolis were often cut off from networks of support such as family and friends, and women's wages were typically significantly lower than men's, and their jobs less secure (The Proceedings of the Old Bailey, 2018b: [Online]).

It was stated that throughout the period 1674–1913, female defendants at the Old Bailey.

> account for a significant proportion of the accused in only a small number of offences, particularly certain kinds of theft (pickpocketing, shoplifting, theft from lodging houses, theft from masters, and receiving stolen goods) and coining, kidnapping, keeping a brothel, and offences surrounding childbirth. On the other hand, relatively few women were accused of deception, other sexual offences, breaking the peace, and robbery (The Proceedings of the Old Bailey, 2018b: [Online]).

This situation was in part explained by the prescribed gender roles (with passivity being emphasised as a female attribute which tended to reduce their involvement in crimes of violence) and to the different nature of the lives led by men and women-

> Women, for example, were less likely to carry weapons or tools, or to spend time in alehouses, so they were less likely to become involved in spontaneous fights, and when they did they rarely had a lethal weapon to hand. Since they spent more time in the home they may have had fewer opportunities to commit crime, particularly temptations to steal (The Proceedings of the Old Bailey, 2018b: [Online]).

In agreement with Beattie (1975) it was argued that life styles also influenced the way in which men and women carried out specific types of crime in London -

> It is certainly likely that male and female patterns of theft differed, owing to the different types of work and leisure engaged in by each sex. Thus prostitutes stole from their clients and were accused of pickpocketing; female servants stole from their masters; and female customers, possibly motivated by desires to keep up with the latest fashions, stole from shops. In addition, women's participation in trading networks gave them skills suitable for buying and selling stolen goods. On the other hand, men were far more likely to be involved in thefts from places of work such as ships, warehouses, docks, and places of manufacture; and, in rural areas, thefts of livestock (The Proceedings of the Old Bailey, 2018b: [Online]).

Box 2.3: Gender, Crime and Employment Opportunities

It has been noted above that female criminality was influenced by employment opportunities.

Drawing on archival research on women in Aberdeen and Edinburgh, Colchester and Kingston-Upon-Thames, Simonton noted that women worked in a myriad of ways during the eighteenth century, with husbands, in families, and as independent workers, both married and single. Middling women 'left bequests...managed household economies, bought luxury goods and fostered cultural production. They were also - and significantly- active in urban commerce and their status as traders was widely recognised' (Simonton, 2013a: 95–6).

'Women dominated certain areas of urban activity, such as clothing trades, food trades, innkeeping, midwifery, and service, also having roles in the informal and sometimes illegal economy, also playing a central part in the development of both local and international commerce in several towns of England in the eighteenth and early nineteenth centuries.

Examining agency as a mosaic of changing opportunities, Simonton and Montenach addressed different local and national contexts, and the constraints and obstacles with which women had to fight or cope - such as laws, guilds or hierarchical relationships - in the private and public spheres' and accommodated, negotiated or manipulated social rules and gender roles' (Simonton & Montenach, 2013: 5).

In their study of female servants in eighteenth-century European towns, it was suggested that women utilised 'diverse strategies, to accommodate, negotiate or manipulate social and gender regulations and restrictions, in order to gain access to major social resources such as work and mobility (both physical and hierarchical), thereby illustrating both the constraints and opportunities presented to women in an urban environment' (Simonton & Montenach, 2013: 5–6).

It was noted that 'As places that disseminated and fostered key social, economic, political and cultural developments, towns were central to the creation of gendered identities and the transmission of ideas across local, national and transnational boundaries' (Simonton, 2013b: 2).

The Role of Receivers

The crime with which women were especially associated which included shoplifting was also often conducted by some form of criminal gang (Shore, 2003: 150). Young children also operated in gangs whose stolen goods were passed on to receivers. This suggested that crime in the late seventeenth and early eighteenth centuries possessed a degree of organisation.

The way in which crime was alleged to be organised focused on factors which included family or neighbourhood links or criminal networks in which receivers (sometimes called 'fences') were deemed to play a crucial role (Shore, 2003: 155).

Many early eighteenth-century commentators felt that the criminal law was poorly structured in the way it dealt with receivers:

> receiving was not actually a felony in common law; the inherent problem was in the link between the receiver and the offender. Thus to convict a receiver, the thief had first to be convicted of felony. By 1718 receivers who were found guilty of being accessories to a felony could be transported for fourteen years. However, there were substantial difficulties in convicting receivers .... Receivers were portrayed as a central feature of the world of organised crime, an agent linking the individual criminal to the broader networks of crime in the city (Shore, 2003: 153–4).

Those who were accused of receiving tended to be pawnbrokers, old clothes shop keepers, publicans and lodging-house keepers, persons who 'occupied roles, ran trades or small businesses, at the heart of the community' (Shore, 2003: 154). Receivers were described as 'central players in the interlinking of community and criminal networks in the metropolis' (Shore, 2003: 154).

It is finally important to point out that crime was not confined to the urban working class. Fraud and forgery were two examples of what we would now refer to as white-collar crime (McLynn, 1989: 133) while offences such as arson and animal maiming afflicted rural areas.

Conclusion

The eighteenth century was often depicted as a period when the customary activities of the poor 'increasingly came under the orbit of the criminal justice system' (Shore, 2003: 137). This especially applies to the activities of the rural and labouring poor (Shore, 2003: 138) whose customary rights and perquisites were eroded' (Shore, 2003: 143) by the twin processes of urbanisation and industrialisation (McLynn, 1989: 301). The erosion of customary rights and 'perks' especially affected rural and coastal locations.

Such a sentiment is compatible with an attempt to draw a distinction between two distinct types of offence and offenders—many forms of which have been considered above—'good criminals' (which included rioters, poachers, smugglers and primitive rebels in industry) to which the term 'social crime' (where 'the perpetrators operated within a broad local or customary consensus of right') (Hay et al., 2011: xlviii) was applied and those who committed crime without qualification—such as thieves, robbers, highwaymen, forgers, arsonists and murderers (Hay et al., 2011: xv-xvi), activities that were branded 'individualistic, selfish or cruel' (Hay et al., 2011: xlviii).

It was argued that those engaged in social crime often did so in support of a traditional way of life which drew them into conflict with the propertied classes and which was likely to secure a degree of support from the local community in which the crime was committed (Hay et al., 2011: xvi). It was remarked about smugglers, for example, that they were overwhelmingly plebian-

> Drawn from the labouring poor of the countryside … far from being seen as criminals, they were held to be defending traditional and customary rights, as well as resisting unpopular authorities and an evolving national market. (Hay et al., 2011: xxviii)

It was further suggested that poaching, wrecking as well as smuggling 'often had the support of or silent acquiescence of significant parts of the community giving rise to them' and sometimes involved 'a tinge of redistributivism' (Hay et al., 2011: xxviii).

There was, however, some degree of fuzziness at the edges of a distinction between social and other forms of criminal activity, as witnessed by events that included manifestations of popular support for criminals such as Jack Shepherd (a thief, burglar, pickpocket, highwayman and shoplifter) when he was executed in 1724.

? Summary Question

Evaluate changes to the character and occurrence of crime that took place in the period 1689–1750.

References

Agozino, B. (2005). Crime, criminology and post-colonial theory: Criminologial reflections on West Africa. In J. Sheptycki, and A. Wardak (Eds.), *Transnational and comparative criminology*. GlassHouse Press.

Andreas, P., & Nadelmann, E. (2006). *Policing the globe: Criminalization and crime control in international relations*. Oxford University Press.

Barker, T. (1954). Smuggling in the eighteenth century: The evidence of the Scottish Tobacco Trade. *The Virginia Magazine of History and Biography, 62*(4), 387–399.

Bassiouni, M. C. (1991). Enslavement as an international crime. *International Law and Politics, 23*, 445–517.

Beattie, J. (1975). The criminality of women in eighteenth century England. *Journal of Social History, 8*(4), 80–116.

Beattie, J. (1986). *Crime and the Courts in England 1660–1800*. Oxford University Press.

Beattie, J. (2012). *The first English detectives. The Bow Street Runners and the Policing of London, 1750–1840*. Oxford University Press.

Brain, J. (undated). *"Bow Street Runners" HistoricUK.[Online]* https://www.historic-uk.com/HistoryUK/HistoryofBritain/Bow-Street-Runners/. Accessed 8 Oct 2020.

Cohen, L., & Felson, M. (1979). Social change and crime rate trends: A routine activity approach. *American Sociological Review, 44*(4), 588–608.

Craton, M. (1974). *Sinews of empire: A short history of British slavery*. Anchor Books.

Curtin, P. (1969). *The Atlantic slave trade*. University of Wisconsin Press.

De Souza, P. (1999). *Piracy in the Greco-Roman World*. Cambridge University Press.
Deflem, M. (2011). *Policing world society: Historical foundations of international police cooperation*. Oxford University Press.
Dolin, E. (2018). *Black flags, blue waters: The epic history of America's most notorious pirates*. Liveright Publishing Corporation.
Durkheim, E. (1893). *De la division du travail social (On the Division of Labour in Society)*. Alcan.
Durkheim, E. (1897). *Le suicide (Suicide)*. Alcan. Re-published as Durkheim, E. (1979). *Suicide: A study in sociology*. Routledge & Kegan Paul.
Felson, D., & Kalaitzidis, A. (2005). A historical overview of transnational crime. In P. Reichel (Ed.), *Handbook of transnational crime and justice* (pp. 3–19). Sage Publications.
Fiske, J. (1897). *Old Virginia and her neighbours*. Houghton Mifflin.
Gosse, P. (1946). *The history of piracy*. Tudor.
Hardt, M., & Negri, A. (2001). *Empire*. Harvard University Press.
Hay, D. (2011). Property, authority and the criminal law. In D. Hay, P. Linebaugh, J., Rule, E.P. Thompson, and C. Winslow (Eds.), *Albion's fatal tree. Crime and society in eighteenth century England*, Revised edn.. Verso, originally published in 1975.
Hay, D. Linebaugh, P., Rule, J., Thompson, E., & Winslow, C. (2011). *Albion's Fatal Tree. Crime and Society in Eighteenth Century England*, Revised edn. Verso, originally published in 1975.
Gray, D. (2015). *Crime, policing and punishment in England, 1660–1914*. Bloomsbury Academic.
Joyce, P. (2017). *Criminal justice: An introduction* (3rd ed.). Routledge.
Joyce, P., & Laverick, W. (2023). *Criminal justice: An introduction* (4th ed.). Routledge.
Laverick, W. (2016). *Global injustice and crime control*. Routledge.
Linebaugh, P. (2006). *The London Hanged: Crime and Civil Society in the Eighteenth Century*, 2 edn. Verso Books.
McLynn, F. (1989). *Crime and punishment in eighteenth century England*. Oxford University Press.
Merton, R. (1938). Social Structure and Anomie. *American Sociological Review, 3*(5), 672–682.
Nadelmann, E. (1993). *Cops across borders: The internationalization of U.S. criminal law enforcement*. Pennsylvania State University Press.
Norton, R. (2003). *The Georgian Underworld. A Study of Criminal Subcultures in Eighteenth Century England.* Ricktornorton.co.uk. [Online] https://rictornorton.co.uk/gu13.htm. Accessed 29 Sept 2022.
Pearce, C. (2014). The Unlucky Wrecker: William Pearce of St Gennys, Cornwall. *Troze, 5*(2), 3–16.
Platt, R. (2007). *Smuggling in the British Isles: A History*. Tempus Publishing.
Platt, R. (2011). *Smuggling in the British Isles: A history* (2nd ed.). The History Press.
Pogge, T. (2008). *World poverty and human rights*. Polity Press.

Radzinowicz, L. (1945). The Waltham Black Act: A study of the legislative attitude towards crime in the eighteenth century. *The Cambridge Law Journal., 9*(1), 56–81.

Rule, J. (1977). Wrecking and Coastal Plunder. In D. Hay, P. Linebaugh, J. Rule, E.P. Thompson, and C. Winslow (Eds.), *Albion's fatal tree: Crime and society in eighteenth-century England.* Penguin.

Savage, W. (2018). Poachers in the 18th Century. *Pen and Pension.* [Online] https://penandpension.com/2018/10/10/poachers-in-the-18th-century/. Accessed 7 Oct 2020.

Shore, H. (2003). Crime, criminal networks and the survival strategies of the poor in early eighteenth century London. In: S. King and A. Tomkins (Eds.), *The Poor in England 1700–1850. An Economy of Makeshifts.* Manchester University Press.

Simon, R. (2023). Hell on High Waters. *History Magazine*, January, pp 28–34.

Simonton, D. (2013a). Widows and Wenches: Single Women in Eighteenth-Century Urban Economies. In D. Simonton and A. Montenach (Eds.), *Female agency in the urban economy: Gender in European Towns, 1640*–1830. Routledge.

Simonton, D. (2013b). *Gender in the European Town. Ancien regime to the modern.* Routledge.

Simonton, D., & Montenach, A. (2013). Introduction. In Female Agency in the Urban Economy: D. Simonton, and A. Montenach (Eds.), *Female Agency in the Urban Economy: Gender in European Towns, 1640*–1830. Routledge.

Smugglers' Britain "Guide Book – South-West England". Smuggling.co.uk. [Online] http://www.smuggling.co.uk/gazetteer_sw.html. Accessed 12 Oct 2020.

The Proceedings of the Old Bailey. (2018a). "A Population History of London". *Old Bailey Proceedings Online.* [Online] https://www.oldbaileyonline.org/static/Population-history-of-london.jsp. Accessed 9 Oct 2020.

The Proceedings of the Old Bailey. (2018b). "Gender in the Proceedings". *Old Bailey Proceedings Online.* [Online] https://www.oldbaileyonline.org/static/Gender.jsp. Accessed 13 Jan 2023.

UK Parliament. (2023). "Turnpikes and Tolls". *Parliament UK.* [Online] https://www.parliament.uk/about/living-heritage/transformingsociety/transportcomms/roadsrail/overview/turnpikestolls/#:~:text=The%20first%20such%20Act%2C%20of,roads%20from%20London%20were%20turnpiked. Accessed 7 Jan 2023.

Ultimate History Project Staff. (undated). Crime and Criminals in Eighteenth Century London. *Ultimate History Project*. [Online] http://ultimatehistoryproject.com/crime-and-policing-in-18th-c-london.html. Accessed 26 Sept 2020.

Vagg, J. (1995). Rough seas? Contemporary piracy in South East Asia. *British Journal of Criminology, 35*(1), 63–80.

Vold, G., Bernard, T., & Snipes, J. (1998). *Theoretical criminology* (4th ed.). Oxford University Press.

von Essen, E. Hansen, H., Nordström Källström, H., Peterson, M., & Peterson, T. (2014). Deconstructing the poaching phenomenon: A review of typologies for understanding illegal hunting. *The British Journal of Criminology, 54* (4), 632–651.

Williams, K. (2001). *Textbook on Criminology* (4th ed.). Oxford University Press.

3

Urban Policing

Introduction

It has been argued that the term 'police' in the eighteenth century 'implied a … general system of government the task of which was to regulate broad aspects of communal existence with the aim of establishing the common good of the community and was closely associated with maintenance of the moral order, security and the maximisation of national resources' (Dodsworth, 2008: 583–4). Although this entails functions beyond that of maintaining law and order, these were key roles performed by the policing apparatus.

In the late seventeenth century and early eighteenth century, the system of policing was antiquated and adequate to combat the new crime problems that were then emerging, mainly in urban Britain. It relied very heavily on voluntary effort which took the form of parish constables, watchmen and the hue and cry. The origins of this are Anglo-Saxon (a period that stretches from A.D. 410 to 1066) but the approach was updated in the 1285 Statute of Winchester. But it was not effective and it has been remarked that 'parish-based policing touched but lightly on everyday life' (Taylor, 1998: 2). Accordingly, initiatives such as the employment of paid night watchmen were introduced to provide a more effective response to crime. Initiatives that were associated with crime detection, especially the role of 'thief takers' in the early eighteenth century, will also be investigated.

Drawing on key episodes of public disorder in the early eighteenth century, the chapter will also consider state responses to serious episodes of public

P. Joyce and W. Laverick, *History of Policing, Crime, Disorder, Punishment*,
https://doi.org/10.1007/978-3-031-36892-9_3

disorder, including the 1714 Riot Act and the role of the military in maintaining order.

The 1285 Statute of Winchester

The 1285 Statute of Winchester (which is also referred to as the 1285 Statute of Westminster II) stood at the peak of developments in dealing with law and order that date back to the twelfth century, in particular King Henry II's 1164 Assize at Clarendon. This led to Judges being appointed (then termed 'Judges of Eyre' and later 'Royal Judges' who subsequently became incorporated into the Assize court structure in 1293) who would tour all areas of England and try cases related to serious crime.

Box 3.1: The Statute of Winchester

The 1285 Statute of Winchester established several important principles and practices regarding how law and order should henceforth be administered.

It emphasised the importance of communal responsibility for protection and law enforcement (which was based on the Anglo-Saxon procedure known as 'frankpledge' and which can be traced back to King Canute who ruled England 1016–1035) which it wished to see delivered in a standardised manner throughout England through practices.

These included the appointment of constables at the level of the Hundred and Tything (these would now correspond to the present system of chief constables—the term 'High Constable' was applied in the seventeenth and eighteenth centuries and these were often persons of high social standing—[Emsley, 2018: 226] and ordinary or 'petty' constables derived from the Anglo-Saxon office of Tythingman), the responsibility to participate in the hue and cry and the sheriff's *posse comitatus* and to possess and train in the use of arms in order to implement it.

It also required the appointment of a night watch in walled towns which might also raise the hue and cry. The development of Justices of the Peace in 1361 (building upon a reform of Richard I's which created Keepers of the Peace in 1195) gave these officials a major role in the superintendence of Parish Constables in the late seventeenth and early eighteenth centuries.

A further consequence of the 1285 Statute relates to viewing the task of law enforcement (and national defence in general) as a male responsibility. McCormack (2012: 61) discussed the importance of masculinity when thinking about the military, citizenship and policing in eighteenth-century England. A tract by Granville Sharp written in 1781 argued that

> Just as civilian men were expected to provide their own policing, so they were expected to act in their country's defence. The citizen was required by ancient laws such as the Statute of Winchester to keep up a proficiency in arms and to associate and intervene in order to restore the king's peace. Granville Sharp reasoned that if men were anciently obliged to be able to use a long bow, why not 'require the exercise of ALL MEN in the use of the present fashionable weapons, the musquet and bayonet'?

The Stature of Winchester was the start of important developments that aimed to standardise the system of law enforcement across the country and the same King wrote to all sheriffs (the chief royal official in the Counties or—to give them their Anglo-Saxon name—'Shires') to try and ensure that the law was applied in a similar—or standardised—way throughout England.

The system of administration in England at that time entailed the country being divided into Counties or Shires. By the eighteenth century, power in the counties was wielded by the Lords Lieutenant, who were responsible for raising the militia and for administering the law. The day-to-day business of the latter fell on the sheriff, a demanding and unpaid role that was held for only a year (McCormack, 2012: 58–59).

The counties were in turn divided into Hundreds (settlements containing around 100 families) which were in turn divided into tythings (a settlement of around 10 families). A tything might be divided into 'vills'. A 'Vill' (or 'tun' in Anglo-Saxon) was the smallest unit of administration in this period.

The court system mirrored this structure with the Shire Court (presided over by the Sheriff) and the Hundred Court (presided over either by the sheriff or the lord of the manor to which the Hundred was attached). At the very top of the legal structure was the Royal Court.

Law enforcement, in turn, mirrored this administrative structure and was the responsibility of the Hundred Man in the Hundred and the Tything Man in the tything.

This administrative structure applied to rural England which in the twelfth and thirteenth centuries constituted most of the country. But there were some towns such as London and York which posed particular issues for law enforcement and which required special arrangements (termed 'watch and ward').

By the time of the eighteenth century, several amendments had been made to the system of medieval government. Manors tended to replace the tything and performed an important role in delivering justice through one of the two manorial courts—the Court Leet whose jurisdiction in these matters replaced the role of the Hundred Court and which appointed the constables: the other court, which mainly dealt with issues that were mainly concerned with agricultural matters and issues such as lord–tenant relationships, was the Court Baron. The development of parishes from units of administration used by the Church into units of civil administration, a development especially associated with the Tudor period (1485–1603), led to them playing a major part in locally administered law and order which included the appointment of parish constables—a development associated with the seventeenth and eighteenth centuries. A parish could be coterminous with a manor or might be one of several within the manor's boundaries.

Key developments relating to crime and order that derived from the 1285 Statute of Winchester will be examined in more detail in the next section. This discusses the hue and cry and *posse comitatus*, the system of night watch in the towns and the Parish Constable system that operated across the country.

The Hue and Cry and Posse Comitatus

The early eighteenth-century system of policing relied heavily on the voluntary principle and emphasised communal responsibilities for the upkeep of law and order, a situation that was especially apparent in the 1285 State of Winchester which contained a requirement for hue and cry to be raised when a constable or a private citizen witnessed a crime taking place (although this method of crime prevention derives from the Anglo-Saxon period). Those involved with the hue and cry were required to apprehend the criminal even if this involved chasing the criminal from the vill in which it occurred to neighbouring vills when s/he had left the scene of the crime.

The operations of the hue and cry in the Anglo-Saxon period are discussed in connection in what is now the County of Gloucestershire—procedures which were continued after 1285

> If anyone in the tything saw a crime being committed they had to raise the 'hue and cry' – by making as much noise as possible to alert everyone else. Upon hearing this, everyone had to stop what they were doing and pursue the criminal. If the offender escaped, then the whole tything was punished, usually being fined. When the offender was caught they would be taken before a court (or 'moot' as it was known) and judged by the elders of the village/hamlet. If the offence was deemed to be serious, the offender would be taken by the tythingman and presented to the 'hundred court' (a hundred was a subdivision of a shire for legal, administrative and military purposes and is roughly akin to a District Council today). Alternatively, they could be taken to the Shire court.

> The head of the hundred court was a 'reeve', while the head of the Shire and Shire court was the 'Shire-reeve' or 'Sheriff'. The latter was responsible to the King for keeping the peace in the Shire (Gloucestershire Archives, undated: [Online]).

The hue and cry and *posse comitatus* were different things. Both were used, however, in the eighteenth century and both had their roots in the 1285 Statute of Winchester. The hue and cry was a spontaneous reaction to a crime, enrolling any bystanders who were at the scene by the cry of 'stop thief'. The *posse comitatus*, as in America, was more of a delayed/reactive response whereby males aged 16–60 could be mobilised by the sheriff after a crime had occurred in order to track down the perpetrator. It was also used in connection with suppressing public disorder. The power to raise the *posse comitatus* in relation to apprehending felons was later codified by provisions contained in the 1887 Sheriffs Act but was later repealed by the 1967 Criminal Law Act.

McCormack (2012: 61) noted that 'It is striking that Georgians so routinely returned to [...] common law principles when discussing policing and home defence' and stated that the notion of the *posse comitatus* featured prominently in Sir William Jones' writing on policing (1782) and subsequently continued to be influential 'it informed plans to prevent invasion in the 1790s and to deal with riots in the 1810s and even 1830s'.

Parish Constables, Night Watchmen and Beadles

Parish Constables

The above consideration of the Statute of Winchester considers the basis of the Parish Constable system which was the bedrock of policing in the late seventeenth and early years of the eighteenth century. Constables were appointed locally. The local appointing authority varied—usually householders within a parish but also by Courts Leet where these existed and, in Westminster, by the Court of Burgesses (London Lives, 2018a, b: [Online]). Their jurisdiction was usually only within the parish that appointed them, although in London what was termed the 'custom of London' authorised them to operate throughout the city (London Lives, 2018 : [Online]).

Their supervisory arrangements also varied—often by Magistrates although sometimes by High Constables. Both Westminster and Middlesex used this arrangement whereby High Constables were appointed by the Court of Burgesses or the Sessions (London Lives, 2018a: [Online]). It also existed in some Counties, where the High Constables were often men of high social standing who exercised a variety of tasks, the most important of which was the collection of the County rates. Their role sometimes included primitive detective work (Emsley, 1986: 70).

The constables were viewed as the Magistrates' subordinate (McLynn, 1989: 19) in the sense that they were responsible for executing warrants issued by Magistrates and also had the power of arrest used against persons guilty of any crime which included vagrancy where constables might also be required to transport the vagrant out of the parish. The Constables' powers in relation to vagrancy were extended by the 1744 Vagrancy Act. In London it was reported that under orders issued by the Justices, the work of the constables could be directed against a wide range of what would be considered moral transgressions directed at prostitutes, vagrants, disorderly persons, gamblers, those who permitted excessive drinking in alehouses, 'profane swearers and cursers, those who worked on the sabbath, and a range of nuisance and regulatory offences' (London Lives, 2018a: [Online]).

The Parish Constable system made policing a highly decentralised affair, the heritage of which remains: England and Wales possess 43 separate police forces rather than having one centralised police organisation.

The Night Watch

The night watch was a component of a system known as 'watch and ward' which applied to urban areas. The 'watch' component provided for public safety at night (by guarding the city gates and apprehending strangers) and the 'ward' component (provided by the constables who also supervised the night watch) provided for security during the day. This system was not unique to England in this period and was adopted in other countries including cities located in the—then—UK colonies in America such as Boston and New York.

Traditionally, towns and cities across England were policed by night watchmen (often referred to as 'Charleys'), a system that originated in the medieval period dating from an Ordinance of 1233 which required the appointment of watchmen to arrest persons who entered 'Vills' at night and were armed. A later Ordinance of 1252 also included 'disturbers of our peace' as targets for the night watchmen (Rich, 1977: 50). The system was reinforced in the 1285 Statute of Winchester which required towns and boroughs to provide a body of men on the streets after dark.

The role of the watchmen was preventive (Emsley, 1986: 71): by the mid-eighteenth century the traditional halberd (a spear with an axe blade) had been replaced with a stick or staff and they were also equipped with a lantern and rattle: 'their job was to literally keep an eye on their designated section of roadway, as a defence against the common perils of crime and fire. In London, they patrolled from late evening until sunrise and were required to challenge persons looking suspicious and if appropriate bring them to the parish watchhouse (London Lives, 2018a: [Online]). In addition, they had the job of calling out the time and describing the weather' (Knowles, 2016: [Online]). They were supervised by constables or beadles. Beattie noted, with reference to London, the social superiority of constables over watchmen—'constables, however poor, were householders, watchmen were more likely to be lodgers' (Beattie, 2001: 205).

Watchmen performed the duty on a rota basis. This harmed the overall efficiency and effectiveness of the office. In theory it was the householders' obligation to provide night watch who would perform the task on a rota basis. However, a tendency arose during the seventeenth century whereby wealthier citizens would appoint deputies to serve in their place which served to transform, the watch into a lowly paid role which by the eighteenth century tended to be paid from a central fund rather than fines levied on those initially chosen to fulfil the role (McCormack, 2012: 60).

By 1700 towns, although in terms of their growth reflected in their population size were much in their infancy, put a strain on the parish constable system of policing and placed additional importance on the night watch.

Beadles

Beadles were described as a 'petty officer of police that may be said to have merged from the ancient parish crier' (Pryne, 1827: 137). They were parish officers responsible for carrying out a wide range of responsibilities that included executing the Vestry's orders (the Vestry being the governing body of the parish) and which often included supervising Parish constables and the night watch. They might also perform policing functions. In London, for example.

> Their responsibilities included a range of policing activities: organising and supervising the night watch; controlling crowds; prohibiting the sale of goods on Sundays; prosecuting nuisances; arresting and prosecuting prostitutes, beggars and vagrants; and even arresting men and women on more serious charges (London Lives, 2018a: [Online]).

Special Constables

The mechanism of appointing Special constables was also available to supplement the parish constable and night watch system of policing. Their origins date to the period of Alfred the Great in the ninth century and men were appointed to this role when there was a perceived need to increase the level of law enforcement. Local men were compulsorily appointed as Special Constables by Justices of the Peace and could be fined for refusing the position (Hands, 2020: [Online]). They were often appointed to help maintain public order, but their responsibilities also sometimes extended beyond this to combat crime. They were in fairly regular use in the late seventeenth and early eighteenth century. It was recorded that

> In 1698 the porters of the London Workhouse were appointed as constables. From 1711 constables were appointed by the commissioners of excise for the port of London in order to prevent pilfering from the docks, and in the 1750s the West India Company appointed "merchants' constables" for the same purpose. In the early 1760s members of Society for the Reformation of Manners were sworn in as extra constables for the prosecution of vice … In the second half of the century the City appointed additional special or deputy constables in order to police crowds during public punishments and demonstrations, under the charge of the City Marshal. Their number expanded dramatically during the 1780s, following the Gordon Riots and the move of public executions to in front of Newgate Prison, and after 1793, owing to fears of insurrection prompted by the trials of members of the reform societies for high treason. The most important role of these constables, however, appears not to have been in preventing riot and disorder, but in arresting pickpockets and vagrants (London Lives, 2018a: [Online]).

Privately Funded Police Work

Deficiencies in the operations of the prevailing system of policing in the eighteenth century sometimes prompted the creation of policing arrangements by private citizens. In London, for example, groups of private citizens sometimes banded together to create their own watch schemes to supplement the parish policing arrangements. One example was the creation of the privately maintained watch in the 'Great Square' of St Giles in the Field, London, in 1691. Societies for the Prosecution of Felons also sometimes hired watchmen to patrol their localities. Private watchmen were also employed by the merchants who owned warehouses in London dockland to prevent the theft of their goods (London Lives, 2018a: [Online]).

The Erosion of the Voluntary Principle

Although throughout the eighteenth century there was considerable support for the voluntary provision of policing (in part on grounds of wishing to avoid the costs that were inherent in a professionalised system), the above discussion of the night watch has referred to the erosion of the voluntary principle as the basis for the preservation of law and order by the employment of deputies. A similar practice also affected the Parish Constable system, arising from the preference of those who were appointed to avoid performing the duties of a constable by hiring a substitute whom they paid or by paying a fine which could fund a replacement (a practice which also arose when the chosen householder was female) (McCormack, 2012: 59). In London, it was reported that

> the practice of hiring substitutes, or deputies, became more common in the first half of the eighteenth century. By 1730, four out of every ten constables in the City of London were hired, many of whom engaged in repeated service, often holding the post for years, effectively become professional policemen (London Lives, 2018a: [Online]).

This led to the conclusion that 'systems of fines and substitutions maintained the fiction of gentry service, when in reality the duties were increasingly being performed by paid functionaries of a lower social rank' (McCormack, 2012: 59).

Additionally, what was termed a 'Tyburn Ticket' provided a means to avoid serving as a constable. By an Act of 1699, any person who successfully prosecuted a felon to a capital conviction would be awarded a certificate that exempted him from parish and ward civic duties (such as serving as a constable or juror) for life in the parish where the felony had taken place. The intention of this measure was to combat crime by encouraging persons to prosecute offenders.

However, those in possession of such a certificate sometimes sold them to a person who did not wish to serve in a civic office and the practice tended to devalue to effectiveness of the ancient system of policing. The measure granting these exemptions was repealed in 1818.

Deficiencies in the operations of the night watch also cast doubt on the usefulness of the voluntary principle affecting the policing of towns at night.

In 1735, an Act of Parliament related to London allowed the appointment of paid night watchmen in St James', Piccadilly, and St George's, Hanover Square. A total of 38 watchmen were initially appointed, superintended by 4 Beadles and one watch house keeper (Knowles, 2016: [Online]). This measure was followed by other Acts which ultimately provided a system of paid night watchmen covering most of London. The cost of the watch was passed on to householders through the rates they were obliged to pay the parish.

The professional watchman's job involved more tasks than his historic predecessor performed. The Act of Parliament that set up the St Martin-in-the-Fields watch said they were 'to prevent as well the Mischiefs which may happen from Fire, as Murders, Burglaries, Robberies, and other Outrages and Disorders' (Reynolds, 1998: 24). Typically, they patrolled in pairs from 9 pm until sunrise. It was not, however, regarded as a particularly effective form of urban policing and contributed to a situation in which 'many Londoners turned to crime because the chances of being caught and punished were relatively low' (Ultimate History Project Staff, undated: [Online]).

Between late September 1769 and March 1770 there were 104 house burglaries in London. This led to the appointment of a committee 'to enquire into burglaries and robberies in Westminster and London and whether it is a growing evil'. The report, published in 1770, evidenced the insufficiency of the reforms that had been introduced into Westminster. It was argued that

> The Watch is insufficient; their Duty too hard, and Pay too small.... That as they are paid Monthly, they borrow their Money of a Userer once a Week.... That the Watch in Westminster is in every Parish under the Direction of a separate Commission:-That Commissioners of the respective Parishes appoint the Beats of their Watchmen without conferring together, which leaves the Frontiers of each Parish in a confused State (Journal of the House of Commons, 1770, Vol XXXII, page 879, cited in Lyman, 1964: 142).

Reforms to the Watch in Westminster were introduced by legislation in 1774 when the Westminster Watch Act established a number of minimum standards affecting the recruitment, pay and conditions of work of the watchmen. Further reform came in 1783 in terms of establishing a minimum wage for the night watch, regulating hours of duty and defining duties. Although, it was concluded that the Act 'changed nothing nor improved anything' (Lyman, 1964: 142–3), the Select Committee that inquired into the state of the Police of the Metropolis heard complimentary accounts of the Watch that was employed in Marylebone, St James's and St George's Hanover square. They were mainly ex-soldiers, 'tall stout fellows' who were below 40 years of age (Parliamentary Papers, 1828: cited in Emsley, 1986: 72).

Elsewhere in England, paid watchmen and also constables could be provided for by local Improvement Acts.

The Detection of Crime

Thief Takers

Historically, individual citizens were expected to report and also prosecute anyone they witnessed carrying out a felony. However, during the eighteenth century there was a reluctance to do so (in part because of fears about violent criminals) so informers and thief takers played an increasingly important role in the prosecution of crime (London Lives, 2018a: [Online]). Informants were especially associated with the activities of the Societies for the Reformation of Manners that were active in the late seventeenth and early eighteenth centuries in their fight against drunkenness and sodomy which they perceived as dangerous vices. These were effectively officers of such societies (London Lives, 2018b: [Online]).

Detective work in early eighteenth-century England was chiefly performed by thief takers. They were private individuals (usually men) who lived from the rewards obtained for bringing offenders to justice which was either paid by the courts or by victims of crime whose property had been returned by the thief taker (Emsley, 1986: 73).

Both informers and thief takers, therefore, shifted the onus of policing and prosecution away from private individuals and onto persons who earned a wage from doing so.

One of the most infamous of the period was Jonathan Wild (or Wilde) who gave himself the title 'Thief Taker General of Great Britain and Ireland' in 1718.

Box 3.2: Jonathan Wild, Thief Taker

Jonathan Wild acted in the manner akin to that of a double agent. On the one hand, he took an active part in combating thieves but his motives were far from public-spirited. His aim was to dominate the London underworld by controlling all criminals in the capital. They could then be organised to steal goods and he would reap the profit by returning them to their rightful owners who would then pay him a reward. Wild also performed a useful service to thieves who might otherwise find it difficult to sell their stolen goods.

The system of rewards then in operation fuelled the profits Wild made from his double dealing. These rewards came from a combination of government money (a system initiated in 1692 in connection with highway robbers and which, at Wild's behest was considerably raised in 1720 to combat the rise in crime for which Wild was partly responsible) and that put up by private individuals whose goods had been stolen.

Those who wouldn't do business with him (the most well-known of whom was Jack Sheppard) would be the ones he would turn over to the authorities. In other cases, Wild would approach those who had been victims of crime and secure the return of the goods (which doubtless he was already in possession of) in return for a reward they would give him. But he did this under the guise of acting in the public good as a thief taker and even had his office in the Old Bailey courtroom complex, serving under the City of London's Under Marshall, Charles Hitchen (who had also been a thief taker) until the two men fell out and became rivals.

However, his deeds were discovered. An Act of Parliament (The Transportation Act) passed in 1718 made it a capital offence for a person to receive a reward for the return of stolen goods in cases where no one was convicted for having committed the crime. This curtailed his activities to an extent and he was finally arrested in 1725 in connection with an attempt to secure the freedom of one of his accomplices. Once arrested and placed in prison, other gang members came forward to give evidence against him. He was executed in 1725, his connection with the political establishment of that period making him a well-and-truly hated person by the mob.

Nonetheless, Wild's activities—even if motivated by personal greed—did have an impact on reducing crime. Additionally, there were ways that other thief takers could use to get around the 1718 Act, for example, by 'fitting up' a person to commit a crime and then arresting him or her (McLynn, 1989: 30).

Public Order Policing

It has been observed that rioting was 'endemic' throughout the eighteenth century (Hay, 2011: 23). The problem was scarcely a new one, it being noted that in the years between the accession of James I in 1601 and Charles' departure from London in 1642 'few years passed without at least one disturbance on the streets of … London and its suburbs serious enough to merit official concern' (Lindley, 1983: 109).

Several riots occurred in the early years of the eighteenth century. However, the policing apparatus that consisted of Parish Constables supplemented by other initiatives such as voluntary or paid night watches were insufficient either in numbers or organisation to be able to respond to major episodes of disorder and there was thus a reliance on other means.

Historically, trained bands (dating from 1571 and which were part time militia organised on a county basis who met and drilled on a regular basis) could be used in such situations, but most of them were dissolved during the eighteenth century. They remained in London, however, composed of householders who maintained arms to be used in the defence of the city. The London trained bands were under the control of the Lord Mayor of London and was commanded by officers appointed by the City Aldermen or the Lord Mayor. They could be called upon in times of civil emergency, although greater reliance was placed on the military. This tended to mean that their use against civilians often led to casualties and served as a reason for the development of a full time force of unarmed police officers to maintain the peace. This issue is explored in greater detail in Chapter 4.

Alternatively, the military could be used and there were several examples of this (Linebaugh referring to a number of examples from the 1740s through to the 1760s). The use of the military will be dealt with more fully in Chapter 4 (Linebaugh, 2011: 100).

Box 3.3: The 1714 Riot Act

Disorders that occurred in the early years of the eighteenth century prompted the government to enact the Riot Act of 1714. It came into force in 1715.

This legislation was designed to 'prevent tumultuous and riotous assemblies' and did so through a procedure known as 'reading the Riot Act'.

When faced with a serious public disorder that involved 12 or more persons who were deemed to be acting in a riotous manner, a local law official (usually a Magistrate but which could also be the Mayor, the Sheriff or a bailiff) was required to read out a proclamation to the crowd. This proclamation, as contained in the 1714 Act, stated

> Our Sovereign Lord the King chargeth and commandeth all persons, being assembled, immediately to disperse themselves, and peaceably to depart to their habitations, or to their lawful business, upon the pains contained in the act made in the first year of King George, for preventing tumults and riotous assemblies. God Save the King!

The 'pains' referred to in the Act treated the continued presence of the crowd as a felony offence to which the sentence of death applied. This 'sentence' was often carried out on the spot as a result of soldiers firing into an illegally assembled crowd.

Upon the reading of the Proclamation, the crowd had one hour to disperse. However, if the situation deteriorated during that period, all those who were present (whether soldiers or civilians) retained the pre-existing obligation to intervene to stop further mischief from occurring and to apprehend those who were carrying them out. However, in practice the military refused to intervene until the Riot Act had been read. The 1714 Act augmented existing powers with a new felony offence of failing to disperse after the proclamation had been read. Persons could be charged with riot only if the Proclamation had been read.

Its use was not without difficulties—in particular under-reaction by the Magistrates in reading the proclamation could result in a fine for criminal negligence whereas an instruction that the troops should open fire could lead to a trial for murder. The possibility that a soldier who fired into a crown could also be indicted for murder posed the further problem that the knowledge of this might lead to refusal to obey the order, in which case he could be shot for disobedience (Palmer, 1978: 208–9).

The 1714 measure was last used in Birkenhead in August 1919 in connection with events associated with the second police strike (The Times, 1919). It was repealed in England by the 1967 Criminal Law Act and in Scotland by the 1973 Statute Law (Repeals) Act and riot became a common law offence. It became a statutory offence once more following the passage of the 1986 Public Order Act.

Examples of Early Eighteenth-Century Disorders

This section aims, using a small number of examples, to provide a snapshot which identifies some of the major disorders which occurred in the early eighteenth century, what these were concerned with and how the eighteenth-century state sought to maintain or restore law and order. It illustrates arguments contained in the following chapter that relate to the role performed by the crowd in eighteenth-century political activity and acts as a prelude to further examples of crowd disorder which are presented in Chapter 4.

The Sacheverall and High Church Riots (1710)

The riots which were triggered in response to the prosecution of Dr. Henry Sacheverall whose impeachment trial for high crimes and misdemeanours was held in the House of Lords in 1710. Sacheverall was a High Church Anglican who had preached two sermons in 1709 (one in Derby and the other in London) condemning what he regarded as threats posed to the Church of England. The bulk of his attack was directed against Nonconformists (as opposed to Catholics) and those who gave them support (which he identified with the Whigs). His alleged crime, which prompted his trial, was an accusation of preaching against the Glorious Revolution of 1688 and his penalty, arising from his conviction, was that his sermons should be burned in public by the common hangman and that he should be barred from preaching for 3 years (although he was able to continue with his other clerical duties). This was, however, viewed as a lenient sentence and was deemed as a triumph for him and the High Church (Billingham, 2009: [Online]).

Riots broke out across England while the trial—which lasted for 3 weeks—got underway. The rioters have been described as a '"Church" Mob' (Holmes, 1976: 59) who were concerned regarding threats posed to the Church of England and to the social and moral order that it underpinned. They were Tory supporters and their targets were the homes and meeting houses of native Dissenters (as opposed to Dissenters of foreign extraction), especially Presbyterians whose congregations tended to support the Whig Party. The underlying causes of their grievances was what Anglicans regarded as the growth of Dissenters (which included Baptist, Presbyterian and Independent congregations) in the wake of the Toleration Act of 1689 (which is discussed in Chapter 1).

Other grievances also inspired those who rioted. These included the increased taxation levied by the Whig government to finance the protracted War of the Spanish Succession (1701–1715), the recent arrival of around 10,000 Calvinist refugees from the Palatinate region of Germany (most of whom settled in the London area) and the growth of what was termed the 'monied interest' among the city business community which had arisen as a consequence of the increased sophistication of international finance, a development which was linked to the occurrence of two long wars. This latter concern was linked to an element of xenophobia since many members of the 'monied interest' were of foreign extraction (Holmes, 1976: 61).

In many ways, the composition of the rioters and their motivations was at variance with contemporary and later events of this nature. Although it has been argued that by 1710, 'the hardships caused by the war with France were causing social unrest in England and the cost of living was rising alarmingly (Billingham, 2009: [Online]), it was asserted that grievances of the poorer classes—such as the price of bread—were hardly raised as an issue (Holmes, 1976: 68) and the London riot on 1–2 March 1710 has been described as 'probably the most respectable urban disorder of the century' and certainly was not a 'protest of the miserably poor and inarticulate' (Holmes, 1976: 73).

It was further argued that the London lower social orders were not conspicuous for their devoutness or church going (Holmes, 1976: 70). The disturbances were supported by those of the Anglican clergy—especially the London clergy—who believed that the Whig government would sell out the Anglican inheritance to dissenters and who made a significant contribution to the hysteria which accompanied Sacheverall's trial and the subsequent disorders (Holmes, 1976: 69).

Rioting commenced in London on 1 March 1710, entailing an attack on a Presbyterian meeting house. From that location in Lincoln's Inn Fields, the rioters moved into London's West End. The Bank of England was under threat of being attacked and looted. The events in London on 1–2 March have been described as 'the second worst disturbance of the century' (Holmes, 1976: 55) (the worst being the Gordon Riots of 1780). Subsequently in March, disorders spread outside the capital to Wrexham, Barnstaple, Gainsborough (Holmes, 1976: 55) where Presbyterian meeting houses were targeted and frequently destroyed.

In the Spring 1710 riots, disorder was restored in London by the deployment of 3 units of Guards, (comprising Life Guards, Coldstream Guards and the Second Horse Grenadiers) many of whose soldiers had served with Marlborough in his campaigns. Their discipline was observed to have been 'excellent' (Holmes, 1976: 56) and accounted for the relatively few casualties that consisted of 2 deaths and around 50 rioters wounded (Holmes, 1976: 56). The London Trained Bands were not deployed until the military had the situation well under control (Holmes, 1976: 56). It has also been argued that the absence of a Riot Act (which was not implemented until 1715) may have contributed to the low fatality and injury toll since in 1710 soldiers—or any person coming to their aid—was not indemnified if they killed a person who was later proven innocent.

Subsequently in March 1710 in London, additional military aid was deployed alongside the militia who were kept on the streets for around 3 weeks (Holmes, 1976: 58). The Trained Bands were also mobilised.

Subsequent events occurred during the summer and autumn months of 1710, the autumn riots occurring in tandem with the 1710 general election contest in which the Tories swept aside the Whig government, securing a Parliamentary majority of 151 in the House of Commons (Billingham, 2009: [Online]). One of the new government's early actions was to enact the 1711 Occasional Conformity Act which prevented Dissenters from evading the provisions of the Test Acts by occasionally taking Anglican communion.

Disorders relating to opposition towards Dissenters did not end in 1710 but continued in the early years of the Hanoverian dynasty, following the accession of George I in 1714 following the death of Queen Anne, thereby perpetuating the Protestant succession. Some Tories and High Churchmen harboured Jacobite sympathies (which aimed to return the Stuart dynasty to the throne of England), a situation that led George I to sympathise with the Whig political cause which secured victory in the 1715 general election.

Against a background of George I's unpopularity with his British subjects and social and political unrest, riots against Dissenters re-surfaced in 1715, the Midlands especially suffering from these disturbances in April 1715 which were triggered by the threat of a Jacobite invasion. These events took the form of religious riots, directed at Dissenters and their meeting houses. It was recorded that

> chapels in the West Midlands were ... attacked including those at West Bromwich, Oldbury, Dudley, Cradley, Bilston and Kingswood. The justices and constables were powerless before the mob and in order to restore order, the Warwickshire justices called out the *posse commitatus,* but the force of about 1,000 men which the constables were able to turn out, proved to be itself 'tumultuous and mutinous...being made up of chiefly of mercenary rabble', so it was not until July 26 that the High Sheriff accompanied by some mounted gentlemen and 60 horse of the late militia arrived in Birmingham and put a stop to the riots (Billingham, 2009: [Online]).

What was termed 'insurrections' which took the form of 'religious riots' directed against Dissenters' chapels, occurred elsewhere in the Midlands in Worcestershire, Warwickshire, Shropshire and Staffordshire which were allegedly encouraged, if not fomented by local gentlemen and manufacturers (Billingham, 2009: [Online]).

The events that took place in 1715 followed a sermon preached by George Sacheverell at Sutton Coldfield in October 1714 to a congregation that was mostly Jacobite in terms of political sympathies (the term 'Jacobite' referring to those who supported the claims of James II and his descendants to be the rightful heirs of the British throne). This resulted in attacks on Dissenters' chapels in Birmingham in 1714 which were a prelude to events that occurred in 1715. However, it has been argued that Sacheverell did not instigate these events but, rather, used existing social unrest to 'fan the flames of his cause' and for this reason the events that occurred in relation to his trial in 1710 to the disorders in 1715 'bear his name' (Billingham, 2009: [Online]).

The Spitalfields Weavers' Riots 1719

Disorder regularly occurred during the eighteenth century, Thornberry (1878) drawing attention to riots among the weavers in Spitalfields (East London) being a common occurrence. It was observed that throughout the seventeenth and eighteenth centuries, the Silk Weavers of the East End conducted a long-running battle with their employers and that an early method of dissent was the 'right of search' whereby weaving produced by outsiders was searched out and in some cases destroyed (Alex, 2012: [Online]).

In the early eighteenth century, disorder was underpinned by opposition to the import of silk goods and clothing manufactured from other materials including calico. One example that occurred in 1719 illustrated the problems faced by the authorities in combating disorder, having to rely on voluntary companies of militia (enrolled into Trained Bands) or the army-

> On 13 June a mob of about 4,000 Spitalfields weavers paraded the streets of the City attacking all females whom they could find wearing Indian calicoes or linens, and sousing them with ink, aqua fortis, and other fluids. The Lord Mayor obtained the assistance of the Trained Bands to suppress the rioters, two of whom were secured by the Horse Grenadiers and lodged in the Marshalsea Prison. As soon as the Guards left, the mob re-assembled, the weavers tearing all the calico gowns they could meet with. The troops were hurried back from Whitehall, and new arrests were made. The weavers then attempted to rescue their comrades, and were not deterred by volleys of blank cartridge fired by the soldiers; one of the troops then fired ball, wounding three persons. The next day four of the mob were committed to Newgate for rioting, and on Sunday night two more were sent there for felony in tearing the gown off the back of one Mrs. Beckett (Page, 1911: [Online]).

Disorders linked to this issue continued into 1720, resulting in the passage of the Calico Act, a protectionist measure which led to a ban on calico and penalties for persons convicted of wearing printed calicoes (Ashley, 2012: [Online]).

Conclusion

This chapter has discussed the way in which the law enforcement system in the early to mid decades of the eighteenth century functioned, drawing especial attention to the origins of the voluntary system that underpinned the operations of Parish Constables and the night watch and also considered how this principle was undermined by the use of substitutes and deputies by those not wanting to fulfil the responsibilities of the office they had been chosen to perform. The chapter also considered how public disorder was handled, indicating the important role of the 1714 Riot Act. This theme will be adopted in the following chapter which examines the occurrence of public disorder and the state's response to it in the period c 1750–1850.

? Summary Question

Evaluate the effectiveness of methods used between 1689 and 1750 to combat crime and public disorder.

References

Alex. (2012). Bold Defiance. *Bristol Radical History Group*. [Online] https://www.brh.org.uk/site/articles/bold-defiance/. Accessed 8 January 2023.

Ashley, I. (2012). The Spitalfields Silk Weavers: London's Luddites ?. *brh.org.uk*. [Online] https://www.brh.org.uk/site/wp-content/uploads/2012/11/THE-SPITALFIELDS-SILK-WEAVERS.pdf. Accessed 12 May 2022.

Beattie, J. (2001) *Policing and Punishment in London 1660–1750. Urban Crime and the Limits of Terror*. Oxford University Press.

Billingham, R. (2009). The Background to the Sacheverall Riots of 1710 and 1714 in Birmingham and the Sutton Coldfield Connect. *Sutton Coldfield Local History Research Group*. [Online] https://sclhrg.org.uk/images/stories/proceedings/V9-Spring_2009-3.pdf. Accessed 30 May 2022.

Brain, J. (undated). Bow Street Runners. *HistoricUK*. [Online] https://www.historic-uk.com/HistoryUK/HistoryofBritain/Bow-Street-Runners/. Accessed 8 October 2020.

Dodsworth, F. (2008). The Idea of Police in Eighteenth Century England: Discipline, Reformation, Superintendence, c 1780–1800. *Journal of the History of Ideas, 69*(4), 583–604.

Emsley, C. (1986). Detection and Prevention: The Old English Police and the New 1750–1900. *Historical Social Research*, (37), 69–88.

Emsley, C. (2018). *Crime and Society in England 1750–1900* (5th ed.). Routledge.

Gloucestershire Archives. (undated). The Judicial System. *Gloucestershire Archives*. [Online] https://www.heritagehub.org.uk/media/2057/the_judicial_system-56102.pdf. Accessed 7 September 2022.

Hands, S. (2020). Background History of the United Kingdom Specials. *Gloucesterpolice Archives*. [Online] https://gloucestershirepolicearchives.org.uk/content/finding-your-police-ancestors/special-constabulary-finding-your-police-ancestors/background-history-of-united-kingdom-specials. Accessed 8 September 2022.

Hay, D. (2011). Property, Authority and the Criminal Law. In D. Hay, P. Linebaugh, J. G. Rule, E. P. Thompson, & C. Winslow (Eds.), *Albion's Fatal Tree*.

Crime and Society in Eighteenth Century England (Revised ed.). Verso, originally published in 1975.

Holmes, G. (1976). The Sacheverall Riots: The Crowd and the Church in Early Eighteenth Century London. *Past and Present*, (72), 55–85.

Jones, W. (1782). *An Inquiry into the Legal Mode of Suppressing Riots. With a Constitutional Plan of Future Defence*. John Fairburn, this work was published posthumously in 1819.

Knowles, A. (2016). Georgian Watchmen—Security on the Night-Time Streets. *Regency History.* [Online] https://www.regencyhistory.net/2016/08/georgian-watchmen-security-on-night.html. Accessed 26 September 2020.

Lindley, K. (1983). Riot Prevention and Control in Early Stuart London. *Transactions of the Royal Historical Society, 33*, 109–136.

Linebaugh, P. (2011). The Tyburn Riot Against the Surgeons. In D. Hay, P. Linebaugh, J. G. Rule, E. P. Thompson, & C. Winslow (Eds.), *Albion's Fatal Tree. Crime and Society in Eighteenth Century England* (Revised ed.). Verso, originally published in 1975.

London Lives. (2018a). Policing. *Londonlives.org.* [Online] https://www.londonlives.org/static/Policing.jsp#top. Accessed 28 September 2022.

London Lives. (2018b). Reformation of Manners Campaigns. *Londonlives.org*. [Online] https://www.londonlives.org/static/Reformation.jsp. Accessed 28 April 2023.

Lyman, J. (1964). The Metropolitan Police of 1829. *Journal of Criminal Law and Criminology, 55*(1), 141–154.

McLynn, F. (1989). *Crime and Punishment in Eighteenth Century England*. Oxford University Press.

Page, W. (Ed.). (1911). *A History of the County of Middlesex: Volume 2, General; Ashford, East Bedfont With Hatton, Feltham, Hampton With Hampton Wick, Hanworth, Laleham, Littleton.* Victoria Country History, sourced from *British History Online* http://www.british-history.ac.uk/vch/middx/vol2/pp132-137. Accessed 12 May 2022.

Palmer, S. (1978). Calling out the Troops. The Military, the Law and Public Order in England, 1650–1850. *Journal of the Society for Historical Army Research., 56*(228), 198–214.

Parliamentary Papers. (1828). *Select Committee on the Police of the Metropolis* (Vol. 6 series [533]). House of Commons.

Pryne, W. (Ed.). (1827). *The World in Miniature: England, Scotland and Ireland.* (Vol. 1). R. Ackerman.

Reynolds, E. (1998). *Before the Bobbies—The Night Watch and Police Reform in Metropolitan London, 1720–1830*. Macmillan.

Rich, R. (1977). *Essays on the Theory and Practice of Criminal Justice*. University Press of America.

Sharp, G. (1781) *Tracts Concerning the Ancient and Only True Legal Means of National Defence, by a Free Militia*, London, 1781, p. 1, 5 cited in McCormack, M. (2012). A Species of Civil Soldier: Masculinity, Policing and the Military in 1780s England. In D. Barrie & S. Broomhill (Eds.), *A History of Police and Masculinities 1700–2010*. Routledge.

Taylor, D. (1998). *Crime, Policing and Punishment in England, 1750–1914*. Palgrave/Macmillan.

The Times. (1919). 4 August cited in "The Last Reading of the Riot Act on Mainland UK. *History House*. [Online] https://historyhouse.co.uk/articles/riot_act.html. Accessed 13 May 2022.

Thornbury, W. (1878). Spitalfields. In *Old and New London* (Vol. 2, pp 149–152). Sourced from *British History Online* http://www.british-history.ac.uk/old-new-london/vol2/pp149-152. Accessed 12 May 2022.

Ultimate History Project Staff. (undated). Crime and Criminals in Eighteenth Century London. *Ultimate History Project*. [Online] http://ultimatehistoryproject.com/crime-and-policing-in-18th-c-london.html. Accessed 26 September 2020.

Part II

Crime and Disorder 1750–1850

4

Crowd Disorders, 1750–1800

Introduction

'Ordinary' crimes such as robbery and burglary were not the only criminal justice issue of the period 1750–1850. Disorder also exerted a considerable pressure on reforming Britain's archaic system of law enforcement and this chapter will consider arguments that relate to the involvement of the crowd in disturbances, illustrating and amplifying these arguments with major events that occurred between 1750 and 1800.

The Crowd in Eighteenth-Century Politics

In an era when most people were denied participation in conventional activity as they did not possess the right to vote, crowds performed an important aspect of political behaviour. It has been argued that 'Crowd activity, both peaceful and violent, was a major form of group expression by the common people of eighteenth-century Britain' (Dickinson, 1994: 125). Although the gathering of crowds on the streets was frequently peaceful and recreational, crowds could gather together in a more aggressive and hostile mood in order to engage in social protests and political demonstrations. One aspect of such collective activity was riots which were 'endemic, widespread and frequent throughout the eighteenth century' (Dickinson, 1994: 125).

P. Joyce and W. Laverick, *History of Policing, Crime, Disorder, Punishment*,
https://doi.org/10.1007/978-3-031-36892-9_4

The term 'mob' was generally applied to rioters in the eighteenth century, a term first applied to rioters in the 'Exclusion Crisis' (1678–1681) (Shoemaker, 1987: 273) and one definition subsequently ascribed to it described the mob as 'an omnibus term for the "lower orders", common people, "inferior set of people" … in brief, the lower strata of society in the pre-industrial age' (Rudé, 1959: 1). The term was also indiscriminately applied 'to crowds engaged in riots, strikes or political demonstrations' (Rudé, 1959: 1).

Although historical research traditionally often viewed riots as mindless and irrational acts of hooliganism (a view reflected in the conservative perspective regarding riots in the latter decades of the twentieth century) (Benyon, 1987: 26–7), pioneering works by George Rudé (for example, 1964 and 1970) and Edward Thompson (for example, 1963 and 1971) challenged this opinion.

Thompson, in reference to the 1795 rural disorders that constituted food riots, developed the concept of moral economy, viewing these disturbances as being triggered by rising prices, malpractices by dealers or hunger but which were formulated 'upon a consistent traditional view of social norms and obligations, of the proper economic functions of several parties within the community, which, taken together, can be said to constitute the moral economy of the poor' (Thompson, 1971: 79), an economy rooted in paternalistic values whose operations were being undermined by the operations of the free market (Thompson, 1963: 67–73)—an economic system viewed as immoral and the cause of hunger and deprivation. He argued

> It is possible to detect in almost every eighteenth century crowd action some legitimizing notion…. The men and women in the crowd were informed by the belief that they were defending traditional rights and customs; and in general that they were supported by the wider consensus of the community (Thompson, 1971: 78).

Such opinions emphasised the purposeful nature and rationality of such activities, depicting them as 'rational and legitimate protests against a variety of grievances and as an expression of the social attitudes and the political will of the common people' (Dickinson, 1994: 126). These were often conducted according to 'commonly accepted codes of behaviour' (Shoemaker, 1987: 275). However, the opinion that actions undertaken by the mob were widely supported by the community within which they emerged has been challenged by the argument that, at least as far as London was concerned, riots often supported contradictory points of view and might be considered as 'less an expression of existing community solidarity than an attempt to generate such solidarity where it was weak' (Shoemaker, 1987: 302).

Rudé's studies of crowd behaviour focused on the character of those involved in rioting. He concentrated on urban rioting (whereas food riots and riots against enclosures and ridings were rural in character) (Shoemaker, 1987: 275). Although contemporary views of rioting associate them with activities conducted by those at the lower end of the social scale—those now depicted as constituting the underclass, the structural definition of which suggests that this comprised the unemployed and the unemployable' (Joyce, 2002: 103)—Rudé suggested (in connection with research into the Wilkesite and Gordon riots) that those involved in eighteenth-century riots constituted a preponderance of the respectable working class—'sober workmen and apprentices' (Rudé, 1971: 282–3)—when the issue at stake was political or religious as opposed to disorders triggered by purely economic motivation. This view was compatible with the Sacheverall and High Church Riots (1710) which were considered in Chapter 3.

Shoemaker (1987: 284) argued that the term 'mob' when applied to rioters 'could be used to specifically describe the lower class or to insult people regardless of their social status'—in other words a term decrying collective behaviour as opposed to social class. He suggested that most participants to mob behaviour were drawn from the middle and lower classes but insisted that 'rioting was not an exclusively lower class occupation' (Shoemaker, 1987: 284–5). It was also argued that women were frequently involved in riots related to sexual morality and economic issues in the late seventeenth and early eighteenth century, mirroring their involvement in food and enclosure riots in rural areas in that period (Shoemaker, 1987: 285).

The scale of rioting in the eighteenth century was considerable. One historian stated that there was a dramatic increase in the number of riots in London between 1690 and 1710:167 riots were prosecuted at Middlesex Quarter Sessions in 1720 and, on average, a riot that resulted in a criminal prosecution occurred every other day in London (Shoemaker, 1987: 276). Another historian identified over 1000 between 1790 and 1810 (Bohstedt, 2010: 5). They were frequently triggered by specific grievances and increased in number as the eighteenth century progressed (Dickinson, 1994: 126).

Shoemaker (1987: 277–9) suggested that in addition to riots that were politically inspired, they occurred as the result of private grievances (such as disputes arising in taverns, brothels and gaming houses) and also public grievances (which included attempts to enforce norms related to issues such as marriage and sexual and economic behaviour). Public grievances generally encompassed disturbances arising from disputes with shopkeepers and labour disputes, the latter of which were sometimes associated with activities performed by journeymen and small masters who were outside the guilds then dominated by industrial merchant capitalists and which began to ignore traditional regulations relating to the hire of foreign labour and the numbers of apprentices. Many of these disorders were small scale, involving just a few dozen people (Shoemaker, 1987: 281) but some teetered on the edge of being urban insurrections (Dickinson, 1994: 126). Rudé (1959: 4) also suggested that participants were usually drawn from local communities rather than outsiders.

Shoemaker (1987: 304) observed a tendency in early eighteenth-century riots for them to exhibit 'a weakening of the role of traditional rituals in disorder and an expansion of the range of grievances expressed'—a tendency which culminated in the Gordon Riots of 1780 which had the quality of 'an assault on the symbols of authority' (Pearl, 1979: 5).

The issues raised in this section will be further considered by examining a number of episodes involving crowd disorder in the period 1750–1800, seeking to provide a flavour of the issues raised by such events and those who participated in such activities.

Disorders 1750–1800

Several disorders occurred between 1750 and 1800 and this section examines some of the more important examples that took place, seeking to illustrate some of the general arguments put forward in the previous section.

Food Riots

Thompson (1971: 78–9) suggested that while food riots throughout the eighteenth century were often triggered by 'soaring prices, by malpractices among dealers, or by hunger'-

> these grievances operated within a popular consensus as to what were legitimate and what were illegitimate practices in marketing, milling, baking, etc. This in its turn was grounded upon a consistent traditional view of social norms and obligations, of the proper economic functions of several parties within the community, which, taken together, can be said to constitute the moral economy of the poor. An outrage to these moral assumptions, quite as much as actual deprivation, was the usual occasion for direct action.

Food riots occurred fairly regularly in eighteenth-century Britain, with 12 major outbreaks taking place in the eighteenth century (Rule, 1996: 196). Rudé (1964: 35–6) estimated that of the 275 disorders that took place between 1735 and 1800, two-thirds were concerned with food prices. Major outbreaks occurred in 1709–1710, 1727–179, 1739–1740, 1756–1757, 1766–1768, 1772–1773, 1783–1784, 1794–1796, 1800–1801, 1810–1813, and 1816–1818 (Archer, 2000: 28). Prior to 1766, the previous major outbreak of violence that could be categorised as food riots took place in 1756–1757 in which food stores were looted. In an attempt to preserve the peace, legislation was passed to regulate grain prices and prohibitions were imposed on grain export. These measures were ended in 1759 although a further provision that prevented the use of corn and flour in distilling remained until 1760.

Arguments presented in this section relating to the crowd in history will be illustrated with specific incidents that occurred in the nineteenth century which are considered below and in the following chapter.

The 1766 Food Riots

Grain harvests began to deteriorate during 1760 which caused the price of wheat and other cereals to rise. In response, the government removed the duty on imported wheat and flour and the bounties that were paid for exported wheat.

However, serious disorder occurred across England in 1766 (Bohstedt, 2010: 126), which Shelton (1973: 37) argued constituted the most serious food riots of the eighteenth century. Randall (1985: 72) argued that

> the food riots of 1766 stand out as among the most extensive, the most prolonged and the most difficult to assuage of the century. They came not in one wave but in three, breaking out in January-February, then again in early August, and finally culminating in September in a headlong rush of disturbances which convulsed central southern England, the Midlands and East Anglia.

The riots were sparked by the export of grain in August and peaked around September–October. A total of 131 riots were recorded (Bohstedt, 2010: 122), many of which took place in the South West and Midlands. A feature of these riots was the pressure exerted by rioters to force farmers and traders to sell their products at lower rates (Barnes, 1930: 32), 39 instances of this being recorded in addition to 31 cases where goods were seized and a further 14 instances in which both of these forms of action took place. One example of forced sale at lower prices occurred in Birmingham in September when butter on sale for 10 [Old] pence a Pound was seized and sold for 7 [Old] pence (Bohstedt, 2010: 126). Forty-six of the disturbances commenced from an attempt to enforce market regulations (Bohstedt, 2010: 122).

Although many of the riots were not violent, there were instances where shops and warehouses were looted and mills were destroyed. Flour mills at Devon and Berkshire valued at £1000 were destroyed while at Beckington, near Bath, a mill was burnt down after two rioters had been shot by the farmer (Palmer, 1978: 212). A local historical source discussing the Newbury Bread Riot in August 1766 stated that it was triggered by the actions of the millers and bakers of the town who 'kept up the price of bread much in excess of what was fair and legitimate' (Newbury History, 2022: [Online]). The sense of injustice arising from these practices boiled over -

> On a certain market day in August, during the time the sack of corn were being pitched for sale, the people broke out into wild riot. Upsetting the open stalls, they flung themselves upon the scattered provisions, corn, meat, butter, and eggs, wrecked a couple of houses and so alarmed the bakers that they at once lowered the price of bread, and promised a further reduction. But the spirit of the mob was not easily to be managed. They proceeded to break into the mills, and throw the corn into the river; windows were broken, and damage to the extent of £1000 was done. Several persons were injured in the fray, one of them fatally. The military had to be summoned before this disturbance could be quelled (Newbury History, 2022: [Online]).

It was recalled at Norwich

> A general insurrection began … provisions of all sorts were scattered about by the rioters in heaps; the new mill … which supplies the City with water, was attacked and pulled down; the flour to the number of 150 sacks, thrown sack after sack into the river; and the proprietor's books of accounts, furniture, plate and money, carried off of destroyed; the bakers' shops plundered or shattered; a large malt-house set fire to, and burnt; houses and warehouses pulled down; and the whole city thrown into the greatest confusion (*Annual Register*, IX, 139 cited in Rudé, 1964: 42–3).

Elsewhere, at Nottingham an event known as the Great Cheese Riot occurred on 2 October when local citizens aimed to physically prevent merchants from Lincolnshire from taking away cheeses they had purchased at the City's Goose Fair in order to sell in their locality. Shops and other premises (including a boat loaded with cheese) were looted and large amounts of cheese wheels were rolled through the streets. The Mayor was unable to restore order and called on military assistance. Soldiers opened fire on the crowds and one man was killed and several were wounded. Elsewhere (at Birmingham in October, for example) Special Constables were enrolled to preserve the peace.

The response of the Whig governments (initially led by the Marquess of Rockingham and subsequently by William Pitt the Elder) was to reduce taxes on imported grain thus lowering the cost of food. Pitt also prohibited the use of grain in distilling and suspended a number of other import duties. Subscriptions were raised to provide charitable relief to subsidise food for the poor (to a greater extent that had happened at previous food riots) (Bohstedt, 2010: 152) but the military was also deployed across the country in an attempt to deter violence.

The Riot Act was read on seven occasions in 1766 and eight people were shot dead by the military during the disturbances (Bohstedt, 2010: 158).

Randall (1985: 72) emphasised the significance of the disturbances, arguing that they

> stretched the resources of the forces of law and order past breaking point. Indeed, the Secretary at War, Lord Barrington, at one point feared a general insurrection. From the reports reaching him and in the press it is easy to see why. Everywhere, it seemed, mobs were seizing grain, flour and foodstuffs, taking over markets, marching from granary to granary, preventing the transportation of food, and attacking and frequently destroying corn mills. From every county magistrates demanded troops to put down riots or to prevent their outbreak. Not until the end of October was order restored.

The twin measures of charity and military repression served to quell the riots by October, although more reduced violence occurred in the following years, again in response to poor harvests. A Special Commission of the Court of Assize (which visited the worst affected counties) as well as Quarter Sessions were used to try those arrested during the disturbances. Fifty-nine persons were convicted (Bohstedt, 2010: 161). Although many were condemned to death, only eight men were hung. The others were either pardoned (which included two pregnant women) (Bohstedt, 2010: 161) or were subjected to transportation.

Food Riots in the 1790s

In his study of food riots in North Western England between 1790 and 1801, Booth (1977: 84–5) asserted that changes occasioned by the 'cotton revolution' were to the detriment of wheat production so that even in times of good harvests, there was a reliance on imports of grain to keep the local population fed and that there was always 'a delicate balance … between existence and starvation'. He further stated that in the event of a failed harvest 'scarcity was certain and hardship sure to follow' (Booth, 1977: 85). His problem was further compounded by changes in the eating habits, especially of people in the larger towns in the South of the North West region, whereby bread manufactured from wheat became the preferred choice over the traditional fare of poor people, bread made from barley or oatmeal (Booth, 1977: 86 - 7). Booth concluded that virtually all of the food riots that occurred in 1795 and 1800 were concerned with the 'subsistence' crops of oats and wheat (Booth, 1977: 87).

Weather conditions caused there to be a poor wheat harvest in 1796 in Lancashire, although barley and oats fared better. The poor wheat crop caused there to be a greater reliance on oats, serving to drive up prices (Booth, 1977: 87–8). Most food riots in the region took place in July and August 1795, coinciding with a period of high prices, and occurred in the manufacturing districts of the region (Booth, 1977: 89). Areas in the North West that had switched their reliance to bread made of wheat experienced severe disorders in 1795/6. In total, around 23 disturbances occurred between 1795–6 (Booth, 1977: 89).

Price levels then lowered in 1797 and 1798 but rose again in 1799 (Booth, 1977: 88) when adverse weather conditions resulted in low yields of all types of grain and also potatoes which, in turn, caused prices to rise (Booth, 1977: 88–9). Rioting again broke out: one estimate suggested that around 50 food-related disturbances occurred throughout the country in 1800–1801 (Quinault & Stevenson, 1974: 37), although Booth (1977: 89) argued that this figure underplayed the scale of such disorders in the North West which he estimated consisted of 20 between 1799 and 1801 (Booth, 1977: 89), mostly in the industrial areas located in the south of the region (Booth, 1977: 89–90).

Problems affecting food prices were compounded by declining wages: Booth suggested that food riots in Rochdale and Saddleworth were influenced by low wages and high unemployment (Booth, 1977: 91) but that such factors became critical in explaining the disorders that took place between 1799 and 1800 since by 1800, wages were at their 'lowest ebb for the whole decade while prices had risen by some 300 per cent'. This resulted in 'privation and hardship' although whether these factors translated into rioting was in part dependent on the state of policing in a township and the local magistracy's provisions for relief (Booth, 1977: 91).

Thompson argued that it was possible

> to detect in almost every eighteenth-century crowd action some legitimizing notion. By the notion of legitimation I mean that the men and women in the

crowd were informed by the belief that they were defending traditional rights or customs; and, in general, that they were supported by the wider consensus of the community. On occasion this popular consensus was endorsed by some measure of licence afforded by the authorities. More commonly, the consensus was so strong that it overrode motives of fear or deference (Thompson, 1971: 78).

Motives of this nature were discerned by Booth who stated with regard to food riots in the North West in the late eighteenth century that particular resentment was vented against corn dealers and speculators who came into the region to buy produce which was then sold elsewhere and also the farmers who grew rich on the high prices they secured for their crops (Booth, 1977: 92).

Booth (1977: 100) further noted that by 1800 popular protest was also being directed against the Magistracy and clergy in events of this nature as these were viewed as key elements of the propertied classes.

Thompson referred to the tactic of forced sales, stating that in 1795 there were a number of occasions when the militia or troops supervised forced sales, sometimes at bayonet point while their officers looked 'steadfastly the other way'. What was described as *taxation populaire* might also be superintended by a constable (1971: 112). Actions of this nature led Thompson to conclude that 'it is the restraint, rather than the disorder which is remarkable: and there can be no doubt that the actions were approved by an overwhelming popular consensus' (Thompson, 1971: 112).

Price fixing was also a common tactic of food rioters in the North West both in 1795 and 1800 whereby shipments of grain would be seized on the highways and sold in a scenario that was akin to that of a public auction. Booth (1977: 95) cited examples in Oldham in both 1799 and 1800 when the crowd seized flour and meal and then handed over the money they had collected to the owner. In areas which exported grain (such as Cheshire and Cumberland), anti-export riots might prevent grain being taken from a locality, Booth (1977: 96–7) citing an example of this action in Chester in May 1795 which was carried out by a body of women. Thompson's broader discussion of crowd behaviour in the eighteenth century argued that the instigator of riots were, very often, women (Thompson, 1971: 115) and women were also argued to have played a part in all riotous events throughout the North West in the late eighteenth century (Booth, 1977: 98).

Thompson (1971: 114) also alluded to food rioters often attacking mills and granaries not to steal the food but to punish the proprietors. This was also a feature of disorders in the North West in the late eighteenth century, the houses of local grain dealers were attacked and other targets included the warehouses and corn mills of the dealers. Looting shops was a far rarer occurrence in the region (Booth, 1977: 93–5). His study of rioters' tactics in food riots in the North West led Booth (1977: 98) to conclude that 'whether spontaneous or planned, the development of the food riot manifested a definite discipline of action'.

It was argued that those involved in rioting in the North West (Booth, 1977: 99) did not constitute those at the bottom rungs of society but, rather, constituted a representative cross section of the labouring classes. Booth (1977: 99) stated that the most complete information regarding the social composition of food rioters was provided from Stockport in 1795 and 1799 where 'among those arrested were weavers, cotton-spinners, colliers and "navigators" working on the nearby canal. In similar vein, Thompson's broader study of riots in the eighteenth century led him to conclude that 'the occupational make up of the crowd … was … fairly representative of the occupations of the "lower orders" in the rioting areas' (Thompson, 1971: 118). Booth (1977: 99) also stated that several food rioters in 1799 were from outside the narrow confines of the town itself'.

Booth (1977: 100–1) argued that while the political element in the food disturbances in the North West was 'almost non-existent', these contributed to the politicisation of the poor with early leadership being provided by the United Englishmen 'who offered a particularly vigorous brand of political radicalism, and of a militant trade unionism and whose views became more influential by the end of the eighteenth century against a background of economic distress in 1800 and 1801.

Archer (2000: 28) stated that outside of the Celtic Fringe, food riots declined fairly rapidly after 1818, to be replaced by other forms of protest. Thompson (1971: 128–9) argued that by 1812, the traditional English food riots overlapped with Luddism while it was observed that by the early years of the nineteenth century, food riots ceased to be a separate entity and 'henceforth food rioting increasingly became intertwined with other branches of protest as Luddism was to reveal in 1811–12' (Booth, 1977: 104). The food riot 'became an integrated part of a wider conception of working class protest' (Booth, 1977: 107), aspects of which will be considered below.

Spitalfield Weavers' Disorders

The scale and nature of public disorder as well as crime exerted a considerable influence on the reform of policing. Disorders were frequently linked to adverse economic conditions so that 'Any decline of prices, or opposition in trade, set these turbulent workmen in a state of violent effervescence' (Thornbury, 1878: [Online]). One example of this concerns disorders associated with weavers in Spitalfields, whose disorderly activities earlier in the century have been referred to in Chapter 3.

By the 1760s, disorder in Spitalfields was characterised by conflict within the ranks of the weavers (often referred to as 'cutters' [militant journeyman weavers who engaged in direct action]) regarding rates of pay they would accept for their work from the master weavers as well as between the journeymen weavers (who were frequently of Irish descent) and the master weavers (who were often of French Huguenot extraction). The use of machinery by the masters with which to manufacture silk goods, and its destruction by the cutters has led to these disorders being characterised as Luddite in nature (Ashley, 2012: [Online]) (a term which is considered below), albeit around 4 decades before the Luddite agitation commenced. An example of the latter aspect of this form of violence occurred in October 1763 when

> several thousand journeymen assembled in Spitalfields and broke open the house of one of the masters. They destroyed his looms, cut to pieces much valuable silk, carried his effigy in a cart through the neighbourhood and afterwards burnt it, hung in chains from a gibbet (Page, 1911: [Online]).

Weavers banding together in what were de facto unions was also a feature of the disorder that took place.

A significant episode involving around took place in 1765 when

> on the occasion of the king going to Parliament to give his assent to the Regency Bill, they formed a great procession, headed by red flags and black banners, to present a petition to the House, complaining that they were reduced to starvation by the importation of French silks. They terrified the House of Lords into an adjournment, insulted several hostile members, and in the evening attacked Bedford House, and tried to pull down the walls, declaring that the duke had been bribed to make the treaty of Fontainebleau, which had brought French silks and poverty into the land (Thornbury, 1878: [Online]).

On this occasion, order was restored by reading the Riot Act and calling in the military (in the form of the Guards). This caused the mob to flee but at a cost—'many being much hurt and trampled on' (Thornbury, 1878: [Online]). However, the military presence was only of a temporary nature and violence resumed later, and it was recorded that

> At a yet later date mobs of Spitalfields weavers used to break into houses and cut the looms of men who were working with improved machinery. Many outrages were committed by these "cutters," and many lives lost in scuffles and fights (Thornbury, 1878: [Online]).

It was recorded that throughout May 1765 the weavers' disorders.

> kept London in such a state of general alarm that the citizens were compelled to enrol themselves for military duty. 'Monday night,' says a contemporary newspaper, 'the guards were doubled at Bedford House, and in each street leading thereto were placed six or seven of the Horse Guards, who continued till yesterday at ten with their swords drawn. A strong party of Albemarle's Dragoons took post in Tottenham Court Road, and patrols of them were sent off towards Islington and Marylebone, and the other environs on that side of the town; the Duke of Bedford's new road by Baltimore House was opened, when every hour a patrol came that way to and round Bloomsbury to see that all was well (Page, 1911: [Online]).

In the wake of the 1765 disturbances, an Act was passed declaring it to be a felony and punishable with death to break into any house or shop with intent maliciously to damage or destroy any silk goods in the process of manufacture. However, this did not halt the violence and similar outbreaks occurred in 1767 (when 'cutters', broke into workshops, cutting the work off the looms, and dangerously wounding several who endeavoured to arrest their progress) (Page, 1911: [Online]).

In 1768–1769, the 'Cutters' Riots' witnessed

> a prolonged struggle, with bitter violence, rioting, intimidation of workers and threatening letters to employers, and hundreds of raids on factories and small workshops. Strikers in other trades joined in the mayhem. In 1768 crowds of weavers also forcibly set their own prices in the food markets, in defiance of high prices. It would end in shootouts in a pub, and executions (Ashley, 2012: [Online]).

These episodes further attest to the state's difficulties in maintaining order. In September 1769, soldiers were deployed in an attempt to arrest a meeting of weavers that was being held in a public house in Spitalfields. In the resulting melee, the soldiers opened fire, killing two weavers and capturing a further four. Two of those detained, John Doyle and John Valline, were hung for their involvement in this meeting.

Subsequently, the government enacted legislation in 1773, 1792 and 1811, collectively known as the Spitalfields Acts, the first of which empowered the Aldermen of London and the Magistrates of Middlesex to settle the wages of journeymen silk weavers in Quarter Sessions (Page, 1911: [Online]). It was argued that 'One major result of the Acts, at least between 1773 and 1824, seems to have been an end to weavers' riots and cuttings… or any strikes at all' (Ashley, 2012: [Online]).

The John Wilkes Agitation (1768)

John Wilkes was a radical MP who had been elected for Aylesbury in 1757. The agitation with which he was associated with, culminating in events in 1768, were founded on concerns in which 'a catalogue of unrighteous Ministerial actions' were perceived as constituting 'a network of interwoven evidence pointing to a definite plot against English liberties' (Maier, 1963: 384). Wilkes, therefore, drew support from those who viewed his actions as those of a defender of liberty in the face of arbitrary action by the executive. As will be argued later in this book in connection with police reform, the defence of liberty was an emotive subject which possessed the potential to rally widespread public support.

In 1763 Wilkes was committed to the Tower of London for publishing a pamphlet which was deemed to have committed seditious libel on the King, George III, arising from an attack Wilkes mounted in his newspaper the *North Briton* (number 45) on the speech delivered by the Monarch's when opening Parliament in 1763 which supported the terms of the Treaty of Paris. His detention (which was based on a general warrant issued by the King which did not require any specific person to be named) resulted in riots and, pleading Parliamentary privilege, he was released.

Following his release, he again fell foul of the authorities for his part in co-writing a poem deemed to be pornographic. Before he was expelled from Parliament or charged with regard to the poem, he moved to France where his daughter lived. In January 1764 he was expelled from Parliament (thus terminating his Parliamentary privilege). In February 1764 he was tried *in absentia* and found guilty of obscene and impious libel (in connection with the poem) and seditious libel (relating to the number 45 issue of the *North*

Briton) and was declared by the House of Lords to be an outlaw (thus beyond the protection of the law) by leaving the country and thus impeding justice.

Riots, primarily fuelled by economic distress, resulted in sporadic outbreaks of rioting in subsequent years (1763–1768). Wilkes returned to London in 1768 and in April was re-elected to Parliament for the County of Middlesex. Waiving his re-newly acquired Parliamentary immunity, he voluntarily surrendered to the Keeper of the King's Bench Prison. He was then tried for the 2 outstanding libel charges and sentenced to 2 years' imprisonment and fined £1000. The sentence of outlawry was, however, overturned on a technicality (events discussed in Cash, 2006: 204–26).

Box 4.1: The St George's Field Massacre (1768)

Perceptions that Wilkes' imprisonment in 1768 epitomised the injustices associated when arbitrary government overrode the traditional rights and liberties of English people triggered rioting in London for around 2 weeks and the authorities were fearful that an attempt would be made to free him from prison. Accordingly, the Secretary of War informed the Surrey Magistrates that troops would be placed at their disposal to suppress any efforts of this nature.

On 10 May 1768, the King was due to formally open Parliament. The situation was flavoured by adverse economic conditions which led to industrial action in London involving workers in several industries that included the Thames watermen, coal-heavers and Spitalfields weavers (an episode that is considered above). A crowd estimated to number around 15,000 initially assembled at St George's Fields (situated in Southwark, South London), calling for the release of Wilkes whom, it was assumed, would then be triumphantly escorted to take his seat at Westminster.

However, there was no intention on the part of the authorities to enable Wilkes to be freed. Surrey Magistrates with Constables in attendance arrived at the scene. The removal by the constables of posters attached to the prison wall in support of Wilkes provoked the crowd into violence. Soldiers drawn from the Horse Grenadier Guards were summoned and the Riot Act's proclamation was read. An altercation between a soldier and supporters of Wilkes led to the fatal shooting of a civilian, William Allen.

What has been described as 'the heightened tensions produced by this event' (Thomas, 1978: 221) triggered intensified violence outside the prison. More troops (this time from the 3rd Regiment of Foot, the Scots Guards) were summoned and the Riot Act Proclamation was read for a second time. On this occasion, the soldiers were ordered to open fire. It was recorded that.

> Two volleys of musketball were shot into and over the crowd. Seven died that day, including a woman orange seller and a man driving a hayrack, unluckily hit by a ball fired over the people's heads (White, 2013: 525).

The incident became known as the Massacre of St. George's Fields. Samuel Gillam (the Magistrate who had read the Riot Act) was subsequently indicted for murder, although he was acquitted of this crime. Two soldiers involved in the death of William Allen were also brought before a Grand Jury at the Surrey Assizes and charged with his murder although neither was indicted on this charge.

The agitations associated with Wilkes took place against a background of a rise in the cost of living (especially bread) in the early part of 1768 and agitation for higher wages, although his appeal was broad-based, securing support from 'large and small property-owners in City and County, but among the small shopkeepers, craftsmen and wage-earners as well' (Rudé, 1959: 10). Rudé (1959: 13) also noted that these riots provided the opportunity for a 'rough form of social justice' in which 'the windows of lords and ladies of opulence and fashion were smashed with gay abandon'.

In February 1769, Wilkes was expelled from Parliament, on the grounds that when elected he had been an outlaw even though this sentence was later overturned. However, he was re-elected that month and when the House of Commons expelled him for being incapable of taking his seat, he was again re-elected in March. Expelled yet again, he was re-elected in April. On this occasion, however, the House of Commons ruled that all votes cast for him were invalid so his court-backed opponent, Colonel Henry Luttrell was duly declared Member for Middlesex.

Following his release from prison in 1770, Wilkes continued with a career in politics, becoming an Alderman of the City of London in 1769 and Lord Mayor of London in 1774. Although (based on his prior attack on general warrants and his belief that electors rather than Parliament had the right to determine who should be a member of the House of Commons) he initially used his position in City of London Politics to support radical causes which included printing Parliamentary debates and subsequently (under the auspices of the Society for the Defence of the Bill of Rights which had been formed in 1769 to support his cause and help off his debts) to embrace a programme of political reform which included the abolition of 'pocket' boroughs, a wider franchise and shorter Parliaments. He advocated this programme in his successful election contests at Middlesex in 1771, 1780 and 1784.

However, he subsequently became less associated with radical politics. He opposed the French Revolution on the grounds of the killings that it entailed and was in charge of the military who defended the Bank of England during the Gordon riots of 1780. He died in 1797, having served in his latter years as a Magistrate.

The Gordon Riots (1780)

Crime and disorder became major concerns towards the end of the eighteenth century when crime rose with the sanction of transportation temporarily in abeyance, and the nation faced an 'acute political crisis' arising from the American War of Independence when the country 'after numerous defeats and counter-alliances found itself virtually isolated' (Rudé, 1956: 93).

Concerns regarding increased levels of crime were aggravated by widespread public disorder in London in the form of the Gordon riots in 1780. These commenced as resistance to the Catholic Relief Act of 1778, a Whig measure passed by Lord North's government which repealed anti-Catholic legislation that dated back to the seventeenth century and excused Catholics from having to swear an oath of allegiance on joining the army. The main rationale for this Act was that Britain's involvement in overseas wars (and in particular tensions between the United Kingdom and France/Spain) required the recruitment of additional soldiers and this measure was designed to remove an obstacle to secure this aim.

In 1780, Lord George Gordon, leader of the Protestant Association, called for this measure to be repealed and on 2 June 1780 he led a crowd of around 60,000 people, which had assembled at St George's Field, Southwark, to the House of Commons to present a petition calling for the 1778 legislation to be repealed (Rudé, 1956: 94–5). The petition argued this measure encouraged 'popery' and threatened to undermine the position of the Church of England. This petition was ultimately rejected by 192:6 votes.

This sparked anti-Catholic riots in London which were initially inspired by religious fanaticism and directed at Catholic targets such as Churches and homes, the homes of supporters of the 1778 measure including Lords Rockingham, Devonshire, Mansfield and Savile. However, as the disorders took hold, the targets became more diversified –

> Great destruction was wreaked in Southwark. The King's Bench prison was burnt out; the ancient Borough Clink was burnt to the ground and never rebuilt; the Southwark New Prison was emptied of prisoners, the Marshalsea attacked but saved by the military, the roundhouses in Borough High Street and Kent Street pulled down and fired (White, 2011: [Online]).

Other targets included the Bank of England and Newgate. The Fleet and New Bridewell prisons were set on fire and prisoners released. Violence was climaxed on 3 June (known as 'Black Wednesday') when 'destruction was widespread: in Westminster, the City and the Middlesex "out parishes", houses, shops and offices occupied by Catholic merchant, shopkeepers, businessmen and justices were attacked and pulled down or damaged' (Rudé, 1956: 97).

Although this might suggest that religious (and to an extent related anti-Irish) impulses initially triggered the riots which subsequently gave way to different inspirations of a material nature (Rudé, 1956: 106), it has been argued that there was no significant change in the character of the disorders. There was no indiscriminate targeting of London's Catholic or Irish population in general and the targets selected were, instead, directed at 'persons of substance' (Rudé, 1956: 109). This led to the conclusion that 'behind the slogan of "No Popery" and other outward forms of religious fanaticism there lay a deeper social purpose: to settle accounts with the rich, if only for a day, and to achieve some rough kind of social justice' (Rudé, 1956: 111). Lyman (1964: 143) endorsed this view, arguing that 'the bitter frustration of the bitter, unrepresented lower classes now had an outlet in religious bigotry' so that 'the prisons, the Inns of Court, the Bank and the houses of Magistrates were all hated and assaulted as symbols of oppression, riches, and dishonest power' (Hibbert, 1958: 18).

Additionally, economic factors such as wages and food prices may have served as a stimulant to disorder (Rudé, 1956: 113, Lyman, 1964: 143), although it was stated that there was no obvious evidence of dissatisfaction with low wages or high prices (Rudé, 1959: 11). It is also possible that participants used the episode as an opportunity to vent their anger at the political establishment in general which they deemed responsible for high taxes that were required to pay for foreign wars, repressive laws and compulsory military service in the army and navy.

Inaction by the Magistrates (Palmer, 1978: 213), perhaps in part because an early intervention by Justice Hyde to read the Riot Act and sending in the Guards to disperse the crowd on 2 June led to the destruction of his town house by the rioters Rudé, (1956: 96–7) and subsequently his country house too. Rudé (1959: 15) also alluded to the case for the repeal of the Catholic Relief Act not being confined to a cause articulated by the 'lunatic fringe' but, rather, having relatively widespread appeal that locates them within the Whig-radical tradition. Thus it was 'little wonder that Magistrates were chary of risking their necks or reputations in order to protect Catholic property or that troops were unwilling to fire on citizens engaged in destroying Catholic chapels and schools'. Thus 'King mob' was able to take control of the streets and to burn and loot property across London until the government called in troops and imposed martial law in the capital Rudé, (1956: 100).

Box 4.2: 'King Mob' and the Gordon Riots

The events in 1780 have been described as 'an uprising of the London poor' whose anger was especially vented against 'the institutions of justice, cruellest symbols of class oppression in eighteenth-century London' (White, 2011: [Online]).

However, the appropriateness of describing the rioters as a 'mob' has been challenged (Rudé, 1956: 94). Although based on a small sample of those engaged in rioting Rudé (1956: 106) concluded that they were mainly not associated with the very poorest sections of the working population. Rudé (1959: 6) asserted that two-thirds of the Gordon rioters were wage earners—journeymen, waiters, apprentices, domestic servants or labourers. Most of the remainder were small employers, independent craftsmen or petty tradesmen.

The unemployed, vagrants and dregs of society hardly figured in the disorders of 1768 or 1780 and led to the conclusion that these events witnessed the first beginnings of a mass radical movement, a key subsequent development being the establishment of Hardy's Corresponding Society in 1792 which provided a 'stable base...for the Radical movement among the petty-craftsmen and wage-earners of the Metropolis' (Rudé, 1956: 17–8).

Aftermath and Consequences of the Gordon Riots

It took a week for the disturbances to be quelled. Inadequacies in the machinery of law enforcement in the capital consisting of constables meant that a reliance was placed on the military at the outset, an early role being the use of the Guards to protect members of the House of Lords and Commons from mob violence when the petition was under consideration in Parliament (Rudé, 1956: 95). Eventually around 12,000 troops were deployed to quell the disorders, at the end of which 250 were killed outright, 75 died of their wounds in hospital and 173 were injured (Rudé, 1956: 99). The costs of damage to property were estimated to be £100,000 (Palmer, 1978: 212–3)—which amounts to around £18 Million in today's money.

Those arrested totalled 450: of these 62 were sentenced to death (although only 25 were executed), 12 were sentenced to varying terms of imprisonment, one was sentenced to a private whipping and 85 were found not guilty (Rudé, 1956: 99). Lord George Gordon was acquitted of High Treason by the King's Bench in February 1781 and was thus unpunished for his role in these events.

The Gordon riots also led to a shift in views concerning the desirability of whipping up a 'mob' to achieve political aims, Rudé (1956: 102) asserting that one of Gordon's aims was perhaps to secure the overthrow of the administration. The use of the mob to secure political objectives was common at the start of the eighteenth century, but in the wake of the riots, the concern that an unruly crowd could easily get out of control and cause severe disorder made political figures less keen to use this and instead to resort to public meetings and voluntary societies to argue the case for political reforms. One aspect of this argument was the assertion that the mob in 1780 was not centrally organised although some organisation existed at local level, wielded by local 'captains' (Rudé, 1956:103), described as 'men whose personality, speech, dress or momentary assumption of authority marked them out as leaders' (Rudé, 1959: 295).

One consequence of these disorders was that in 1787, George III issued a Proclamation against drunkenness, gaming, profane swearing and cursing, lewdness, profanation of the sabbath and other dissolute, immoral or disorderly activities (London Lives, 2018: [Online]). This reflected the view that immorality was the source of crime and disorder and gave rise to the Proclamation Society in 1787 whose purpose was to give practical effect to the King's sentiments.

Additionally, it was argued that the disorders created 'powerful arguments…in favour of a professional police force' (Rudé, 1956: 94) since they made it 'glaringly and irrefutably apparent that the police system was inadequate and that there was no civil force capable of restraining disorder' (Lyman, 1964: 143).

However, this sentiment was not acted upon at the time. Rudé (1959: 14) argued that the disorder prompted property owners and householders in the City of London to demand the right to set up voluntary associations commanded by their own officers to protect their rights and properties from both the depredations of rioters but also the encroachment of government: this spirit of 'sturdy independence and hostility to the executive was shown in the flat refusal of a majority of the City Companies to contribute financially to the upkeep of troops quartered in the City during the disturbances'. Such feelings would help to undermine the case for the development of professional policing in the wake of these disturbances.

Conclusion

This section has discussed the role performed by the crowd in late eighteenth-century politics and has provided a snapshot of disorders that occurred in the period 1750–1800. This provides a basis from which to consider further aspects of crowd disorder in the period 1800–1850 and then to evaluate the resources that were available to the state to combat the threat and actuality of disorder in the period covered by both Chapters 4 and 5.

? Summary Question

Based on the material in this chapter, do you consider crowd disturbances between 1750 and 1800 as purposeful acts designed to bring about social and political change or mindless acts of hooliganism?

References

Archer, J. (2000). *Social unrest and popular protest in England, 1780–1840*. Cambridge University Press.

Ashley, I. (2012). The Spitalfields Silk Weavers: London's Luddites ? brh.org.uk. [Online] https://www.brh.org.uk/site/wp-content/uploads/2012/11/THE-SPITALFIELDS-SILK-WEAVERS.pdf. Accessed 12 May 2022.

Barnes, D. (1930). *A history of English Corn laws: From 1660–1846*. Routledge.

Benyon, J. (1987). Interpretations of civil disorder. In J. Benyon and J. Solomos (Eds.), *The roots of urban unrest*. The Pergamon Press.

Bohstedt, J. (2010). *The politics of provisions: Food riots, moral economy and market transition in England c 1550–1850*. Ashgate Publishing Ltd.

Booth, A. (1977). Food riots in the North West of England 1790–1801. *Past and Present, 77*(1), 84–107.

Dickinson, H. (1994). The politics of the crowd. In H. Dickinson (Ed.), *The politics of the people in eighteenth-century Britain*. Palgrave Macmillan.

Hibbert, C. (1958). *King Mob*. Longmans-Green.

Joyce, P. (2002). *The politics of protest. Extra-parliamentary politics in Britain since 1970*. Palgrave/Macmillan.

London Lives. (2018). Policing. Londonlives.org. [Online] https://www.londonlives.org/static/Policing.jsp#top. Accessed 28 September 2022.

Lyman, J. (1964). The Metropolitan Police Act of 1829. *Journal of Criminal Law and Criminology, 55*(1), 141–154.

Maier, P. (1963). John Wilkes and American Disillusionment with Britain. *William and Mary Quarterly, 20*(3), 373–395.

Newbury History. (2022). The Bread Riot at Newbury During 1766. *Newbury History.co.uk*. [Online] http://www.newburyhistory.co.uk/bread-riot. Accessed 17 Dec 2022.

Page, W. (Ed). (1911). *A history of the county of Middlesex: Volume 2, General; Ashford, East Bedfont With Hatton, Feltham, Hampton With Hampton Wick, Hanworth, Laleham, Littleton*. Victoria Country History, sourced from *British History Online* http://www.british-history.ac.uk/vch/middx/vol2/pp132-137. Accessed 12 May 2022.

Palmer, S. (1978). Calling out the troops. The military, the law and public order in England, 1650–1850. *Journal of the Society for Historical Army Research., 56*(228), 198–214.

Pearl, V. (1979). Change and stability in seventeenth century London. *London Journal., 5*(1), 3–34.

Quinault, R., & Stevenson, J. (1974). *Food riots in England 1792–1818*. Routledge.

Randall, A. (1985). The Gloucestershire Food Riots of 1766. *Midland History, 10*(1), 72–93.

Rudé, G. (1956). The Gordon Riots: A study of the rioters and their victims. The Alexander Prize Essay. *Transactions of the Royal History Society, 6*, 93–114.

Rudé, G. (1959). The London 'Mob' of the eighteenth century. *The Historical Journal, 2*(1), 1–18.

Rudé, G. (1964). *The crowd in history: A study of popular disturbances in France and England, 1730–1848*. John Wiley and Sons.

Rudé, G. (1970). *Paris and London in the eighteenth century: Studies in popular protest*. Fontana.

Shelton, W. (1973). *English Hunger and industrial disorders: A study of social conflict during the first decade of George III's Reign*. University of Toronto Press.

Shoemaker, R. (1987). The London "Mob" in the early eighteenth century. *Journal of British Studies., 26*(3), 273–304.

Thomas, P. (1978). The S. George's Fields 'Massacre' of 10 May 1768: An Eye-Witness Report. *The London Journal, 4*(2), 221–226.

Thompson, E. P. (1963). *The making of the English working class*. Victor Gollancz.

Thompson, E. P. (1971). The moral economy of the English crowd in the eighteenth century. *Past and Present, 50*(1), 76–136.

Thornbury, W. (1878). Spitalfields. *Old and New London, 2*, 149–52. Sourced from *British History Online* http://www.british-history.ac.uk/old-new-london/vol2/pp149-152. Accessed 12 May 2022.

White, J. (2011). The Gordon Riots, 1780. *London Historians*. [Online] https://www.londonhistorians.org/index.php?s=file_download&id=45. Accessed 3 Sept 2022.

White, J. (2013). *A great and monstrous thing. London in the eighteenth century*. Harvard University Press.

5

Public Disorder and the state's Response, 1800–1850

Introduction

This chapter will continue the discussion of the previous chapter and discuss the role of the crowd in early nineteenth-century politics. The period 1800–1850 witnessed several disorders, some of which were associated with the industrial revolution (such as Luddism), others with plots and conspiracies (such as the 1802 Despard conspiracy and the 1820 Cato Street conspiracy) that were deemed as treason and which also events that were associated with the cause of political reform. Rural disorder, in particular the 'Swing Riots' of 1830–1831 will be discussed.

The chapter will also discuss the way in which the state responded to events of this nature, drawing attention to its ability to criminalise protest through measures such as 1819 Six Acts enacted in the wake of Peterloo. It will also discuss the physical forces it had at its disposal to counter disorder (including the military, the militia, the yeomanry and—where they existed—professional police forces). It will additionally evaluate the nature of the early nineteenth-century secret state and activities such as spying and infiltration through which the state monitored groups and individuals deemed to be engaged in subversive activity.

P. Joyce and W. Laverick, *History of Policing, Crime, Disorder, Punishment*, https://doi.org/10.1007/978-3-031-36892-9_5

Disorders in the First Half of the Nineteenth Century

Disorders associated with crowds have been discussed in Chapter 3 with reference to the period 1750–1800. Such activities continued to perform an important aspect of political conduct in the first half of the nineteenth century. This section will provide a snapshot of the range of disorders that occurred in this period which resulted in some form of state intervention.

The Industrial Revolution and Public Disorder

It has been argued that

> The period 1750–1830 saw the rapid rise of the market economy in Britain. During this same period, as capitalism tightened its grip on the emerging working class, so the first signs of real resistance against this new form of economic oppression began to develop. During the early part of the 19th Century, there was a radical period in Britain, and the working class started organizing themselves and trying out methods of resistance (Solidarity Federation, n.d. [Online]).

The aim of this section is to illustrate how social transformations and developments associated with the industrial revolution were responsible for the development of activities which were viewed by those in power as threatening to their status and which were therefore criminalised and dealt with in a harsh manner. These events played an important role in the development of professional policing in early nineteenth-century England.

Luddism

The industrial revolution entailed the use of technology within large units of production (usually urban-based) and was thus at the expense of small-scale production in which textile production was a cottage industry performed by outworkers that was conducted within the homes of those involved in the trade (spinners, weavers, dyers and tailors) or in very small workshops. It was argued, with reference to Lancashire, that one consequence of the industrial revolution that the cotton 'revolution' displaced long-standing local industries such as the wool trade in Rochdale, sailcloth manufacture in Warrington and silk production in Stockport (Booth, 1977: 84). It further affected agriculture which became increasingly commercialised with 'industrial enterprise' becoming 'the paramount concern' (Booth, 1977: 85). Such motives also underpinned the Highland Clearances in Scotland (which took place from the mid-eighteenth until the mid-nineteenth centuries) whereby landowners displaced crofter communities in order to use the land for commercial sheep and cattle farming.

Other industries such as coal mining and metal production also traditionally took place on a small scale. The industrial revolution posed a significant threat to these traditional ways of production and also to the 'perks' and privileges of those who performed the work whereby left over materials would be retained by the worker. Practices formerly associated with outworking (such as retaining left over materials) were outlawed by a series of embezzlement acts, fourteen of which were passed between 1725 and 1800 affecting the wool industry alone (McLynn, 1989: 300–2) which were designed to impose a wage economy at the expense of outworking.

Such perks had been custom and practice in many industries. In agriculture, it took the form of gleaning (that is, gathering grain left over following a harvest) by farm labourers. In the mining industry, miners took small quantities of coal for their own use. However, the relationship between industrialisation and wage labour led to such practices being challenged by those who owned the means of production and who sought to subjugate the working class to the discipline and regimentation of the factory system.

In 1788, the Court of Common Pleas (in the case of *Steel v. Houghton*) ruled that there was no specific right in common law for a farm worker to glean without the permission of the landowner (Emsley, 2018: 147–9). Although in many places practices of this nature continued, in other industries it was sharply curtailed: for example, between 1835 and 1860 prosecutions for industrial theft in the Black Country rose from 10% of all prosecutions in one year to 33% and to facilitate prosecution, the 1855 Criminal Justice Act authorised summary trial for what was no longer regarded as a customary right but was now deemed to constitute employee theft.

The Luddites emerged in the early nineteenth century. They consisted of weavers and textile workers. These were skilled craftsmen who had spent many years learning their trade whose livelihoods threatened to be undermined by machinery which was being introduced into the textile industry in the form of the flying shuttle (1733), the spinning jenny (1762), the water frame (1762), the steam engine (1769), the cotton gin (1792) and the Jacquard loom (1804).

The Luddites destroyed the machinery used in the new factories, fearing that the cheaper cost of these goods would undercut their market and destroy their way of life, a problem that was compounded by factory production requiring fewer workers than old-style means of production, meaning that those driven out of work could not always easily find comparable alternative employment in their trade. The condition of employment in the new factories was also a source of grievance.

This form of action was not new: weavers had a long history of direct action that dated from the destruction of engine rooms in 1675 (Shoemaker, 1987: 280) and machine breaking had been the subject of punitive legislation since 1721. The late eighteenth century had also witnessed the destruction of textile machinery making textile goods which prompted the government to pass the 1788 Protection of Stocking Frames, etc. Act.

The Luddite movement started in Nottingham in 1811 (involving textile workers) and spread to the West Riding of Yorkshire (targeting the wool industry) and Lancashire (targeting the cotton mills) in the period 1811–1815. The term 'Luddite' comes from the name of a worker, Ned Ludd. He may well have been a fictional character, a latter-day Robin Hood but in his name mechanical weaving machines were destroyed in the late 1770s. Subsequently, a more general uprising known as the Pentrich Rising and led by Jeremiah Brandreth occurred in 1817 is associated with Luddism although it was not specifically targeted at the use of machinery used in an industrial context.

Luddism was met with extreme violence by mill owners and eventually the protest was suppressed by the use of military force. It was remarked by one eminent historian that the 12,000 soldiers who were made available to combat Luddism far exceeded the size of the army that Wellington had made available to him in 1808 to conduct the Peninsula War against France (Hobsbawm, 1952: 58).

The government sought to eliminate the movement with a trial in January 1813 of over 60 alleged Luddites in January following an attack on Cartwright's mill at Rawfolds, near Cleckheaton, West Yorkshire. Although 30 defendants were acquitted, those found guilty were sentenced either to execution or transportation. Subsequently, the 1812 Frame Breaking Act made any form of machine breaking a capital offence while the 1812 Watch and Ward Act introduced procedures to beef up the system of watch and ward in areas where Luddite disturbances had occurred or were anticipated. Members of the public were permitted to enrol as Special Constables to maintain law and order for which purpose they could be armed.

Trade Unionism and the Tolpuddle Martyrs

An important consequence of the industrial revolution was the growth of trade unions. A key event in this history of trade unionism affected rural workers in Dorset whose grievances reflected those of protesters associated with the 'Swing Riots' (which are considered below). Their actions occurred against the background of rural poverty and the exploitation of the poor by unscrupulous landlords who paid their workers what amounted to starvation wages. However, rather than adopt the tactics of direct action associated with the 'Swing' rioters, they resorted to a peaceful means of remedying their grievances—forming a trade union.

In 1799, the Combination Act was passed which prevented workers from collectively bargaining either in groups or through trade unions for higher wages or improved working conditions such as reduced hours of labour. This did not prevent the development of unions (often under the guise of Friendly Societies) but did result in actions they implemented (most notably the withdrawal of labour or 'strike') being severely clamped down upon and frequently led to union leaders being imprisoned.

The 1799 Act was repealed in 1824 which led to a growth of trade unionism and a wave of strikes. This prompted Parliament to pass an Amending Act in 1825 which restricted the freedom of trade unions but allowed them to continue in existence to bargain about hours or conditions of work provided they did not 'obstruct' or 'molest' employers or fellow workers.

In the wake of repeal, Robert Owen formed the Grand National Consolidated Union (GNCU) in 1834 which aimed to place all unions under one broad umbrella—an action which made it possible to envisage a general strike involving all component unions as a threat to employers. This was not the first venture to consolidate unions—there had been a number of attempts in the 1820s and in 1830 the National Association for the Protection of Labour had been formed. The government (which after 1832 was a Whig government led by Lord Grey) was concerned to prevent the spread of trade unionism and in 1834, six men in Tolpuddle, Dorset, were prosecuted in connection with the formation of the Friendly Society of Agricultural Workers which was affiliated to the GNCU.

As there was no specific law to prevent anyone from joining a trade union, they were prosecuted under antique law of 1797 (the Unlawful Oaths Act) designed to deal with mutinies on ships of the Royal Navy which forbade the taking of secret oaths. The men were transported for 7 years. The Home Secretary, Viscount Melbourne, did not interfere with the sentence and it was carried out.

This episode illustrates how the criminal justice system can be used to ensure that an economic system that was based upon exploitation and social injustice could be upheld by criminalising the activities of any of those who fought against these evils, regardless of whether they used peaceful or violent methods. Juries that were composed of landowners made sure that a conviction would be obtained, thereby illustrating the concerns of late twentieth critical criminology whose prime concern was the power structure of society and how this was maintained and in particular 'the causal significance of capitalism in the generation of, and responses to crime' (White & Haines, 2004: 197).

However, in this instance, the government went too far. A demonstration took place in London and 800,000 people signed a petition protesting against the sentences imposed. This pressure had some success: the men were pardoned (an event highlighting the arguments in Chapter 1 regarding the role of mercy in maintaining social stability) and returned to England having served two years of their sentence.

Key Events Associated with the Radical Politics—Plots and Conspiracies

Radical politics embraced actions that would in the contemporary period be viewed as terrorism. Two key events, and the response by the state, are considered below.

The Despard Conspiracy (1802)

One early nineteenth-century example of this was the so-called Despard Plot of 1802, led by Colonel Edward Marcus Despard. In 1802, the court heard evidence that this plot intended to assassinate George III and seize major institutions in London, including the Bank of England, the House of Commons and Tower of London which would trigger an uprising in London. However, the government became aware of the plot and Despard and his co-conspirators were arrested by the Bow Street Runners a week before the attack was planned. Despard and six co-conspirators were found guilty and executed in 1803.

In planning a rising, 'a group of hardened conspirators' (Elliott, 1977: 53) sought to build upon popular discontent arising from food shortages, the 1799 and 1800 Combination Acts (which forbade societies or amalgamations of persons for the purpose of political reform, and was especially directed at the London Corresponding Society, and also made it illegal to interfere with commerce and trade) and the 1801 Cotton Arbitration Act, enabling them to attach to their movement 'a discontented and malleable proletariat' (Elliott, 1977: 53), thereby giving 'a temporary, but substantial, accession of popular strength to an otherwise élitist conspiracy' (Elliott, 1977: 53). Their overall aim was an Anglo-Irish rebellion in support of a French invasion.

Problems that included the absence of a constant level of French enthusiasm for an invasion of England at the beginning of the nineteenth century and the role played by the domestic intelligence system spies (whose spies were argued to have operated even more reliably than the government was prepared to accept) (Elliott, 1977: 61) thwarted the progress of the revolutionary movement. However, it was concluded that the threat was real enough, with activities in London forming 'merely one aspect of a wider conspiracy' which was manifest in Ireland in 1803 in the form of Emmett's Rising. Nonetheless, Despard's part in these events has been argued to have been overstated and it has been concluded that there was no *Despard* conspiracy in 1802—there was a conspiracy around that time but it was not of Despard's making and neither was it planned to take place in November 1802 (Elliott, 1977: 61).

Radical politics suffered a blow with the events in 1802/1803 in England and Ireland, although it has been argued that (based on findings derived from London) there was a continuity of radicalism from 1790 until its revival in the 1820s (Hone, 1982).

The Cato Street Conspiracy (1820)

In the wake of Peterloo, a plot to blow up the cabinet at Cato Street (when they were supposedly having a communal dinner at the home of the Earl of Harrowby) and then seize London was unearthed, led by Arthur Thistlewood. This plot was associated with a group of ultra radicals who followed the ideas of Thomas Spence. It took place against a background of economic distress (which especially resulted in high food prices).

This group had been infiltrated by the informant, George Edwards, who channelled information back to Lord Sidmouth, illustrating the use of 'high policing' against actions deemed to be seditious. As the Cabinet did not socially mix for events such as this, the public announcement of this event was a hoax, designed to bring the ultra-radical conspirators into the open where they could be apprehended. The plotters were seized by Bow Street Runners (one of whom was killed), with a detachment of Guards on standby.

Exemplary sentences were passed on the leaders of the conspiracy. Thistlewood and four other plotters were hanged at Newgate prison and their bodies were then beheaded (formerly after hanging they would have been drawn and quartered). Three other leading plotters were transported to America.

Key Events Associated with Radical Politics—The Reform of the Conventional Political System

Until the enactment of political change in the 1832 Reform Act, very few people were entitled to vote in Parliamentary elections and even the 1832 Act failed to make significant differences to the situation. Accordingly, much political activity was conducted outside of the Parliamentary arena and such actions were in the form of extra-parliamentary political action.

Extra-parliamentary political actions associated with demands for political reform were viewed as radical in the early nineteenth century were frequently depicted as seditious by the authorities, illustrating the arguments later associated with critical criminology of the way in which the state could maintain the control of the ruling elite by its ability to define actions or values that conflicted with the social and economic status *quo as* 'criminal'). The methods employed to combat such actions constituted 'high policing', a term that is discussed in Chapter 11.

In 1795, the Treason Act ('An Act for the Safety and Preservation of his Majesty's Person and Government against treasonable and seditious Practices and Attempts') was enacted. It was passed following the stoning of George III in 1795 on his way to open Parliament. It was enacted alongside the 1795 Seditious Meetings Act which provided that any public meeting of more than 50 persons had to be authorised by a Magistrate and gave the Magistrates the discretionary power to disperse any public meeting. Both were often referred to as the 'Gagging Acts' or the Grenville and Pitt Bills and were directed against radical politics which was often equated with Jacobism in that time.

The Treason Act was a temporary measure, made permanent in 1817. It provided that physical actions aiming to harm or imprison the Monarch could be punished by the offender being hung, drawn and quartered (as was the case for High Treason) and also created a new offence of bringing the monarch, the constitution or his government into contempt which merited the sentence of 7 years' transportation.

Sedition was widely used against radical politics in this period. Between 1792 and 1801 there were over 200 prosecutions for sedition, which was a considerable increase over the number in the previous decade (Emsley, 2018: 25).

This section provides a brief snapshot of some of the key episodes associated with radical political action that aimed to enable increased numbers of citizens to participate in the conventional political system by extending the franchise. However, such demands were deemed to constitute sedition in the early years of the nineteenth century.

Spa Fields

In 1816, in the wake of an economic slump following the end of the Napoleonic Wars, disorder, including machine breaking, occurred in many parts of the country. A group of radical politicians, followers of Thomas Spencer and known as the Spencean Philanthropists, whose main policies advocated the nationalisation of land and the abolition of all taxes save the income tax, intended to hold a meet at Spa Fields in London and then to present a petition to the Prince Regent. They hoped to invite a radical speaker called Henry Hunt, known as 'Orator' Hunt because of his speaking abilities when addressing large crowds of people. Hunt, however, refused to speak unless he could advocate the Radical Programme that viewed Parliamentary reform (in the form of the vote for all men) as the key to all other reforms.

Accordingly, two meetings took place—one by the Spenceans and the other by Hunt and the political Radicals. These attracted large numbers of people who became disorderly and marched towards the City of London. Some rioting occurred before a force collected by the Lord Mayor succeeded in restoring order.

This prompted the government to suspend *habeas corpus* (which had been reinstated in 1815) and enact measures against seditious meetings. These were known as the 'Gagging Acts'. They banned meetings of over 50 people (The 1817 Seditious Meetings Act) and made permanent the 1795 Treason Act and additionally defined as High Treason the assassination of the Prince Regent (The 1817 Treason Act). Their aim was to suppress manifestations of radical politics.

Peterloo

Economic difficulties and unemployment formed the backdrop to a further protest mounted in 1817 in which the unemployed in Manchester planned to march to London in order to petition the Prince Regent for reform and the relief of distress and for the cancellation of the Home Secretary's recent measures of repression. The marchers carried blankets in which to sleep as they progressed towards London. The protest commenced with a meeting held in St. Peter's Field, Manchester but was immediately broken up by troops and the leaders arrested.

The end of 1817 witnessed improved economic conditions and Parliament restored habeas corpus in 1818. However, in 1819 unemployment again increased which fuelled working-class demands for political reform. Economic change (causing the growth of towns) formed the basis for calls for political reform, in particular wrestling power from the landed classes in rural England to those who worked in the towns.

An important event was planned for St. Peter's Field, Manchester at which Henry Hunt would voice political demands for suffrage reform whereby all workers would have the right to vote (although at that time, 'workers' meant males). Demands of this nature were viewed as revolutionary by those who held power in early nineteenth-century England—hence the overreaction of the Magistrates in writing out a warrant to arrest Hunt and ordering soldiers to disperse the assembled crowd.

The meeting was well organised and intended to be peaceful although the authorities had soldiers and volunteers formed into the Manchester and Salford Yeomanry ready for any disturbances. The decision to arrest Hunt when he was speaking and the resultant chaos this caused led the Magistrates to order the cavalry to charge the crowd, in consequence of which 15 people including two women and a child were killed and a very large number were injured (the precise figure is unknown and estimates range from around 140 to 700).

The term 'Peterloo' was a sarcastic reference to the 'glorious' victory secured by the local Magistrates, military and yeomanry in defeating unarmed people, killing 15 and injuring very many, comparing it to the victory won by the Duke of Wellington against Napoleon at Waterloo some four years earlier. Some in the crowd supporting reform would have been soldiers who fought in that battle in 1815. Subsequently, the military commander at Peterloo, Lt Col George L'Estrange, stated that he decided not to use his infantry against the crowd since they would have shot protesters. Instead, he limited military intervention to the cavalry who merely cut and slashed them (House of Commons, 1819: item 36). Infantry was, however, deployed to rescue the yeomanry from possible 'annihilation' by the angry crowd (Palmer, 1978: 213).

The government fully supported the action of the Magistrates and passed the so-called 'Six Acts' which sought to suppress the radical movement.

Box 5.1: The Six Acts

These Acts, passed in the wake of Peterloo, 1819, indicated the manner in which radical politics was labelled as 'seditious' and hence criminalised. These Acts

- made military training illegal
- limited rights to hold political meetings of more than fifty people
- gave magistrates powers to undertake household searches without a warrant
- newspaper duties were increased further and extended to cover all cheap publications—a measure that was especially aimed at the *Register* that had been edited by the radical politician William Cobbett
- strengthened the laws against blasphemous and seditious libel by adding a clause authorising banishment for seven years on a second conviction
- initiated steps to speed the process from indictment to trial and conviction for offenders.

(Philp, 2020: [Online]).

The Act relating to newspaper duties aimed to prevent the circulation of radical ideas of political reform which might encourage debate and inflame the mood of workers living in the newly established towns.

The 1831 Bristol Riots (October 29–31)

In 1830, following the death of King George IV and the accession of William IV, a Whig government headed by Lord Grey took office. It was committed to a moderate measure of political reform that would provide political representation to the emerging middle class and put forward a Bill to achieve this purpose in March 1831. Defeats in the House of Commons prompted the government to resign but it was returned in the subsequent general election and put forward a slightly revised version of the original Bill. This passed the House of Commons but was defeated in the House of Lords in October 1831.

The cause of reform was supported by a large number of political unions that were located throughout the country. These were inspired by the Birmingham Political Union, formed by Thomas Attwood in 1829 and which adopted the name of the Political Union for the Protection of Public Rights towards the end of that year. The Union advocated the cooperation of middle and working classes and their key policies were shorter term Parliaments to increase the accountability of MPs to their constituents, the abolition of the property qualification required of MPs, the payment of salaries to MPs and the vote for all men who directly or indirectly contributed to local or national taxation (UK Parliament, 2022a: [Online]).

They sought to operate within the law so that the government lacked the pretext to ban them. Their activities took the form of mass meetings, demonstrations and petitions to Parliament advocating reform. Although supporters of the Political Unions wanted a measure of reform that was more radical than the Whigs were willing to concede, they were willing to endorse the measure as being the first step in political reform that would make a dent in aristocratic privilege and which could be built upon at a later date. Thus the defeat of the Bill resulted in several disorders throughout the country (UK Parliament, 2022b: [Online]).

They occurred in places that included London, Yeovil, Birmingham (where the Scots Greys were deployed to restore order), Nottingham (where a combination of constables and military restored order, but only after Nottingham Castle, owned by the Duke of Newcastle who opposed Parliamentary reform, had been set on fire). Other disorders occurred at Sherborne, Exeter, Derby and Bristol (Beckett, 2021: [Online]; Caple, 1990: 242–3,).

Bristol was a city containing around 100,000 inhabitants but was represented by just two MPs. Only 6000 men had the right to vote (Brantley, 2016: [Online]). The arrival on 24 October in Bristol of George Henry Law, Bishop of Bath and Wells (who had voted against the Reform Bill in the House of Lords) threatened disorder. The forces of law and order numbered around 100 Constables (Thomas, 1974: 3). There were problems in recruiting large numbers of Special Constables who traditionally came from the ranks of the middle classes (Thomas, 1974: 18) and they declined to summon the yeomanry. Some volunteers were recruited (Thomas, 1974: 3) but, additionally, a request was made for military assistance. Around 90 soldiers from the 14th Light Dragoons and the 3rd Dragoon Guards (commanded by Lt Col Thomas Brereton) arrived in the city.

Against this already tense background, the arrival of Judge Charles Wetherell (a known opponent of Parliamentary reform) on 29 October 1831 was the trigger for three days of disturbances. Wetherell's carriage was attacked and violence escalated, one aspect of which was an attack into the crowds by the Special Constables in which one person was killed (Thomas, 1974: 3). The Town's Mayor, Charles Pinney, attempted to defuse the situation but was eventually forced to read the Riot Act (Thomas, 1974: 3).

During that night and continuing into the next day (October 30), the Mansion House was stormed in response to which the 14th Light Dragoons charged into the crowds with their swords drawn and one man was killed (Brantley, 2016: [Online]). On 30 October, Pinney ordered the formation of a *posse comitatus* but this proved to be ineffectual. A small contingent of the Dodington Yeomanry also arrived that day but were withdrawn before they became involved in quelling the disorder. The leader of the Bristol Political Union, William Herapath, also sought to reason with the crowd, but to no avail (Thomas, 1974: 11). Actions against the crowd by the 14th Light Dragoons resulted in the death of two men and Brereton ordered the unit's withdrawal. However, the remaining soldiers from the 3rd Dragoon Guards were insufficient in numbers to prevent the town's goals from being attacked and their prisoners freed (Thomas, 1974: 8). Other civic property and the Bishop's Palace were also attacked. Private property was also attacked, perhaps being the spur for the formation of a large (3000 strong) *posse comitatus* (Thomas, 1974: 11).

More troops from the 14th Light Dragoons also arrived and their charge into the crowd effectively ended the disorders. The *posse comitatus* then was able to restore order, before the arrival of several hundred more soldiers led by General Sir Richard Downes Jackson (Thomas, 1974: 12). He remained in Bristol for the following 4 months, in order to maintain law and order in the absence of the Corporation setting up an effective police force to do so (Thomas, 1974: 24).

The riots were described as the worst in England since the Gordon Riots in 1780 (Thomas, 1974: 1). At least 12 people were killed, a large part of the Town centre was destroyed and damage estimated at around £300,000 occurred (Thomas, 1974: 1), which is about £24 million in today's money. Subsequently, the city's Mayor, Charles Pinney (who as a Whig supported reform), was tried for having failed to prevent the riot but was acquitted. Charges that were intended to be brought against the remaining Magistrates who governed the city were then dropped (Thomas, 1974: 26). The military commander, Lt Col Thomas Brereton was court-martialled on a similar charge but committed suicide before he was sentenced.

An analysis of those engaged in the rioting suggests that

> the rioters seem to have been mostly men in their twenties and thirties rather than women or young boys, and they were certainly not part of the criminal underworld; only one of those arrested had any previous conviction. Of those who were found guilty for their part in the riot, at least thirty-one were in regular employment and only one was mentioned as being out of work: Six of them owned property of some sort, while the remainder were unskilled or semi-skilled workmen such as porters, labourers, carpenters and journeymen-bakers (Thomas, 1974: 23).

It was concluded that

> The active rioters ... were drawn neither from the semi-criminal elements of the city nor from the mechanics and artisans of the Political Union, but from Bristol's poorer working classes. They were the men who could be found out in the streets on any occasion of great public excitement (Thomas, 1974: 24).

In January 1832, 102 persons involved in the rioting were tried, of which 31 received the death sentence, although only 4 hangings were carried out. Twenty-two persons were transported to Australia and 43 received prison sentences.

The Bill was represented to the House of Commons again in December 1831. It passed in March 1832 and was sent back to the House of Lords. On 7 May a major meeting convened by the Political Unions (known as the Gathering of the Unions or the Meeting of the Unions) took place on Newhall Hill, Birmingham. This was a large demonstration involving 200,000 people and 40 Unions (UK Parliament, 2022b: [Online]). Despite this massive show of popular support for the Bill, it was defeated by the Lords on the same evening. As a result, Grey resigned and the King called upon the Duke of Wellington to form a new government and bring forward a diluted measure of political reform that would serve to neuter popular unrest.

The resignation of the Whig government triggered widespread political agitation across the United Kingdom, some commentators believing that the country was on the verge of revolution. The Birmingham Political Union, headed by Charles Attwood, threatened a campaign of tax withholding. Francis Place (a radical activist who in the 1790s had headed the London Corresponding Society that campaigned for political reform and who in 1831 set up the National Political Union to try and coordinate the work of the existing Political Unions) urged a mass run on the banks to withdraw deposits and thus threaten the financial stability of the government. His slogan that was placarded around London and elsewhere read 'To Stop the Duke, go for gold' whereby people were advised to draw their balances from the Bank of England and to demand payment in gold (Ervine, 1912: 23). In anticipation of disorder, many towns were garrisoned in order to maintain public order.

Wellington, however, was unable to form a government and William IV was forced to recall Grey who took office on the understanding that the Monarch would threaten to create a sufficient number of Whig peers to outvote the Tory ones if they continued to reject reform. On Wellington's instructions, Tory Peers stayed away from Parliament while the Whig measure was being debated and their abstentions in the vote enabled the third Bill for Parliamentary reform to be passed in May 1832, becoming law on 4

June 1832. It was a modest measure that overall increased the electorate from around 435,000 to 652,000. It set up uniform (although differential) franchises in the counties and the boroughs and reduced the number of rotten boroughs (places that had few inhabitants but which returned one or two MPs to the House of Commons), allocating the seats to the expanding industrial towns.

It was concluded that

> No period of British History has been as tense, as politically and socially disturbed, as the 1830s and early 1840s, when both the working class and the middle class, separately or in conjunction, demanded what they regarded as fundamental changes. From 1829 to 1832 their discontents fused in the demand for Parliamentary Reform, behind which the masses threw their riots and demonstrations, the businessmen the power of economic boycott (Hobsbawm, 1999: 55).

A comparison was also drawn between these disorders and those occurring in rural Britain known as the 'Swing Riots' which are considered below:

> The farm labourers directed their anger at the machines and agricultural features which they experienced in their working daily lives. For the urban worker, their revenge was as indiscriminate as it was targeted; entire areas of cities looted and burnt, whilst also specifically attacking the property of those in the political classes who sought to frustrate change (Beckett, 2021: [Online]).

After 1832, when several of the demands of the middle-class radicals were met, the worker's movement fought and failed alone (Hobsbawm, 1999: 55). Middle-class dissent, especially in the form of the Anti Corn Law League, articulated its views through non-violent methods which involved selling their case through education in the form of pamphlets, articles and speeches.

Chartism and the Policing of Political Disorder

While the 1832 Reform Act gave the vote to the urban middle class who thus were given the ability to exert political control over the localities in which they lived, it ignored the urban working class. In total, the 1832 Act increased the percentage of the male population in the United Kingdom who could vote from around 10% to 18% (Knaggs, 2020: [Online]).

This meant that most men (and all women) did not possess the ability to vote and this situation led to the development of political organisations which aimed to further extend the right to vote to include them. The reason for arguing for political reform was that this would ensure that the needs and issues faced by working-class people at that time would be properly addressed in Parliament.

An important movement of this nature was Chartism.

Box 5.2: Early Feminist Thought

Chartism was not the only political movement to challenge the social and economic *status quo* in the early decades of the nineteenth century. This period also witnessed the development of early feminist thought.

In 1792, the feminist philosopher, Mary Wollstonecroft, published *A Vindication of the Rights Of Women* (1792). This asserted that women should not be viewed as ornaments to society or commodities to be bought and sold in marriage but must be regarded as human beings who should rightfully possess the same fundamental rights as men and must be given equal opportunities as men in education, work and politics. To ensure this, she argued that women should be educated equally to men.

Subsequently, Harriet Martineau published a nine-volume work Illustrations of Political Economy. This studied the relationship between economics, politics and social morality and argued that the economic system of England required reform. She provided a model for feminist sociology, addressing key issues of politics, government, newspapers, the economy, slavery, manufacture and commerce, class, women and minorities and religion and identifying four anomalies—the institution of slavery, the unequal status of women, the pursuit of wealth and the fear of public opinion.

These ideas would underpin various aspects of feminist criminologies in the twentieth century, in particular discussions that related to examinations of the discriminatory practices of the criminal justice system towards women, the concerns of radical feminism in highlighting female oppression and victimisation and the manner in which socially constructed gender roles influence the scale and nature of female criminality.

The chartist movement commenced in 1836 when the London Working Men's Association was formed. It represented skilled working men and its leaders were William Lovett and Francis Place. Similar organisations which shared the programme of political reform put forward by the London Movement were set up throughout the country, perhaps the most important being in Birmingham led by Thomas Attwood and the former Irish MP, Feargus O'Connor.

The London Working Men's Association was responsible for drawing up a six-point programme of political reform which was called the 'People's Charter' (or 'The Charter for the Emancipation of the People of the British Isles'). This inspired the creation of the Chartist movement which was initiated in a meeting held in Glasgow in May 1838, reportedly attended by 150,000 people. Its demands were further popularised by the anger generated from the introduction of the 1832 Poor Law Amendment Act which attempted to force all those thrown out of work because of factors such as factory closures or increased mechanisation into workhouses (Solidarity Federation, n.d. [Online]).

Box 5.3: The Chartist Movement

The Charter contained 6 political demands.

- All men to have the vote (universal manhood suffrage)
- Voting should take place by secret ballot
- Parliamentary elections should take place every year, not once every five years
- Constituencies should be of equal size
- Members of Parliament should be paid
- The property qualification for becoming a Member of Parliament should be abolished.

The preamble to the petition presented to Parliament in 1839 referred to the failure of the measure of the 1832 Reform Act to improve conditions of life for poorer people. It also warned that revolution was possible if the government failed to pursue policies designed to promote the good of the many.

To people of wealth and property in the 1830s and 1840s, suggestions that workers and labourers should possess the right to vote was viewed as political extremism. Those who advocated it were viewed with hostility since their demands threatened the status and economic power of the propertied classes. Disorders and riots associated with Chartism fuelled fears that this was a revolutionary movement, aiming to seize control by force, and thus viewed as akin to sedition. Such concerns were justified by the existence within Chartism of a revolutionary current whose aim was insurrection. It was argued that

> Many in the insurrectionist wing argued for the establishment of a French style Republic and this resulted in a split in the Chartist movement in 1839. From the insurrectionist side of the split, a Convention of the Industrial Classes was organised as a workers' alternative to Parliament, and a movement emerged which argued that the charter could only be achieved by force. ...the main aim was political reform and the establishment of a Government based on equal representation. (Solidarity Federation, n.d. [Online])

It was further stated that

> within Chartism there were those who viewed capitalism as an important source of working class oppression as well as unrepresentative Government. In particular, the unions involved in the Chartist movement contained currents of such awareness. These included followers of Thomas Spence, a revolutionary who argued that land and property should be forcibly taken from the aristocracy and returned to the people. It was from the Spencian current within Chartism that the idea of the general strike was developed as a means of achieving the charter. (Solidarity Federation, n.d. [Online])

For such reasons, Chartism was placed on the receiving end of a physical response by the law enforcement machinery and was also the subject of state surveillance carried out by a range of bodies.

Chartism and Political Disorder

The demands of the Chartists were incorporated into a petition.

Petitions in themselves are not revolutionary instruments. However, to add weight to this document, those associated with the insurrectionist wing within Chartism organised a Convention of the Industrial Classes as a workers' alternative to Parliament which initially met in London, aiming to supplement signatures on the petition with the physical weight of those who endorsed its demands. This met in 1839 and initiated meetings throughout the United Kingdom to gain further support for the Charter. One of these took place in Birmingham which led to disorder and rioting.

The Home Secretary despatched 100 Metropolitan Police Officers to the city to help suppress it. As their powers did not extend beyond London, they had to be enrolled as Special Constables before being deployed in Birmingham. In conjunction with the military they used sabres to do so (Steedman, 1984: 7).

Box 5.4: The Birmingham Bull Ring Riots

The National Convention composed of Chartist delegates from across the country and first met in London in February 1839, effectively being a 'mock' parliament. Following its cessation, its members moved to other locations, including Birmingham. In May meetings advocating the Chartist cause were regularly held at the Bull Ring.

The Chartist petition was presented to Parliament on 14 June and there was a strong possibility of disorder arising from Chartist meetings that were taking place in Birmingham. Between 2000 and 3000 Special Constables were enrolled and troops were placed on standby to enforce the ban. However, the meetings resumed in July and on 4 July a detachment of London's Metropolitan police, 90 in number, was sent to augment local responses to disorder.

A contemporary account recorded that

> On the day in question [4 July] an unusually large meeting was held … when banners and flags, bearing mottoes and other insignia, were displayed. Speeches were made, in which the most inflammatory language was employed; but, in the midst of the meeting, the London police … presented themselves and required the dispersion of the crowd. The order was peremptorily given, but no effort was made to obey it, and force was resorted to, to clear the spot of its present occupants. The mob resisted with success, for although the police were a well organised body, and most determined in their efforts, the number of Chartists to whom they were opposed, and their evident preparation to meet any attack which might be made, led to their temporary defeat. For about ten minutes the conflict was dreadful, and individuals on both sides sustained severe and dangerous injuries. The police were driven back … and, for a time, an attack on the prison by the mob was apprehended. Fortunately, however, the 4th Royal Irish Dragoons …accompanied by Mr. Scholefield, the mayor, arrived in time to afford assistance to the civil authorities, and to prevent the riot proceeding to any more dangerous lengths. The dragoons were soon aided by the Rifle Brigade, and their formidable appearance quickly inspired alarm where confidence the moment before had been displayed. The mob quickly took to flight (The Newgate Calendar, 1839: [Online]).

Sporadic outbreaks of violence continued in the following days and the Metropolitan police played an important part in helping to maintain order. However, their presence was not welcomed by the Chartists attending the General Convention in Birmingham stated

> That this Convention is of opinion that a wanton, flagrant, and unjust outrage has been made upon the people of Birmingham by a bloodthirsty and unconstitutional force from London, acting under the authority of men who, when out of office, sanctioned and took part in the meetings of the people, and now, when they share in the public plunder, seek to keep the people in social slavery and political degradation (Resolution Number 1 of the General Convention in Birmingham, cited in Newgate Calendar, 1839: [Online]).

The rejection by the House of Commons of a Motion to refer Attwood's petition—signed by around 1. 25 million people—to a Committee of the Whole House by 253:26 votes (UK Parliament, 2022c: [Online]) on 12 July prompted the return of violence.

Riots took place across the country, including Birmingham where disorder was especially severe on 15 July. Property was attacked and arson attacks occurred. Claims for property damage totalled £20,000. The riot Act was read (UK Parliament, 2022c: [Online]) and the Metropolitan police in conjunction with the military were deployed to combat the rioters and restore order. Criticisms were, however, made of the conduct of the London police, an unnamed journalist present during the disturbances stating the views made to him by 'operatives' (typically machine minders who were employed in factories as semi-skilled workers) that

> it was a shame to bring the London police amongst them; that the police had acted very badly; that they attacked them without telling them to disperse; that many innocent men, some bringing home their work to their employers, were struck down by the police; and that in short the town would never be quiet again until the London police were sent away (anonymous journalist cited in Newgate Calendar, 1839: [Online]).

Complaints were also made of inaction by the Magistrates in connection with the events of 15 July, whereby the police and soldiers not 'called upon to act for a considerable time after the riots prevailed' (Earl of Warwick, 1839: col 371), a view reinforced by the Duke of Wellington who attributed this situation to the Magistrates having been appointed by the Home Secretary out of the ranks of persons who sympathised with Chartist demands (Duke of Wellington, 1839: col 375). Ultimately, order was restored and in the aftermath of the disturbances sentences of imprisonment and transportations followed (UK Parliament, 2022c: [Online]). Some participants were sentenced to death but the sentences were subsequently commuted to transportation.

The question of what to do next split the Chartist leaders. Some were willing to endorse only a constitutional road to achieving their objectives whereas others were willing to support the use of violence to achieve it. Attempts—initiated by the latter—were made to organise what would amount to a general strike—termed the 'Sacred Month'—which might form the nucleus of a popular upheaval or revolution, an idea popularised with the 1832 publication of a pamphlet entitled 'The Grand National Holiday and Congress of the Productive Classes', written by William Benbow, a physical force Chartist. In 1839, endorsed by the Chartist National Convention, Benbow embarked on a speaking tour to organise the strike. However, in late July he was arrested and subsequently tried in Chester for Sedition for which he received a penalty of 16 months' imprisonment.

His arrest and the absence of widespread support within Chartism for this course of action led the Convention to abandon the strike shortly before it was due to commence on 12 August. The strike was opposed by those Chartists who feared its revolutionary implications as well as by those who supported the strike but feared it would fail through the absence of sufficient advanced preparations, especially the arming of the working class (Solidarity Federation, n.d. [Online]).

Box 5.5: The Newport Rising (1839)

There was, however, a consequence of this event which perhaps illustrates the revolutionary potential—or at the very least the revolutionary zeal—of some of those involved in the Chartist movement.

In November 1839, an attempt was made to organise a rising which entailed taking over Newport, which was seen as a prelude to a more general revolution throughout England and Wales. It was spearheaded by John Frost who had served a sentence of imprisonment for libel and who was subsequently elected Mayor of Newport in 1837 and also became a Magistrate. Those involved consisted mostly of iron and coal miners who were suffering from economic distress.

This event was associated with physical force Chartism, one of its objectives being to release the Chartist leader, Henry Vincent, from goal together with other imprisoned Chartists. Vincent had been convicted in 1839 of unlawfully meeting together, intending to disturb the peace and tranquillity of this realm, and to excite disaffection and hatred to the government and constitution of the country for which he had received a prison sentence of one year (The Newgate Calendar, 1840: [Online]).

However, the authorities were aware of the Newport plot and police officers, Special Constables and soldiers were deployed to crush it (The Newgate Calendar, 1840: [Online]). Accordingly, when the insurrectionists entered the town they were driven back by soldiers, resulting in 24 of the crowd being killed (Palmer, 1978: 213). Frost was condemned to death for high treason for the part he played in the rising but his sentence was commuted to transportation.

Other risings, including rumours of risings which never actually occurred, took place in London, Sheffield and Dewsbury in early 1840. These required interventions from both police and the military. Regarding events in Sheffield on 11 January 1840, a contemporary source recorded that

> In the outskirts of the town it was found that the Chartists had assembled in great numbers, and were prepared to undertake any mischievous attack which might appear to their leaders to be proper. The police, who were stationed in the roads to gain intelligence of their proceedings, were repeatedly fired upon and wounded… In the

course of the night a great many persons were taken into custody, and a large quantity of muskets, pikes, daggers, a species of instrument intended to impede the progress of horse soldiers, with three long and sharp prongs, called a cat, with powder, balls, and hand-grenades, were secured. In the darkness of the night large bodies of men, armed with muskets and spears, were seen moving from various points towards the town; but, upon their approaching as far as the pickets which had been thrown out, they appeared to come to the conclusion that their scheme had been discovered, and that therefore their attack would be repelled, and they turned back and marched off into the country districts. During the whole of Saturday night and of Sunday, the greatest degree of excitement prevailed throughout the neighbourhood of Sheffield, and frequent seizures of combustibles and arms took place in houses in the suburbs (The Newgate Calendar, 1840: [Online]).

The Chartist Revival (1842)

Chartism revived in 1842 when a second petition—this time containing 3,300,000 signatures—was presented to Parliament by Thomas Duncombe. In addition to demanding the enactment of the 6 points, the petition also complained about the 'cruel wars against liberty'; and 'unconstitutional police force'; the 1834 Poor Law; factory conditions and church taxes on Nonconformists. It also included an attack on Queen Victoria, contrasting her income of '£164 17s. 10d. a day' with that of 'the producing millions' (cited in Simkin, 1997: [Online]).

However, the petition was again rejected and this sparked off a wave of industrial unrest which has been referred to as the 1842 General Strike which commenced as a protest against wage cuts occasioned by the 1841–1842 economic depression and increased food prices. It started in the Staffordshire Coalfield, and thence in August to Scotland. It also embraced direct action in the Lancashire and Yorkshire textile industry which were known as the 'Plug Plot' riots, so called because it entailed removing the drain plugs of steam boilers installed in the mills, thereby preventing steam from being raised and thus making it impossible for work to be conducted at the mills since there was no power with which to drive the machinery. This became used as a generic name to embrace all industrial actions associated with the 1842 strike. Overall, the disturbances affected twenty-three counties between early July and late September, and led the authorities to view the actions as a 'semi-revolutionary strike movement' (Mather, 1972: 5–27). A key concern of those engaged in strike action was to secure the implementation of the demands of the Charter on the grounds that only political reform could secure economic justice (Irving, 2011: [Online]). This led to a view that the strike of 1842 was essentially an insurrectionary movement with political reform as embodied in the Charter becoming a key objective (Jenkins, 1980: 144).

Although the government was initially divided in how to respond to these events (Peel favouring a non-intervention approach whereas Wellington argued for the deployment of troops) the Plug Plot strike was eventually met with the robust use of force (in the form of the army comprising Hussars, Lancers and Infantry who opened fire on the strikers) and repression—in the North West over 1500 participants were put on trial (Jenkins, 1980: 119), out of whom seventy-nine were sentenced to between 7 and twenty-one years' transportation (Simkin, 1997: [Online]).

By the end of August, the rioting ended. Most strikers returned to work but the cotton operatives of Lancashire and the Staffordshire miners held out for another month (Simkin, 1997: [Online]). Subsequently, many Chartist leaders involved themselves in another of the key issues of that time, agitating in favour of the repeal of the Corn Laws.

The Chartist Revival (1848)

The final wave of Chartist agitation occurred in 1848, triggered by news of events from abroad in which the French King, Louis Philippe, was toppled in a revolution. This initiated popular revolts against absolutist government across Europe and led to the third and final Chartist petition being launched which was intended to be presented to Parliament following a procession that started at Kennington Common. The government was concerned about the revolutionary potential of this latest wave of Chartist agitation. The Duke of Wellington, then almost 80 years old, superintended the defence of London and thousands of citizens enrolled themselves into the Special Constabulary.

The government eventually allowed the meeting at Kennington to take place but O'Connor presented the petition to Parliament which was conveyed in 3 taxis. Although it was said to contain 6,000,000 signatures, the true figure was nearer 2,000,000, many of which were forgeries (including those of the Queen, the Duke of Wellington and the glove puppet, Mr. Punch.)

The circumstances surrounding the third petition triggered actions by extremists that included a meeting at Bishop Bonner's Fields (now called Victoria Park) in East London which was intended to be used as a cover from which a crowd would launch an attack on Whitehall. The police were forewarned of this action and blocked the exit from the fields. Subsequently a further plot to seize London was unearthed, possibly planned by an agent provocateur.

Chartism subsequently declined as a political force. An economic upturn took the sting out of the motives underpinning the demand for Parliamentary reform and the Chartists were deprived of their enigmatic leader, Fergus O'Connor, who died in 1855.

The cause of political reform which underpinned Chartism was not, however, a pointless one. By 1918 all demands made by the Chartists, save that of annually elected Parliaments, had been implemented. And in that year some women (when aged 28) were also given the right to vote.

Rural Disorder

Disorder was not confined to the towns but also occurred in the countryside. This section will examine some of the major manifestations of rural disorder in the early decades of the nineteenth century.

A combination of economic factors in 1829 and 1830 (poor harvests, low wages and high unemployment) caused considerable hardship to agricultural workers whose actions were perhaps inspired by ideas associated with the French Revolution. These economic problems occurred against the backdrop of the loss of common land from 1760 onwards and the introduction of mechanisation to rural industries such as the threshing machine which meant that workers who had formerly performed the task of separating grain from the stalks became redundant and, because they were hired for less than one year were unable to claim on the Poor Rates which had the effect of accentuating rural poverty (Eastbourne Prosecuting Society, n.d. [Online]).

The situation that led to the disorders of the 1830s has been attributed to changes between 1750 and 1850 whereby the rural worker

> was simultaneously proletarianized—by the loss of land, by the transformation of his contract and in other ways—and deprived of those modest customary rights as a man …to which he felt himself to have a claim. This happened at a time when his economic situation deteriorated sharply. He became not merely a full proletarian, but an underemployed, pauperised one (Hobsbawm & Rudé, 1969/2001: 15).

These adverse circumstances led to rural disorders that occurred in the mid-1790s, in 1816 in the Eastern counties and in East Anglia in 1822 (Hobsbawm & Rudé, 1969/2001: 16). Disorders again broke out in 1830. It was asserted that the purpose of these events 'was not revolutionary. Their immediate purpose was economic' (Hobsbawm & Rudé, 1969/2001: 16).

In 1830, rioting started in Mildenhall in Suffolk in February 1830 and then moved to Kent and adjacent counties, especially Sussex. They are known as the 'Swing Riots', named after 'Captain Swing', a fictional person who was the symbol of the anger and resentment felt towards well-to-do farmers and landowners by impoverished rural workers. These disturbances were at their height in 1830–1831 but continued sporadically throughout this decade.

Their demands included higher wages and the abandonment of the use of machinery in the farming industry. These demands were enforced by threats which often transformed into acts of violence involving arson (especially rick-burning), the destruction of machinery as well as wages meetings, attacks on magistrates and overseers (the latter administered the pre-1834 system of poor relief), riotous assemblies to extract money or provisions or to enforce a reduction in rents or tithes (Hobsbawm & Rudé, 1969/2001: 97). The latter reflected Luddite protests against the use of machinery in the manufacturing industry and it was argued that 'the rising of 1830 was the greatest machine-breaking episode in English history' (Hobsbawm & Rudé, 1969/2001: 17).

Initially, the authorities (in the form of Magistrates) were lenient towards offenders, but as the violence increased, so did the severity of the response, including offering large rewards to apprehend those responsible for the damage (Fig. 5.1).

Ten Pounds
REWARD.

WHEREAS late last Night, or early this Morning, the Premises of Mr. RICHARD MARSH, of the Parish of RIPPLE in the County of Kent, were unlawfully entered by some Person or Persons at present unknown, and a

Thrashing Machine
THEREIN WAS
Feloniously Broken and Destroyed;

THIS IS THEREFORE TO GIVE NOTICE,—That active Exertions are now making to discover the Offender or Offenders, and a REWARD of TEN POUNDS is hereby offered to be paid by the said RICHARD MARSH, to any Person who will give such Information as will lead to the Conviction of such Offender or Offenders.

Ripple, 5th August, 1831.

Fig. 5.1 A poster directed at those responsible for actions undertaken in the 'Swing riots' is reproduced above (*Source* https://www.henleyherald.com/2019/04/09/hahg-lecture-the-swing-riots/?doing_wp_cron=1605959625.8789939880371093750000)

Box 5.6: The Swing Riots

An example of the violence associated with the 'Swing Riots' is contained in an account published by the Eastbourne Prosecuting Society, an organisation for Prosecuting Thieves, Felons, and Receivers of Stolen Goods. It offered substantial rewards to anyone providing information leading to the prosecution of arsonists, thieves and receivers of stolen goods.

One example of arson in Eastbourne at the height of the Swing Riots occurred at Colstocks Farm Meads, occupied, by Mr. Moses Filder. The Society's account is as follows:

> On the evening of Thursday 10 February 1831 at about 6.45pm the whole of the property save the farmhouse was discovered to be on fire. The large farmhouse itself was put at great risk due to the intense heat and was only saved by the workers greatest exertions.
>
> It was reported in several newspapers, including The Times, that a stack of straw in the rickyard was 'feloniously and maliciously' set on fire together with one wheat stack, one oat stack, six hay-ricks, two straw stacks, a double barn containing a barley mow, sixteen quarters of threshed wheat in sacks and about thirty quarters of unthreshed barley, a fatting-lodge, a wagon lodge with granary above containing barley and malt etc and an outhouse containing about one thousand bushels of potatoes all of which were destroyed. All that remained from the general wreckage was part of one wheat stack.
>
> A reward of Fifty pounds was offered by Moses Filder and a further Fifty pounds by the East-Bourne Prosecuting Society 'to any person who shall discover the said offender or offenders, so that he, she or they may be apprehended and convicted of the said Offence'.

Additionally,

> a notice was published from Whitehall on February 22 1831, stating that in order to bring the person or persons to justice His Majesty would graciously pardon anyone of the persons involved, who would give information, except the person who actually set the fire. This was signed by the Home Secretary Viscount Melbourne.

Source: http://eastbournehistory.org.uk/eastbournehistoryarchive/eastbourne-archive-files-001/east-bourne-prosecuting-society.pdf

The response by the authorities to the disorders, whatever form they took, was subject to wide variation. In some areas, the military was deployed but it was argued that 'they were intended to guard towns rather than villages or farms' (Hobsbawm & Rudé, 1969/2001: 254). Accordingly, 'outside a few strategic centres, the justices were largely left to fend for themselves' which they did by inviting farmers to enrol in the yeomanry, form voluntary associations, enrol as Special Constables or set up a night watch (Hobsbawm & Rudé, 1969/2001: 253–5).

It was argued, however, that the replacement of the Tory government with Lord Grey's Whig government in 1830 led to 'a more resolute intervention in the suppression of disturbance' in part arising from the fear that the actions in rural England might spark disturbances among the industrial workers in the north and west. The actions undertaken included offering rewards to bring rioters and incendiaries to justice. Additionally, a special Commission was set up to try those arrested for involvement in the disturbances in Hampshire, Berkshire, Dorset and Buckinghamshire (Hobsbawm & Rudé, 1969/2001: 258).

In total, 1976 prisoners were tried by 90 courts sitting in 34 counties: 252 were sentenced to death (although only 19 suffered this fate), 505 were sentenced to transportation (although only 481 were actually transported, 644 received prison sentences, 7 were fined and 1 was whipped (Hobsbawm & Rudé, 1969/2001: 262). It was concluded that 'from no other protest movement of the kind—from neither Luddites not Chartists, nor trade unionists—was such a bitter price exacted' (Hobsbawm & Rudé, 1969/2001: 263).

Public Order Policing, 1750–1850

The following two sections consider the mechanisms that existed to deal with crowd disorder and radical and seditious politics in the period covered by Chapters 4 and 5, 1750–1850.

The response was two-pronged—a physical response by the forces of law and order (which will be considered in this section) and an intelligence-gathering process (which will be discussed in the following section).

The Physical Response to Disorder

The 'Old' Policing System

In urban areas, the system of watch and ward would sometimes be utilised to suppress minor disorders it being observed that historically constables would often be one of the first officials to come into contact with rioters (Lindley, 1983: 117). They were at their most effective in dealing with small-scale disorders but there were examples (even in the early seventeenth century) of them failing or refusing to take action against rioters (Lindley, 1983: 118).

Historically, the 'old' policing system could be reinforced by additional officials, especially in times of disorder. One of these in the City of London was the office of City Marshall, whose origins date to 1570 when 2 were appointed to deal with beggars. The City Marshall wore a uniform and was paid, serving under the Lord Mayor and whose responsibilities included supervising the night watch and apprehending vagrants and suspected criminals. Subsequently an Under Marshall and a small number of Marshalmen were appointed. During the 1770s, the role of the City Marshall was increased and he assumed leadership of the day patrol in 1785 by which time he headed a force of 10 men (Beattie, 2001: 158–62). The office remains to this day, performing ceremonial duties, policing functions having been transferred to the City of London police force when it was created in 1839.

Additionally, provost marshals were sometimes utilised. The office (which was salaried) was initially a military one whose role was to deal with soldiers and ex-soldiers. However, during the sixteenth century, their role was extended to administer 'something like martial law throughout the Country' (Bullock, 1927a: 67). This practice was especially used during the Spanish invasion scares of 1588 and 1599 (Bullock, 1927a: 68).

In the 1590s, the responsibility of provost marshals was extended to deal with civilians who threatened the peace (such as vagrants, vagabonds and beggars who often pretended to be soldiers), one example relating to what has been described as a 'crisis' affecting London between 1594 and 1597, characterised by high prices, food shortages, heavy taxation and wars waged against Spain and in Ireland which created 'unusual difficulties for London' (Bullock, 1927b: 125; Power, 1985: 371). Disorders in the Summer of 1595 arising from these circumstances (in which apprentices played a prominent part) resulted in the appointment of Sir Thomas Wilford as Provost Marshal in 1595 in order to apply martial law who

> patrolling the streets with an armed force, apprehended many rioters, of whom five were executed on Tower hill; which intimidated the rest, and restored quiet to the city. This extra-judicial method of proceeding was a sure indication of a bad domestic government, and of an imperfect police (Noorthouck, 1773: [Online]).

They were intermittently appointed in the City of London in the late sixteenth and early years of the seventeenth century (Power, 1985: 380), appointed by the Monarch upon application of the Court of Common Council (Bullock, 1927b: 124–5).

The Military

The military (and also the militia and yeomanry) could be summoned by the civil authority (a Magistrate) to deal with public disorder. The Magistrate was commonly a local one since only the larger cities possessed Stipendiary Magistrates, the first of whom was appointed for Manchester in 1813: subsequently, the 1835 Municipal Corporations Act enabled incorporated Boroughs to request that a similar appointment should be made.

The procedure of military aid to the civil authority was first used in 1717 in connection with revenue collection and subsequently to help quell riots at Taunton in 1721. Between 1721 and 1766, the request for military aid required approval from the Secretary at War (Palmer, 1978: 204) after which time a general warrant made it possible for the Magistrate to approach the local military commander directly in order to speed up the process of getting soldiers onto the streets or wherever they were required (Palmer, 1978: 206).

It has been remarked that 'the combination of Magistrates and the military would be the single most important instrument for the maintenance of order until the middle of the nineteenth century' (Palmer, 1978: 200). It has been estimated that throughout the eighteenth century, around 17,000 troops were available for 'domestic policing in peacetime Britain' (Palmer, 1978: 206). Subsequently, during the period of chartist agitation the military was deployed especially in Northern England and also when risings (such as that in Newport in 1839) took place. Palmer (1978: 199) cited Colonel T. J. Wemyss who commented, in relation to Chartist disturbances, that 'the only security for life and property in these populous districts is to have more troops at hand'.

Reliance on the military to suppress disorder, however, posed difficulties, the most obvious being the United Kingdom's involvement in wars. The Seven Years War (1756–1763) which pitted the United Kingdom and her allies against France and her allies led the government to seek to beef up the militia to combat internal disorder as well as to defend the country against potential invasion from France. This development is considered below. However, the cessation of hostilities led the government to revert to the use of the military to suppress disorder, such as the riots against high bread prices that took place in rural England in 1766. It was estimated that military intervention resulted in 19 rioters being killed and 200 arrested (Palmer, 1978: 205–6).

A further issue affecting the use of troops in civil situations was where to station them. In January 1840, 7500 troops were stationed in 31 towns in the Military's Northern District (Palmer, 1978: 200). They could be housed in temporary camps or billeted in private homes and public houses, but mixing with the civilian population in times of emotive political discourse and activities carried the risk of undermining military discipline. The alternative was to build more permanent barracks in which to house the soldiers. A building programme was thus embarked upon commencing in the latter decades of the eighteenth century (Palmer, 1978: 20) which between 1816 and 1847 entailed the construction of 21 barracks, most of which were located in Northern England which was particularly associated with disorder (Palmer, 1978: 200). By the end of the nineteenth century, there were 40 local barracks housing around 20,000 troops (Geary, 1985: 15).

One corollary of the building of barrack style accommodation was legislation that aimed to prevent the spread of sexual diseases within the armed forces, a procedure initiated by the 1864 Contagious Diseases Act. This provided for the arrest and compulsory medical checks of any woman suspected of being a prostitute in ports and army towns.

The Militia

The militia (or 'general levy') consisted of a part time force organised at County level. Its officers were drawn from the ranks of nobility and gentry and the rank-and-file theoretically consisted of yeoman but generally was composed of persons from the 'lower orders' of society. The militia could be summoned by the Lord Lieutenant of the County to go to the aid of Magistrates in areas experiencing disorder (Palmer, 1978: 203) and it has been observed that 'the militia was the bulwark of public order from the Glorious Revolution [1688] to the Hanoverian Succession [1714]' (Palmer, 1978: 203). Additionally, the militia was also used in connection with combating crimes that included smuggling and protecting turnpikes.

However, by the middle of the eighteenth century, its overall effectiveness was questioned for reasons that included lack of training and the reluctance of the rising middle class to wish to devote their time and energies into voluntary service. Although the numbers could be maintained by recruiting those lower down the social ladder, there arose the possibility that such recruits might have a personal interest in the disturbances (Palmer, 1978: 203) in the sense of sympathising or even siding with the 'dangerous classes' and the cause that was being articulated (Geary, 1985: 14).

A series of militia Acts passed from 1757 to 1762 sought to revitalise the militia by imposing a quota on each county which would be met by the introduction of compulsory service determined by a ballot from able-bodied men aged 18–45 (although designating a substitute on payment of

£10 was allowed) (Palmer, 1978: 205). However, this led to disorders by those opposed to compulsion (including an attempt by Northumberland miners in 1761 to stop the ballot from taking place). Additionally, where substitutes were used, they often consisted of 'local drunkards and village idiots who had no other way of earning a living'. Thus the militia, although cheap 'was hardly reliable and consequently from the mid eighteenth century the public order maintaining role of the militia was taken over by the regular army' (Geary, 1985: 14–15).

The Yeomanry

In 1794, a new force, the Yeomanry, was developed as a force of volunteer cavalryman to combat a French invasion—a role they performed only once when the Castlemartin yeomanry were deployed in response to a small French landing at Fishguard, Pembrokeshire, in 1797 (Talbot, 2001: 45). Its members came from the ranks of the urban and rural propertied classes and numbered around 36,000 by 1803 (Talbot, 2001: 45–6).

The absence of an effective police force to deal with episodes of public disorder in the early decades of the nineteenth century—especially when associated with demands deemed radical by the propertied classes—resulted in the Yeomanry being retained following the end of the Napoleonic wars (Talbot, 2001: 46). It was reported that between 1819 and 1827 they were used on 156 occasions and between 1841 and 1846, 216 members were used for a total of 486 days (Palmer, 1978: 199). Talbot (2001: 48–9) lists 44 major actions in which the yeomanry were used in support of the civil power between 1819 (Peterloo) and 1867, sometimes (on 17 occasions) in conjunction with the military and on other occasions acting in isolation. The years 1831 (in connection with disorders associated with political reform) and 1839 (relating to Chartism) witnessed the use of the yeomanry on several occasions.

However, they became associated with 'the enthusiastic application of maximum repression' (Geary, 1985: 15) and their class composition and their brutality was said to have undermined their legitimacy (Geary, 1985: 15). The organisation 'never recovered from the stigma of Peterloo' (Palmer, 1978: 199) and this (together with other weakness that included the Yeomanry's infrequent training, their local interests and prejudices, the demands on their time imposed by their employment and the cost that was involved in deploying men who had to be paid for their services) meant that they tended to be used only if regular troops were unavailable (Palmer, 1978: 199). Many corps disbanded following the end of the Napoleonic wars. When used they usually operated under the supervision of the local magistracy and Lords Lieutenant (Talbot, 2001: 50).

The development of professional policing in the middle decades of the nineteenth century made their role in support of the civil power largely redundant and from around 1830 onwards they were resorted to only in cases of 'extreme need' (Geary, 1985: 15). Accordingly, they reverted to fulfilling their military role. By 1898 the yeomanry consisted of 11,724 men organised into 38 regiments (Talbot, 2001: 51).

Professional Police Forces

It has been estimated that although professional policing was well-developed in the incorporated Boroughs under the provisions of the 1835 Municipal Corporations Act (so that by 1842, 80% of incorporated Boroughs had their own forces), only 25% of Boroughs was the force large enough to be effective in relation to quelling disorders. In the counties, the situation was worse: the 1839 Rural Constabularies / County Police Act provided the discretionary power to Magistrates to establish professional forces but by 1842 there were only 1700 professional police officers and by 1848 only 14 of the 40 Counties in England and Wales possessed a professional police force (Palmer, 1978: 198).

One way around this deficiency was for an area experiencing disorder to 'borrow' police officers from another force. At Birmingham in 1839 officers of the Metropolitan Police force were deployed to handle disorder that occurred in the Bull Ring and overall, around 2000 London police officers were deployed to deal with Chartist disturbances between June and December 1836 (Geary, 1985: 16).

Disorders that included Chartism provided the rationale for extending the system of professional policing across England and Wales. Palmer (1978: 199) cited Colonel T.J. Wemyss who, in relation to Manchester, argued that a more numerous regular police force ought to be established. In addition to the 1856 County and Borough Police Act making the establishment of professional police forces compulsory across England and Wales, a further inducement to do this in connection with public order was the reluctance displayed by the Home Office to authorise the despatch of officers from the Metropolitan Police to places outside of London in the latter decades of the nineteenth century (Geary, 1985: 16).

The Special Constabulary

In 1831 legislation (The Special Constables Act) was enacted relating to the appointment of part time police officers who were enrolled into the Special Constabulary.

Box 5.7: The Special Constabulary

Although the origins of the modern Special Constabulary date from 1831, its history can be traced back much further than that. It is compatible with the principle of citizens policing their own communities by voluntary effort, a concept which dates back at least as far as the 1285 Statute of Winchester.

Measures in 1673 and 1820 provided for the temporary (but compulsory) enrolment of citizens to deal with specific emergencies. The 1673 Act authorised Magistrates to summon citizens and swear them in as a Special Constable and to fine or jail them if they refused.

The 1831 Special Constables Act permitted Magistrates to enrol Special Constables in times of emergency. This legislation is the basis of the modern Special Constabulary.

The 1831 Act retained the element of compulsion but this was abandoned in 1835 when legislation made membership of the Special Constabulary a voluntary choice. It was used to combat disturbances associated with Chartism.

It was observed, however, that the Special Constabulary was hardest to recruit in the areas where it was most needed, a problem arising from the lack of a numerous middle class in the towns.

Ad Hoc Initiatives

Actions undertaken by the Whig government which took office in 1830 to counter the 'Swing' riots included mobilising out-pensioners of Chelsea hospital and Ordnance pensioners into service (Hobsbawm & Rudé, 1969/2001: 256–7). Subsequently, to counter the Chartist disturbances, the 1843 Enrolled Pensioners Act provided for the compulsory enrolment of out-pensioners of Chelsea hospital as Special Constables as a response to public order emergencies. A further Act of 1846 made similar provisions for out-pensioners of Greenwich hospital (Mather, 1959: 87). However, it has been argued that these men were 'often undisciplined, physically infirm, and sometimes politically unreliable' (Palmer, 1978: 199).

Political Policing—1750–1850

Political policing is a key aspect of 'high policing'—a term that will be considered more fully in Chapter 11. One aspect of this was to amass information on those individuals and groups involved in extra-parliamentary political activities, on the pretext that such actions were seditious in intention.

The Eighteenth- and Early Nineteenth-Century Secret State

An important resource to counter the threat of politically motivated disorder is intelligence which provides the police or other bodies charged with upholding public order with advance knowledge which may enable them to nip an event in the bud before it has the chance to take hold. In the period 1750–1850, such advance knowledge could be provided by a number of sources and was especially directed at working-class political organisations. However, the secret state was not an invention of the early nineteenth century. Deacon (1980: 15–18) documented the history of a range of agencies that comprise what he described as the 'British Secret Service', arguing that it developed from counter-espionage work introduced by Henry VII whose reign 'marked an inauspicious beginning to national intelligence' which was primarily focused on his personal protection.

Informants/spies

In the eighteenth and nineteenth centuries, governments made use of informants who acted as spies to gather intelligence on those engaged in political dissent. This development was especially associated with Viscount Sidmouth (1759–1844) who served as Home Secretary between 1812 and 1821 (and had briefly served as Prime Minister in 1801 when called Henry Addington). Richard Ford (Chief Magistrate at Bow Street 1800–1806) played an important role in analysing intelligence gathered by spies and other domestic intelligence sources in relation to the activities of the United Irishman and United Englishmen (documented in Hone, 1982: 50–65). Some were directly employed by the government and others by local magistrates.

Sidmouth's use of informants must be seen in the context of the French Revolution and the desire of a Tory party that was resistant to social, economic and political change that such should not be repeated in the United Kingdom. Their use during the time when England was at war with France was not especially controversial as it was viewed as an extension of the war with Jacobin France (McKenzie, 2016: 83) but became so when the war was ended and their target was that of internal dissent in the form of radical politics. Government paranoia that a revolution was imminent in the United Kingdom led to the appointment of a Committee of Secrecy in 1817.

Information provided to the government on radical politics by informants supplemented the role performed by state functionaries such as Magistrates and Lord Lieutenants who communicated to Sidmouth accounts of radical political movements and their views, opinions and actions that were undertaken at a local level. This information was based on first-hand information through observations they made but also from their own local informants. As documented by Bunyan (1977: 102–4) and Geary (1985: 20), these practices continued into the nineteenth century whereby Lord Lieutenants in the Counties and Magistrates in the towns sent the Home Office reports of political activities that took place in their areas and Magistrates could and did offer rewards to informants whose activities resulted in convictions.

A set of papers submitted as part of the record of Parliamentary proceedings in the House of Commons on 24 November 1819, a few months after Peterloo (House of Commons, 1819), evidenced how information on those holding radical political views was obtained and also why it was obtained, echoing the sentiments expressed above that demands that included working-class enfranchisement were viewed as revolutionary in this period. One source stated

> I have great reason to believe, that the lower orders in this part of the country are very much irritated by the laudable conduct of the civil and military authorities at Manchester, and warmly espouse the cause of the Revolutionists; for such they are. Speaking entirely of the actual labouring class, I have not a doubt that a very great majority have the above feeling, and would act upon it if they dared, at this moment (House of Commons, 1819: item 53).

These papers also provide details as to what forces were available to uphold order—reference is made to the 'regular' (that is, Parish) Constables, to Special Constables, the yeomanry and military and also to watch and ward.

The key danger with the use of informants is that they may act as *agents provocateurs* and encourage or instigate an action that would not otherwise have taken place to justify their existence or to allow an action to continue rather than nip it in the bud. Additionally, it was argued that agents created plots in order to justify the government crackdown on dissent and radical politics (McKenzie, 2016: 84).

Government informants—especially William Oliver, sometimes referred to as 'Oliver the Spy' and described as 'the most hated government operative of the period' (McKenzie, 2016: 82)—played an important role in the instigation and then suppression of a rising in Derbyshire in 1817, known as the Pentrich Rising which has been referred to in connection with Luddism.

Oliver sought to mobilise radicals in Northern England by telling them of the scale of preparations in other parts of the region. His actions prompted a small disturbance in Huddersfield in 1817 but a more significant event in Derbyshire where unemployed textile workers led by Jeremiah Brandreth sought to capture Nottingham Castle. Soldiers easily quelled the disturbance. Brandreth and three of the leaders were beheaded, 14 were transported and others were imprisoned.

Infiltration

Initially, the Home Office was the main agency concerned with intelligence on political activities. However, the formation of the Metropolitan police in 1829 provided a new avenue of information-gathering through the infiltration of political organisations by serving police officers.

In the early 1830s an organisation called the National Political Union of the Working Classes (the NPU) came to the attention of the police. They organised political meetings and demonstrations, one of which—at Cold Bath Fields in London—was broken up by the police who charged the crowd with batons. In the melee, one of their number, PC Culley, was stabbed to death. Subsequently, the Inquest Jury returned a verdict of justifiable homicide. Although the government successfully appealed this verdict at a higher court, this episode starkly revealed the level of popular scepticism regarding the desirability of professional policing in England and Wales.

The response of the police towards this political organisation was not confined to a physical one. The organisation had been infiltrated by a plain clothes officer, Sgt William Popay. He attended meetings (where he was alleged to have made inflammatory speeches urging 'radical and violent' actions) (Emsley & Shpayer-Makov, 2006: 7) and attended demonstrations and sent reports of NPU activities back to his superiors at Scotland Yard which were in turn forwarded to the Home Secretary. The NPU became aware of his role as an informant and Parliament set up a Select Committee to investigate this issue of infiltration.

Little came of this inquiry, save 'the vilification of Popay and not his bosses, whose instructions he had been obeying' (Bunyan, 1977: 63). Popay's reward for his part in this affair was that of dismissal. In a debate in the House of

Commons on 22 August 1833, it was stated that Popay's actions were not isolated and that 'it certainly did appear that twenty of them had been so employed at different times, for the purpose of detecting felonies, but the twenty had never been employed all at one time' (Lamb, 1833).

Other Sources of Information

In addition to the use of spies/informants and infiltration other sources existed to gather intelligence on political organisations and activists. The army utilised a separate intelligence network. General Charles Napier, who commanded troops in the North of England in the early nineteenth century was especially adept at doing this by asking his officers for reports derived from their soldiers regarding the mood of the 'labouring classes' in the areas in which they were garrisoned. The officers, in turn, relied on their soldiers for information, many of whom were billeted with local people or drunk in the pubs they frequented (Bunyan, 1977: 103, Mather, 1959: 183).

Other state agencies included the Post Office (which on the authorisation of the Home Secretary could intercept and open mail) and Factory Inspectors (appointed under the provisions of the 1833 Factory Act). It was later recorded that between 1838 and 1842, 69 mail interception warrants were issued (Bunyan, 1977: 103). If a situation appeared threatening, the Home Office could send its own agents to an apparently disaffected area and report on what they found there.

Conclusion

This chapter has highlighted the extent of political dissent in the period 1800–1850 and the various forms that it assumed. Although many of these forms of dissent would be viewed as legitimate sources of protest in the contemporary period, in this period these actions were labelled as subversive and justified the government taking robust action to put them down. Accordingly, the state employed a number of mechanisms through which intelligence was gathered on organisations and individuals whose views were regarded as seditious in the sense of seeking fundamental changes to the political, economic and social order. These mechanisms included informants and infiltrators whose work is considered in this chapter.

Reference has been made in this chapter to the development of the Metropolitan Police Force which paved the way for the birth and growth of professional (sometimes referred to as 'new') policing across the United Kingdom. This development will form the subject of Part 3 of this work.

? Summary Question

Evaluate the effectiveness of the state's response to public disorder in the period 1800–1850.

References

Beattie, J. (2001). *Policing and Punishment in London, 1660–1750: Urban Crime and the Limits of Terror*. Oxford University Press.

Beckett, M. (2021). Inflamed Passions: Organised Violence Against UK Country Houses (Part 2/3)—Reform Act Riots 1831. *The countryseat.org* [Online]. https://thecountryseat.org.uk/2021/06/18/inflamed-passions-organised-violence-against-uk-country-houses-part-2-3-great-reform-act-riots-1831/. Accessed 3 November 2022.

Booth, A. (1977). Food Riots in the North West of England 1790–1801. *Past and Present, 77*(1), 84–107.

Brantley, T. (2016). Commemoration of the 1831 Bristol 'Riots' at Queen Square. *Brh.org* [Online]. https://www.brh.org.uk/site/2016/11/commemoration-1831-bristol-riots-queen-square/. Accessed 3 November 2022.

Bullock, H. (1927a). The Provost-Marshal 1513–87. *Journal of the Society for Army Historical Research, 7*(27), 67–69.

Bullock, H. (1927b). Provost Marshal. *Journal of the Society for Army Historical Research, 6*(24), 124–127.

Bunyan, T. (1977). *The History and Practice of the Political Police in Britain.* Quartet Books.

Caple, J. (1990). *The Bristol Riots of 1831 and Social Reform in Britain.* E. Mellen Press.

Deacon, R. (1980). *A History of British Secret Service*. Granada.

East-bourn Prosecuting Society (n.d.). East-bourn Prosecuting Society. *Eastbourne History Archive* [Online]. http://eastbournehistory.org.uk/eastbournehistoryarchive/eastbourne-archive-files-001/east-bourne-prosecuting-society.pdf. Accessed 10 January 2022.

Elliott, M. (1977). The "Despard Conspiracy" Reconsidered. *Past and Present, 75*, 46–61.

Emsley, C. (2018). *Crime and Society in England 1750–1900*. 5th edn. Routledge.

Emsley, C., & Shpayer-Makov, H. (Eds.). (2006). *Police Detectives in History 1750–1950*. Ashgate.

Ervine, S. G. (1912). *Francis Place. The Tailor of Charing Cross.* The Fabian Society, Biographical Series Number 1.

Geary, R. (1985). *Policing Industrial Disputes 1893–1985*. Methuen.

Hobsbawm, E. (1952). The Machine Breakers. *Past & Present, 1*(1), 57–70.

Hobsbawm, E. (1999). *Industry and Empire: The Birth of the Industrial Revolution.* New Press.

Hobsbawm, E., & Rudé, G. (1969/2001). *Captain Swing*. Phoenix Press.

Hone, J. (1982). *For the Cause of Truth: Radicalism in London 1796–1821.* Oxford University Press.

House of Commons. (1819). Papers Relevant to the Internal State of the Country, 24 November 1819. *Parliament UK* [Online]. https://hansard.parliament.uk/Commons/1819-11-24/debates/0ff523ed-31b2-461a-acc3-4b2b70976ab3/PapersRelativeToTheInternalStateOfTheCountry

Irving, S. (2011). Manchester's Radical History. *Radical Manchester* [Online]. https://radicalmanchester.wordpress.com/2011/10/23/the-1842-strike-part-1/. Accessed 14 January 2023.

Jenkins, M. (1980). *The General Strike of 1842.* Lawrence and Wishart.

Knaggs, P. (2020). The People's Charter. Labour Heartlands [Online]. https://labourheartlands.com/the-peoples-charter/#:~:text=In%201838%20a%20People's%20Charter,the%20vote%20(universal%20manhood%20suffrage).

Lamb, G. (1833). Speech in the House of Commons 22 August. *Historic-hansard/Commons* [Online]. https://api.parliament.uk/historic-hansard/commons/1833/aug/22/the-police-popay. Accessed 17 January 2022.

Lambert, T. (2020). A History of English Population. *Localhistories.org* [Online]. http://www.localhistories.org/population.html. Accessed 9 October 2020.

Lindley, K. (1983). Riot Prevention and Control in Early Stuart London. *Transactions of the Royal Historical Society, 33*, 109–136.

Mather, F. (1959). *Public Order in the Age of the Chartists.* Manchester University Press.

Mather, F. (1972). The General Strike of 1842: A Study of Leadership, Organisation and the Threat of Revolution during the Plug Plot Disturbances. In J. H. Porter (Ed.), *Provincial Labour History.* Exeter: University of Exeter, Exeter Papers in Economic History No. 6.

McKenzie, K. (2016). Exit Pursued by a Bear: Oliver the Spy and the Imperial Context of British Political History. *History Australia, 13*(1), 80–94. https://doi.org/10.1080/14490854.2016.1156187

McLynn, F. (1989). *Crime and Punishment in Eighteenth Century England*. Oxford University Press.

Noorthouck, J. (1773). Book 1, Ch. 9: Elizabeth. In *A New History of London Including Westminster and Southwark* (pp. 130–144). British History Online [Online]. http://www.british-history.ac.uk/no-series/new-history-london/pp130-144. Accessed 26 September 2022.

Palmer, S. (1978). Calling out the Troops. The Military, The Law and Public Order in England, 1650–1850. *Journal of the Society for Historical Army Research, 56*(228), 198–214.

Philp, M. (2020). The Six Acts 1819. University of Warwick [Online]. https://agmed.lnx.warwick.ac.uk/items/show/102. Accessed 12 October 2020.

Power, M. (1985). London and the Control of the 'Crisis' of the 1590s. *History, 70*(230), 371–385.

Publishing Company.

Publishing Ltd.

Shoemaker, R. (1987). The London "Mob" in the Early Eighteenth Century. *Journal of British Studies., 26*(3), 273–304.

Simkin, J. (1997). Plug Riots. *Spartacus-educational* [Online]. https://spartacus-educational.com/CHplug.htm. Accessed 17 January 2022.

Solidarity Federation. (n.d.). Britain—The Radical Tradition. *Solfed* [Online] http://www.solfed.org.uk/a-s-history/unit-2-britain-the-radical-period-1750-1840. Accessed 8 January 2023.

Steedman, C. (1984). *Policing the Victorian Community: The Formation of English Provincial Forces, 1856–80*. Routledge and Kegan Paul.

Sullivan, M. (n.d.). The Swing Riots. University of Kent [Online]. https://blogs.kent.ac.uk/ageofrevolution/riots/the-swing-riots/. Accessed 18 October 2020.

Talbot, P. (2001). The English Yeomanry in the Nineteenth Century and the Great Boer War. *Journal of the Society for Historical Army Research, 79*(317), 45–62.

The Newgate Calendar. (1839). The Birmingham Riots 13th of July 1839. *Exclassics.com* [Online]. https://www.exclassics.com/newgate/ng895.htm. Accessed 2 October 1839.

The Newgate Calendar. (1840). The Chartist Riots 1839–1840. *Exclassics.com.* [Online]. https://www.exclassics.com/newgate/ng896.htm. Accessed 10 October 2022.

Thomas, S. (1974). *The Bristol Riots*. Bristol Branch of the Historical Association, Bristol University.

UK Parliament. (2022a). Birmingham Political Union. *Parliament UK* [Online]. https://www.parliament.uk/about/living-heritage/transformingsociety/electionsvoting/chartists/case-study/the-right-to-vote/thomas-attwood-and-the-birmingham-political-union/birmingham-political-union/. Accessed 3 November 2011.

UK Parliament. (2022b). Reform and the Birmingham Connection. *Parliament UK* [Online]. https://www.parliament.uk/about/living-heritage/transformingsociety/electionsvoting/chartists/case-study/the-right-to-vote/thomas-attwood-and-the-birmingham-political-union/reform-and-the-birmingham-connection/. Accessed 3 November 2022b.

UK Parliament. (2022c). The Bull Ring Riots. *Parliament.uk*. [Online] https://www.parliament.uk/about/living-heritage/transformingsociety/electionsvoting/chartists/case-study/the-right-to-vote/the-chartists-and-birmingham/the-bull-ring-riots/. Accessed 1 October 2022c.

Warwick, E. G. (1839). Speech in the House of Lords 16 July. HL Debs, series 3, Vol. 49, cols 370–371.

Wellington, D. C. (1839). Speech in the House of Lords 16 July. HL Debs, series 3, Vol. 49, cols 373–376.

White, R., & Haines, F. (2004). *Crime and Criminology: An Introduction* (3rd edn.). Oxford University Press.

Wollstonecroft, M. (1792). *A Vindication of the Rights of Women*. The Humboldt.

6

Reform of Prisons, the Penal Code and Legal System

Introduction

This chapter will consider the pioneering efforts of prison reformers such as John Howard, Elizabeth Fry, Sir George Onesiphorus Paul and Jeremy Bentham and the reforms that they inspired and helped to bring about. Their opinions regarding prison reform were voiced within the context of broader considerations which derived from two key influences—religion and classicist criminology. In the latter, reform was underpinned by secular thoughts and considerations, not inspired by religious beliefs or opinions.

The commencement of the period covered by this chapter was the heyday of what was termed the 'Bloody Code': in theory (but not in practice) almost all crimes carried the death penalty. However, much inspired by classicist criminology, reforms took place which vastly reduced the number of capital offences by 1850, a development that is considered in the context of Émile Durkheim's views regarding changes to the nature of punishment as society transitioned from the mechanical to the organic (terms that are defined in Chapter 2) and Max Weber's discussion of bureaucratic rationality.

This chapter will also examine the operations of the legal system in the eighteenth and nineteenth centuries and discuss the nature of changes that occurred in the early decades of the nineteenth century.

P. Joyce and W. Laverick, *History of Policing, Crime, Disorder, Punishment*,
https://doi.org/10.1007/978-3-031-36892-9_6

Sociological Perspectives to the Punishment of Offenders: Durkheim and Weber

Émile Durkheim and Max Weber provide theoretical perspectives that seek to explain why reforms to the operations of the criminal justice system and in particular to methods of punishment were put forward in the first half of the nineteenth century.

Durkheim

Durkheim believed that social cohesion was based upon the division of labour and consequent specialisation of tasks arising from it. He argued that a mechanical society characterised by little division of labour and consequent uniformity in the work and beliefs of most of its members. The solidarity of this society was maintained by the pressure for uniformity exerted by the majority against the minority who held different standards.

In a society in which consensual values were adhered to by most of its members—which was the feature of a mechanical society, although it might also arise in stable organic societies whose characteristics could thus be described as 'tending towards the mechanical'—diversity was inevitable.

Crime was useful in a mechanical society as the negative views held by the majority of lawabiding citizens towards those who contravened its legal or moral standards helped to promote a sense of social solidarity by affirming the boundaries of what society regarded as right and wrong behaviour. This gave rise to a legal system that was repressive in nature (since crime offended what Durkheim referred to as the 'conscience collective') (Durkheim, 1893).

As Chapter 1 has argued, severity characterised the overall response to crime in the early eighteenth century since for the most part a mechanical society prevailed in most of the country in which social order was maintained by traditional methods that included deference and transgressions were punished by a harsh penal code, albeit one that was tempered through the application of mercy.

However (as is argued in this chapter) as urbanisation accelerated during the early years of the nineteenth century, the consequences of the transition from a mechanical to an organic society became more far-reaching in relation to methods of punishment. By the early nineteenth century, the severity of the criminal code (and especially the circumstances under which the death penalty could be used) became lessened since the intensity of the 'conscious collective' lessened in a society that became characterised by moral diversity and the interdependence of cooperating individuals (Garland, 1990: 37).

Weber

Whereas Durkheim viewed changes to the methods of punishment in the context of society's transition from feudalism to capitalism, Weber (1922) focused upon the concept of authority (that is, how widespread compliance with the demands made by those in positions of leadership was achieved).

Weber argued that legal-bureaucratic (or legal rational) authority was most appropriate to a modern capitalist society characterised by the division of labour and the differentiation of tasks. He believed that this source of authority was the key characteristic of an efficient, legitimately governed, modern state whereby 'judgements must be made according to rules; authority is vested in position-holders rather than in people themselves' (Hudson, 2003: 106).

Legal-bureaucratic authority rested upon a system of bureaucratic rationality. This was characterised by features that included 'impersonality, the interchangeability of officials, routinization of procedure and a dependency on the existence of recorded information' (Cavadino & Dignan, 2002: 75). This was contrasted to the irrational means of social control that he contended were found in primitive societies.

Bureaucratic rationality was thus seen as the hallmark of advanced societies and this characteristic was mirrored in its modes of punishment that were administered in a dispassionate, impartial and consistent manner by the professional functionaries of the central state.

It was argued that aspects of the application of the principle of bureaucratic rationality in modern societies were found in attempts to eliminate the discretion wielded by professionals in areas such as sentencing and in changes to the methods of punishment, which were guided 'not so much by progress in humanitarianism as progress in bureaucratized rationalism, necessary to meet the social control needs and legitimacy conditions of modern society' (Hudson, 2003: 107).

Prison Reformers

There had been attempts in some places to implement prison reform in the earlier part of the century and thus there was considerable local variation in the way in which the criminal justice system operated in the late seventeenth and eighteenth centuries. This section will evaluate the reforms that were delivered on more of a national basis.

An influential figure in promoting reform—in which prisons were viewed as places where prisoners could be reformed and then rehabilitated—was John Howard. John Howard was a Quaker who was driven by his religious impulse, viewing criminals as 'lost souls estranged from God', and believing that 'men could be changed by awakening their consciousness of sin' (Ignatieff, 1978: 67). He put his ideals into practical reforms that aimed to turn around the lives of those placed in prison which would be achieved through the implementation of 'a strict regime of routinization and repetition' that would lead to 'the internalisation of moral duties' (Shelden & Vasiliev, 2018: 150) performed within what Goffman (1961) referred to as a total institution, a place where people are isolated from society and whose conduct is controlled by those who are in charge of them.

Howard's interest in prison conditions began when he was appointed as High Sheriff of Bedfordshire in 1773. His inspection of the county goal made him aware of the squalid conditions that existed at that time which led him to conduct other inspections further afield. The following year, 1774, he gave evidence to a Select Committee of the House of Commons on prisons which helped influence two Goal Acts in 1774 which sought to end the system whereby goalers relied on fees from prisoners for their income and to improve conditions in prisons. Its provisions were, however, widely ignored by those who run prisons in that period. Following further visits to prisons in the United Kingdom and abroad, he published *The State of the Prisons in England and Wales, With An Account of Some Foreign Prisons* in 1777.

Based on extensive travels visiting English and Welsh prisons, this work pointed out that prisoners were not separated by gender or by the type of crime they had committed, many prisoners were dying of illness and disease (it being stated that in 1782, three times as many prisoners died of goal fever at Gloucester prison as were executed) (May, 2006: 8 and 11), too few people were employed to guarantee prisoner safety, many gaolers were corrupt and many prisoners stayed in prison beyond their sentence as they could not afford to pay the gaoler the release fee that was required in order to secure their release.

Ignatieff argued that Howard sought to remove discretion, cruelty and abuse from the guards, arguing that 'gentle discipline [was] commonly more efficacious than severity' (Howard, 1777: 39). He advocated increasing their accountability and formal regulation—both guards and inmates were to be routinised by formal regulations, so that in place of 'the unwritten, customary, and corrupt division of power between criminals and their custodians', both would be subjected to 'the disciplines of a formal code enforced from the outside' (Ignatieff, 1978: 77). He also aimed to secure this objective by attacking the fee system and through the introduction of mandatory quarterly inspections by Magistrates (Ignatieff, 1978: 77). Rules of this nature were intended to win back the prison from both the criminals and their keepers.

Howard put forward a number of recommendations that included gaolers should be paid (a reform that was embodied in the 1815 Goals Fees Abolition Act whereby the salaries for goalers were to be provided out of the County rate or an equivalent authority), that prisoners should have access to medical treatment, secure an improved standard of food and receive visits from churchmen and that prisons should provide clean and hygienic conditions with access to running water, echoing the views of the hospital reformers who were active in the latter decades of the eighteenth century. He advocated prison regimes based on the principles of solitary confinement, religious instruction and hard labour. Not all of these ideas were original: prison reform was debated by several reformers in the latter decades of the eighteenth century, Samuel Hanway putting forward the argument 'solitude in imprisonment, with profitable labour, and a spare diet' was

> the most humane and effectual means of bringing malefactors who have forfeited their lives or are subject to transportation, to a right sense of their condition (Hanway, 1776: 4).

Howard believed that the purpose of prisons was not simply retributive—to punish—but also to bring about the prisoner's reform and rehabilitation. Perhaps his main contribution to the development of prisons in the criminal justice system was to popularise them as a central part of the penal system, serving as alternatives to either transportation or execution (May, 2006: 11). It was argued that 'his reports caught the public imagination and were in tune with a rising swell of evangelical religion' (May, 2006: 11), although others have downplayed his contribution to prison reform, it is alleged that that prison reform in the second half of the eighteenth century arose from factors other than Howard's writings—

> Population rose; crime rose; the prison population grew, especially when transportation of felons was drastically interrupted by American independence […]. And the upshot of overcrowding was typhus […] it was epidemics not Howard that got reform rolling (Porter, 1995: 14–16).

Howard's ideas influenced the 1779 Penitentiary Act which set forward a penal regime bearing many resemblances to that proposed by Howard in 1777. Although this measure failed to provide an immediate blueprint for prison reform, it has been argued that Howard promoted the prison to centre stage in the delivery of responses to crime 'shifting all other forms of punishment to the margins' (McGowen, 1998: 79). Ignatieff argued that the theory of the penitentiary offered 'to restore the legitimacy of the legal system that they feared was jeopardized by the excessive severities and gratuitous abuses of the Bloody Code' (Ignatieff, 1978: 55), although he was critical of the penitentiary 'as a machine for the social production of guilt' (Ignatieff, 1978: 213). Foucault (1977) similarly depicted this approach as central to the shift in criminal justice policy away from capital punishment and the spectacle of terror but he was critical of the new age of confinement and discipline that it inaugurated.

Sir George Onesiphorus Paul

A further influential prison reformer in the late eighteenth century was Sir George Onesiphorus Paul (1746–1820). He was a textile manufacturer who became High Sheriff of Gloucestershire in 1780. He published a book in 1784 called *Thoughts on the Alarming Progress of the Jail Fever which he republished with amendments in 1817.*

His concern was voiced against the background of the American revolution which resulted in the loss of a destination for transported convicts (Paul, 1817: 21). Accordingly, this sentence was substituted for long periods of imprisonment for convicts which led to the overcrowding of these institutions with the disease being 'an infallible result' (Paul, 1817: 21). He argued that while he believed it was possible for the disease, once generated, to be prevented from 'rising to a state of contagion' to achieve this it was necessary for there to be

> A strict police amongst the prisoners, and a regulation in the conduct of their keepers, which is not attainable under the principle of construction of our present prisons (Paul, 1817: 22).

He argued that the preservation of health in prisons

> Must depend on the possibility of introducing air, and separating the prisoners, with due regard to their safe custody: how far these two objects are reconcilable to each other, must depend on the system of regulation attainable from the construction of the prison (Paul, 1817: 21).

His belief that the prison design could combat fever led him to draw up plans for a new county goal, an accompanying penitentiary and—initially—a House of Correction (or Bridewell) that were opened in 1791 in the

County under the provisions of the 1785 Gloucestershire Act (Evans, 2013: [Online]).

The prison was based on the separate system with prisoners in individual cells. It was secure and had separate areas for male and female prisoners, as well as a chapel, an infirmary and exercise yards. Prisoners received visits from chaplains and doctors. His prisons included isolation sections to check new inmates for disease, good ventilation and an exercise yard. Workrooms were provided for debtors and provision was made for inmates to obtain work from manufacturers.

Elizabeth Fry

Prison reform was also promoted by the Quaker, Elizabeth Fry, whose concerns stemmed from the treatment of female prisoners in London's Newgate Prison. Here women prisoners were housed in wards within the prison, convicted prisoners mixed with those awaiting trial and prisoners lacked basic necessities such as beds and blankets. She undertook a range of practical measures within the prison that included providing clothes and bedding, establishing a chapel and school in the prison and teaching women practical skills such as knitting and sewing. In 1817, she established the Association for the Reformation of Female Prisoners in Newgate.

The context of her concerns to improve prison conditions stemmed from a belief that the intention of harsh responses to crime such as public executions or transportation were ineffective means of deterrence and also that the increased use of prisons as responses to crime necessitated consideration to be paid to what exactly was trying to be achieved by this mode of punishment.

Rejecting the retributivist function of punishment, she embraced the rehabilitative ideal, believing that prisons were places where the lives of those who had done wrong could be turned around. In 1816 she funded a prison school for the children who were imprisoned with their mothers and in 1817 she helped found the *Association for the Reformation of the Female Prisoners in Newgate*.

With specific reference to women prisoners at Newgate, she urged a regime of religion, employment in tasks such as knitting and sewing (with materials provided by the Association referred to above) and rewards as the ways to make those who had broken the law become valuable members of society. Teaching prisoners self-respect was an important objective she worked towards. Her ideas were not totally dissimilar from those of John Howard's, but she believed that prisoners should mix together whereas Howard believed in keeping them apart by the use of single cells.

Her reforms were achieved by her being an extremely influential lobbyist. She lobbied Parliament, giving evidence to a House of Commons Committee on Prison Conditions (which focused on prisons in London) in 1818. Although her views did not make much headway while Viscount Sidmouth was Home Secretary (since he believed it was necessary to instil fear into the criminal classes), his successor, Sir Robert Peel, was far more receptive to what she was saying. The 1823 Goals Act promoted by Peel was inspired by her pioneering work.

Box 6.1: Legislative Reform Affecting Prisons

In 1779 Parliament passed the **Penitentiary Act**, which authorised the building of one or more national or state-run penitentiaries characterised by strict discipline and hard labour. An important feature of the penitentiary was that prisons were given a purpose, that of turning around the lives of those convicted of a crime.

This noble objective was not, however, acted upon in the late eighteenth century since no state-administered penitentiaries were ever built, although some local ones were. However, the new Coldbath House of Correction (which opened in 1794) did seek to bring about the reform of those convicted of a crime.

The prison population grew during the early nineteenth century reflecting the increased use of imprisonment as a penalty for crime at the expense of older forms of corporal punishment that fell into disuse. This resulted in renewed interest in prisons and led to the enactment of the 1823 Goals Act.

This legislation required that prisons should be safe and secure, that gaolers should be paid, that female prisoners should be separated from male prisoners and be superintended by female wardens, that prisoners should be regularly visited by doctors and chaplains and that efforts should be devoted to reform prisoners who would no longer be confined in chains or irons.

However, the impact of this legislation was limited.

It did not apply to all prisons—town jails and debtors prisons were not covered by this measure.

Additionally, there was no mechanism to ensure these measures were adhered to. This was only provided when the 1835 Prison Act set up the Prison Inspectorate.

In 1835, Elizabeth Fry gave evidence to a Select Committee of the House of Lords. She stated that despite the 1823 measure 'in many instances their condition is melancholy…they may truly be called schools for crime'. She bemoaned the fact that some still had 'no instruction, no employment, no classification [of inmates]…and they get into a most low and deplorable state of morals'. She feared that many prisons could be characterised in this manner (Fry cited in Isba, 2010: 139–144).

The 1823 Act led to the construction of many new prisons during the century which followed a fairly similar design in which prisoners were housed in single cells. These new prisons included Millbank Prison (which opened in 1821), Beaumaris Prison (opened in 1830), Cardiff Prison (opened in 1832) and London's Pentonville Prison (opened in 1842).

A further Act, the 1839 Prison Act, provided for visits by chaplains, gave salaries to gaolers, prohibited the use of irons and manacles and provided for women wardens to supervise female prisoners.

Jeremy Bentham

The philosopher Jeremy Bentham made important contributions to prison reform through his suggestion of the blue print he referred to as the Panopticon. His ideas on this matter were consistent with the impulses of the Enlightenment, a key aspect of which viewed humans as rational beings (Emsley, 2018: 10–11). This issue is considered more fully in Chapter 1.

Despite important differences regarding prison reform between Howard and Fry, both believed in the importance of religion in bringing about a change of habit. This was totally absent in the ideas of Bentham—he was a 'secular' prison reformer, believing that the reform of criminal habits would occur because of the nature of the prison regime, in particular the important role that surveillance played in this process. Contrasting the views of Howard against those of Bentham, Ignatieff noted that both denied criminal incorrigibility but from diametrically opposed positions—one (Howard) accepting the idea of original sin, the other (Bentham), denying it. For Bentham 'criminals were "froward children, persons of unsound mind", who lacked the self-discipline to control their passions according to the dictates of reason' (Ignatieff, 1978: 67), while for Howard (as has been argued above), men could be changed by awakening their consciousness of sin.

Bentham put forward the Panopticon (which means 'all-seeing') design. This entailed a circular building with prisoners' cells arranged around the outer wall. The entire structure was overseen by a central inspection tower (or inspection lodge). From the tower, prison guards would be able to observe the prisoners and monitor their behaviour at all times. Power over the prisoners derived from this form of observation is termed surveillance.

This design enabled the guards to be placed centrally within the prison where they could view the prisoners but—crucially—where the prisoners could not see them. The belief by prisoners that they were being watched even when they were not, was crucial to the self-regulation principle upon which the Panopticon operated.

Ignatieff argued that

> Materialist philosophy implied that a regimen applied to the body by the external force of authority would first become habit and then gradually be transformed to a moral preference. Through routinization and repetition the regimens of discipline would be internalized as moral duties'. (Ignatieff, 1978: 67)

The knowledge of the possibility of being constantly watched by those in prison was meant to make prisoners adopt conforming standards of behaviour since constant observation could result in punishment for those who failed to comply. Constant surveillance would 'coerce the inmates into adjusting their own behaviour' (Cutieru, 2020: [Online]). Eventually, the socially correct ways of behaving would become second nature to the prisoner who would thus go on to lead a socially useful life when released. This is referred to as 'internalised authority' and would be aided and was further aided by the prison design preventing prisoners from mixing with each other and also from the availability of work for them.

Box 6.2: Jeremy Bentham and the Panopticon

In 1791 Bentham wrote a three-volume work, *The Panopticon* (which was subsequently amalgamated into one volume), in which he devised a blueprint for the design of prisons in order for them to be able to bring about the transformation of the behaviour of offenders.

Central to his idea was the principle of surveillance whereby an observer was able to monitor prisoners without them being aware when they were being watched. This 'invisible omniscience' secured the constant conformity of inmates since they were unable to discern when their actions were not being observed. It induced in inmates 'a state of conscious and permanent visibility that assures the automatic functioning of power'. Surveillance was thus 'permanent in its effects, even if it is discontinuous in its action' (Foucault, 1977).

To achieve this function, Bentham proposed that prisons should be designed with a central tower which housed the observers from which rows of single cells arranged in tiers and separate blocks would radiate. These cells would be isolated from each other.

Michel Foucault was heavily influenced by Bentham's ideas, especially in connection with the way in which power and knowledge were intertwined: he argued that the disciplinary surveillance of the prison created knowledge of the convict's body thus creating a new kind of power (Foucault, 1977: 27). This power was exercised through the fear of being the constant subject of observation—'he is seen, but he does not see; he is the object of information, never a subject in communication' (Foucault, 1977: 201).

Bentham promoted the Panopticon design in connection with plans to construct Millbank Penitentiary which was opened in 1821. This became the first national penitentiary, responsible for holding convicted persons awaiting transportation (May, 2006: 21). However, Bentham was not responsible for its construction which abandoned the Panopticon model. One problem was that the blueprint to achieve the objectives desired by Bentham were hard to translate into a practical design.

The design of Pentonville Prison (opened in 1842) was, however, influenced by this concept. However, as distinct from Bentham's Panopticon, this design did not let prison guards see into the individual cells—the method of the prison's construction was primarily designed in order for prisoners to have individual cells rather than to provide for a system of surveillance by the prison guards.

Bentham was criticised for developing a design from prisons which was mechanistic but not necessarily humane. Prisons, he believed, were machines that would 'grind rogues honest' (Bentham, cited in Ignatieff, 1978: 68)—and reform would be achieved not through the intervention of God but by the convicted person internalising new ways of behaving which were taught to him and her by the way in which the prison regime 'educated' a convicted person to conform to the socially acceptable standards of behaviour of the day.

The Separate and Silent Systems

Concerns regarding the growth of crime (estimates suggested that the 5000 offences committed each year in 1800 had risen to 20,000 each year by 1840) and public scepticism regarding transportation as an incapacitative solution to this problem resulted in a new emphasis being placed on prisons as a key mechanism of punishment. The prison estate expanded whereby 90 new institutions were constructed between 1842 and 1877 (National Archives, undated: [Online]). Prisons in this period were either convict prisons or local prisons. Convict prisons were controlled by the central government (and were where sentences of penal servitude were carried out) and local prisons were controlled by local Magistrates.

The prison regimes that operated in the growing prison estate followed two models—the separate system and the silent system. These regimes were governed by Acts of Parliament. The 1835 Prison Act favoured the separate system but legislation enacted in 1837 undermined this approach by prohibiting solitary confinement for more than one month (or for three months in any one year). Further legislation enacted in 1839 facilitated the use of a separate system and led to the construction of Pentonville Prison, London, between 1840 and 1842 which utilised this prison regime (May, 2006: 14). By 1856, two-thirds of prisons in England had adopted the separate scheme in whole or in part (May, 2006: 16).

In the separate system (based on the system used in Cherry Hill Prison, Pennsylvania, United States), prisoners were isolated from contact with other prisoners and spent much time alone in their cells, commonly 23 hours each day. Work, however, was available to prisoners who asked for it. Religion was designed to play an important part in helping to change the behaviour of the offender. They were allowed out to exercise and attend church services but when exercising had to wear masks and in chapels were made to sit in booths so that they were physically separate from other prisoners. Accordingly, the kind of work they performed while in prison was of the sort that had to be carried out in their cells.

There were several perceived benefits from this regime, including the intention to prevent hardened criminals from influencing other prisoners and that harsh conditions of this nature would serve as a deterrent to committing crime. In particular, it was assumed that in this condition of solitude, prisoners would reflect on their actions that led to their imprisonment and were encouraged to change their habits by visits undertaken by prison chaplains. Moral reform, achieved through religion, therefore, was viewed as the key to changing the habits of a convicted offender (Emsley, 2018: 286). The separate regime also served a control purpose since prisoners separated in this manner were easier to control (May, 2006: 15).

The silent system was associated with 1865 Prison Act which reflected a move towards the use of harsh punishments to exact retribution on offenders. This issue is considered more fully in Chapter 12. It was based on a model derived from Auburn Prison, New York which was subsequently adopted at Sing Sing prison also in New York. Under the silent regime, prisoners were not allowed to communicate in any way with each other but they did perform tasks of work together which meant that it could be performed in places such as prison workshops.

In reality, there was not a great deal of difference between the manner in which the separate and silent systems operated. It was the motives that underpinned them that were the key difference—the separate system was more concerned with reforming the habits of prisoners by opening their minds to religion which caused them to reflect on their wrongdoings whereas the silent system was underpinned by a philosophy of retribution in which breaking a prisoner's will and punishing them for their crimes was viewed as a main purpose of prisons.

To achieve this purpose, prisoners might be subjected to the treadmill whose use was initially authorised by the 1779 Penitentiary Act but was not widely used until the nineteenth century. By 1824, there were 79 of these wheels in 49 prisons. These could be used for agricultural purposes (such as grinding corn) or for non-productive tasks until the use of treadmills for non-productive tasks was abolished in 1899.

In addition to the nature of the prison regime, the conditions inside the prison were harsh. Problems faced by prisoners included overcrowding and disease. The latter included what was then termed 'goal fever' (which would now be termed typhus) a disease caused by bacteria that was spread through the bites of lice and fleas. It caused a rash, headache and fever.

The Eighteenth and Early Nineteenth-Century Legal System

As has been stated in Chapter 1, in the eighteenth century, a distinction was drawn between felonies (regarded as serious criminal offences which carried the death penalty), misdemeanours (lesser criminal offences sometimes referred to as petty larcenies and which included the theft of goods valued at below one shilling and assault/brawling to which the death penalty did not apply) and summary offences which especially embraced economic regulation.

However, as has been argued in Chapter 1, the full rigour of the law was not consistently brought against offenders through the application of mercy as a key tactic through which the ruling elite sought to maintain the existing power structure of society—'mercy was part of the currency of patronage' (Hay, 2011: 45). It was noted that

> In a rural parish with a relatively settled population there were many alternatives to a rigorous prosecution. The accused man could be made to post a bond not to offend again, or be given the choice of leaving the neighbourhood. The threat of prosecution could be held over his head to ensure his future good behaviour. He might also be allowed to escape the law by making compensation for his crime (2011: 41).

Pardons (especially in relation to convictions that would have carried the death penalty) were frequently used in this period, especially when supported by 'opinion and evidence from employers, respectable farmers, and neighbouring gentlemen, not mere neighbours and friends' (Hay, 2011: 42). They performed a key role in 'the ideology of mercy' (Hay, 2011: 46).

The Court System

Box 6.3: The Structure of the Courts
Felonies were tried in Assize Courts. These were presided over by Judges. These were appointed to try cases in geographic areas termed circuits (of which there were seven, covering a number of counties in England and Wales) which they would visit regularly, their authority to try cases being derived from a commission of *oyer and terminer* (sometimes referred to as *audiendo and terminado*).

On these occasions, prisoners would be presented to the court by writ of 'general goal delivery' (May, 2006: 5). Juries were used to determine whether a person was innocent or guilty of the offence they were of accused of having committed. Under the operations of the 'Bloody Code' a large number of felonies carried the death penalty, even if it was not consistently carried out.

Misdemeanours were tried in a court of Quarter Session. These were presided over by Magistrates (at least two), who were appointed by the Crown, typically from the nobility and gentry. Unlike the Magistrates' courts of today, juries were used. Its main workload was concerned with cases such as fraud, embezzlement, assault and theft to which the death penalty did not apply. Fines were a relatively common punishment imposed by Magistrates.

Minor offences were tried in courts of Petty Sessions. These were also presided over by Magistrates (in the eighteenth century, often one) but juries were not used. Courts of Petty Sessions were responsible for trying minor offences such as drunkenness or vagrancy and for which the penalty included whipping, the pillory or being sent to a house of correction.

This fairly neat division of responsibilities between these three types of court began to break down: after 1750, for example, Quarter Sessions were able to try some felonies including theft. In the nineteenth century and in 1842 an attempt was made to re-assert the difference between them by requiring cases that carried the death penalty or those where the sentence was life in prison to be reserved for Assize Courts. However, it was not until the late twentieth century that the UK's modern judicial system consisting of Magistrates' and Crown Courts was set up.

The historic difference between crimes and misdemeanours no longer applies in England and Wales. It was formally abolished by the 1967 Criminal Law Act. Instead, a distinction is drawn between summary and indictable offences, the former of which, constituting the less serious crime, are heard in a Magistrates' courts while the latter are tried in Crown Courts.

The structure of the eighteenth-century courts followed the differentiation of crimes into felonies, misdemeanours and summary offences.

The Court of Assize

Felonies were tried in the Assize Court. Outside of London and Middlesex, this sat twice each year in each county. For purposes of administration, England was divided into six circuits (which consisted of a group of counties) and trials were presided over by a royal judges (from a total of 12 for the entire country). Two judges handled Assize Court work, one dealing with criminal cases and the other with civil ones. These judges were members of the three central courts (comprised of King's Bench, Common Pleas and Exchequer) and whose bread-and-butter work was mainly civil in nature (Langbein, 1987: 18). In London and the adjacent county of Middlesex, criminal cases were held at the Old Bailey, which in status was an Assize Court, presided over by the Recorder of London (but who shared the presiding role with two or three royal judges) and which met eight times each year (Langbein, 1987: 18–19).

There was no system of legal representation and those accused of a crime were required to defend themselves, even in cases where their lives were at stake. This especially discriminated against poorer people whose upbringing and lack of education meant they were ill-equipped to deal with the formal procedures of the courts.

During Peel's tenure as Home Secretary, after 1823 the number of judges was increased and he instituted a Third Assize to lessen delays in bringing prisoners to trial.

The Court of Quarter Sessions

The Court of Quarter Sessions (so-called because it met four times each year in each County) dates from 1388 and was responsible for hearing those criminal cases that fell between the boundaries of serious (carrying the death penalty and which were heard at the Assize Court) and petty (which were tried summarily at the Court of Petty Sessions by magistrates without a jury). It has been observed that eighteenth-century Magistrates were untrained and their practices were informal and lacking in uniformity across the country (Taylor, 1998: 107).

Cases for the court of Quarter Sessions were sent to the court on indictment and were heard by two or more Magistrates and a jury. These cases included theft, highway robbery, drunkenness, profanity, assault and rioting. Courts of Quarter Sessions also acted as a court of appeal regarding decisions taken by justices in Petty Sessions, which often included decisions related to the administration of the Poor Law.

The Assizes and Quarter Sessions remained functioning until replaced by the Crown Court under the provisions of the 1971 Courts Act.

Trial Procedure

Trial procedure was very different from the current system in which the police service and crown prosecution service play major roles in the investigation and prosecution of offences.

In the eighteenth century, 'the victim played a major role in most prosecutions' (Langbein, 1987: 20), and the system of rewards was designed to provide an incentive to prosecute those who had suffered from crime (Brain, undated: [Online]). However, local associations for the prosecution of felons could sometimes provide aid to poorer people in bringing prosecutions and there was also some degree of official support in the form of coroners (relating to murders) and Magistrates (also known as Justices of the Peace or JPs) and constables (relating to property crimes). It has been stated that from the sixteenth century, the Magistrate played an important role in the pretrial procedure, his powers being derived from an Act of 1555 which authorised the Magistrate to examine the accused and the accusers in felony cases and to produce a record of the investigation to the court, to order the accused to be arrested and held for trial and to require witnesses to appear at the trial.

It was concluded that 'in the eighteenth century pretrial criminal investigation was the work of amateurs—the victim, the lay constable, and the lay JP' (Langbein, 1987: 21). Additionally, a system which relied on the system of private prosecution was biased towards those in higher social positions: equality before the law was an accepted principle, but access to it was differential: prosecution was not an 'equal opportunity game' (Hay et al., 2011: xxxviii): those who initiated prosecutions came from the upper end of the social ladder and successful prosecutions were especially associated with those from the top third of the social scale (Hay et al., 2011: xxxviii). This led to a conclusion that 'the notion that the poorer half of the population, because they sometimes could prosecute, believed that the law was basically just, seems most unlikely' (Hay et al., 2011: xxxviii–xxxix).

Crimes of special concern to the state were handled somewhat differently—the Royal Mint and Post Office employed professionals (usually solicitors) to investigate and prepare cases related to counterfeiting and mail robbery and the revenue authorities used similar methods relating to smuggling. Cases involving treason and seditious libel were investigated and prosecuted by government law officers in the form of the Attorney General and Solicitor General (Langbein, 1987: 21), while coining offences involved the Treasury Solicitor.

Grand Juries

Juries played an important role in the legal process. The concept of the jury system was associated with reforms introduced into Britain following the Norman conquest in 1066, although it may have existed prior to this period. In connection with civil cases, the principle of trial by jury was established by the 1166 Assize of Clarendon.

The role of the jury in English legal proceedings was substantially enhanced by Article 39 of the Magna Carta that was signed by King John in 1215. There the King agreed that no person would be 'amerced' without the judgement of his peers: the word 'amerced' is now obsolete but in legal terms meant 'punished by being fined' although in more general language simply meant 'be punished'. The intention of this article was to place a limit on the power of the monarch who henceforth would have to abide by the rule of law. By the fourteenth century, 'law judgement of peers' became understood to mean a trial before a jury.

Initially, the Grand Jury was responsible for considering an indictment that was drawn up following the process of pretrial investigation (however, this was conducted) and for determining whether the case should go to trial before the Court of Assize or Court of Quarter Sessions. This role gave them an alternative name, that of 'presentment jury' as their ultimate role having considered the facts available to it would be to 'present' the accused person to the courts.

By the eighteenth century, Grand Juries were composed of 23 persons and a simple majority determined whether an indicted person should be sent for trial. To determine this they would question those who were party to bringing the accusation. They customarily met at the opening of the Assize Court and the process of a Grand Jury was also used in connection with summary offences tried at Quarter Sessions (Langbein, 1987: 22–3).

Although most of the functions of the Grand Jury were ended by the 1933 Administration of Justice (Miscellaneous Provisions) Act, it was not totally abolished until the enactment of the 1948 Criminal Justice Act. However, it has been argued that its role in criminal procedure had become 'unimportant' by the late eighteenth century in that it largely rubber stamped decisions made by those who had conducted the prior pretrial investigation. The Grand Jury thus became more of a ceremonial and social gathering in which local elites could socialise and 'to be seen participating in the pageantry of the assize courts' (Langbein, 1987: 24).

Trial (or Petty Juries)

Cases that went to trial at the Assize Court (and also Quarter Sessions) were heard by a jury that consisted of twelve persons.

Trial by jury replaced trial by ordeal. In 1215, the Church forbade the use of water and fire ordeals to prove guilt or innocence (although trial by battle remained sanctioned), thus popularising the use of trial by jury. Initially, the Grand Jury also acted as the trial jury until a distinction was drawn during the fourteenth century which ultimately led to two distinct juries—the grand jury and the trial jury—being involved in a criminal trial.

Trial juries were solely composed of males aged between 21 and 70 and were required to own property that produced a stipulated annual income (which by an Act of 1692 was £10 per annum in most parts of the country). This tended to mean that juries were typified by the occupations of 'farmer, artisan, and tradesman' which made them 'neither aristocratic nor democratic' (Langbein, 1987: 25).

Hay emphasised the importance of the property qualification for jury service—

> All men of property knew that judges, justices and juries had to be chosen from their own ranks. The jury, the supposed guarantee that an Englishman would be tried by his equals, had a sharp property qualification. The reason …

> simply put, was that the common Englishman could not be trusted to share in the operation of the law. A panel of the poor would not convict a labourer who stole wood from a lord's park, a sheep from a farmer's fold, or corn from a merchant's year (Hay, 2011: 38).

Accordingly,

> The cottager who appeared in court charged with theft had no illusions about being tried by 'his equals and neighbours' … The twelve men sitting opposite him were employers, overseers of the poor, propertied men. In most cases they were the equals and neighbours of the prosecutor, not the accused, and this was especially true in the case of theft. The point is not that such juries convicted against the evidence, but rather that a more democratic jury might not have convicted at all (Hay, 2011: 38).

The names of those eligible to serve were compiled under the supervision of the Magistrates annually in each county in a Book of Freeholders and names were selected from this list by the sheriff. Those who were selected as potential jurors were termed 'veniremen'. During the eighteenth century, the use of prosecuting and defence barristers was not common (although it became more so towards the end of that century) and it thus fell to the trial judge to question the witnesses to elicit their version of events and to probe for any contradictions in their accounts.

At the end of the trial, the judge would sum up proceedings for the benefit of the jury and instruct them regarding the law. Although initially judges might intervene and determine guilt or innocence in cases where the jury was divided, by the fourteenth century it had been established that in order to convict, all twelve jurors were required to be in agreement: in cases where this was not possible, theoretically a new trial would be held although it is argued this hardly ever happened as unanimity was usually secured (Langbein, 1987: 38). It was also argued that 'Judge and jury virtually never disagreed about anything' although such a consensus was strained by political cases, especially that of seditious libel (Langbein, 1987: 39) during the eighteenth century.

Juries exercised—through the procedure known as 'pious perjury'—an important role in sentencing whereby they exercised choice regarding what offence they determined the defendant had committed. A key purpose of this was to enable a sentence other than death to be passed, thus tempering a harsh penal code with the application of mercy.

Reform of the Penal Code in the Nineteenth Century

The 'Bloody Code' entailed a large number of criminal offences carrying the death penalty. In 1818, over 200 statutes provided this outcome for a wide range of offences (225 in total).

Box 6.4: The 'Bloody Code'
Persons could be hung for committing offences that included

- murder
- arson
- forgery
- cutting down trees
- stealing horses or sheep
- destroying turnpike roads
- stealing from a rabbit warren
- pickpocketing goods worth a shilling (roughly £30 today)
- being out at night with a blackened face
- being an unmarried mother concealing a stillborn child
- stealing from a shipwreck
- wrecking a fishpond (National Justice Museum, 2020: [Online]).

However, very few people (around one in twenty in 1810) were actually executed (Glazebrook, 2001: [Online]), emphasising the important role accorded to mercy in maintaining eighteenth-century social relationships. However, it has also been stated that more people were being hanged in early nineteenth-century England than at any time since the early modern era (Gattrell, 1994).

Box 6.5: Jeremy Bentham and Penal Reform
Classicist criminology placed considerable emphasis on explaining their views regarding the appropriate response to crime.

Writings of Jeremy Bentham, investigated by Bedau (2004), highlighted his views regarding punishment that were intended for a work entitled *Theory of Punishment* that was never published. The views put forward by Bentham included

- Punishment may be defined as an evil inflicted on an offender by persons in authority.
- Punishment may be justified, if at all, as the least worst use of coercion in the name of securing public safety, in the belief that the gain in security—the satisfaction of living in a secure society—outweighs the loss in punishment, which involves deliberately causing harm to offenders. In short, an increase in public safety is achieved through general deterrence and individual reformation of convicted offenders.
- 'All punishment is mischief: all punishment in itself is evil', and therefore is to be reduced to the minimum in severity (intensity, duration) consistent with securing its ends.
- Thus punishment is a practice essentially forward-looking (to prevent crime and secure public safety), not a practice essentially backward-looking (to render retribution based on desert). It has three goals: prevention of crime, correction of offenders and compensation of victims.
- Punishments must be apportioned to crimes so that the would-be offender is always given an incentive to commit a less serious crime (such as rape) rather than a more serious one (such as rape and murder).
- Afflictive punishments, the chief of which is the death penalty, are to be avoided wherever possible in favour of less brutal interventions.
- 'The value of a punishment must be not less in any case than what is sufficient to outweigh that of the profit of the offence' (Bentham, unpublished manuscripts for *Theory of Punishment*, cited in Bedau, 2004: [Online]).

The first and second of these propositions have been summarised by the statement that 'Bentham believed that sometimes punishment is right, which is to say that sometimes the painfulness of a punishment is sufficiently outweighed by the pleasure it causes or the pain it prevents' (Sverdlik, 2022: [Online]).

The importance placed by classicist criminology on the law being applied in a consistent manner so that potential offenders knew in advance what the consequences of their actions would be was consistent with the aim of 'making the punishment fit the crime'. This objective became an influential concern in the late eighteenth and early nineteenth century and the chief objective was to reduce drastically the number of capital offences, thus enhancing the deterrent aspects of reductivist strategies of punishment which were considered in Chapter 1.

However, it has been argued that an approach which sought to eliminate discretion in the operations of the criminal justice system underplayed its role in maintaining the power of the propertied classes, whereby justice was tempered with the application of mercy (Hay, 2011: 39). This led Hay to conclude that

> that the criminal law more than any other social institution, made it possible to govern eighteenth-century England without a police force and without an army. The ideology of the law was crucial in sustaining the hegemony of the English ruling class (Hay, 2011: 56).

Legal scholarship adopted a quizzical approach to the penal code in the late eighteenth century, an important contribution being made by William Eden (1744–1814) whose book, *Principles of Penal Law* was published in 1771. This work put forward a critique of the structure of English law and the principles that underpinned it. In line with the classicist thinking which inspired him, he argued that penalties should be informed by the seriousness of the offence that had been committed and he went on to identify a very wide range of offences that he argued ought not to be capital ones.

Within Parliament, influential roles in the reform of the penal code were played by Samuel Romilly (1757–1818) and James Mackintosh (1756–1832), both of whom were heavily influenced by the ideas of Jeremy Bentham and classicist criminology.

In 1808, Romilly—unsuccessfully—moved in Parliament for the repeal of a 1565 Act that made pickpocketing a capital offence. This helped stimulate public debate regarding legal reform. In 1810—again unsuccessfully—he sought to remove capital punishment for three petty offences.

In 1819, James Macintosh was successful in getting Parliament to appoint a Select Committee 'to consider so much of the criminal laws as relates to capital punishments in felonies'. Subsequently, the committee made several recommendations which supported the repeal of capital punishment for a relatively small range of offences. Parliament failed to act on these recommendations but they were pursued by Home Secretary Robert Peel after he committed the government to the reform of the penal code in 1823.

A number of other reforms to the legal system were pursued after 1823. Lyman (1964: 149) recorded that in 1823, Peel consolidated into one statute the laws dealing with theft and destruction of property, and did the same with the laws dealing with offences against the person. There were 130 statutes concerning larceny which were condensed into one Act. In total whereby 316 Acts of Parliament concerned with criminal law were consolidated into four statutes between 1827 and 1830.

Prison discipline laws and transportation laws were also consolidated, and Peel tried to prevent abuses. Additionally, Peel made it easier for victims of sexual offences to get justice by abolishing the requirement that certain embarrassing proofs be furnished (Lyman, 1964: 149). A number of obsolete laws were also repealed. It was concluded that when Peel 'finally left office in 1830 he had reformed and consolidated practically the whole of the Criminal Law of England' (Ramsay, 1928: 68). Further consolidation did not take place until 1861.

Under Peel's guidance during the 1820s, a number of offences also ceased to be capital offences, amounting to around 100 in total (Lyman, 1964: 149). These included two that had been proposed by Romilly in 1810 and eight recommended by the Parliamentary Select Committee. It has been observed that a key reason for the reform of the penal code in this period was the fear of revolution that might be brought about by 'brutal and unequal punishment' (Emsley, 2018: 11). Benefit of Clergy was also abolished in 1827 along with the distinction between grand and petty larceny, the practical effect of which being that a second conviction for the theft of more than 12 pence ceased to be a capital offence.

However, it has been observed in Chapter 1 that although reforms to the penal code that involved reducing the number of offences that carried the death penalty ought theoretically to have ensured that better protection was afforded to property arising from the greater certainty that proscribed penalties would be consistently enforced by sentencers (thus enhancing the deterrent effect of punishment), there was extreme reluctance on the part of the eighteenth-century ruling elite to sanction such a course of action.

There were several reasons that explained this reluctance, one of which was that this would almost inevitably have set in motion a wholesale reform of the criminal justice system, entailing the creation of professional police forces which carried with it the potential of enhancing the power of central government in the localities that were controlled by local elites. But, as was discussed in the Introduction, the key reason was that the system of social relations was underpinned by a criminal justice system whose severity was tempered by mercy derived from the use of discretion (the use of which was also opposed by classicist criminologists). Accordingly, wholesale reform of the criminal justice system threatened to erode the power wielded by the English ruling class.

It has been argued that legal reformers had a particular appeal to the 'middling men'—persons who earned between £25 and £150 per year in the mid-eighteenth century but who created more than half of England's wealth and whose property was the prey of thieves undeterred by terror (Hay, 2011: 60). Such persons deemed their property to be more at risk than that of the land-owning class who could afford to tolerate small losses which did not threaten their livelihood and whose power could be enhanced by applying mercy in cases of small-scale depredations. Their ability to secure action on their concerns was provided by the 1832 Reform Act.

The 1832 Reform Act modestly extended the franchise, adding around 217,000 new male voters to the existing 435,000 (Joyce, 2004: 4). This reform (and the redistribution of seats that was also an aspect of the 1832 measure) was to the benefit of the urban middle class that had emerged as a consequence of the industrial revolution and urbanisation. Unsurprisingly, therefore, a government relying on support from the new electorate would seek to address their concerns, one of which centred on legal reform.

In 1832, a Whig government headed by Lord Grey took office. Under his premiership, a large number of criminal offences ceased to be capital so that by 1839 the only offences that carried this penalty were 'treason, riot, arson of naval ships and of naval and military stores, murder and other offenses involving attempts on or risks to life, rape, buggery, sexual intercourse with girls under ten years of age, and robbery and burglary when accompanied by personal violence—much the same list as that proposed by Eden in 1771' (Glazebrook, 2001: [Online]). In 1840, rape ceased to be a capital offence. Correspondingly, there was an expansion of summary justice by the mid-nineteenth century (Taylor, 1998: 2).

Abolition of the Death Penalty

On 5 March 1840 (House of Commons, 1840: [Online]) a debate calling for the abolition of capital punishment was moved on a motion presented by William Ewart, the MP for Wigan. He was an opponent of the death penalty and during his Parliamentary career, had some successes in repealing capital punishment for specific offences such as cattle stealing. But he wanted to remove this penalty in its entirety.

In his speech, he presented a number of important arguments against capital punishment. Many of his sentiments were inspired by the beliefs of classicist criminologists—querying whether such an extreme penalty was required for the safety and security of society and suggesting that it was an excessive response to crime and arguing that the certainty of punishment, when sanctions other than the death penalty were used, was the best way to reduce crime—and in this respect he cited examples from France and India. He also provided statistics in his speech that suggested a reduction in the number of offences that carried the death penalty in early nineteenth-century Britain had not led to an increase in crime (the very opposite in fact).

Providing the case against the abolition of capital punishment in this debate was former Liberal Home Secretary Lord John Russell. He argued that there was no reliable way to prove whether the death penalty was a more effective deterrent to crime than lesser penalties. He also argued that suggestions that public executions had a brutalising effect on those who watched them should be balanced against the view that the removal of this penalty from many offences in the early nineteenth century meant there were far fewer executions taking place, thus lessening the brutalisation argument.

It was argued that the movement away from the death penalty in this period rested on a number of concerns that included changing sensitivities and concerns regarding elite views of the reactions of spectators, the 'simple pragmatism' that derived from an awareness of the ineffectiveness of capital punishment as a deterrent and the limits to the number of people who could be hanged without undermining the legitimacy of the justice system (Taylor, 2010: 153). It was also a reform that was associated with the Quakers (which included John Howard) arising from 'their doctrinal concern to set strict limits on the use of state force' (Ignatieff, 1978: 59).

Arguments against the death penalty were compatible with twentieth-century responses to crime associated with abolitionist criminology. This approach wishes to replace punitive responses to crime with one that views it as a social problem whose remedy rests on programmes that focus on the reintegration of offenders.

Consolidation of the Legal Code

The need to consolidate the legal code has been summarised as follows

> The form of the law was chaotic and extremely obscure. In 1821 it was estimated that there were 750 acts of Parliament concerning the criminal law in force, together with another 400 relating to proceedings before magistrates. These statutes were the product of three centuries of parliamentary activity. Not only had almost all of them been enacted without regard to any of the others, but they also presupposed the "unwritten" common law of crime, without a knowledge of which the statutes themselves were more often than not quite unintelligible (Glazebrook, 2001: [Online]).

One example of the need for consolidation related to forgery which in the early nineteenth century was governed by over 100 statutes.

Peel as Home Secretary set about the task of consolidating the criminal laws, initiating what might be termed a 'bonfire of legislation' whereby a large number of statutes became consolidated into a small number of Acts. In 1827 he brought forward four Bills designed to consolidate and amend the law regarding theft and related offences, to amend the law relating to wilful and malicious injury of property and to consolidate and amend the laws relating to remedies against the hundred. The fourth Bill aimed to repeal all statutes that would be superseded by the first three of his proposed measures (Peel, 1827: col 632–633).

Peel's work in consolidating the criminal law was guided by his belief in the need for consistency in its application. In his speech in 1827, he suggested that the distinction between petty and grand larceny (whereby the theft of goods below the value of one shilling could be tried by Magistrates whereas the theft of good above this value was triable by a higher court with power to impose the death penalty) resulted in the law being evaded by courts and prosecutors who stated in their indictment that the goods were valued at below one shilling. His first Bill sought to remedy this issue by abolishing the distinction between petty and grand larceny with a maximum punishment of 7 years transportation. A person who committed grand larceny for a second time would receive the penalty of transportation for life rather than the then-current sentence of capital punishment.

Peel's reforms to consolidate the criminal law were entwined with the removal of the death penalty. He argued that the situation in which men were condemned to death for crimes but whose sentence was never intended to be carried out was a 'mockery' which could be remedied by erasing capital punishments from the Statute-book and providing milder punishments in every available instance (Peel, 1827, col 635). This concern led him to propose in the first Bill he put forward in 1827 that the death penalty for stealing goods from a dwelling house to the value of forty shillings should be raised to a higher amount 'by which means the number of capital convictions for this species of crime would be considerably diminished' (Peel, 1827, col 635).

Reform to Other Punishments

Brandings

Branding continued as a means of punishment (covering crimes that included bigamy and manslaughter) and in the latter decades of the eighteenth century was sometimes used as an alternative to transportation (Cumbrian Characters, 2020 [Online]). However, its usage in connection with bigamy and manslaughter largely died out—in the case of the former crime by the end of the eighteenth century and in relation to the latter crime, was ended by legislation in 1822.

Fines

Historically, fines had been used as punishments for misdemeanours but their usage in connection with more serious crimes was increased following the enactment of the 1779 Penitentiary Act which allowed a fine to substitute for branding. Thereafter, fines were often used as a penalty for crimes such as imprisonment, manslaughter, petty larceny and simple grand larceny. The amount of fine (which varied from below a shilling to hundreds of Pounds) could be adjusted by the judge to take into account both the severity of the offence and the financial means of the offender (The Proceedings of the Old Bailey, 2018: [Online]).

Whipping

Whipping continued as a form of punishment into the early nineteenth century, although these were mainly conducted in private. The public whipping of women was ended in 1817 and of men was formally ended in 1862 (although in practice had ceased in the early 1830s) (The Proceedings of the Old Bailey, 2018: [Online]). Whipping conducted in private (usually a prison) continued, usually as a punishment for male offenders and was not formally abolished until 1948.

William Garrow and Reforms to Legal Procedure

The early part of the nineteenth century saw some important changes in the way in which trials were conducted took place. These were especially associated with William Garrow (1760–1840).

Garrow had an extremely full career, serving as a Member of Parliament and becoming Solicitor General in 1812 and Attorney General in 1813. However, it is his work as a defence lawyer that is of particular importance to the conduct of legal procedure which he pioneered at the Old Bailey between 1783 and 1793. Trials were conducted in the late seventeenth and early years of the twentieth century very differently than they are in the contemporary period.

Judges and also juries played a very active part in proceedings and there was no legal representation for those on trial for felonies, even though their lives were at stake: perhaps curiously, legal representation was allowed in cases involving misdemeanours and also for High Treason. Those on trial for felonies could consult a lawyer, but he could not appear in court on the defendant's behalf. The system has been referred to as 'a lawyer-free contest of amateurs' (Langbein, 1999: 314). The prosecution was also usually unrepresented by a lawyer.

The victim of the crime usually served as the prosecutor, aided by other witnesses and sometimes by the constable (Langbein, 1999: 314). Many criminal trials in the early part of the eighteenth century were founded on falsehoods—on evidence supplied by persons such as thief takers whose motives were often to make financial profits rather than secure justice. But in a time when those on trial had to defend themselves as best they could, the prosecution would normally 'win the day' and that the odds were stacked against acquittal.

Gradually, however, in the early decades of the eighteenth century, judges began to allow defendants to employ defence counsel to question those giving evidence against them. This practice began in a hesitant way in the 1730s and by the 1780s it was not unusual to have barristers for the defence appearing at criminal trials at the Old Bailey. However, they were not allowed to address the jury by way of summing up on the defendant's behalf. Garrow got around this restriction by adopting a lengthy style of cross examination in which he posed extended questions which turned into mini-speeches directed at those who were to pronounce verdict. Although this style was deemed aggressive for its time, it sought to ensure that evidence was thoroughly tested in court in order to help guarantee that the trial ended in a fair outcome and that justice was served.

Operating on the belief that the accused was innocent until proven to be guilty, this style of cross-examination helped inaugurate what is now a fundamental principle of our legal procedure—the adversarial system. It also helped establish another key aspect of our legal process, that of rules of evidence—what evidence is, and what is not, permitted to be brought forward during the course of a trial.

A contemporary lawyer, Geoffrey Robertson KC, described Garrow in this way

> In 1783, when he burst upon the Old Bailey stage, defendants had no rights other than to a counsel who could merely ask polite questions of prosecution witnesses. No speeches were allowed, there were few rules of evidence and

> absolutely no prosecution disclosure even of the depositions taken in Magistrate's Court. It was Garrow's genius to change all that and to inject for the first time an element "equality of arms" in what eventually became a true adversary process (Robertson, 2009: [Online]).

Robertson further argued 'That he appeared at a time when the English Penal Code was at its most barbaric, with several hundred minor felonies carrying the death penalty, made his achievement all the more necessary and all the more dramatic' (Robertson, 2009: [Online]).

Robertson asserted that

> He was certainly no "trickster", as Langbein mistakenly labelled him, but rather an advocate who came into court equipped with savage wit, a fearless capacity to object to unfair evidence, and clever tactics. He crashed through the barriers of class, overcame judicial hostility and popular jury prejudice, and his courage soon inspired other barristers to adopt similar strategies. In due course, it was this pressure from the Bar that won increased latitude for the defence and made trials more fair, as counsel insisted upon evidential rules (such as the rule against hearsay, equal rights for defence barristers and the transformation of the role of the judge from that of active inquisitor and jury-director to that of a more neutral umpire) (Robertson, 2009: [Online]).

After 1793, Garrow's life took a different path as is noted in the article. He became an MP and served in a Tory government, first as Solicitor General (1812) and then as Attorney General (1813). But his contribution to the cause of advocacy was enormous, his quest for fairness and justice in the courtroom being reflected in the contemporary importance attached to human rights.

His career paved the way for important legal changes to courtroom procedure and advocacy. In 1836, the Prisoner's Counsel Act (discussed by Gray, 2015: 264) permitted a counsel or solicitor who was representing a defendant charged with a felony to address the jury on his or her behalf. Later, in 1848 and 1849, legislation set out procedures and standards to be applied in Magistrates' courts.

Conclusion

This chapter has focused on the topic of prison reform and has discussed the contribution made in the late eighteenth and early nineteenth century by four key reformers, John Howard, Elizabeth Fry, Sir George Onesiphorus and Jeremy Bentham. Although they differed regarding the causes of crime and how this problem could be combated, all exercised considerable influence in the subsequent operations of the criminal justice system and focused on the architecture and design of prisons as key factors that influenced the nature of the prison regime and the purposes they wished it to fulfil.

This chapter then considered the operations of the legal system in the period 1760–1850, including the structure of the courts and the role played by the jury system. It has drawn particular attention to the way in which the strict application of a harsh penal code was tempered by the use of discretion in order to sustain deference and thus to maintain existing social relationships. The chapter has also examined key reforms to the system of punishment that were especially associated with classicist criminology and which were implemented by reformers that included Home Secretary Robert Peel. The significance of developments associated with William Garrow concerned with court procedure have also been evaluated.

The following chapter, constituting the commencement of Part Three of this book, will consider a related issue, namely the reform of policing in the late eighteenth and nineteenth centuries.

? Summary Question

Critically evaluate reforms put forward between 1750 and 1850 that promoted prison and penal reform.

References

Bedau, H. (2004). Bentham's Theory of Punishment: Origin and Content. *Journal of Bentham Studies, 7*. Semantics Scholar. [Online] https://pdfs.semanticscholar.org/9ef9/1356c3915c46e2b52a6511dd5aea8b669e43.pdf. Accessed 1 Oct 2022.

Bentham, J. (1791). *Panopticon or the Inspection House*. T. Payne.

Brain, J. (undated). Bow Street Runners. *Historic UK*. [Online] https://www.historic-uk.com/HistoryUK/HistoryofBritain/Bow-Street-Runners/. Accessed 8 Oct 2020.

Cavadino, M., & Dignan, J. (2002). *The Penal System: An Introduction* (3rd ed.). Sage.

Cumbrian Characters. (2020). Branded, Burned, Hanged—Punishments in the Eighteenth Century. *Cumbrian Characters*. [Online] http://crimesofthecenturies.com/index.php/2018/04/19/branding-punishment-1700s/. Accessed 5 Oct 2020.

Cutieru, A. (2020). The Architecture of Surveillance: The Panopticon Prison. *ArchDaily*. [Online] https://www.archdaily.com/937611/the-architecture-of-surveillance-the-panopticon-prison. Accessed 16 Dec 2021.

Durkheim, E. (1893). *De la division du travail social* [On the Division of Labour in Society]. Alcan.

Emsley, C. (2018). *Crime and Society in England 1750–1900* (5th ed.). Routledge.

Evans, J. (2013). HMP Gloucester: A Brief History (Updated). *Gloucestershire Crime History*. [Online] https://gloscrimehistory.wordpress.com/tag/george-onesiphorus-paul/

Foucault, M. (1977). *Discipline and Punish: The Birth of the Prison*. Allen Lane.

Garland, D. (1990). *Punishment and Modern Society*. Clarendon Press.

Gattrell, V. (1994). *The Hanging Tree: Execution and the English People 1770–1868*. Oxford University Press.

Glazebrook, P. (2001). Criminal Law Reform: England. In J. Dressler (Ed.), *Encyclopaedia of Crime and Justice* (Vol. 1, 2nd ed.). Macmillan. [Online] https://www.encyclopedia.com/law/legal-and-political-magazines/criminal-law-reform-england. Accessed 18 Dec 2021.

Goffman, E. (1961). *Asylums: Essays on the Social Situation of Mental Patients and other Inmates*. Anchor Books.

Gray, D. (2015). *Crime, Policing and Punishment in England, 1660–1914*. Bloomsbury Academic.

Hanway, J. (1776). *Solitude of Prison with a Proper Profitable Labour and a Spare Diet*. J. Bow.

Hay, D. (2011). Property, Authority and the Criminal Law. In D. Hay, P. Linebaugh, J. G. Rule, E. P.Thompson & C.Winslow (Eds.), *Albion's Fatal Tree. Crime and Society in Eighteenth Century England* (Revised ed.). Verso, originally published in 1975.

Hay, D., Linebaugh, P., Rule, J., Thompson, E. P., & Winslow, C. (2011). *Albion's Fatal Tree: Crime and Society in Eighteenth Century England* (Rev. ed.). Verso, originally published in 1975.

House of Commons. (1840). *Historic Hansard*. [Online] https://api.parliament.uk/historic-hansard/commons/1840/mar/05/abolition-of-capital-punishments. Accessed 18 Dec 2021.

Howard, J. (1777). *The State of the Prisons in England and Wales, With An Account of Some Foreign Prisons*. William Eyres.

Hudson, B. (2003). *Understanding Justice* (2nd ed.). Open University Press.

Ignatieff, M. (1978). *A Just Measure of Pain: The Penitentiary in the Industrial Revolution 1750–1850*. Pantheon Books.

Isba, A. (2010). *The Excellent Mrs. Fry: Unlikely Heroine*. Continuum International Publishing Group.

Joyce, P. (2004). *British General Elections 1832–2001*. London: Methuen.

Langbein, J. (1987). The English Criminal Trial Jury on the Eve of the French evolution. In A. Schioppa (Ed.), *The Trial Jury in England, France, Germany 1700–1900*. Duncker & Humblot. Law.yale.edu [Online] https://www.law.yale.edu/sites/default/files/documents/pdf/Faculty/langbein_theTrialJury.pdf. Accessed 11 Apr 2022.

Langbein, J. (1999). The Prosecutorial Origins of Defence Counsel in the Eighteenth Century: The Appearance of Solicitors. *Cambridge Law Journal, 58*(2), 314–365.

Lyman, J. (1964). The Metropolitan Police Act of 1829. *Journal of Criminal Law and Criminology, 55*(1), 141–154.

May, T. (2006). *Victorian and Edwardian Prisons*. Shire Publications.

McGowen, R. (1998). The Well-Ordered Prison. In N. Morris & D. Rothman (Eds.), *The Oxford History of the Prison: The Practice of Punishment in Western Society*. Oxford University Press.

National Archives. (undated). A Victorian Prison. *National Archives*. [Online] https://www.nationalarchives.gov.uk/education/resources/victorian-prison/

National Justice Museum. (2020). What Was the 'Bloody Code ? [Online]. https://www.nationaljusticemuseum.org.uk/what-was-the-bloody-code/. Accessed 12 Oct 2020.

Paul, Sir G. O. (1817). *Observations on the Alarming Progress of the Goal or Typhus Fever*. D. Walker and Sons.

Peel, Sir R. (1827). Speech in the House of Commons 22 February. HC Debs XVI [NS], cols 632–642.

Porter, R. (1995). Howard's Beginning: Prisons, Disease, Hygiene. In R. Creese, W. Bynum, & J. Bearn (Eds.), *The Health of Prisoners: Historical Essays*. Rodopi.

Ramsay, A. (1928). *Sir Robert Peel*. Constable and Co Ltd.

Robertson, G. (2009). Foreword to William Garrow. *Geoffrey Robertson.com* [Online] https://geoffreyrobertson.com/foreword-to-william-garrow/

Shelden, R., & Vasiliev, P. (2018). *Controlling the Dangerous Classes. A History of Criminal Justice in America*. Waveland Press Inc.

Sverdlik, S. (2022). Bentham and Criminal Law. In R. Y. Chappell, D. Meissner, & W. MacAskill (Eds.), *An Introduction to Utilitarianism*. utilitarianism.net. [Online] https://www.utilitarianism.net/guest-essays/bentham-and-criminal-law. Accessed 10 Jan 2022.

Taylor, D. (1998). *Crime, Policing and Punishment in England, 1750–1914*. Palgrave/Macmillan.

Taylor, D. (2010). *Hooligans, Harlots and Hangmen: Crime and Punishment in Victorian England*. Praeger.

The Proceedings of the Old Bailey. (2018). Punishment Sentences at the Old Bailey. In: *Old Bailey Proceedings Online*. [Online] https://www.oldbaileyonline.org/static/Punishment.jsp#:~:text=It%20is%20alleged%20that%20sometimes,applied%20when%20it%20was%20cold.&text=Branding%20as%20a%20punishment%20for,of%20clergy%20ended%20in%201779. Accessed 27 Sept 2020.

Weber, M. (1922) *Wirtschaft und Gesellschaft* [Economy and Society]. J. C. B. Mohr.

Part III

The Development of Professional Policing from the Late Eighteenth Century—1856

7

Police Reformers and Police Reform in the Late Eighteenth and Early Nineteenth Centuries

Introduction

This chapter will analyse the arguments that were put forward to justify the creation of professional policing across England and Wales. It will examine the context within which these ideas were put forward (in particular urban population growth and the views put forward regarding the causes of crime by classicist criminologists) and discuss the proposals that were made by police reformers (the Fielding Brothers, Patrick Colquhoun and Jeremy Bentham) and the measures with which they were associated to reform policing in the eighteenth century. The chapter will also evaluate an early—but abortive—attempt to reform policing in 1785 following the Gordon Riots of 1780 (an event which is discussed in Chapter 4).

The Context of Crime and Disorder—Urban Population Growth

The overall population of Britain grew from around five million people in 1700 to nearly nine million by 1801 (White, 2009: [Online]).

Much of this growth took place in the second half of the eighteenth century and led to the growth of towns as people moved from the countryside in order to take advantage of the employment opportunities caused by the industrial revolution. A further factor that caused urban growth was

P. Joyce and W. Laverick, *History of Policing, Crime, Disorder, Punishment*, https://doi.org/10.1007/978-3-031-36892-9_7

the operations of the 1834 Poor Law Amendment Act which sought to move unemployed rural workers into the towns where work was available—and also to reduce the costs of poor law administration on urban ratepayers.

Thus in the second half of the eighteenth century, the size of towns grew considerably. London's population increased from around 750,000 in 1760 to 1,096,784 in 1801 and 1,400,000 by 1815 (The Proceedings of the Old Bailey, 2018: [Online]). The population of other towns also grew—but at a smaller rate. In 1800, the population of Liverpool was around 77,000, Birmingham 73,000, Manchester 70,000, Bristol 68,000, Portsmouth 32,000, Sheffield 31,000, Leeds 30,000, Exeter 20,000 and Leicester 17,000 (Lambert, 2020: [Online]).

A corollary of this was the decline in rural employment—the proportion of the population engaged in agriculture fell from an estimated 80% in 1500 to 40% in 1800 (Shaw-Taylor et al., 2010: [Online]).

The population growth was most spectacular in the period 1800–1850, growing to 17.9 million overall in England and Wales in 1851 (which is almost 3 times the figure in 1750). The expansion of towns was significant—London had a population of 2,320,000 in 1850, Liverpool 425,000, Manchester 416,000, Glasgow 345,000, Birmingham 294,000, Dublin 263,000, Edinburgh 191,000, Leeds 184,000, Bristol 150,000, Sheffield 141,000 and Wolverhampton 114,000 (Barke & Taylor, 2013: [Online]).

Urbanisation was also an important factor in fuelling the demand for political reform as well as providing the context for the growth of crime arising from severed bonds of deference. It also required the development of methods to combat it.

Eighteenth-Century Views Regarding the Causes of Crime and Responses to It

Prior to the eighteenth-century crime tended to be viewed as a sin, an action that arose because a person's actions were controlled by an evil force. This view legitimised the use of severe punishments to eradicate what was seen as the root cause of all manifestations of criminal behaviour.

This chapter focuses on the pioneering efforts of key police reformers. However, it is important to appreciate that their views concerning police reform were influenced by broader reforming endeavours that sought to address the causes of crime.

These included religion (England witnessing an evangelical revival during the 1730s and 1740s) and the efforts of various organisations that aimed to reform manners that first emerged in 1690 in Tower Hamlets in the form of the Society for the Reformation of Manners and whose aims of seeking moral reform were adopted by similar campaigning organisations during the eighteenth century. Both of these approaches to reform were inspired by the belief that immorality was the key source of crime. John Fielding (who is discussed below in connection with the Bow Street Runners) was a supporter of the Society for the Reformation of Manners which was re-formed in 1757, initially to combat sabbath breaking but which subsequently expanded its campaign to combat swearing, gambling and prostitution (London Lives, 2018: [Online]).

Additionally, during the eighteenth-century classicist criminology emerged. Although the emphasis of this approach was on responses to crime delivered through the criminal justice system, by implication classicist criminology addressed the causes of crime, arguing it was caused by inconsistencies in the way in which the criminal justice system of that time operated. The origins and key tenets of classicist criminology and the contribution of a key exponent of this approach in the United Kingdom, Jeremy Bentham, will be explored in more detail in this chapter.

Box 7.1: Social Contract Theory

In 1513, Machiavelli wrote *The Prince*, a handbook on ruling and the exercise of power (which was not published until 1532). In this work he described men as 'ungrateful and fickle, dissemblers, avoiders of danger and greedy of gain' (Machiavelli, [1532] 1997: 65).

This view of human nature is also evident in the work of Thomas Hobbes (1588–1678) who argued that people naturally pursue their own self-interests without consideration of others. Self-preservation is man's primary interest, resulting in a 'war of each against all' leading to distrust and fear for one's own safety (Vold et al., 1998: 15).

Viewed as rational beings, and faced with such hostile conditions, men, it is suggested, turn to the state to find security collectively (Waltz, 1959). The civil state is therefore the solution for Hobbes as men sacrifice some liberties by entering into a social contract, defined as a guiding idea, which serves to legitimise the state to use force to enforce the contract.

Hobbes' ideas provided the basis of right, the basis of law and state legitimacy and power. Prior to the nineteenth century, monarchies appealed to the doctrine of divine right in order to justify their power, arguing that monarchies were ordained with authority directly from God (Bodin, 1987: 40, cited in Reus-Smit, 2011: 282).

Hobbes' views effectively dismissed God's will as the foundation of modern law, placing in its stead the will and desire of man and rational endeavours to organise collectively to generate social stability in the face of the human condition (Laverick, 2016: 64).

The ideas that were put forward by Hobbes further influenced the conduct of international relations. In the absence of God, and within an international order characterised by a situation of anarchy and the absence of political authority, both men and states were regarded as fearful and self-interested.

It is necessary to place this concern in its political context. Hobbes lived during a period of conflict known as the Thirty Years War, which began in 1618. Initiated by the Austrian Habsburgs in their efforts to impose Roman Catholicism on their Protestant subjects, the war ended with the signing of the Peace of Westphalia in 1648.

The Peace of Westphalia has been regarded as responsible for delimiting the political rights and authority of European monarchs, establishing the sovereign state as the singular mode of constitutional authority, thereby also 'signalling the defeat of religion as a scheme for organising international authority' (Tickner, 2014: 153–154).

It is within this context that the new conceptualisation of law as a reciprocal accord was embedded within major European states with contractual international law evolving to become a foundation of modern international politics. International law is therefore regarded as the product of negotiations between sovereign states who enter into binding agreements reflecting the mutual will of the nations concerned, rather than ordained by God, or within the body of the ruler (Reus-Smit, 2011: 282).

The treaties associated with Westphalia consequently consolidated a number of organising principles governing international relations including non-interference in the sovereign affairs of others; legal equality of sovereign states and the right to make and enter into treaties.

Secularisation prohibited religious and imperial interference, providing a legislative framework for a new international order and a method for securing peace between equal and sovereign states within an anarchic and hostile international environment—reflecting the 'will of all' to organise collectively to generate social stability within a condition of anarchy, a position similarly adopted to regulate behaviour internally, within states (Laverick, 2016: 65–66).

Classicism developed out of the Enlightenment movement of late eighteenth century Europe. Its political expression was liberalism. Society was viewed as a contract voluntarily entered into by those who were party to it rather than being a structure handed down by God. Government emerged as the result of a rational choice by those who subsequently accorded their consent to its operations, and this belief ensured that the rights of the individual were prominent concerns of liberal and classicist thinking. Crime was viewed as an act that infringed the legal code whose rationale was to safeguard the interests of those who were party to the social contract, especially the preservation of their personal safety and property.

In such a contractual society, the equality of all citizens before the law and the presumption of the innocence of a person accused of criminal wrongdoing were viewed as cardinal principles to safeguard individual rights and liberties. Reflecting the concerns of utilitarian philosophy, classicist criminologists argued that the state was entitled to intervene in the lives of its citizens in order to promote their happiness and to combat actions that would cause them harm.

A key exponent of classicist criminology was Cesare Beccaria, who endorsed social contract theory and put forward several views concerning crime and how the state should respond to it (Beccaria, 1764). These included the following:

- Crime was an act undertaken by a rational being: individuals possessed free will and the decision to commit the crime was viewed as the consequence of a logical thought process in which a person calculated the benefits to be derived from a criminal action compared with the personal costs it might involve. Classicists assumed that rational beings sought to maximise their pleasure and avoid inflicting pain on themselves. Accordingly, they advocated measures that guaranteed that crime would inevitably result in sanctions.
- Crime required a uniform and consistent response: classicists argued that the most appropriate solution to crime was a clearly defined and consistently applied legal code and a criminal justice system that was predictable (and also swift) in its operations. This would ensure that potential criminals were aware of the inevitable personal cost of committing a crime. In the United Kingdom, uniformity was promoted by giving central government an important role in the criminal justice system that it initially discharged through the process of inspection.
- Discretion was to be avoided: the emphasis on a uniform and consistent approach to crime inevitably rejected the exercise of discretion by professionals such as magistrates and judges. Beccaria argued that punishments laid down in law should never be exceeded and that the role of judges was to apply, but never to interpret, the law (or act in accordance with what a judge might subjectively view as the spirit of a law).

- Punishments should fit the crime: the harm which a particular criminal action did to society was the classicist yardstick by which they judged the appropriateness of punishments. Classicism focused on the offence and not the person who carried it out, thus intent was deemed irrelevant. It was further argued that the degree of punishment to be inflicted on a wrongdoer should be no more than what was required to outweigh any advantage which the criminal action might bring.
- Deterrence: the main aim of state intervention against crime was to deter persons from committing wrongdoings rather than to punish them after they had transgressed.

In Britain, Jeremy Bentham (1748–1832) was a leading classicist criminologist. The reforms with which he and his followers were identified included the reform of the penal code and police reform. These two reforms were underpinned by the principle of general deterrence: the belief that the certainty of arrest and subsequent conviction would enable all citizens as rational beings to make informed decisions not to offend. Bentham (1843a, 1843b) was condemnatory of discretion, especially when this was underpinned by the application of mercy, arguing that

> To the vocabulary of tyranny belongs the word mercy. The idea expressed by this word is a sort of appendage to, and antagonizes with, the idea designated by the word justice. The word justice, as but too commonly employed, matches with the word deserved, as applied to punishment. In this sense, penal justice is exercised by the application of punishment on the occasion on which, and in the quantity in which, it is deserved. This case, if mercy be exercised, it is in opposition to, and at the expense of, justice: in so far as mercy is exercised, justice is not done.

It has been concluded that classicist criminology, following Hobbes and other social contract philosophers such as John Locke (1633–1704), represented an endeavour to counter the arbitrary administration of justice and abuses of power and cruel punishments from within the nation-state—

> Classical criminologists are therefore social reformers protesting against inconsistency in the application of justice, advocating the creation of a coherent and rational criminal justice framework. Law was accordingly deemed legitimate to the extent that it was authored by those subject to the law (the will of all of us) or their representatives, rather than a command of God...classical criminologists rejected the religious basis of state legitimacy and legislative authority. (Laverick, 2016: 66)

The approach adopted by classicist criminology has been criticised for its assumption that all individuals were able to act rationally since crime might be caused by medical factors that include mental illness or through social factors such as disadvantage rooted in class, race or gender inequalities that might override free will and further erode equality of access to the law.

The contribution of Jeremy Bentham to police reform will be evaluated below.

Police Reformers and Police Reform

Henry and John Fielding and the Bow Street Runners

Henry Fielding (1707–1754) was a renowned English novelist and playwright. In 1748 he was appointed Magistrate for Westminster and Middlesex, whose office was based at Bow Street, London. This was not a salaried post and its occupants derived a living from the fees they were able to charge for their services. This situation was prone to corruption since the unscrupulous magistrate could exploit the office—especially derived from goal fees (McLynn, 1989: 19)—for financial gain and was referred to as a system of 'trading justices'.

In 1751, Fielding published a report entitled *An Enquiry into the Causes of the Late Increase of Robbers, &c. With Some Proposals for Remedying this Growing Evil,* etc. This argued there were several reasons to explain the increase in crime, including a large number of people moving to London and expecting an easy life, the corruption within government, people choosing crime over legitimate forms of employment, the ineffectual nature of the Parish Constable system (Brain, undated: [Online]) and the effect of demobilising around 80,000 soldiers and sailors following the end of the Austrian War of Succession in 1748 following the Treaty of Aix-la-Chapelle. Lyman (1964: 141–2) also cited the new policy regarding gin as a contributory factor to the 'severe London crime wave about the time of his appointment' whereby, commencing in 1745, distillers were able to pay a £5 licence fee in order to retail which led to a 'shocking increase of gin consumption due to its cheapness'.

Henry Fielding especially pointed to immorality as the prime cause of crime. Although immorality, he believed, was not confined to the lower orders of society, he believed that this social category contained persons who were able to work but unwilling to do so, and he put forward remedies that included tougher controls of the drink trade to counter drunkenness and for the stricter control of vagabondage (a term that was identified with vagrancy) (Fielding, 1751). This work argued in favour of preventive policing, although it did not use the term 'police' (Dodsworth, 2008: 588). He especially drew attention to the role of professional criminals in accounting for much crime at that time.

Henry was joined by his half-brother John (1721–1780) as his assistant Magistrate in 1750.

The Bow Street Runners

In 1749, Henry set up a small foot patrol force to supplement the historic policing system that operated in London which became known as the 'Bow Street Runners'. Described as 'regularly paid detectives functioning as a police force' (Lyman, 1964: 142), their initial role was to attend crime scenes, detect and apprehend offenders and take them to Bow Street to be examined and, if appropriate, committed for trial. By the end of the eighteenth century, they consisted of a force of 68 men (Emsley, 1986: 72).

Although their work was similar to that of thief takers (and officers were permitted to undertake paid private work from persons and businesses such as banks) (Moss & Skinner, 2013: 7), Fielding's force was formally attached to his office and operated under his supervision thus offering a solution to the corruption that had been previously associated with thief taking, especially through the activities of Jonathan Wild. Additionally, the official intervention of the nature put forward by Fielding meant that those who had experienced crime were no longer solely responsible for apprehending and prosecuting the perpetrator (which was both difficult and dangerous if a criminal gang was involved)—now they could report the incident to the Bow Street office and the Runners would take the matter over.

Henry Fielding also used his literary and communication skills acquired as a novelist to found *The Covent Garden Journal* (first published in 1752) which asked those who had been the victim of crime to send details of the incident, and in particular a description of the perpetrator, to his office. It has been argued that this publication 'served to make people aware, allowing them to assist in solving a crime and operating almost as a neighbourhood watch, helping to reduce the likelihood of a crime being committed' (Brain, undated: [Online]), thus enhancing increasing the risk of detection and serving as a mechanism of general deterrence as is discussed in Chapter 1.

The Runners were initially funded without government support, their income being derived mainly from rewards received following a conviction and also by private citizens to whom stolen goods were returned. However, in 1753 the government made a financial contribution towards the cost of the work of the office (which covered both thief taking, the circulation of information regarding criminals, initially in a publication called the *Covent Garden Journal* but subsequently in a newspaper called *Public Advertiser* and for the maintenance of clerks at the Bow Street office to record details of criminal activity that were reported to them by the public).

John Fielding succeeded Henry as Magistrate in 1754, holding this office until 1780. He was a prominent criminal justice reformer whose particular interests focused on youth crime. In 1758 he established the Asylum for Orphan Girls in Lambeth, South London. He wrote fairly widely on the subject of policing in works that embraced *An Account of the Origins and Effects of a Police* (1758); *Extracts From Such of the Penal Laws as Relate to the Peace and Good Order of This Metropolis* (1762) and *A Plan for Preventing Robberies Within 20 Miles of London* (1775).

Under John Fielding's superintendence the role and scope of the Bow Street Runners were increased. In response to attacks by footpads and highwaymen in the 1750s, the Runners were augmented by foot and horseback patrol. The targeting of highwaymen after 1763 by the horse patrol of the Bow Street Runners played an important part in the reduction of this form of criminal activity. Additionally, Fielding was named in the Commissions of the Peace in Kent, Surrey and Essex which meant that his officers could operate freely outside of London in these areas without the need to seek the sanction of the local Magistrates when wishing to conduct searches or arrests. On occasions, they operated even further afield to transact their work.

In 1772 and 1773, he set up a Gazette known as the *Quarterly Pursuit* (which was circulated throughout the country giving details of criminals who had fled the Metropolis) and the *Weekly Pursuit* (which circulated details of crime, stolen goods and a description of criminals that had been reported to Bow Street and which thus became the clearing house for information about crime across the metropolis) (Beattie, 2012: 85). The latter replaced the previous practice of placing advertisements in the *Public Advertiser* and reflected his belief that an effective deterrent to crime was an effective system of circulating criminal information which would enhance the likelihood of offenders being brought to justice and thus influence persons not to commit a crime (Beattie, 2012: 86).

The circulation of such information was also designed to secure information regarding crime from those who worked in jobs such as gatekeepers on turnpikes and keepers of public houses who were encouraged to inform Bow Street what they knew about crimes that were highlighted in these and other publications. Both publications were granted public funding in 1773 (Waters, 2020: [Online]).

These publications underwent changes of name that included the *The Public Hue and Cry and* the *Hue and Cry* which was published weekly by the chief clerk at Bow Street and was made available to all Magistrates in the Kingdom who wanted it and to the Clerk of the Peace of the Counties and Mayors and functionaries of the great towns (Waters, 2020: [Online]). It thus transformed Bow Street into a clearing house for information regarding serious crime and offenders across the entire country (Emsley, 1986: 73). It became known as the *Police Gazette* in 1828 and Scotland Yard assumed responsibility for its publication in 1883.

Further initiatives augmented the work of the Fieldings and the Bow Street Runners—Peel, for example, creating a day patrol which operated between 9 am and 7 pm, consisting of 24 men who were nicknamed 'Robin Redbreasts' because of the red waistcoats they wore (Emsley, 1986: 74). An important aspect of the work of the Fieldings was to increase the likelihood that those who engaged in crime would be caught and punished. Both Fieldings regarded this as a more effective deterrent than public executions. Emsley argued that some of the Bow Street Runners such as George Ruthven and John Townsend 'acquired formidable reputations as detectives and the apprehenders of offenders' and that the services of the Runners were sought by provincial authorities faced with a spate of robberies, a gang of poachers or a difficult murder (Emsley, 1986: 74).

However, proposals by John Fielding in 1785 to expand the scope of his Bow Street experiment into a more general system of paid professional police officers operating at a greater distance outside London fell on deaf ears, one obstacle being that magistrates sitting on county benches saw no merit such a proposal operating in their own localities—

> provincial England was not London with its urban sprawl and its apparently disproportionate amount of serious crime. What appeared of value from the centre of London to suppress the city's unique crime problem, had little value outside (Emsley, 1986: 73).

Sentiments of this nature would continue to thwart initiatives to reform policing throughout England and Wales into the early decades of the nineteenth century. As Emsley concluded, following the creation of the Metropolitan Police Force in 1829, those in the provinces asked 'what relevance did this metropolitan model have for the rest of the country?' (Emsley, 1986: 75).

Patrick Colquhoun and Police Reform

Patrick Colquhoun came from Dumbarton, Scotland, but moved to London in 1789. He was appointed a Magistrate in 1792 and in 1798 wrote the first edition of his *Treatise on the Police of the Metropolis* in which he suggested that there were around 115,000 persons in London (whose population then numbered around 99,000) 'who are supposed to support themselves in and near the Metropolis by pursuits either criminal illegal-or immoral' (Colquhoun, 1798: 6–10) which included a hard core of around 2000. Criminality among the poor, he believed, arose from their idleness and improvidence.

He drew attention to the inadequacy of the policing system—the constables and watch numbered 1000, and guarded the lives and properties of the inhabitants residing in near 8000 streets. The police were under seventy different trusts, employed by and authorised to act only in their own particular ward, parish or borough. The police themselves were underpaid, often feeble and frequently in league with the criminals (Colquhoun, 1798: 161–4). He argued in favour of a centrally organised police force for London under the direction of the Home Office.

He proposed to augment existing methods of policing based around the Parish Constables by giving each parish the ability to recruit a small professional police force which would be regulated by a central board consisting of 5 Commissioners appointed by the government. The Board would be responsible for keeping records and circulating information about criminals and to publish a *Police Gazette*. His ideas (which entailed a collaboration with Jeremy Bentham) regarding police reform were embodied in a 'Bill for the Establishment of a Board of Police' that was drafted in 1799 but never introduced (Lyman, 1964: 145), one reason being that it sidelined the Magistracy's involvement in policing, thus arousing their opposition (Houghton, 2001: 47–8). However, he was approached by London merchants who traded with the West Indies regarding the prevention of thefts of cargoes from ships that were moored on the River Thames.

Colquhoun estimated that the portion of the river four miles below and two miles above Tower Bridge contained around 8000 vessels at any one time which contained property to the value of around £75 million. He further calculated that in 1797 over £500,000 of this was stolen by various categories of criminal that—using the slang then in use at that time—he described as 'river pirates', 'night plunderers', 'light horsemen' and 'scuffle hunters', who often operated in criminal gangs. It was estimated that theft cost the West Indian merchants around £232,000 per year (around £27 Million in today's money). His solutions were to replace the Legal Quays (where at that time—dating from customs regulations dating to the reign of Elizabeth I—all imports were required to be landed) with securely managed docks where goods could be more speedily offloaded and urged the creation of a River Police force.

Colquhoun was able to persuade these merchants of the benefits of a River Police Force by using cost–benefit analysis, pointing out that their outlay in paying for the policing of the River and quaysides would result in much greater savings.

In 1798, the Committee of the West India Merchants asked Colquhoun to put this scheme into operation. The government—perhaps as it realised then forms of theft to which Colquhoun had alluded was costing it money in lost customs revenue amounting to some £50,000 per year—agreed to support the initiative financially, although initially what was termed the West India Merchants and Planters Marine Police—came into operation through private subscriptions. It consisted of a small force of 80 permanent officers) (Lyman, 1964: 145) who patrolled the River Thames from London Bridge to Blackwall by boat and although its primary purpose was to protect those ships that carried cargoes from the West Indies, their physical presence had a deterrent impact on theft from all ships in that vicinity.

Another of Colquhoun's proposals was acted upon when in 1799 an Act of Parliament created the West India Docks on the Isle of Dogs which aimed to prevent the kind of thefts that had taken place in the Legal Quays. Although this initiative reduced the importance of the Marine Police to the West India Merchants, its success in reducing crime on the River Thames (which was discussed by Colquhoun in his work, *A Treatise on The Commerce and Policing of the River Thames*, published in 1800, to extol the virtues of regulated policing as a method to reduce crime) persuaded the government to take it over entirely, thus providing the central state with a direct role in law enforcement.

The 1800 Depredations on the Thames Act (usually referred to as the Marine Police Act) created the Marine Police Establishment as a public body that would patrol the tidal Thames and its tributaries and provide protection to all shipping that used it. Again, Bentham collaborated with Colquhoun in the drafting of this legislation. Also the River Police occasionally performed policing duties on land, as was the case with their involvement in the 1811 Ratcliffe Highway murders (Joyce & Laverick, 2022: 121).

Following the creation of the Metropolitan Police in 1829, the Marine Police was incorporated into this force in 1839 as its Thames Division and still functions today, policing the River from the same headquarters in Wapping as was used when the Marine Police was founded.

Although the Marine Police is one of Colquhoun's most notable achievements, he was interested—and wrote about—policing and police reform in more general terms. In his *Treatise on the Police of the Metropolis* (1796) he argued that the Bloody Code was ineffective in preventing crime and he estimated that there were some 115,000 people in London supporting themselves by criminal or immoral means (which amounted to a cost to the Metropolis of around £2 million a year). His solutions to this included the classicist belief in the certainty of law enforcement as opposed to the severity and the advocacy of an efficient system of policing whose ethos was to prevent crime. This emphasis on the prevention of crime (as opposed to reacting to it after it had been committed) was adopted as the purpose of the Metropolitan Police when it was formed in 1829.

Colquhoun was aware of the impact of adverse social conditions on the causes of criminal behaviour and in particular drew attention to the importance of indigence to the commission of crime. This led him to conclude that one task of policing was to prevent 'the class of poverty from falling into indigence' (Neocleous, 2000: 715), thus developing the concept of the 'social police' that sought to influence the moral outlook of the poor by inculcating 'bourgeois social values along with the new economic order' (Dodsworth, 2008: 585). Upholding morality by addressing the factors that might undermine it (such as drinking and gambling) was thus viewed by Colquhoun as a key function of the police, albeit one that would be shared by teachers and the Church. The opinion that a reformed policing system would 'act as a form of moral education, compensation for the apparent lack of religious and civil instruction in the general populace' (Dodsworth, 2008: 597) was also shared by John Fielding.

Views of this nature were later expanded upon by Robert Storch (1976) in an article depicting the police as social missionaries. These are compatible with arguments that suggest that the prime role of policing was to challenge values and attitudes that were at variance with the newly emerging capitalist order—that the development of professional policing marked the birth of a disciplinary society which was geared towards 'the disciplining or social control of the population and their compulsion into industry'. Policing was defined as 'the regulation of sites of temptation so as to prevent the acquisition of vicious habits, alongside the assumption that the police function was generally to establish good order and public morals' (Dodsworth, 2008: 586–7).

Colquhoun also favoured the penitentiary ideal to reform those who had committed a crime.

Jeremy Bentham and Police Reform

Jeremy Bentham was a key proponent of Utilitarianism in the United Kingdom who argued that the morality of an action was determined by its utility and that the aim of all conduct and legislation should be to assure 'the greatest happiness of the greatest number'. He regarded this as the true measure of right and wrong and provided the underpinning of his various proposals to reform all spheres of public administration: the key task of political and legal institutions was to deliver the 'principle of utility' by maximising happiness. He believed that mankind was governed by two key motives, pleasure and pain, and that the role of law was to maintain a fair balance between rewards and punishments (Bentham, 1789).

Since he regarded inflicting pain on an individual as an evil, he advocated police reform as a way to prevent criminal action from occurring in the first place, thereby safeguarding the happiness of the majority by 'combating mischief' (Bentham, 1782, cited in Quinn, 2021: [Online]) and minimising the infliction of pain on those who might otherwise be offenders. His advocacy of police reform also put into practice the ideas of classicist criminology concerning the need for an effective system of policing to deter criminals since the certainty of apprehension and punishment would fly in the face of rational behaviour on their part.

Box 7.2: Bentham and Police Reform

In his Constitutional Code, Bentham proposed the creation of a Preventive Service Ministry to give effect 'all ordinances of the Legislature, in so far as they have for their object the prevention of calamity; or of delinquency' (the latter included disease, mortality, 'unhealthy employments', dearth and famine) (Bentham, 1843a: 872–3).

To perform these roles, the Ministry would have control over facilities that included the Offices for Police Directors and their subordinate and Police Station-houses. In order for the Ministry to discharge its responsibilities, the prime minister would be authorised to augment the staff of the Ministry with members of his proposed stipendiary National Defensive Force (comprised of the Land and Sea Forces).

Bentham did not explicitly use the word 'police' in his Constitutional Code but what he described as 'functionaries' of the Preventive Service would possess 'local knowledge, including that of the characters, family circumstances, abodes and haunts of individual delinquents, and persons most in danger of falling into delinquency' (Bentham, 1843a: 876).

Bentham, like Colquhoun and the Fieldings, emphasised the main task of policing was that of preventing crime—termed by Bentham as a 'system of precaution, either for the prevention of crimes or of calamities' (Bentham, 1843b, Vol III,: 167, cited in Quinn, 2021: [Online]), a view that was in line with his opinion that 'preventive justice is ... preferable in all respects to punishing justice' (Bentham, 1765, cited in Quinn, 2021: [Online]).

However, crime prevention was not entirely viewed as a state-administered function, and he identified twenty-five 'crime-preventing' expedients, ranging from street lighting, to registers of travellers, provision of identifying marks for all subjects of the state, regulation of the sale of poisons, establishment of standard weights and measures, publication of accounts and giving publicity to 'proceedings of state' (Bentham undated, cited in Quinn, 2021: [Online]).

The Utilitarian position regarding police reform was not unchallenged. Adam Smith, for example, believed that what entailed a complex and involved system of policing would interfere with the liberty of the individual, especially since state involvement could result in central government using the police to favour a particular interest rather than to serve the general good (Smith, 1759, cited in Houghton, 2001: 50–1). This sentiment inspired an alternative approach to combating crime and disorder which was to reform the criminal law and penal system rather than embarking upon police reform.

The 1780 Gordon Riots and Police Reform

In addition to responding to crime, the creation of a professional policing force could be justified by the need to respond to public disorder, especially when this threatened the status and power of those who enjoyed a privileged position within early nineteenth-century society.

It has been argued that prior to the nineteenth century, urban disorder was not necessarily viewed as subversive of the social order. Riots were especially designed to secure the redress of perceived grievances which, once accomplished, would quieten the disorderly situation (Storch, 1975: 61). Nonetheless, activities of this nature required a response from the state to quell disorder (or potential disorder) arising from crowd situations.

An important lesson learned from the disturbances in 1780 (which are discussed in Chapter 3) was the deficiency of forces to maintain law and order. The Prime Minister, Lord North, failed to mobilise parish constables and thus ultimately had to rely on the military to put down the disorder and it took around one week for the government to muster sufficient soldiers and militia to quell the disorders. However, no Magistrate could then be found who was prepared to face the mob and read the Riot Act in order to enable soldiers to intervene in the disturbances (which was a requirement of the 1714 Riot Act, whereby a magistrate would read a proclamation requiring the rioters to disperse)—an omission for which the Lord Mayor of London—Barkley Kennett—was fined £1000 for criminal negligence. Eventually the King had to use the royal prerogative and declare martial law in order to get troops out on the streets and quell the disturbance by shooting those engaged in disorder.

A number of developments related to the maintenance of law and order were pursued in response to this event. In 1782, the government created the Home Department (which is usually referred to as the Home Office). This reform was designed to create a central focus through which matters relating to crime, disorder and internal security could be dealt with.

An early policing initiative centred on the Bow Street Runners: in 1782/1783, central government funding was provided for an armed foot patrol funded out of the public purse to counter highway robberies. Consisting of 46 men divided into six groups, each of which was controlled by a Captain, these patrolled the major routes into London each night.

William Pitt's government then aimed to introduce legislation in 1785 in the form of '*A Bill for the further Prevention of Crimes, and for the more speedy Detection and Punishment of Offenders against the Peace, in the Cities of London and Westminster, the Borough of Southwark, and certain Parts adjacent to them*'.

The context of this measure was that the government was having 'serious doubts' (Devereaux, 2007: 125–6) that reliance on a harsh penal code was providing an ineffectual response to crime and disorder and sought to handle the problem through other methods that embraced the reform of policing alongside measures that included crime prevention, new approaches to vagrancy and poor relief and the search for alternative forms of punishment including a new destination for transportation (Ward, 2015: [Online]).

The 1785 Bill proposed that three paid Commissioners would be appointed by the government, each of whom would be a Magistrate. They would supervise the selection and work of all other Magistrates in the Metropolitan Police District and also would have the power of veto over appointments to the night watches. London would be divided into 9 police divisions, headed by a Stipendiary Magistrate appointed by the Crown. Each office would have a force of paid petty constables (both foot and horse) numbering around 200 in total (Beattie, 2012: 154) supervised by chief constables. The chief constables reported to one Head Constable who in turn reported to the Commissioners.

The Bill proposed extensive powers to the constables which included the powers of search and arrest on suspicion and authorised the commissioners to grant search warrants to enable the constables to enter any house in search of stolen goods or receivers (Beattie, 2012: 154). It was concluded that this measure 'embodied the ultimate logic of eighteenth-century preventive policing: the surveillance of persons and places, strict punishment of relatively minor crimes, and keeping records on suspected as well as known offenders by a government-controlled, metropolitan authority' (Reynolds, 1998: 74). The ethos of the proposed force was the effective prevention of crime (Beattie, 2012: 155).

An important feature of the 1785 measure was to provide for a measure of central control by unifying the Cities of London and Westminster, the Borough of Southwark and other adjacent areas into one police district, thus placing the burden on delivering policing away from individual citizens and voluntary effort and instead to view it as a function that ought to be administered by the state. However, existing Parish Constables and nightwatchmen were to be retained but their duties would be coordinated with those of the police created by this legislation (Critchley, 1967: 36).

However, the proposed legislation aroused the hostility of the City of London, which viewed the Bill as 'an infringement of the rights of aldermen' and also viewed it 'being too similar to the Paris police system' (Lyman, 1964: 144). The Lord Mayor and Court of Aldermen (cited in Reynolds, 1998: 75) asserted that it subverted the chartered rights of the City of London and was destructive of the constitutional liberties of the citizens of London. It was alleged that the Bill would establish 'a system of policing new and arbitrary in the extreme, creating, without necessity, new officers, invested with extraordinary and dangerous powers, enforced by heavy penalties, and expressly exempted from those checks, and that responsibility, which the wisdom of the law has hitherto thought necessary to accompany every extraordinary power'.

The possibility of re-vamping the militia to provide permanent patrols within the city was put forward as an alternative to the creation of a professional police force (Houghton, 2001: 44–5). Pitt, not wishing to upset the business and commercial interests of the city, withdrew the Bill. Reynolds (1998: 75) concluded that

> Thus ended the first effort by the central government to reform the institutions of law enforcement in London on a metropolitan-wide basis. It had proposed fundamental changes that were seen as too drastic and its framers did not seek

> to consult or lobby local authorities whose interests would have been directly affected and who wielded considerable clout in Parliament.

It did, however, place police reform in London on the political agenda even if it was not acted upon immediately and also served as a blue print for the creation of the Dublin Metropolitan Police in 1786 (which is discussed in Chapter 9).

Following the withdrawal of this reform measure, the 1792 Middlesex Justices Act created seven additional Magistrates' offices modelled on Bow Street. These were situated at Queen's Square (Westminster), Great Marlborough Street (Westminster), Worship Street (Shoreditch), Lambeth Street (Whitechapel), Shadwell (later closed and replaced by an office in Marylebone High Street), Union Hall (Southwark) and Hatton Garden (Open University, 2009: [Online]). The City of London was not included in this new police reform initiative. However, subsequent attempts to expand this Middlesex model more widely failed, Emsley concluding that this was probably because of the cost it entailed (Emsley, 1986: 74).

Each of the new offices had three salaried (Stipendiary) Magistrates who controlled police forces fashioned on the Bow Street Runners who each initially had six constables at their disposal. These were financed by the Home Office. The constables were empowered to arrest thieves and suspected persons. Other initiatives that stemmed from the 1785 Police Bill were the Royal Proclamation on Vice (1787) (Dodsworth, 2008: 589) and the Thames River Police (which is discussed below being a further office created under the auspices of the 1792 legislation).

Bow Street initially enjoyed a privileged position in the new police arrangements, derived from the close proximity of Bow Street to the Home Office and the financial resources that were made available to it. However, the creation of additional police offices under the 1792 legislation diminished the volume of work that was required to be undertaken at Bow Street, which was further diminished when the Metropolitan Police was created in 1829 when the Bow Street patrol was absorbed into the new policing structure so that only the Runners remained. Additionally, central government control expanded over the operations of the Bow Street office, at the expense of power formerly wielded by the Magistrates. The 1839 Metropolitan Police Act absorbed the Runners into the Metropolitan Police force.

Conclusion

This chapter considered some of the key ideas put forward by police reformers in the late eighteenth century. Although the development of crime associated with the growth of towns was advanced as an argument for police reform, it has been suggested that 'the perceived threat of the "criminal classes" was used by commentators in the early to mid-nineteenth century to their own ends' and that what was termed 'moral entrepreneurs', defined by Becker (1963) as someone who makes a career out of rousing public alarm on some particular issue (especially crime), advocating certain necessary reforms and measures (such as establishing a police force) to deal with the problem and putting forward himself as the appropriate person to carry out these reforms and measures effectively. These included Patrick Colquhoun and Edwin Chadwick.

However, this view has been challenged, Bailey (1993: 237–8) arguing that although some historians had displayed a 'strong tendency to write the history of the first half of the nineteenth century in terms of the threat of "the dangerous and labouring classes", and the associated introduction of new instruments of policing and punishment' (Bailey, 1993: 237–8), in reality, in the first half of the nineteenth-century 'fears of an alliance between the criminal and working classes were neither as potent nor as pervasive as most British historians contend; by implication, class fear was less influential than commonly claimed in creating paid constabularies and the prison system' (Bailey, 1993: 230).

As the chapter indicates, some of these proposals resulted in reforms to policing but others did not. These ideas form the background for concrete measures of police reform in the nineteenth century which will be considered in the following two chapters.

? Summary Question

Analyse the factors that promoted interest in police reform in the late eighteenth and early nineteenth centuries.

References

Bailey, V. (1993). "The Fabrication of Deviance: "Dangerous Classes" and "Criminal Classes" in Victorian England. In J. Rule & R. Malcolmson (eds.), *Protest and Survival. The Historical Experience. Essays for E.P. Thompson.* Merlin Press.

Barke, M., & Taylor, P. (2013). "Newcastle's Long Nineteenth Century: A World-Historical Interpretation of Making A Multi-Nodal City-Region". *GaWC Research Bulletin*, 427. [Online] https://www.lboro.ac.uk/gawc/rb/rb427.html. Accessed 9 Oct 2020.

Beattie, J. (2012). *The First English Detectives. The Bow Street Runners and the Policing of London, 1750–1840.* Oxford University Press.

Beccaria, C. (1764). *Dei deliti e delle pene* (*On Crimes and Punishments*), trans. H. Paolucci (1963). Bobbs-Merrill.

Becker, H. (1963). *Outsiders. Studies in the Sociology of Deviance.* Free Press.

Bentham, J. (various documents marked as undated, 1765 and 1782), cited in M. Quinn, (2021) "Bentham on Preventive Police: the Calendar of Delinquency in Evaluation of Policy, and the Police Gazette in Manipulation of Opinion". *Ucl.ac.uk.* [Online] https://discovery.ucl.ac.uk/id/eprint/10060730/1/RPS%20MQ%20JB%20Preventive%20Police.pdf. Accessed 21 Sep 2022.

Bentham, J. (1789). *An Introduction to the Principles of Morals and Legislation.* T. Payne and Son.

Bentham, J. (1843a). *The Works of Jeremy Bentham*, Vol. 9 (Constitutional Code). *Online Library of Liberty.* [Online] https://oll-resources.s3.us-east-2.amazonaws.com/oll3/store/titles/1999/Bentham_0872-09_EBk_v6.0.pdf. Accessed 22 Sep 2022.

Bentham, J. (1843b). *Works of J. Bentham, Published Under the Superintendence of His Executor John Bowring*, 11 vols. William Tait, cited in M. Quinn, (2021). "Bentham on Preventive Police: the Calendar of Delinquency in Evaluation of Policy, and the Police Gazette in Manipulation of Opinion". *Ucl.ac.uk.* [Online] https://discovery.ucl.ac.uk/id/eprint/10060730/1/RPS%20MQ%20JB%20Preventive%20Police.pdf. Accessed 21 Sep 2022.

Brain, J. (n.d.). "Bow Street Runners" HistoricUK. [Online] https://www.historic-uk.com/HistoryUK/HistoryofBritain/Bow-Street-Runners/. Accessed 8 Oct 2020.

Colquhoun, P. (1798). A Treatise on the Police of London. Joseph Mawman.

Critchley, T. (1967). *A History of Police in England and Wales 900–1966*. Constable.

Devereaux, S. (2007). Imposing the Royal Pardon: Execution, Transportation, and Convict Resistance in London, 1789. *Law and History Review, 25*(1), 101–138.

Dodsworth, F. (2008). The Idea of Police in Eighteenth Century England: Discipline, Reformation, Superintendence, c 1780–1800. *Journal of the History of Ideas, 69*(4), 583–604.

Emsley, C. (1986). Detection and prevention: the old english police and the new 1750–1900. *Historical Social Research, 37*, 69–88.

Fielding, H. (1751). *An Enquiry into the Causes of the Late Increase of Robbers, &c. With Some Proposals for Remedying this Growing Evil, etc.* A. Miller.
Fielding, J. (1758). *An Account of the Origins and Effects of a Police.* C. Henderson.
Fielding, J. (1762). *Extracts from Such of the Penal Laws as Relate to the Peace and Good Order of This Metropolis.* A. Millar.
Fielding, J. (1775). *A Plan for Preventing Robberies Within 20 Miles of London.* A. Millar.
Houghton, J. (2001). *Policing and Local Government in England*. Unpublished PhD thesis, Manchester Metropolitan University.
Joyce, P., & Laverick, W. (2022). Bringing History to Life – From 'Old' to 'New' Policing 1689–1839. *Journal of the Police History Society, 36*, 118–125.
Lambert, T. (2020). "A History of English Population". *localhistories.org*. [Online] http://www.localhistories.org/population.html. Accessed 9 October 2020.
Laverick, W. (2016). *Global Injustice and Crime Control*. Routledge.
London Lives. (2018). "Reformation of Manners Campaigns". *Londonlives.org*. [Online] https://www.londonlives.org/static/Reformation.jsp. Accessed 28 Apr 2023.
Lyman, J. (1964). The Metropolitan Police of 1829. *Journal of Criminal Law and Criminology, 55*(1), 141–154.
Machiavelli, N. (1532). *The Prince*. Ware: Wordsworth Editions Limited: This edition was published in 1997.
McLynn, F. (1989). *Crime and Punishment in Eighteenth Century England*. Oxford University Press.
Moss, A., & Skinner, K. (2013). *The Victorian Detective*. Shire Publications Ltd.
Neocleous, M. (2000). Social Police and the Mechanisms of Prevention. Patrick Colquhoun and the Condition of Poverty. *British Journal of Criminology, 40*, 710–726.
Open University. (2009). "Origins of the Metropolitan Police". *Open.ac.uk*. [Online] http://www.open.ac.uk/Arts/history-from-police-archives/Met6Kt/MetHistory/mhPolOffices.html#:~:text=The%20success%20of%20Bow%20Street,six%20paid%20officers%20or%20constables. Accessed 29 Sep 2022.
Quinn, M. (2021). Bentham on Preventive Policing – The Calendar of Delinquency in Evaluation of Policy, and the *Police Gazette* in Manipulation of Opinion. *Ucl.ac.uk*. [Online] https://discovery.ucl.ac.uk/id/eprint/10060730/1/RPS%20MQ%20JB%20Preventive%20Police.pdf. Accessed 21 Sep 2022.
Reus-Smit, C. (2011). "International law". In J. Baylis, S. Smith, P. Owens, (Eds.). *Globalisation of World Politics: Introduction to International Relations*. Oxford University Press.
Reynolds, E. (1998). *Before the Bobbies. The Night Watch and Police Reform in Metropolitan London 1720–1830*. Macmillan.
Shaw-Taylor, L., Davies, R., Kitson, P., Newton, G., Satchell, A., & Wrigley, E. (2010). The Occupational Structure of England 1750–1871 Some Preliminary Results. *Campop.geog*. [Online] https://www.campop.geog.cam.ac.uk/research/projects/occupations/britain19c/papers/paper4.pdf. Accessed 13 Jan 2023.

Storch, R. (1975). The Plague of Blue Locusts: Police Reform and Popular Resistance in Northern England 1840–1857. *International Review of Social History, 20*(1), 61–90.

Storch, R. (1976). The Policeman as Domestic Missionary. *Journal of Social History, 4*, 481–509.

The Proceedings of the Old Bailey. (2018). A Population History of London. *Old Bailey Proceedings Online*. [Online] https://www.oldbaileyonline.org/static/Population-history-of-london.jsp. Accessed 9 Oct 2020.

Tickner, A. (2014). *A Feminist Voyage Through International Relations*. Oxford University Press.

Vold, G., Bernard, T., & Snipes, J. (1998). *Theoretical Criminology* (4th ed.). Oxford University Press.

Waltz, K. (1959). *Man, the State and War: A Theoretical Analysis*. Columbia University Press.

Ward, R. (2015). The Criminal Corpse, Anatomists, and the Criminal Law: Parliamentary Attempts to Extend the Dissection of Offenders in Late Eighteenth-Century England. *Journal of British Studies, 54*(1), 63–87.

Waters, L. (2020). The Police Gazette. *amdigital.co.uk* [Online] http://www.ampltd.co.uk/digital_guides/police_gazette_part_1/Editorial-Introduction.aspx. Accessed 8 Oct 2020.

White, M. (2009). The Rise of Cities in the Eighteenth Century. *Georgian Britain*. [Online] https://www.bl.uk/georgian-britain/articles/the-rise-of-cities-in-the-18th-century#:~:text=The%20population%20of%20Britain%20grew,in%20nearby%20towns%20and%20cities. Accessed 9 Oct 2020.

8

The Development of Professional Policing in London

Introduction

Police reform entailed abandoning the historic Parish Constable system and watchmen (which was dubbed 'insufficient and inefficient' by Lyman, 1964: 142) and replacing it with professional police forces (the term 'professional' denoting that those who performed the task of policing were paid a wage to undertake this work rather than reliance being placed on voluntary effort to prevent and detect crime). As has been argued in Part 2, this development was not completely new and built upon initiatives that included the Bow Street Runners who were paid for the work they performed. This chapter will discuss the key legislation through which this reform was implemented, starting with the 1829 Metropolitan Police Act.

However, professional policing was far from a popular reform in the early nineteenth century and police reformers (especially the Home Secretary Robert Peel) had to tread a very delicate line in seeking to ensure that the police forces they wished to create operated with the consent of the general public and in no way would undermine the rights and liberties of English people. The issues of why this was important and what practical steps were taken to achieve it will be explored in detail in this chapter.

P. Joyce and W. Laverick, *History of Policing, Crime, Disorder, Punishment*, https://doi.org/10.1007/978-3-031-36892-9_8

Background to the Formation of the Metropolitan Police Force

Population Growth

The period c 1750–1800 did not witness any key developments associated with the newer forms of crime in London that were considered in Part 1. The absence of any national crime figures before 1805 makes it hard to estimate the extent of crime across England and Wales (Emsley, 2018: 21). However, much of it was not of a serious nature and an analysis of crimes tried at the Old Bailey between 1810 and 1850 revealed that only 2% were for murder or manslaughter (Taylor, 1998: 27).

However, it was observed that prosecutions of juveniles for theft in London in the late eighteenth and early nineteenth centuries increased and one reason given for this situation was the decline in apprenticeships and living in service (Emsley, 2018: 26). Additionally, the growth of other urban locations made the problem related to newer forms of criminality more widespread across the country. Recognition was also paid to crimes that did not involve property, including that conducted behind closed doors—rape, sexual assault and wife beating. The latter was viewed mainly as a working-class phenomenon (Emsley, 2018: 107–108).

In addition to a crime that was attributed to the lower classes, other forms of criminality also existed. White-collar crime in the nature of fraud was stated to be endemic in railway companies and that legislation that included the 1844 Company Act offered no meaningful protection against it.

Violence and Disorder in London

Chapter 5 has cited a number of key case studies that detail the violence and disorder that occurred throughout Britain in the period 1800–1850. Disorders especially affected London in this period, and this section refers to some of the episodes that played an important part in promoting the reform of policing in the capital in 1829.

Lyman (1964: 146) provided an account of economic conditions in early nineteenth-century Britain. She argued that unemployment and hunger accelerated by Britain's blockade of French ports commencing in 1807, a hard winter in 1810 and a harvest failure in 1812 were acutely felt by the working class. Their initial frustrations were directed at the introduction of machinery, resulting in direct action to destroy it—events associated with Luddism that commenced in 1811 (and which have been discussed in Chapter 5). Although frame breaking became a capital offence, there was no attempt made to reform policing.

Subsequently, Lyman (1964: 146) stated, the years 1815–1822 were a period of economic distress, characterised by trade languishing and unemployment increasing. The labour market was swelled by discharged soldiers and sailors. However, the agricultural interests and landed gentry were the predominant power in Parliament. Fearing a fall in the prices of grain and the decrease in their profits, they rushed through the Corn Laws of 1815. The importation of foreign wheat was prohibited until the domestic price reached eighty-four shillings a quarter. But nothing of substance was done to ameliorate the sufferings of the poor. Although the government repealed the property tax, the taxes most oppressive to the poor—derived from customs and excise duties on sugar, tea, coffee, spirits, beer and tobacco—were not reduced.

Against this background of economic suffering (especially the 1815 Corn Laws), disorders occurred which included rioters assaulting MPs on 6 March 1815. A further disorder at the House of Commons on 5 June 1815 resulted in the High Bailiff of Westminster being summoned to Parliament to explain alleged neglect of duty by the civil power. He explained that 'of his 80 constables, about 50 attended today…; he found this force, joined with all the force of the police offices, quite insufficient to restrain the mob …. He had no power over any constables but his own' (Parliamentary Debates Vol XXX, 1815, cited in Lyman, 1964: 146). No rioters were arrested in this incident.

Although these events might have highlighted the need for police reform, no action of this sort was attempted, Lyman (1964: 147) arguing that this was because of 'opposition to more taxes and government intervention by the upper classes, and a deep-seated fear by the lower classes that law enforcement was just one more measure to protect the privilege and property of a resented and sometimes hated upper class'. Further protests underpinned by economic distress (Lyman, 1964: 147 arguing that by the end of the decade there were around 4 million people in receipt of parish relief out of a total population of 12 million) included outbreaks of Luddism in the textile centres and in agricultural areas and Peterloo resulted in government repression in the form of the Six Acts (which have been discussed in Chapter 5) but still no police reform.

Lyman (1964: 147–148) documented the continuance of violence in the early 1820s. This was especially fuelled by the Queen Caroline affair in which George IV sought the government's support to initiate divorce proceedings against his wife. Lyman (1964: 147) observed that

> Unpopular taxes, suspicions concerning the Duke of Wellington's ambitions, and a licentious and profligate king whose sexual life was a public affront and scandal, roused people of all classes against a Ministry which dared support the trumped-up charges of adultery against the Queen.... To the lower classes, the wronged Queen became an object with whom they could identify as fellow-victims of injustice. To the Radicals, the case was fuel for their political fire.

One aspect of the protest that occurred in conjunction with the trial of Queen Caroline was the appearance of placards—'some were so violent in their implications that revolution seemed possible' (Lyman, 1964: 148). Following the Queen's death in August 1821, clashes occurred between the people and the military at her funeral procession and Lyman (1964: 148) recorded that

> There was more fighting between people and troops in Kensington Church Street and Tottenham Court Road. The parish police who were there were powerless and useless. Instead of the blame being placed where it properly belonged, on the failure to provide effective police legislation, the Chief Magistrate at Bow Street was dismissed.

However, the revolution did not occur, Lyman (1964: 148) suggesting that this was probably because 'the protest against the Ministers was led by the middle class and Whig gentry'. A subsequent government reshuffle (that saw Sir Robert Peel take over at the Home Office) improvement in economic conditions between 1822 and 1825 aided the reduction of tensions in the nation, Lyman (1964: 149) stating that 'as unemployment decreased so did the riots and disorder'.

The bubble of financial speculation between 1823–5 burst, leading to a run on the banks, a fall in wages and unemployment. This situation prompted disorders across the country, that included strikes, riots, the destruction of machinery and looting. The military was called in to quell these disturbances. Further changes in the composition of the government (that saw the Duke of Wellington became prime minister in 1828) and an improvement in economic circumstances (aided by a new Corn Law in 1828) that permitted corn to be imported when the domestic price reached 60 shillings a quarter calmed the disorderly situation down.

However, Peel's return as Home Secretary in 1828 (an office he held from 1822 to 1827) placed police reform on the political agenda, in which he drew upon reforms he had introduced into Ireland when he served as Secretary between 1812 and 1818.

Peel and Police Reform

Peel was aware, however, that 'in London public order and the security of life and property still remained, for the most part solely dependent on troops'. Accordingly, 'Peel's mind turned toward the creation of an adequate police force' (Lyman, 1964: 149). His motive was to improve the system of policing in London since 'Twelve of London's parishes', with a total population of twenty thousand, had no night police. By 1828 one person in every 383 was adjudged to have been a criminal (Lyman, 1964: 149).

Accordingly, Peel instigated the appointment of a Select Committee to study the police, the fourth such Committee since 1803 (the others being 1816, 1818 and 1822). In a Memorandum to this Committee, Edwin Chadwick argued that the existing policing system consisted of 'disjointed bodies of men, governed separately, under heterogeneous regulation, and acting for the most part under the earliest set of experience'. He believed that a good police force was 'a well organised body of men acting upon a system of precaution to prevent crime and public calamities, to preserve public peace and disorder and perform whatever other functions might be comprehended in their duties' (Chadwick, 1829 cited in Houghton, 2001, 51–2).

The Select Committee reported in July 1828. It verified there had been an increase in crime in London and Middlesex and advocated wholesale reform that entailed the establishment of an Office of Police under the Home Secretary, with responsibilities for policing the entire metropolitan area. The Office of Police would be controlled by appointed Magistrates who would not perform normal judicial duties. As Houghton (2001: 53) argued, the involvement of the Home Office in policing was not novel—the re-institution of the Horse Patrol (originally set up under the auspices of the Bow Street Runners) to police main roads leading into London up to a radius of 20 miles and the funding of Thames Police (under the auspices of the 1792 Middlesex Justice Act which further funded the 7 police offices that were created by that legislation) gave the Home Secretary direct control over around 400 paid police officers by the time Peel became Home Secretary in 1822. Additionally, the Home Office could employ Special Constables when circumstances required it (Houghton, 2001: 54).

However, Peel faced formidable hurdles in introducing any scheme of this nature. The City of London was opposed to the idea of a centralised police force for the whole of London on the grounds it infringed their historic rights of self-government. Lyman (1964: 150) also pointed to the opposition of some of the London parishes which had adopted the practice of employing paupers as constables in order to reduce Poor Law Rates. Further afield, some manufacturing interests were concerned that a professional system of policing would cost them money through taxation while opposition also arose from those who believed that a reformed system of policing would be used by Tories to keep themselves in power (Lyman, 1964: 150). Although some Whigs also opposed the Report on the grounds that it had been triggered by a Tory Home Secretary, others supported the Committee's proposals—

> Publicly advocating reform, condemning the use of troops, committed to certain positions because they were representative of middle class business and industrial interests, the Whigs could not completely condemn the Report and its proposals. A number of these interests suffered financial and property losses from the riots, and were therefore interested in measures that would prevent such losses (Lyman, 1964: 150).

The Development of Professional Policing in London

The first professional police force in England and Wales was created by Peel in 1829. Peel was motivated by the view that harsh penalties did not act as a deterrent to crime which would be more effectively prevented by an effective police force. When introducing his Bill into Parliament, he argued that crime had increased 55% in London and Middlesex between 1821 and 1828, as compared to the period 1811–1818, while the population had increased only 19% (Peel, 1829, cited in Lyman, 1964: 151). He attributed this situation to a lax policing system which he proposed to reform. His cause was aided by episodes of rioting and frame breaking occurring while Peel's Bill was being debated in Parliament. Lyman (1964: 152) referred to this incentive for enacting police reform, noting that

> the monarchy was unpopular, republican sentiment was being heard openly, there was fear of revolution, fear of the mob, and apprehension for the security of property. The demand for protection became widespread as business and industrial interests exerted a pressure which transcended party lines, a pressure which Parliament dared not ignore. The Metropolitan Police Act was passed.

The 1829 Metropolitan Police Act

The 1829 Act (whose official title was An Act for improving the Police in and near the Metropolis) provided for the creation of a Metropolitan Police District which covered Westminster and parts of Middlesex, Surrey, and

Kent. The aim of the measure was 'to substitute a new and more efficient system of Police in lieu of such establishments of nightly Watch and nightly Police' (cited in Lyman, 1964: 150). The City of London was exempted from these arrangements and was later provided with its own 'new' policing arrangements by the 1839 City of London Police Act (which is considered below).

The Metropolitan Police was initially supervised by Crown-appointed Justices who later took the title of commissioners. These were Charles Rowan and Richard Mayne. When Rowan retired due to ill health in 1850 he was replaced by Captain William Hay. When Hay retired in 1855, the current practice of having just one commissioner (initially the incumbent Mayne) was adopted.

The new force was under the ultimate control of the Home Secretary and to whom the Commissioners reported directly. This form of policing marked a break from historic models (and also from developments that included the Bow Street Runners) whereby policing had been under the control of Magistrates and it differed from the old model of policing by creating 'a uniformed, paid force under bureaucratic control' (Taylor, 1998: 72). It was financed by a rate levied on property-holders, replacing the former Watch Rate (Lyman, 1964: 151).

The new police force first appeared on the streets of London on 29 September 1829. All existing persons who previously held some form of police office were dismissed from it and although they could apply to join the new Metropolitan Police, it was concluded that most of the initial officers 'came fresh to the job' (Hart, 1955: 420).

Box 8.1: The 1829 Metropolitan Police Act—Key Provisions

The 1829 measure set up a police force that operated in a 7-mile radius from Charing Cross in London (an area which is close to modern-day Trafalgar Square) and was responsible for law enforcement and the maintenance of public order in an area housing around 1.5 million people—about one constable to every 450 persons (Tobias, 1972: 113–114).

By 1 June 1830, the force consisted of 'three thousand, three hundred and fourteen (3314) men' (Lyman, 1964: 153). Although using a military-type rank structure (consisting of sergeants, inspectors and superintendents—initially 323, 68 and 17, respectively) (Tobias, 1972: 1213), the force was organised on civilian lines.

As Houghton observed (2001: 60), the Constable who had previously been an independent officer within the parish, answerable only to the High Constable and local Magistrate, was now 'part of a hierarchical structure answerable to senior officers and subject to regulation and a discipline code governing the performance of his duties'. The parish was now devalued as an important unit of local government both geographically and financially (Houghton, 2001: 65–66).

Further, 'the local connection between the law enforcement system and the community had been broken because now a direct link had been forged in the London area between the Home Secretary and the police, which enabled central government to develop a direct influence on the administration of policing' (Houghton, 2001: 60).

The key features of this measure were (Hart, 1955: 416).

- Placing all the police of London (save the City of London) under one authority
- Providing sufficient but not too many police officers
- Making the police a full-time occupation
- Paying the men fixed weekly wages and not according to the work they performed
- Improving the efficiency of the police by the careful selection and instruction of recruits
- Strict enforcement of discipline of those recruited into the force.

Constables were required to be under 35 years of age, in good health and were forbidden from visiting public houses, talking to prostitutes or making use of informants.

It has been noted that new police requirements for strength, height and appearance of constables codified earlier ideals ensuring masculine qualities, reinforcing class and gender restrictions posed by requirements for constables to be literate and propertied (Dodsworth, 2012: 47–48).

Creation of the City of London Police Force (1839)

The City of London had a proud tradition of local self-government, which pre-dated the Norman Conquest of 1066 and entailed the citizens electing their own Magistrates and appointing persons to keep watch and ward within the city. The royal charter granted to the city by William I in 1067 was viewed as an important landmark in guaranteeing autonomy to the city in these matters since it reaffirmed these historic rights and freedoms to the city. The city was controlled by Alderman (who were initially termed 'burgesses') and the maintenance of law and order was an important aspect of their role.

The city possessed its own police force organised under the Lord Mayor and the City Marshalls (Emsley, 1986: 72).

Historically, the system of night-time policing was based around a number of wards into which the city was divided, each of which possessed a number of watchmen, appointed on the voluntary principle by the city Aldermen. However, the use of deputies by those nominated to perform the role tended to undermine the efficiency of this historic policing system and led to the appointment of paid watchmen. Although this system was initially viewed as ineffective, reforms to the way in which these were organised (including the use of a rank structure similar to that of the Metropolitan Police) helped improve efficiency by the 1830s and served as a rationale for not incorporating the city into Peel's Metropolitan Police Force when it was set up in 1829. Peel later stated in Parliament that

> the ancient privileges of the city of London were powerfully pleaded in exemption, prejudices were awakened respecting interference with the ancient rights of freemen, and eventually the anomaly was established, by which we behold a small civic district, the population of which does not exceed 58,000 or 60,000 inhabitants, permitted to be arbitrarily governed by its own police, or a system different and distinct from that by which the peace and security of the whole surrounding district are preserved. (Peel, 1839: column 1065)

In 1839 Lord John Russell, Home Secretary in a new (Whig) government headed by Viscount Melbourne, introduced a Bill that intended to expand to Metropolitan Police into the City of London. This prompted the city to petition Queen Victoria, arguing that their own police arrangements were equal if not superior to those of the remainder of London. One argument that was presented in Parliament emphasised the nature of governance in the City of London–

> The corporation appointed a committee, which was annually elected—they had the sole control over the police, acting under the instructions of the Lord Mayor, Aldermen, and Common Councilmen; so that the police of a district, containing 123,000 inhabitants, instead of being under one head, was under the control of the Lord Mayor, Aldermen, Common Councilmen, and the committee annually elected (Hawes, 1839: column 1061).

It was further alleged that the expansion of the Metropolitan Police into the city was destructive of the rights of its citizens and dangerous to the constitution since it was based upon the principle of centralisation which was inimical to the liberties of the people.

The Queen assented to the petition and requested the government to bring forward a new measure which would provide for a professional police force to operate within the boundaries of the City of London. The government acquiesced, primarily as it feared the forcible expansion of the Metropolitan Police into the City of London would be detrimental to the force's authority, Lord John Russell (1839: column 1291) stating that

> as a very great outcry had been raised in the City against the introduction of this bill, it was probable that if it were forced on the City the commissioners of police would not have that authority or be so well received in the City as was requisite in order to secure to the public the full benefits of the act.

Russell considered these objections to be a sufficient reason for waiving what he thought would be a very great improvement, namely the creation of a single force for all of London.

Thus a new Bill was brought forward in August 1839 whereby the Mayor, Aldermen and Commons were responsible for appointing (and also dismissing and/or replacing) a Commissioner who would head the new professional police force for the city. Although the exercise of these powers was subject to the approval of the Queen, the absence of Ministerial control over these new arrangements preserved the principle of self-government and local control of policing in the city.

Applicants to the City of London force were required to be under 40 years of age, able to read and write and also to be of a certain height. Although this force was a small one, it was not out of kilter with the size of many police forces which developed in urban and rural England and Wales in the early decades of the nineteenth century.

Subsequent attempts were made to amalgamate the Metropolitan and City of London police forces, including one by Sir George Grey in 1863. However, the weight of local opposition (which entailed 3000 merchants and bakers demonstrating at the Guildhall in 1863) ensured no such reform was enacted then or subsequently.

The Slow Take up of Professional Policing Outside of London

Despite evidence that the new Metropolitan Police succeeded in checking the previous rate of increase in crime in London (Hart, 1955: 414), there was no immediate move to follow the example of London and set up professional police forces elsewhere. A key reason for this was that the old system of policing was not totally inefficient, Taylor observing that there was a degree of 'interparochial cooperation' that offset the fragmentation that stemmed from a parish-based system of policing (Taylor, 1998: 72). Additional considerations are considered below in this section.

Difficulty in Securing Appropriate Recruits

Evidence from the Metropolitan Police Force contained in statistics related to recruitment and retention that suggested many of those attracted into policing were unsuited to the role—'some 3400 men joined the newly formed force in 1829–1830, of whom only a quarter were still in post four years later' (Taylor, 1998: 89). Dismissals and resignations were the main reasons for this high turnover of staff—

> during the first few decades, they [the Metropolitan Police] dismissed massive numbers of employees for the flimsiest transgression of the rules, thereby exacerbating the already high turnover caused by the extensive voluntary withdrawals. Officers also left when found unfit for service because of failing health or deteriorating physical condition .... During the period between 29 September 1830 and 31 December 1831, 1,586 officers were dismissed from the Metropolitan Police, whereas 736 resigned voluntarily (Schpayer-Makov, 2004: 105).

Thus a professional system might not be any more effective than the existing system of policing (Taylor, 1998: 72), since 'high turnover disrupted the normal operating routines and threatened the effectiveness of the overall organization' (Schpayer-Makov, 2004: 104).

Police Reform and Civil Liberties

There was suspicion that a reformed system of policing would trample on the historic rights and liberties of English people (an issue that is explored in more depth below). Storch (1975) whose arguments will be considered more fully in Chapter 10, argued that

> Resistance to a reformed police had root in a number of fears: the traditional fear of a standing army; of the political uses which might be made of such a force; of the effects of police intrusion upon daily neighbourhood life; and fear of the police as an agency which might be used to enforce the New Poor Law. There was also great apprehension about the role the police might play in trade-union affairs and strikes (Storch, 1975: 69).

Haliday observed that

> One of the key elements of reducing crime and instilling more orderly behaviour in the Victorian streets was the visibility of the professional police force, the aspiration being that people might conduct their lives in a more appropriate manner if they could see they were being observed (Haliday, 2017: 57).

However, 'being observed' also raised the spectre of 'being spied upon'. Accordingly, the abolition of the Metropolitan Police became prominent in the Radical platform, London Radical politicians in the 1830s pointing to the danger that 'the traditional liberties of the subject would be eroded, as well as the prerogatives of the old parishes' (Storch, 1975: 66–67). This issue is explored in greater detail below.

Cost

The new policing arrangements were costly. Professional policing entailed paying police officers a wage thus those who would be required to foot the bill were often reluctant to do so—why pay for something that you could get for free? Additionally, the beat system that was used as the basic model of police work meant that extra personnel was required to police large and thinly populated geographic areas, thus serving as a deterrent for police reform in rural areas.

Propping up the Old System

During the early years of the nineteenth century, initiatives were undertaken that were designed to prop up the old system to avoid root-and branch-reform of policing arrangements.

One example, initiated by Peel was contained in the 1829 Cheshire Police Act. This permitted each Hundred in the County to appoint a stipendiary high constable who would control a number of paid petty constables. This reform intended to create a county-wide policing system but lacked any mechanism of coordination to ensure that this outcome would be achieved (Houghton, 2001: 67).

A further example was the 1842 Parish Constables Act. This measure required all males aged between 25 and 55 years to serve as Parish Constables. It further provided for the supervision of Parish Constables (who could be voluntary or paid) of a Petty Sessions division by a superintending constable who was paid for from the county rate and was under the exclusive control of the local Justices. This measure was especially used in rural England, especially after amending legislation was enacted in 1850, so that 14 counties adopted its provisions. Emsley argued that this measure was popular 'because it appeared so much cheaper than a full-blown country constabulary and because it kept control of the police within the smaller traditional units of parishes and petty sessional divisions' (Emsley, 1986: 78).

Local Improvement Acts

In urban areas outside of London, improvements to the old system of policing were possible through measures that included the use of local Improvement Acts which required Parliamentary approval. Legislation of this nature (which is classified as 'private' legislation to distinguish it from public legislation which affected the entire country) typically authorised rates to be collected to pay for a wide range of municipal services whose actions were supervised by an elected body of ratepayers.

An important example of this was the 1792 Manchester and Salford Police Act, which permitted rates to be levied on householders to pay for a range of services that included 'the cleansing, lighting watching and regulation (of) the streets, lanes, passages and places within the towns of Manchester and Salford'. These functions were superintended by an elected body of ratepayers termed 'commissioners'. The policing arrangements provided for by legislation of this nature were typically a night watch that operated alongside a day police controlled by the parish constables, whose appointment remained governed by the historic feudal arrangements. The constables could be aided in their work by paid officials such as beadles.

Although Improvement Acts were costly to secure and were an option usually confined to large and wealthy towns, the 1833 Lighting and Watching Act provided a general power for the ratepayers in any parish.

> To elect a committee of between three and twelve 'Inspectors' to light and watch the parish. The Inspectors could raise a rate for their work and were given very wide powers. Parishes could either adopt the lighting or watching provisions, or both if they wished (Davey, 1983: 47).

This legislation maintained the historic link between parish government and policing and its importance to the policing of small towns, typically where the system of Parish Constables had broken down and where residents were willing to make financial sacrifices to solve the problem, is discussed by Davey

(1983). Subsequently, the 1847 Town Police Clauses Act provided a *pro forma* for local legislation related to policing which could be adopted in areas not included in the 1835 Municipal Corporations Act (Steedman, 1984: 15) which required the creation of a paid police force in large urban areas, termed [incorporated] Boroughs. This reform is discussed in Chapter 7.

Police Reform and Civil and Political Liberties

Contemporary discussions that relate to combating terrorism frequently refer to the need to balance liberty with security. These considerations were equally meaningful to many people in Britain in the late eighteenth and early years of the nineteenth century in connection with the development of professional policing.

Although police reform could be argued to be compatible with liberty since crime and lawlessness prevented people from going about their everyday lives, there was a very real fear in this period that a professional system of policing would serve a political purpose: the new police would see their main role as that of serving the interests of the government by 'spying' on the population whose rights and liberties would thus be undermined a contravention of the 1689 Bill of Rights which had prevented the monarch from possessing a standing army in time of peace.

Professional policing, it was feared, would undermine the independence of freeborn Englishmen by providing for the accumulation of excess powers in the executive branch of government (Dodsworth, 2012: 594). It was argued that 'Englishman of all classes generally viewed the Continental monarchy as being based on a police tyranny. Consequently, any measure suggesting a strengthening of the power of the central government was suspect' (Lyman, 1964: 141).

Those who voiced fears of this nature were able, subsequently, to point to the reform of policing in France where what was contemptuously described as a 'Continental' system of policing had been introduced, a system that was 'associated with the suppression of personal liberty and the ubiquity of spies' (Benjamin, 1931: 598). Emsley commented that the presence of a body of policemen patrolling the streets to prevent crime and disorder was an anathema to Englishmen which 'smacked of the absolutism of continental states' (Emsley, 1986: 69), while Palmer (1978: 198) posed the question

> would not a strong centrally-controlled police serve only to destroy English liberties and undermine cherished local governing institutions ? Might not government use this surrogate standing army to enforce arbitrary and unpopular laws ?

Sentiments of this nature helped defeat the intentions of the government to promote police reform in 1785 in the wake of the 1780 Gordon Riots (Critchley, 1967: 36–37) which have been considered in Chapter 7.

Joseph Fouché and the 'Continental Model of Policing'

Josef Fouché (or the Duc d'Otrante) was the main architect of the reformed system of policing in France. He served as Minister of Police 1799–1802, 1804–1810, 1814 and 1815. The system of policing with which he was associated emphasised the importance of intelligence gathering and spying on the French population as key ways to ensure that governments were not overthrown by those who were opposed to its rule.

The emphasis that Fouché placed on safeguarding the interests of the government as opposed to dealing with routine crime ensured that political policing was a prime concern of his office. However, this emphasis was not entirely new and can be traced back to the creation of the office of Lieutenant of Police in 1667 by Louis XIV and the role the police performed under the auspices of Nicolas de La Reynie (who held the post between 1667 and 1697) in which much use was made of informants.

Fouché became Minister of Police in 1791 and subsequently played a key role in the operations of what would now be termed 'high' policing (a term defined in Part 4 of this work). He served in every government between 1792 and 1815, being wonderfully skilled in changing sides. Although serving as Minister of Policing during Emperor Napoleon's brief return to power in 1815, he worked for the return of the Bourbon Monarchy which was restored in 1815 following the Battle of Waterloo.

Fouché was rewarded by briefly becoming Minister of Police and in this role superintended what was termed a 'White Terror' against enemies of the Bourbon restoration in the Summer of 1815. He drew up lists of those who should be punished for their support of the French Revolution and Napoleon, many of whom were executed, including Marshal Michel Ney. However, it is also argued that behind the scenes, he did his best to aid many of those on the wanted lists to escape from France (Montgomery, 2019: [Online]).

However, his stay in office was brief as royalists could not forgive him for supporting the execution of Louis XVI in 1793 during the French Revolution. He spent his remaining years in self-imposed exile.

Box 8.2: Joseph Fouché and 'High Policing'

Brodeur (1983: 507) wrote extensively about the difference between high and low policing.

Brodeur argued that Napoleon's Minister of Police, Joseph Fouché, who expressed the concept of high policing, 'made an explicit distinction between establishing a political order ("faire **la** police") and doing piecemeal policing ("faire **de la** police") (Madelin, 1930: 490)'.

Brodeur (2007) stated that at that time 'a three-tiered construction: (a) "the police", the dominant political regime and prevailing order of things; (b) "policing", conceived as sundry police actions directly devoted to bolstering the political regime or indirectly pursuing this end through the prevention and repression of various kinds of crimes and disorder - in short, the production of security; and (c) "police", this last word referring to the individual members of hybrid policing organizations using both public state police and private entrepreneurs (mainly informants) of all kinds'.

Those whom he referred to as 'THE police' protected the political order of the realm and 'were performing "high policing" tasks, as they were the executive arm of the monarch'.

Those police who performed the wide range of duties related to community security which Fouché referred to as the policing of lamp-posts (since prostitutes often stood close to them)—were doing what he referred to as 'low policing' and were accountable to the judiciary.

Brodeur concluded that 'high and low policing originally referred to a scale of prestige according to how close to the seat of power the police was' (Brodeur, 2007: 25–26).

The desire to avoid implanting a 'Continental' system of policing in England in the early nineteenth century has been summarised as follows:

> Fouché...commanded the French police who were the strong right arm of Napoleon's dictatorship. His men became an army of spies and agents provocateurs, spreading insidious terror and repression throughout France. For six years between 1804 and 1810 his method of control dominated the internal life of the country. There was, understandably, a very real fear in Britain that the formation of any sort of police force would result in the same fearful invasion of privacy and liberty that had occurred in France. (Manwaring-White, 1983: 3)

It was for this reason that England and Wales adopted a model of policing which emphasised the need for policing to secure popular legitimacy and consent.

Initial Popular Dissent Towards Policing

Although great care was taken to ensure that the new professional model of policing that was being developed in early nineteenth-century London was not the same as the Continental system of policing, this was not how many people viewed the situation at that time. This situation can be verified by a brief examination of the following anti-police posters that were circulated in the early decades of the nineteenth century (Figs. 8.1, 8.2 and 8.3).

The Philosophy of Policing—Legitimacy and Consent

The Legitimacy of the Police

In order for the police to perform their tasks effectively in society, they require legitimacy—an acceptance by the public (or the majority of it) that they have the right to exercise their functions even if specific actions they undertake do not meet with the approval of those on the receiving end of them.

Legitimacy derives from one or other of two sources—'the police are seen either as servants of the government ... or as officials whose source of authority derives from the general public .... The former is referred to as a *Roman law* (or Continental) model of policing and the latter as a *common law* model of policing' (Joyce, 2012: 175).

In Roman law models of policing, the police are typically controlled by and accountable to the central government. They act as *servants of the state* and their main purpose is to ensure that threats to the government (perhaps posed by politically motivated protests) are effectively neutered and to perform this function they will use weaponry and other coercive methods, acting in a manner similar to the military.

In common law models of policing, the police are typically subject to a degree of local control and accountability. They are *servants of the citizens* whose main purpose is to act in the interests of the general public by tackling problems of common concern (such as the prevention and detection of crime). They are [routinely] a non-militaristic force which actively seeks the

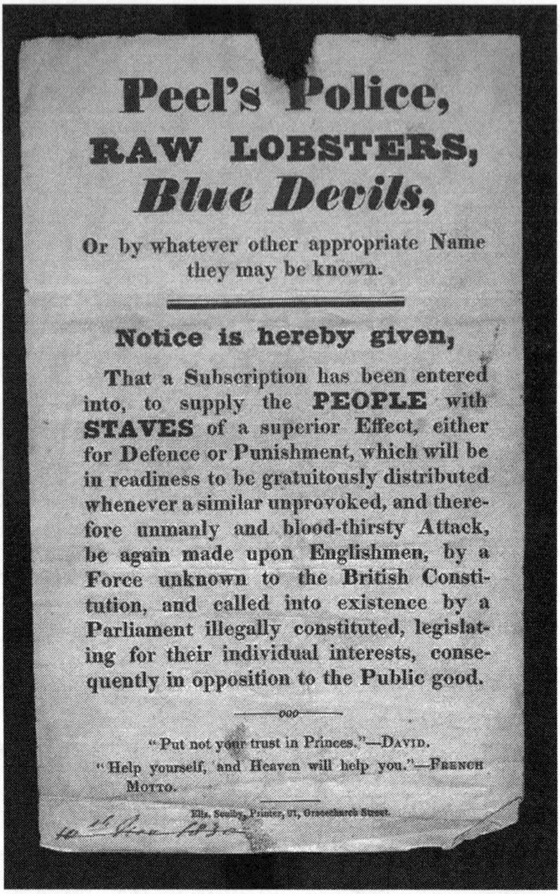

Fig. 8.1 The reference to 'raw lobsters' in this poster refers to the situation that when fresh lobsters are boiled, they turn red. Great care was taken in the design of police uniforms in the formative years of professional policing to avoid using the colour red as this was associated with the military which wore red tunics in this period. This poster sought to convey the impression that although Peel's police were dressed in blue uniforms ('blue devils'), when any form of law and order crisis arose (when a situation 'boiled over'), they would become transformed into soldiers and deploy military-style tactics against civilians. The poster goes further to suggest that it was perfectly justifiable to resist by force of arms any interventions made by police officers (*Source* https://digital.nls.uk/jma/gallery/title.cfm?id=24)

cooperation of the public when performing their tasks. Their guiding philosophy is that of policing by consent (in contrast to the Roman law model's philosophy of policing by coercion).

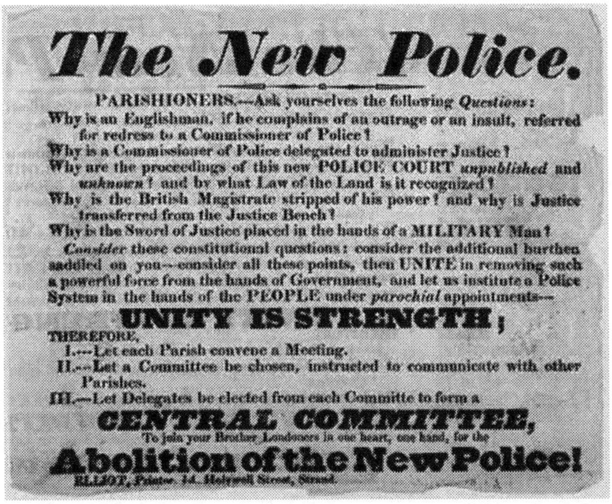

Fig. 8.2 This poster alludes to the loss of power by the Magistracy and parishes in London over Peel's Metropolitan Police Force which, it is argued, was now under the control of a military man (one of the first Commissioners being Colonel Charles Rowan). It calls for the abolition of the Metropolitan Police which was ultimately under the control of central government (the Home Secretary acting as the Police Authority) and the restoration of local (parish) control over policing (*Source* https://www.nationalarchives.gov.uk/education/candp/prevention/g08/g08cs2s3.htm)

Peel's Nine Principles of Policing

In a common law model of policing, consent is the crucial underpinning of legitimacy.

The 1829 Metropolitan Police Act gave the Home Secretary considerable power to develop the constitution of the new police force in accordance with his own beliefs regarding how the Metropolis should be policed (Houghton, 2001: 57). Considerable care was taken to dispel any view of the police as a repressive force under the command of the government.

But most important of all was the need for the police to operate with the consent of the public. Accordingly, 'from its inception in 1829, the essential civilian character of the police was stressed; public service, self-control, and the importance of gaining the public's trust were emphasized' (Lyman, 1964: 153).

The purpose of the police and the manner in which officers should discharge their duties was defined at the inception of the Metropolitan Police in 1829 in the form of 'General Instructions' written either by Peel or the two initial Commissioners of Police in London (Richard Mayne and Colonel

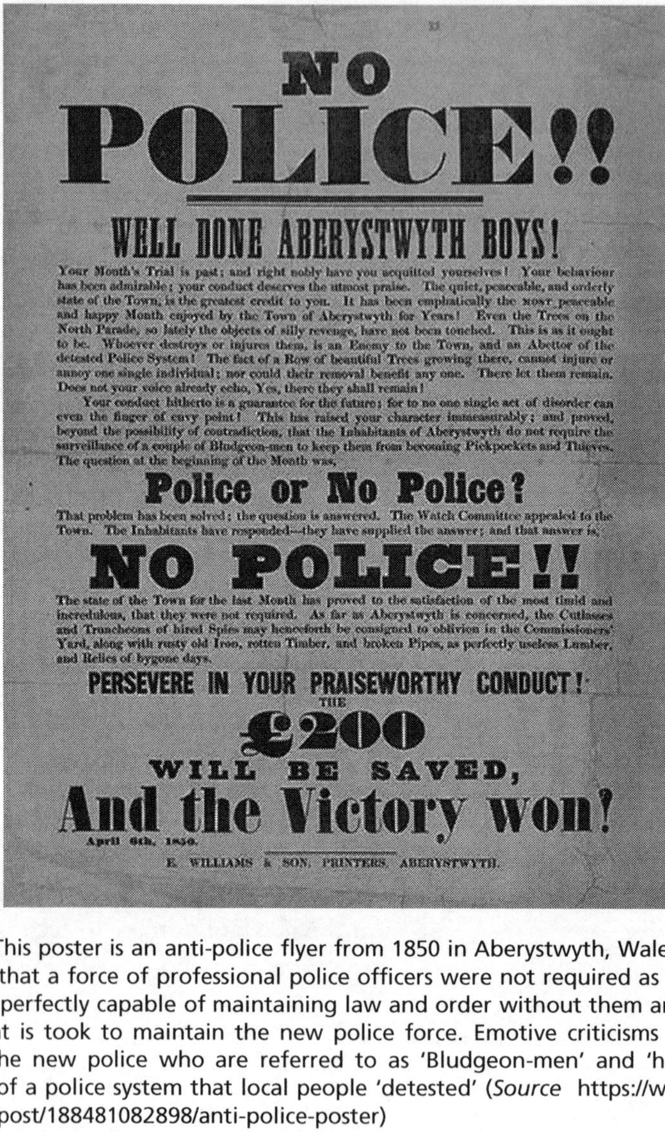

Fig. 8.3 This poster is an anti-police flyer from 1850 in Aberystwyth, Wales. It makes the point that a force of professional police officers were not required as the towns-folk were perfectly capable of maintaining law and order without them and the cost (£200) that is took to maintain the new police force. Emotive criticisms are voiced towards the new police who are referred to as 'Bludgeon-men' and 'hired spies', members of a police system that local people 'detested' (*Source* https://worldhistoryfacts.com/post/188481082898/anti-police-poster)

Charles Rowan). These principles emphasised the importance of the police securing the consent of the public. They were widely adopted outside of London as professional policing was extended in the early decades of the nineteenth century (Emsley, 1986: 80).

Box 8.3: Peel's Nine Principles of Policing

These were as follows:

- To prevent crime and disorder, as an alternative to their repression by military force and severity of legal punishment.
- To recognise always that the power of the police to fulfil their functions and duties is dependent on public approval of their existence, actions and behaviour, and on their ability to secure and maintain public respect.
- To recognise always that to secure and maintain the respect and approval of the public means also securing of the willing cooperation of the public in the task of securing observance of laws.
- To recognise always that the extent to which the cooperation of the public can be secured diminishes proportionately the necessity of the use of physical force and compulsion for achieving police objectives.
- To seek and preserve public favour, not by pandering to public opinion, but by constantly demonstrating absolutely impartial service to law, in complete independence of policy, and without regard to the justice or injustice of the substance of individual laws, by ready offering of individual service and friendship to all members of the public without regard to their wealth or social standing, by ready exercise of courtesy and friendly good humour and by ready offering of individual sacrifice in protecting and preserving life.
- To use physical force only when the exercise of persuasion, advice and warning is found to be insufficient to obtain public cooperation to an extent necessary to secure observance of law or to restore order, and to use only the minimum degree of physical force which is necessary on any particular occasion for achieving a police objective.
- To maintain at all times a relationship with the public that gives reality to the historic tradition that the police are the public and that the public are the police, the police being only members of the public who are paid to give full-time attention to duties which are incumbent on every citizen in the interests of community welfare and existence.
- To recognise always the need for strict adherence to police-executive functions, and to refrain from even seeming to usurp the powers of the judiciary, of avenging individuals or the State, and of authoritatively judging guilt and punishing the guilty.
- To recognise always that the test of police efficiency is the absence of crime and disorder, and not the visible evidence of police action in dealing with them (taken from Reith, 1956: 140).

Theory into Practice—The Underpinnings of Policing by Consent: Creating Trust and Confidence

In order to achieve policing by consent, the professional police forces that emerged during the nineteenth century adopted a number of key measures which served as the pillars on which the principle of policing by consent was constructed. These sought to create public trust and confidence in the police which would ensure consent for their work and ultimately bestow legitimacy on professional policing. The key measures on which policing by consent was based (discussed in Joyce & Laverick, 2021: 14–16) are considered below.

The extent to which these measures succeeded in establishing a more or less universally approved system of policing by consent by the end of the nineteenth century is, however, debatable. This issue is explored in Chapter 10.

Local Organisation, Control and Accountability

As has been argued above, outside London (where the Home Secretary served as the police authority between 1829 and 1999) policing was organised locally and controlled by local people who were initially drawn from the property-owning classes and to whom the police were accountable. Watch Committees in the towns and Magistrates in rural areas exercised considerable authority over policing in its formative years in an attempt to remove fears that the reformed system would act as the agent of the government, trampling roughshod over the rights of the people.

The Preventive Style of Policing

One of the main objectives of policing was to prevent crime and this was performed by the home beat method, whereby police officers patrolled small geographic areas on foot. Their task was essentially passive, based on the belief that their physical presence was sufficient to deter the commission of a crime. They were not encouraged to pursue a more active role within the community since actions regarded as an unnecessary intrusion in people's lives would have had an adverse impact on popular support for the reformed system of policing.

Accordingly, patrol work was central to the preventive functions of the newly formed police forces—'the very idea of patrol as a mechanism of crime prevention was that criminals would be deterred because they never knew whether or not a watchman or later a police officer was approaching, and that there was always one within easy reach should anyone call for assistance' (Dodsworth, 2012: 593). Patrol work of this nature was adopted by other forces as professional policing expanded during the nineteenth century.

The emphasis that was placed on preventive policing was at the expense of detective work, which was given a relatively low profile in early nineteenth-century police forces—

> the detective policeman, wearing plain clothes 'smacked of things French, of the sinister, snooping practices of Napoleon's police minister Joseph Fouché, and this fostered the public's fear of the undercover men among the Bobbies'. (Emsley, 2009: 63)

The Rule of Law and Police Powers

From its outset, the performance of professional police officers in England and Wales was subject to constraints imposed by the rule of law. Police officers were required to use formalised procedures against those who had broken the law, and to apply those procedures without fear or favour to those who had transgressed.

Additionally, at the outset of professional policing, officers were given no special powers with which to discharge their duties. The spectre of police officers equipped with an array of powers that might be used in an arbitrary manner was thought to be inconsistent with the ability of citizens to exercise their civil and political liberties. Accordingly, the police were initially able to exercise only common law powers. This emphasised their image as 'citizens in uniform' (Royal Commission on Police Powers and Procedure, 1929), who were 'paid to give full-time attention to duties which are incumbent on every citizen in the interests of community welfare and existence' (Reith, 1956: 288).

Minimum Force

The desire to dispel the image of the reformed police service as an arbitrary and overbearing force extended beyond the powers given to police officers and affected the weaponry with which they were provided. It was assumed that there was an inverse correlation between the resort to physical force and obtaining the cooperation of the public for the task of policing. As a result, police officers were not routinely armed and merely carried a truncheon which was designed for their personal protection.

The absence of weaponry that could be used in an offensive posture was designed to ensure that when the police were required to intervene to uphold law and order, they would initially rely on 'persuasion, advice and warning' (Reith, 1956: 287) and only if this failed would they use physical force, which should be the minimum that was required to achieve their objective. This concern was also evident in the choice of colour for police uniforms, which were frequently blue or brown but never red, the colour associated with the military.

The Service Role of Policing

Although a reformed policing system that more effectively protected life and property would appeal to all law-abiding persons, the latter role was clearly of most benefit to the wealthy, who owned property that required protecting. Accordingly, in order to 'sell' policing to a wider audience (and in particular to the working classes), its task extended beyond law enforcement. This was the origin of the 'social service function of the police' (Fielding, 1991: 126), in which a diverse range of activities (some of which were designed to tackle the social causes of crime and others which were not crime-related) were pursued by officers in order to befriend the community, resulting in the police providing 'a host of friendly supportive services to people in need' (Reiner, 1994: 13). This role aimed to dispel the image that police work was exclusively concerned with the exercise of coercive authority against the lower social classes.

Recruitment

'Peel felt that retired non-commissioned army officers with good character certificates would be suitable recruits; it was important that the moral character of the police be above suspicion' (Lyman, 1964: 152). This meant that the 'character and conduct of the police was vigilantly supervised'. Between 1829 and 1831, eight thousand men had been enrolled, and over three thousand had been discharged for unfitness, incompetence or drunkenness. (Lyman, 1964: 153).

Initially, police forces deliberately recruited their personnel from persons who 'had not the rank, habits or station of gentlemen' (Peel, 1829, cited in Gash, 1961: 502), save for the most senior ranks of the service who in the formative years of the reformed system were frequently ex-army officers. This situation meant that police work initially had the status of a job, the performance of which required little training.

This policy of recruiting 'fools dressed in blue' (Steedman, 1984: 7) was partly pursued for economic reasons (since working-class recruits could be paid less than members of higher social groups) but was also a means through which members of the working class could be incorporated into the machinery of the newly emerging capitalist state. The tendency for officers below the rank of chief constable to be selected from serving policemen offered the possibility that police work could be an avenue, albeit a very limited one, of social mobility for working-class people.

Working-class recruitment also ensured that police officers would act deferentially to those who were their social superiors and act in accordance with their interests and instructions with a particular objective of providing 'an ordered and supervised system of control'. This was especially directed against the regulation of vagrants (since these were regarded as potential criminals) (Steedman, 1984: 58–59), but also extended towards behaviour such as prostitution and drunkenness since immoral and disorderly behaviour offended the propertied classes who viewed such actions as deviant. It was remarked that the police

> Were placed among the working classes to monitor all phases of working-class life – trade-union activity, drinking, gambling, sports as well as political activity. The overall mission of the police was to place working-class neighbourhoods under a constant and multifaceted surveillance (Storch, 1975: 66).

Monitoring moral behaviour in working-class communities was an important role that sought to secure securing the consent of 'respectable' people to the new system of policing: but performing it cast the police as moral censors. It has been argued that

> police activity in the field of morality is a normal rather than an exceptional occurrence....There have been those who have argued that the survival of the state, of civilized life itself, turns upon the degree and extent of unregulated immorality in a nation's private and public life'....The government, in the name of the state...claims...a monopoly upon what is deemed to be 'right' conduct (Bowden, 1978: 72–73).

Storch stated that

> The implantation of a modern police in the new industrial districts of Northern England resulted from a new consensus among the propertied classes that it was necessary to create a professional bureaucratically organized lever of urban discipline and permanently introduce it into the heart of working-class communities. This was to be accomplished by the creation of a powerful and quite modern device - a bureaucracy of official morality (Storch, 1975: 61).

Additionally, the recruitment of police officers from the working class might also aid the attainment of consent between the police and the lower classes. Police officers who were drawn from the lower end of the social scale might find it easier to relate to fellow members of the working class with whom they came into contact, and to discharge their duties without displaying a sense of class hatred towards them. Similar sentiments underpinned the desire to recruit police officers from minority ethnic communities in the late twentieth century.

Conclusion

This chapter has considered the development of professional policing in London.

In 1834 a Select Committee of the House of Commons investigating the Police of the Metropolis reported that 'an efficient and systematic establishment of police, has been practically attained'. It was reported that violent offences had decreased, the detection of more minor ones had increased—achievements that were 'to be expected from a good system of preventive Police' (House of Commons, 1834, cited in Lyman, 1964: 154).

As has been argued in this chapter, much of the work of professional policing in London was directed at working-class communities, especially seeking to regulate their moral habits. The perceived need of the propertied classes to regulate the working class was an important factor in expanding professional policing across England and Wales and also impacted on the extent to which the ideal of policing by consent was achieved by the end of the nineteenth century (an issue explored in Chapter 10).

This situation had arisen because traditional lines of authority and deference had been ruptured (Storch, 1975: 63) and by the 1830s and 1840s, 'dread of the "dangerous classes" could be transformed into near hysteria at times of great social and political tension' (Storch, 1975: 62). Accordingly, many of the propertied classes were willing to accept the introduction of new agencies of social discipline which a reformed policing system would provide—

> In short, the very fabric of society was thought to be threatened. By this period [the 1840s] popular disorder of any type, even manifestations usually devoid of any overt political content—public-house affrays, dog fights, races, popular fêtes of any type—seemed to constitute a clear and present danger to the social order (Storch, 1975: 62).

The resultant expansion of policing across England and Wales is the topic considered in the next chapter.

? Summary Question

Evaluate the significance of Peel's Nine Principles of Policing on the subsequent development of policing in London in the early decades of the nineteenth century.

References

Benjamin, H. (1931). The Internal Police Administration of England II—The Police Bill of 1785 and Subsequent Reform in the Metropolis to 1829. *The Police Journal, 4*(4), 598–622.

Bowden, T. (1978). *Beyond the Limits of the Law*. Penguin Books.

Brodeur, J.-P. (1983). High Policing and Low Policing: Remarks about the Policing of Political Activities. *Social Problems., 30*(5), 507–520.

Brodeur, J.-P. (2007). High and Low Policing in Post-9/11 Times. *Policing, 1*(1), 25–37.

Chadwick, E. (1829). "Preventive Police". *London Review, 1*(1), pp 252–308, cited in J. Houghton (2001) *Policing and Local Government in England* [Unpublished Ph.D. thesis] Manchester Metropolitan University.

Critchley, T. (1967). *A History of Police in England and Wales*. Constable.

Davey, B. (1983). *Lawless and Immoral: Policing a Country Town 1838–1857*. Leicester University Press.

Dodsworth, F. (2012). "Masculinity as Governance." In D. Barrie & S. Broomhill (Eds.), *A History of Police and Masculinities, 1700–2010*. Routledge.

Emsley, C. (1986). Detection and Prevention: The Old English Police and the New 1750–1900. *Historical Social Research, 37*, 69–88.

Emsley, C. (2009). *The Great British Bobby: A History of British Policing from the 18th Century to the Present*. Quercus.

Emsley, C. (2018). *Crime and Society in England 1750–1900* (5th ed.). Routledge.

Fielding, N. (1991). *The Police and Social Conflict: Rhetoric and Reality*. Athlone Press.

Gash, N. (1961). *Mr. Secretary Peel: The Life of Sir Robert Peel to 1830*. Faber.

Haliday, G. (2017). *Victorian Policing*. Pen and Sword History.

Hart, J. (1955). "Reform of the Borough Police 1835–1856". *English Historical Review, 70*(276), 411–427.

Hawes, B. (1839). Speech in the House of Commons 28 May. *HC Debs, 47*, column 1060–3.

Houghton, J. (2001). *Policing and Local Government in England* [Unpublished Ph.D. thesis] Manchester Metropolitan University.

House of Commons. (1834). "State of the Police of the Metropolis." *Reports from Committees, XVI*, 4, cited in J. Lyman (1964), "The Metropolitan Police Act of 1829". *Journal of Criminal Law and Criminology, 55*(1), 141–154.

Joyce, P. (2012). *Criminology: A Complete Introduction.* Hodder and Stoughton.

Joyce, P., & Laverick, W. (2021). *Policing: Development and Contemporary Practice* (2nd ed.). Sage.

Lyman, J. (1964). "The Metropolitan Police Act of 1829". *Journal of Criminal Law and Criminology, 55*(1), 141–154.

Madelin, L. (1930). *Fouché, 1759–1820, 2*. Librairie Plon, cited in J-P Brodeur, (2007) "High and Low Policing in Post-9/11 Times". *Policing, 1*(1), 25–37.

Manwaring-White, S. (1983). *The Policing Revolution: Police Technology, Democracy and Liberty in Britain.* The Harvester Press.

Montgomery, D. (2019). "The White Terror". thesiecle.com. [Online]. http://thesiecle.com/episode5/. Accessed 7 Jan 2022.

Palmer, S. (1978). Calling out the Troops: The Military, The Law and Public Order in England, 1650–1850. *Journal of the Society for Historical Army Research, 56*(228), 198–214.

Peel, Sir R. (1829). Parliamentary Debates XXI, New Series, 1829, p. 871, cited in Lyman "The Metropolitan Police Act of 1829". *Journal of Criminal Law and Criminology, 55*(1), 141–154.

Peel, Sir R. (1839). Speech in the House of Commons 28 May. *HC Debs, 47*, column 1064–1065.

Ramsay, A. (1928). *Sir Robert Peel*. Constable and Co Ltd.

Reiner, R. (1994). "The Dialetics of Dixon: The Changing Image of the TV Cop". In M. Stephens & S. Becker (Eds.), *Police Force, Police Service*. Macmillan.

Reith, C. (1956). *A New Study of Police History*. Oliver and Boyd.

Royal Commission on Police Powers and Procedure. (1929). *Report of the Royal Commission on Police Powers and Procedure*. Cmd 3297. HMSO.

Russell, Lord J. (1839). Speech in the House of Commons 3 June. *HC Debs, 47*, col 1291.

Schpayer-Makov, M. (2004). "Job Stability and Career Opportunities in the Work-Life History of Policemen in Victorian and Edwardian England". In D. Mitch, J. Brown, & M. van Leeuven (Eds.), *Origins of the Modern Career*. Ashgate.

Steedman, C. (1984). *Policing the Victorian Community: The Formation of English Provincial Forces, 1856–80*. Routledge and Kegan Paul.

Storch, R. (1975). "The Plague of Blue Locusts: Police Reform and Popular Resistance in Northern England 1840–1857". *International Review of Social History, 20*(1), 61–90.

Taylor, D. (1998). *Crime, Policing and Punishment in England, 1750–1914*. Palgrave/Macmillan.

Tobias, J. (1972). *Nineteenth Century Crime: Prevention and Punishment*. David and Charles.

9

The Development of Professional Policing in England and Wales (Outside of London)

Introduction

Progress in developing a professional system of policing in which police officers were paid a wage was slow and hesitant during the early decades of the nineteenth century.

Initiatives that sought to prop up the old system of policing rather than introduce root-and-branch reform met with varying degrees of success. Night watches provided for under Improvement Acts, for example, sometimes offered a relatively effective form of policing (Joyce, 1993: 199–201), some features of which (such as the use of beat patrols) became a subsequent feature of professional police forces when these were introduced, serving to blur the distinction between 'old' and 'new' policing systems. Other reforms were, however, less effective. The 1842 Parish Constables Act, for example, was branded a 'complete failure' (Brown, 1998: 178). Overall, there was no consistency in the way in which policing was delivered throughout England and Wales.

Additionally, public disorder was a concern that served as an inducement to bring about police reform. Problems of this nature were of particular concern to the rural elites and urban manufacturers as their status and economic position required a working class that was obedient and servile in performing waged labour rather than engaging in disorder and rebellion. For them, the need for security would often outweigh the desire to sustain traditional rights and liberties. This served as a spur to the development of

P. Joyce and W. Laverick, *History of Policing, Crime, Disorder, Punishment*, https://doi.org/10.1007/978-3-031-36892-9_9

professional policing and the chapter discusses the pressures of this nature that prompted police reform and the key measures through which it was accomplished culminating with the 1856 County and Borough Police Act.

Pressures for Police Reform

The Imposition of Social Discipline on the Working Class

Arguments derived from Marxist perspectives regarding the role of the criminal justice system suggest that an important imperative to justify the nationwide creation of professional policing related to the need to impose social control over the working class, subjecting them to the discipline of waged labour conducted within the factory system. A key piece of legislation that was designed to achieve this intention was the 1834 Poor Law Amendment Act.

Box 9.1: The 'Old' System of Poor Relief
The pre-1834 system of poor relief was administered by parishes or townships (of which there were more than 14,000 in England) by churchwardens (who were chosen by the Vestry or committee of parishioners) and overseers of the poor who were appointed by the Justices). Parish officials were legally obliged to relieve their poor—

> Under the supervision of the justices, the churchwardens and overseers levied the poor tax, applied for writs of removal, provided relief in the form of cash or gifts in kind, arranged apprenticeships for poor children, and accounted annually for their expenditures (Ely, 1986: 3 and 20).

Accordingly, public assistance measures stressed local responsibility and management by unpaid amateur officials. In the absence of a central governing body, 'the poor laws effectively carved England into thousands of petty jurisdictions' (Ely, 1986: 3). As the system operated, Justices at Quarter Session could issue a warrant to direct a parish to 'receive' a pauper, although the parish could appeal to Quarter Sessions against such a warrant. It was concluded that

> No system as complex as the old poor laws could function long without friction. There were endless possibilities for conflict – between parishes, between overseers and magistrates, and between town overseers and magistrates (Ely, 1986: 17).

The 1834 Poor Law Amendment Act sought to discourage early Victorians from becoming a 'burden' on the local ratepayers. The main provisions of the legislation were designed to prevent persons from receiving money or any other form of aid in relation to poverty unless they entered a work house.

Under the 1834 Act, every parish (or sometimes a group of parishes grouped in what was termed a 'union') had to have such a facility. It was supervised by a Board of Guardians that was elected by the inhabitants of the parish (or union) who would levy a poor rate from the local inhabitants to fund the new arrangements. Central supervision in the form of inspection by a Poor Law Commission appointed by the government was also an important aspect of this 1834 Act. This aimed to ensure that the new law was enforced in a consistent way across the country: local variation in the way in which paupers were treated was viewed as an undesirable feature of the existing (1601) system of poor relief which commonly took the form of outdoor relief although some larger parishes did possess 'poor houses' for the receipt of indoor relief (Ely, 1986: 19).

Conditions inside the new workhouses were made as harsh as possible in order to deter anyone from going there unless they were really desperate. Underpinning the philosophy that inspired the 1834 Act were beliefs that poverty was the product of foolishness and that the failure to engage in lawful forms of employment, and instead to see begging and vagrancy as a kind of alternative career structure, arose from personal choice which workhouses and the conditions associated with them sought to discourage.

The new situation has been summarised as follows:

> Under the new poor law, the workhouse was designed to be 'an uninviting place of wholesome restraint... thus making the parish fund the last resource for the pauper, and rendering the person who administers the relief the hardest task-master and the worst paymaster that the idle and dissolute can apply to'. The classification and separation of paupers, the imposition of strict rules and the overbearing monotony of day-to-day life in the workhouse were central facets of this deterrent policy (Green, 2006: 137).

It was argued that running parallel with this disciplinary system came innovations in workhouse design and construction that served to allocate and separate paupers according to their particular status and form of treatment. 'Inmates were taught to know their place, from the ritual of initial application through to the medical examination that confirmed their status as able bodied or infirm and determined their physical separation in separate spaces inside the workhouse' (Green, 2006: 137).

Opposition to the imposition of the 1834 Act was especially found in the industrial north where the Anti-Poor Law Movement was formed whose key motivation was a belief that the new Act took away the 'right' available to poor labourers for relief in times of economic distress. Some opposition in Northern England was associated with what were termed 'Tory Radicals' such as David Sadler and Richard Oastler who believed this legislation undermined the social bond of paternalism which required the rich to aid the poor in order to maintain the existing structure of a society that was essentially unfair but which could be maintained if the wealthy gave the poor a few crumbs of comfort in times of need or hardship.

The tactics associated with the Anti-Poor Law Movement included attempting to prevent the election of Guardians, intimidating the new Boards so they did not elect clerks and thus no business could be carried out and physically obstructing the poor law officials. Riots against its implementation occurred. Disorders occurred especially in the period 1837–1839 in places that included Huddersfield, Oldham, Dewsbury and Bradford, and on occasions the military, police and Special Constables had to be used to restore order.

The New Poor Law and Police Reform

The 1834 Act was relevant to police reform in two ways.

First, the use of the military to quell regular outbreaks of disorder was undesirable. As Storch (1975: 64) observed

> By 1830 the deficiencies of the army in order keeping were manifest. The inflexibility of the military, its inability to act with anything less than the maximum of force when compelled to intervene, and the consequent and frequent refusal of its commanders to act; but more important its inherent unsuitability to the task of providing the daily protection now demanded made its use increasingly inappropriate except in pressing emergencies.

Thus the disorders associated with the implementation of the 1834 Act were an important factor in supporting either the creation or the extension of professional police forces.

Second, however, it was explicitly argued that the role of a reformed policing system should be to enforce the implementation of the New Poor Law. This view suggested that it was the legitimate task of professional policing to deal with both the causes and the manifestations of behaviour that discouraged or served as a disincentive to persons engaging in lawful forms of productive employment. This provided the grounds for advocating professional policing to implement these two tasks, both of which were put forward by the police reformer, Patrick Colquhoun, whose work is discussed in Chapter 7.

Colquhoun was aware of the impact of adverse social conditions on the causes of criminal behaviour and in particular drew attention to the importance of indigence to the commission of crime. This led him to conclude that one aspect or task of policing was to prevent poverty transcending into indigence which in turn led to the commission of crime. It has thus been argued that he advocated two 'sides' of the police—'whereas the potentially criminal indigent class are to be the main object of the Criminal Police, the class of poverty—the working class—are to be the main object of Municipal Police. The key to prevention is thus not directly preventing crime, but preventing the class of poverty from falling into indigence' (Colquhoun, 1798, cited in Neocleous, 2000: 715). Upholding morality by addressing the factors that might undermine it (such as drinking and gambling) was thus viewed by Colquhoun as a key function of the police, albeit one that would be shared by teachers and the Church. This opinion echoed the views of eighteenth-century Societies for the Reform of Manners which argued that that immorality was a key explanation of crime.

Additionally, for the workhouses to operate as they were intended, a civil force was needed to provide a constant form of opposition to begging and vagrancy. The new Poor Law provided an important incentive to support the universal spread of new policing both in the towns and in the countryside.

Colquhoun argued that the task of policing extended to consolidating 'the existence of a class of wage labour' by closing off 'any access by which the class of poverty might obtain subsistence other than through the sale of its labour' (Colquhoun, 1798, cited in Neocleous, 2000: 724). One aspect of this was to robustly police vagrancy (whereby begging was an alternative to waged labour) which, in turn, would aid the new Poor Law (introduced in 1834) to function more effectively by denying those in need an alternative to the workhouse and in addition to curtail customs and common rights 'such as casual labour for payment in kind, grazing cattle on public byways, pilfering wood, picking fruit or vegetables for either consumption or sale, fishing from rivers without licence, hawking, peddling and street selling', all of which 'became subject to the social police and eventually eliminated' (Carson, 1985: 8, cited in Neocleous, 2000: 723).

It is in this respect that it has been argued that 'Colquhoun's objective was the development of a free market economy and, concomitantly, the commodification of labour' (Neocleous, 2000: 718). It was thus concluded that although he was associated with Jeremy Bentham 'in this context Colquhoun is in fact more Malthusian than Benthamite' (Neocleous, 2000: 715) and that Colquhoun's work 'should be of interest as much to the discipline of social policy as police studies', and that the concept of a 'social police' may be 'a useful way to understand these links' (Neocleous, 2000: 710).

As Storch argued, however, this objective was not lost on the working-class political movements whose leaders feared that professional police forces would be used 'as an agency ... to enforce the New Poor Law' and that 'the police would become the guardians of unfettered capitalist economic development and of a free labour market as defined by orthodox political economy' (Storch, 1975: 69). This thus served as the pretext for opposition to the nationwide spread of professional policing.

The 1835 Municipal Corporations Act

In 1833 a Royal Commission was established to consider the reform of local government—an action that reflected the impulse behind the 1832 Reform Act that it was necessary to ensure that the 'old order' no longer exercised a monopoly of power in urban Britain through the existence of 'close' corporations. While radicals and reformers regarded these as 'strongholds of Anglicanism and toryism' (Finlayson, 1966: 674), Tories (or at least the ultra Tories) viewed them as 'bulwarks of the old order, and re-assuring symbols of its survival against the onslaught of radicalism' (Finlayson, 1966: 675).

The Commission's report detailed corrupt practices and other abuses associated with the unreformed system of municipal administration that consisted of non-elected bodies that exercised 'compulsive powers over the citizens' (S. and B. Webb, 1906: 702–3). The Commission concluded that the existing municipal corporations 'neither possess nor deserve the confidence or respect of your Majesty's subjects' (Municipal Corporations [England and Wales] Report, 1835: 49).

The current state of policing urban areas was also criticised for inefficiency and for failing to maintain public order. Coventry was cited as an example where serious riots and disturbances were frequent in part because 'officers of police, being selected from one political party, are often active in fomenting them' (Municipal Corporations [England and Wales] Report, 1835: 43).

To solve problems of this nature, the Royal Commission recommended that 178 of the existing Royal Boroughs in England and Wales should be given the status of a scheduled town (or chartered Borough) which would be governed by a locally elected council. This provision was provided for in the 1835 Municipal Corporations Act which also provided for the reform of policing in those areas that the Act catered for.

The broader topic of the reform of urban government provided for by the 1835 measure provided the opportunity to accomplish the reform of policing (Hart, 1955: 415). In addition to accusations of inefficiency and corruption levelled against the existing policing arrangements in Royal Boroughs, a further impetus for police reform was a perception at the time that the new Metropolitan Police had driven criminals away from London to urban areas elsewhere (Hart, 1955: 415). This is known as the 'migration thesis', although there is no conclusive evidence that this phenomenon actually occurred (Hart, 1955: 414).

The Act provided for the creation of a committee of the council termed the Watch Committee. In the words used by the legislation (5 & 6 Will 4 c 76), the role of the Watch Committee was to appoint constables who would be responsible for 'preserving the peace by day and by night, and preventing robberies and other felonies, and apprehending offenders against the peace'.

There was no minimum or maximum number set for the number of police officers employed—this was up to local determination (Hart, 1955: 418). The police force was paid for by rates levied on local property owners. The Watch Committee initially exerted a considerable degree of control over local policing arrangements that included hiring and dismissing constables, making regulations for the efficiency of the constables and to direct salaries, wages and allowances to be paid, subject to the overall approval of the Council of the Borough. In order to keep costs down, many of the new Boroughs employed as few constables as they could, paid at low rates of pay that corresponded to the wages of unskilled labourers—decisions that were likely to 'establish forces of indifferent effectiveness' (Houghton, 2001: 72). Matters such as the rank structure of the new forces were left to the determination of the watch committee. Unlike in the Metropolitan Police, the Watch Committees often incorporated persons associated with the 'old' policing system (such as Parish Constables, night watchmen and beadles) into their forces who were of 'doubtful quality' (Houghton, 2001: 72).

Although constables retained their common law powers, they were also required to obey the orders of the Justices, senior members of the police force and the Watch Committee. However, powers such as these could be used inappropriately by the Watch Committee and potentially sowed the seeds of corruption: it was later observed that some Watch Committees interfered with the executive work of the police 'particularly with proceedings against publicans and brewers, and as the liquor interest was often very well represented on the committee, this had a deleterious effect on this aspect of the work of the police' (Hart, 1955: 424).

Unlike the model of police reform that had been provided for by the establishment of the Metropolitan Police in London in 1829, this measure reaffirmed the principle of placing the maintenance of law and order on bodies of local citizens. Nonetheless, this measure did not secure the instant compliance of the towns to which the legislation applied. Only 93 of the Boroughs set up police forces in the two years following the measure (Hart, 1955: 415). However, by the early 1840s, the number of new/professional police forces in the Boroughs had risen to around 140 (Taylor, 1998: 88).

There were several reasons to explain this situation. Hart (1955) raised a number of issues related to the slow progress of police reform in urban England. She refers to matters that include the concern that civil liberties might be undermined by professional police forces, to which could be added concerns that professional policing would be used as an enforcement mechanism regarding the new Poor Law, which was widely unpopular. Additionally, the cost of paying for such forces and the difficulties in securing outside help in setting up police forces and then disseminating good practices between them.

She further discussed issues such as the efficiency (or otherwise) of new urban police forces and argued that those who presented themselves to work as police officers were not always suitable and the small size of many of the police forces (around 250 in number) meant that 'many of them [were] so small that they could not hope to constitute a workable unit'. The lack of central government pressure was a further factor that hindered reform. Following the 1835 measure, there was no central mechanism to inspect and/or audit Boroughs to discover whether they had carried out their legal responsibilities regarding policing. Without this, many simply got away with doing nothing.

The 1839 County Police Act

In 1836, a Royal Commission (composed of Edwin Chadwick, Charles Rowan and Charles Lefevre, Speaker of the House of Commons) was appointed—at Chadwick's instigation—'for the purpose of Inquiring as to the best means of establishing an efficient constabulary force in the counties of England and Wales' (cited in Critchley, 1967: 69). Chadwick was then Secretary of the Poor Law Commissioners and one of his concerns was the suppression disorders that were connected to the administration of relief under the new system (Critchley, 1967: 68).

The commissioners travelled throughout Britain to collect evidence. This was gathered both from 'respectable' persons and also from convicted criminals (Critchley, 1967: 69–70). Information was gathered on issues such as

> The state of crime, the careers of habitual delinquents, the nature of their depredations, the degree of insecurity of travellers on the roads, and the increasing risks opened up in rural areas by the conveyance of valuable cargoes by canal and railway (Critchley, 1967: 69).

The report of the Royal Commission (that was published under the title of First Report of the [Constabulary] Commissioners) argued that the old function of watch and ward had fallen into abeyance 'which is ascribable to the dereliction of the constitutional principle of local responsibility to the supreme executive for the prevention of crime' (First Report of the [Constabulary] Commissioners, 1839: para. 122). Thus the new business middle class could not utilise the hue and cry to combat crime but instead were forced to rely on the Parish Constables who were not deemed fit for the job (Critchley, 1967: 71).

The solution preferred by the Commission was the creation of a nationally administered policing system in the counties. It would be appointed and trained by the Metropolitan Police Commissioners to whom Magistrates at Quarter Session could apply for an allotment of police (to comprise 1 officer for every 2000 of population). The Exchequer would fund one-quarter of the cost and the remainder would be provided by local ratepayers.

The Commission was critical of the one experimental reform of County policing (The 1829 Cheshire Police Act) because it provided for a decentralised form of policing across the County with what amounted to separate constabularies organised at the level of the Hundred (or petty sessional division), each of which was supervised by a paid High Constable who was under the control of local Magistrates.

The Commission further was critical of the role played by the Magistrates in this arrangement, believing that their social status meant they were aloof from knowledge of criminals and in any case could afford to protect their own property without recourse to 'official' policing arrangements. It was also argued that the judicial and executive functions of Magistrates were essentially incompatible and ought not to be fused (Critchley, 1967: 71).

The obvious objection to a centrally directed force was that it would undermine the liberty of individual citizens. It was argued that the defence against this occurrence was that the police would be accountable to the courts and ultimately Parliament when enforcing the law and thus the democratic process would safeguard individual liberties.

The immediate motive for setting up this legislation was disorders associated with Chartism (which were considered in Chapter 8) which prompted the government to temporarily create centrally controlled and financed police forces in Manchester, Birmingham and Bolton, towns which at that time had not received Charters of incorporation under the provisions of the 1835 legislation (Houghton, 2001: 77).

Although many towns possessed professional police forces, their efficiency and geographic control (which initially often did not extend to the suburbs) (both issues discussed in Hart, 1955) meant that rural areas could be prey to rioters who spilt into the countryside from the towns and the only way to defend them would be to use the military. But, as Critchley (1967: 78) argued, the form it took was heavily flavoured by 'political necessities'. The most important concession to county politics was the abandonment of the Commission's desire to set up a centrally organised county constabulary and to sever the control of policing from the Magistrates.

Reform in the shape of the 1839 County Police Act, also referred to as the Rural Constabularies Act or the Rural Police Act (a measure to which Peel gave his support to the Whig government) gave Magistrates at Quarter Sessions the *discretionary* power to establish 'new' police forces throughout the county (or, if desired, particular divisions within the County), paid for out of the rates and controlled by a chief constable whom the Magistrates appointed.

County forces were subject to considerable control by the magistrates, although it was noted that the relationship between Magistrates and police forces was 'not so obviously the master-servant relationship of most boroughs'. One reason for this was that county chief constables were usually 'of more genteel origin that their borough counterparts' (Emsley, 1986: 77) and were often drawn from the military officer class. However, county forces established by this Act were subject to a greater degree of control by the Home Secretary than their urban counterparts so that the Minister was empowered to make rules for the government and pay the constables and to approve the appointment of chief constables. The legislation also stipulated that the police establishment had to consist of one police officer for every 1000 inhabitants (Hart, 1955: 418).

The 1840 County Police Act made provision for the merger of Borough forces with county constabularies under the control of one chief constable and provided that the cost of policing would be borne by a special police rate as opposed to being a charge on the general county rate. Justices at Quarter Session could also resolve to disband the police force if they thought it was no longer required, but this power was never put into practice. The legislation also abolished police forces that had been set up in rural areas under the provisions of the 1833 Lighting and Watching Act.

However, this measure was not widely adopted. By 1841, 24 counties (out of a total of 54, excluding Middlesex and dividing Yorkshire into its three Ridings) (Emsley, 1986: 77) had adopted the measure in whole or in part (that is, covering only selected Hundreds or divisions) but

> The impetus of the Act had been spent by the end of 1841, and from this time onwards a growing body of opinion all over the country was complaining about the cost of rural policing. As a result, during the next fifteen years ... only four more counties adopted the Act (Critchley, 1967: 89).

Accordingly, there were only 1700 professional police officers in rural England in 1842 (Palmer, 1978: 198).

In addition to reasons related to the cost of the new policing arrangements there were other reasons to explain this non-adoption. There was a belief that an increased number of police officers did not necessarily result in a reduction in crime and Magistrates were able to swear in Special Constables to cope with temporary outbreaks of public disorder (Emsley, 1983: 77). Nor, as has been stated above, was public order a sustained problem—it came and went and when the threat was no longer there, the weight of the case for rural police forces diminished. Also, the belief that such would be injurious to liberty remained a potent force against reform, an article in the *Times* Newspaper on 26 July 1836 expressing the opinion that the policing apparatus proposed by the 1839 legislation 'will be very injurious to public and general liberty and the free expression of opinion' (cited in Critchley, 1967: 80).

Voluntary effort (in the form of Voluntary Associations that provided for self-protection and mutual action to apprehending offenders and which comprised of around 500 bodies in 1836) (Critchley, 1967: 72) and the 1842 Parish Constables Act (which is considered in this chapter) were seen in many rural areas as an alternative to the implementation of the 1839 measure.

The 1839 Act was perceived to smack of centralisation, which would entail the loss of the traditional ability of rural elites to retain control over the conduct of their own affairs. Adoption of the measure was also flavoured by political considerations, the Tories being against reform and the Whigs supportive of it.

Special Police Legislation

Disorders associated with Chartism that occurred in Birmingham in 1839 required (as is stated in Chapter 5) aid from the Metropolitan Police Force. Local politics (whereby Birmingham Tories opposed a Charter of incorporation under the provisions of the 1835 Municipal Corporations Act), prevented a professional police force from being established. Joyce (1993: 202) pointed out that under the 1835 legislation, the grant of a Charter was not automatic but required local inhabitants to appeal to the Privy Council in order to obtain it. Although a Charter was granted to Birmingham in 1838, local Tories challenged its validity which meant the newly established Council was unable to levy rates to pay for, among other things, a local police force.

Following the Bull Ring riots (which are considered in Chapter 5), the new Town Council appealed to the Whig government for a loan to establish a police force while the validity of the Charter was heard before the courts. The government, initially supported by the leader of the Tories, Robert Peel, endorsed this course of action but under pressure from Birmingham Tories changed his opinion and instead urged the government to install a government-appointed police commissioner in the city, thus placing Birmingham on a par with London (Critchley, 1967: 82–3), until the issue of the validity of the Charter was resolved. The Whig Home Secretary endorsed this course of action, Critchley speculating that this decision may have been borne out of a compromise whereby Peel would give his support to the County Police Bill then going before Parliament (Critchley, 1967: 83). This course of action was then adopted, to the vociferous objections of the Birmingham Town Council which viewed it as contrary to the principles of local self-government which robbed the people of their liberties (Critchley, 1967: 84).

Similar local political difficulties to those which arose in Birmingham also occurred in both Bolton and Manchester resulting in the passage of three Police Bills that provided police forces in these areas controlled by a government-appointed commissioner and under the direct authority of the Home Secretary (Critchley, 1967: 85; Mather, 1959: 119–27). The rules governing the operations of these three forces were drawn up by the two Metropolitan Police Commissioners.

Box 9.2 considers the background to the enactment of the 1839 Manchester Police Act. The rationale for special legislation affecting Bolton was similar to that of Manchester, it being argued that—'A charter had been granted, the charter was disputed, the rates could not be raised, and an efficient police force could not consequently be maintained' (Melbourne, 1839: column 431).

An additional factor in justifying the enactment of this legislation was the Chartist disturbances in the town in August 1839 that lasted for 3 days and required the intervention of a County Magistrate and police under the control of the borough reeves—although opponents of the measure argued that the problem was inaction by the existing Bolton police arising from the Chartist sympathies harboured by the mayor who had also been appointed as a magistrate by the Whig government (Lyndhurst, 1839: column 429–31). However, the government sought to turn such an argument on its head, arguing that 'if the mayor was not an individual to be trusted, surely this was a reason for appointing another officer to have the management of an independent force' (Melbourne, 1839: column 432).

The Bolton Police Act was enacted in 1839 and the government-appointed Commissioner was Sir Charles Shaw who held a similar role in Manchester. Sir Charles served in Bolton until 1842 when control of the police passed to the Town's Watch Committee (Mansfield, 2019: 135).

Box 9.2: The 1839 Manchester Police Act

The Borough of Manchester comprised six existing townships, all with their own system of government. The campaign to secure a Charter of incorporation was spearheaded by Richard Cobden who authored a pamphlet entitled *Incorporate Your Borough* (1838) which asserted that such a reform would result in expenditure being controlled by gentlemen who had been popularly elected and would prevent the aristocracy and squirearchy from exercising control over the towns of Britain (Cobden, 1838: 9).

Police reform figured prominently in the campaign for incorporation (Joyce, 1993: 202). Under existing arrangements each township possessed its own police force, that of Manchester consisting of a night watch that was controlled by a body of Police Commissioners whose powers derived from the 1792 Manchester and Salford Police Act and a day police that was formally controlled by the feudal institution, the Court Leet presided over by the Steward of the Lord of the Manor which appointed day constables who were controlled by beadles and a deputy constable (Joyce, 1993: 197–8). Other townships that would comprise the Borough of Manchester also had watchmen appointed by local Improvement Acts (Joyce, 1993: 198–9). However, this made for a disjointed system across the area which highway robbers, for example, were able to exploit to their own advantage.

However, incorporation was opposed by local Tories who feared this would result in the townships being forced to sacrifice their independent identities and who suggested that it was possible to provide for a more unified system of policing across the six townships without resorting to a Charter of incorporation.

Accordingly, two petitions were presented to the Privy Council, one opposing incorporation and the other supporting it. The Whig government supported the case for incorporation and granted a Chart of Incorporation in August 1835. But this did not end the dispute as local Tories denied its validity and challenged its legality in the courts. In the meantime, local policing became chaotic: the township of Manchester effectively had two units of local government (the new Borough Council and the old Police Commissioners), both of which issued rate demands. Concerns regarding public disorder associated with Chartism prompted the Whig government into action. Their intervention resulted in the enactment of the Manchester Police Act in August 1839. And in October 1839, the government-appointed Commissioner, Sir Charles Shaw, was appointed to take charge of policing across the Borough.

Although Shaw faced initial problems regarding the hostile attitude adopted towards him personally by local Tories and the underfunding of the police force that he controlled (documented in Joyce, 1993: 205–6), once his force became established, the smaller township authorities declined in significance, serving to legitimise the role of the Borough Council.

Local politics also worked in the reformers' favour. The Tories lost control of the Police Commissions at the end of 1839 which facilitated amalgamating their affairs with those of the Borough Council. The legality of the Charter of Incorporation was affirmed by the case of *Rutter v. Chapman* (1841). The transfer of function from the Manchester Police Commissioners to the Borough Council was agreed at the end of 1842 and accomplished by the 1843 Corporation Transfer Act. In the other townships, the transfer of powers from local bodies to the Borough Council was achieved by deeds of indenture. The Borough Council then assumed control of policing from Sir Charles Shaw on 1 October 1842.

The 1856 County and Borough Police Act

A Select Parliamentary Committee on Police was set up in 1852 to examine the existing situation regarding policing in England and Wales. Evidence was taken from a variety of law enforcement officials but (as Houghton, 2001: 80) pointed out, none was taken from members of Borough Watch Committees.

Although evidence taken suggested that the system of superintending constables created under the 1842 legislation was generally operating satisfactorily (Emsley, 1986: 78–9), the report of the Committee evidenced its acceptance of the 'new' system of policing which it wished to see reinforced. The proposals to do this included making the new system compulsory throughout England and Wales (although Chadwick's attempt to convince the Committee of the desirability of a national policing system was not endorsed). It was recommended that smaller Borough forces should be amalgamated with neighbouring County Constabularies, that the cooperation between forces should be improved upon, that Boroughs and Counties should share a common system of management and that the government should make a financial contribution towards the cost of Policing (Report of the Select Committee on Police, 1853).

The government put forward legislation to implement the proposals of the Select Committee. This reduced the number of Boroughs that were empowered to have their own police forces by over 50% and required the five smallest Counties to amalgamate. Government Inspectors were to be appointed with a remit to regulate policing although no provision was contained in the legislation for central government to make any financial contribution towards the cost of local policing.

Opposition from the Boroughs to the legislation helped to ensure its defeat and a similar fate befell a subsequent attempt to legislate on this matter. A third attempt was made which contained no provisions to abolish the smaller Borough forces. However, this legislation made it compulsory for 'new' (or professional) police forces to be established in all local authority areas, including the counties. Key reasons for this rested on the contemporary concern of the threat of vagrant crime, associated with unemployed soldiers returning from the Crimean War, and the virtual end of transportation which posed the possibility that habitual criminals being released from prison would take to the highways and byways and pose a threat to property.

These issues justified a uniformity in the provision of policing across England and Wales that was lacking under existing arrangements (Steedman, 1984: 26). The fear of vagrancy added to the concern of the rural gentry regarding the disorderly opposition that had been mounted against the implementation of the 1834 Poor Law Amendment Act and encouraged them to accept a reformed policing system (Rawlings, 2008: 125–6).

As an inducement to the degree of compulsion contained in the 1856 measure, central government funding, initially equivalent to one-quarter of the costs of pay and clothing (increased to one-half in 1874), was given to forces certified as efficient by the newly created Inspectorate of Constabulary. Additionally, in most counties, the Petty Sessions divisions (rather than Quarter Sessions) were at the apex of police organisation, thereby retaining the geographic and administrative power of individual magistrates (Steedman, 1984: 47).

There were, however, misgivings, from Boroughs whose police forces were founded upon the 1835 legislation, regarding the desirability of this reform. In Manchester, it was subsequently recorded that they were concerned that

> any power should be obtained by the central authority to interfere with or lessen in any way, directly or indirectly, to control the right of watch committees, subject only to the approval of the Councils, to determine both the numbers and remuneration of the respective police forces in corporate towns (Minutes of the City of Manchester Watch Committee, 1869).

A proposal contained in the Bill that would have given the Home Secretary the power to make regulations for Borough forces as he was able to do for County forces was withdrawn because of opposition from the Boroughs. They accepted the reform on the understanding that the powers of the Home Office were limited whereby efficiency was judged according to the number of officers employed and the discipline of the force (Minutes of the City of Manchester Watch Committee, 1869).

Nonetheless, the 1856 legislation did enhance the degree of central government control over policing. The system of inspection, modelled on systems of inspections used in connection with administering the Factory Acts and Poor Law, became the key mechanism through which central government influence and control was exercised. This issue is explored more fully in Chapter 10.

The 1856 County and Borough Police Act: Summary

The 1856 legislation was significant for ensuring the spread of professional policing across England and Wales, although many of these forces were small in terms of the personnel they employed which thus questioned their efficiency in discharging their duties. However, the legislation did provide the potential for implanting a physical system of social control in each and every neighbourhood. Steedman (1984: 6) argued that as the result of this legislation 'within the space of six months—the winter and early spring of 1856–1857—every community in England became subject to a system of surveillance, some of them for the first time'. It was, as Storch (1975: 76) argued, a development that was not without challenge in the form of anti-police riots in which 'the presence of the police itself' was the key issue of contention. This issue will be further discussed in connection with debates concerning the extent to which policing by consent had been attained by the end of the nineteenth century in Chapter 10.

The Development of Professional Policing in Ireland

The Irish Constabulary

Professional policing was introduced in Ireland under the provisions of the 1822 Irish Constabulary Act. This legislation empowered the Lord Lieutenant to appoint a chief constable to each barony and in turn he appointed a number of constables. County Magistrates retained the power to also appoint constables and sub-constables, but the use of this power was gradually relinquished. The chief constable was required to submit a report to the Lord Lieutenant every three months.

Baronies were grouped into the four provincial areas, and in each the Lord Lieutenant appointed an Inspector General (sometimes referred to as a General Superintendent). The Inspector Generals' role included drawing up general regulations for the police in their area. At first, the full cost of policing was met by the central government, but subsequently county ratepayers met half of the costs.

The style of policing provided by the Irish Constabulary was paramilitary. Constables were armed and housed in barracks and police stations throughout Ireland. The great bulk of constables were from Catholic backgrounds, but the officers tended to be Protestant.

Further reform was provided by the 1836 Irish Constabulary Act. The main effect of this measure was to centralise control over policing. The four provincial areas headed by an Inspector General were replaced by one Inspector General and two deputies, who exercised control throughout Ireland (with the exception of Dublin). A hierarchy was established through the creation of the rank of Head Constable as the highest rank to which those who joined as ordinary constables could aspire. The more senior officers (including chief constables) were usually appointed from outside the force. After 1846 the government fully funded the Irish Constabulary.

Professional policing in Ireland was underpinned by the Roman Law model of policing whose philosophy was that of policing by coercion. Much of the work of the new force was directed at disturbances that were a frequent feature of Irish political life. The role of the Irish Constabulary in dealing with Fenian violence was recognised by Queen Victoria, who renamed the force the *Royal* Irish Constabulary (RIC) in 1867.

Policing in Dublin

Policing in Dublin differed from the system throughout the remainder of Ireland. Dublin became the first area in the United Kingdom to be provided with a 'new' (or professional) policing system. The 1786 Dublin Police Act established the Dublin Metropolitan Police District headed by a High Constable. The Police District was divided into four districts, each headed by a chief constable. A salaried Magistrate was appointed to each of these districts, appointed by the Lord Lieutenant. The police force was armed; officers were paid and were mainly Protestant.

A brief period of local control exerted by the Dublin Corporation over policing was initiated in 1795 but abandoned in 1798 when the four districts were restored. The Lord Lieutenant appointed a Superintendent Magistrate for Dublin and he appointed a High Constable for Dublin and the four chief constables who headed each district. A government-appointed Magistrate (a divisional justice) was also appointed to each of the four districts. The 1808 Dublin Metropolitan Police Act extended the jurisdiction of the force which now operated over six districts.

Subsequent reform replaced the Superintendent Magistrate and Divisional Justices with 18 divisional justices (three per district), 12 of whom were appointed by the Lord Lieutenant and six by the Dublin Corporation. The 1836 Dublin Police Act removed the last vestiges of local control over the force, which was placed in the hands of the Chief Secretary for Ireland, with day-to-day control being vested in the hands of two Magistrates appointed by the Lord Lieutenant.

One of the key roles of the Dublin Metropolitan Police was to control social conduct, and they were frequently accused of doing this in an aggressive manner.

The Ethos of Irish Policing

The Irish policing system was founded on the Roman Law model of policing (which is discussed below). This meant that policing served the interests of the government rather than those of the people. In England and Wales, policing was based on the Common Law model of policing and was designed to act as the servant of the people.

This had important consequences for the philosophy and role of policing in Ireland. Whereas policing in England and Wales was based on the philosophy of policing by consent, in Ireland it was based on the philosophy of policing by coercion.

Several important features reflect this—centralised rather than local control and the carrying of weapons characterised Irish policing. A key concern of Irish policing arrangements was thus to deal with disorder that might threaten the rule of the British state rather than dealing with bread-and-butter issues such as theft and burglary that troubled ordinary people. This role accords with the concept of high policing that will be discussed in Chapter 11, although this chapter has also pointed to the social control function exercised by professional policing in England and Wales.

It was thus concluded that

> The Constabulary of Ireland carried out a full range of policing tasks, but its most important task was that of security, due to the ever-present threat of nationalist insurrection. Due to this it was organised as a colonial constabulary and as an armed, quasi-military force, rather than along the lines of other conventional police forces in the British Isles (Police Service of Northern Ireland, n.d.: [Online]).

For this reason, there was a heavy recruitment of Protestants as opposed to Catholics since the former were loyal to the British Crown and opposed home rule when these demands were made by nationalists (who were identified with Catholicism) during the nineteenth century.

This was further reflected in the manner in which the police were organised. They were housed in barracks across Ireland and were not allowed to serve in the place they (or their wives) came from (Police Service of Northern Ireland, n.d.: [Online]). In England and Wales, the police operated out of police stations which were within the hearts of the communities they policed. But in Ireland, the police were kept physically distanced from the population and the location of barracks across the length and breadth of the country ensured there was an ever-present police presence in each locality whose role included gathering information on episodes that might have disorderly—or even revolutionary—consequences.

The Development of Professional Policing in Scotland

Scottish policing rested on the voluntary principle, the first constables being appointed in 1617. In the cities, the constables were augmented by watchmen to guard the area at night. By the eighteenth century, constables appointed by the Justices performed a range of functions in connection with the maintenance of order and were empowered to summon public aid in order to quell disturbances. Although they were often paid, their tenure in office was of limited duration.

A professional police force was briefly established in Glasgow in 1779, but collapsed because there was no provision for it to be supported by the levying of a local rate (Donnelly & Scott, 2005: 45–6). The 1800 Glasgow Police Act provided for a professional police force for that city, whose underlying ethos was that of crime prevention. It was financed by a rate levied on houses and businesses by the City Council and was under the control of the Lord Provost, three baillies (Magistrates) and nine commissioners who were elected each year from the traders and merchants of the city (Donnelly & Scott, 2005: 47).

Separate Acts of Parliament subsequently established similar policing arrangements for a number of other cities and burghs (the latter being similar in status to an English incorporated Borough). A general power to establish professional police forces in the burghs was provided by the 1833 Burghs and Police (Scotland) Act, which also enabled burghs to adopt powers relating to cleansing, lighting and paving. The Policing of Towns (Scotland) Act 1850 and the General Police and Improvement (Scotland) Act 1862 extended these powers to other urban areas and this resulted in the creation of around 100 burgh police forces.

The 1857 Police (Scotland) Act imposed a compulsory requirement on the commissioners of supply in each county (who performed most of the local government functions in these areas until their replacement by county councils by the 1890 Local Government (Scotland) Act to establish police forces in the counties and also permitted existing burgh forces to be amalgamated with the county force if the Magistrates and town council of the burgh and the commissioners of supply in the county were agreed on this course of action.

These forces were administered by a police committee that consisted of a maximum number of 15 commissioners and the Lord Lieutenant and Sheriff of the county. The commissioners of supply were responsible for levying a 'police assessment' to finance the force and a key role of the police committee was to appoint a chief constable, who was responsible for the day-to-day activities of the force and for appointing and dismissing constables.

Conclusion

This chapter has discussed the rationale for the expansion of professional policing across England and Wales, drawing particular attention to the perceived need to enforce the provisions of the 1834 Poor Law Amendment Act. It has considered the provisions and implementation of the key legislation to secure such reform, namely the 1835 Municipal Corporations Act, the 1839 County Police Act and the 1856 County and Borough Police Act that made professional policing a mandatory requirement across England and Wales. The chapter has also briefly referred to the introduction of professional policing in Ireland and Scotland in the nineteenth century. The following chapter in Part 4 of this book will evaluate issues related to crime, disorder and the state's response in the period between 1850 and c 1920.

? Summary Question

Evaluate the significance of the 1856 County and Borough Police Act to the development of policing in England and Wales.

References

Brown, A. (1998). *Police Governance in England and Wales*. Routledge.

Carson, W. (1985). Policing the Periphery: The Development of Scottish Policing 1795–1900. Part II—Policing and the Production of Social Order. *Australian and New Zealand Journal of Criminology, 18*(1) [Online] https://doi.org/10.1177/000486588501800102. Accessed 7 Oct 2020.

Cobden, R. (1838). *Incorporate Your Borough – A Letter to the Inhabitants of Manchester.* A facsimile copy of this pamphlet is to be found in W. Axon (1907) *Cobden as a Citizen. A Chapter in Manchester History*. T. Fisher Unwin.

Critchley, T. (1967). *A History of Police in England and Wales 900–1966*. Constable and Company.

Donnelly, D., & Scott, K. (eds.) (2005). *Policing Scotland.* Willan Publishing.

Ely, J. (1986). The Eighteenth-Century Poor Laws in the West Riding of Yorkshire. *The American Journal of Legal History, 30*(1), 1–24.

Emsley, C. (1983). *Policing and Its Context 1750–1850*. Macmillan.
Emsley, C. (1986). Detection and Prevention: the Old English Police and the New 1750–1900. *Historical Social Research, 37*, 69–88.
Finlayson, G. (1966). The Politics of Municipal Reform, 1835. *The English Historical Review, 81*(321), 673–692.
Green, D. (2006). Pauper Protests: Power and resistance in Early Nineteenth-century London Workhouses. *Social History, 31*(2), 137–159.
Hart, J. (1955). Reform of the Borough Police 1835–1856. *English Historical Review, 70*(276), 411–427.
Houghton, J. (2001). *Policing and Local Government in England*. Unpublished PhD thesis, Manchester Metropolitan University.
Joyce, P. (1993). The Transition from "Old" to "New" Policing in Early Nineteenth-century Manchester. *Police Journal, LXVI* (2), 197–210.
Lyndhurst, L. J. (1839). Speech in the House of Lords 20 August. HL Debs, Vol. 50, columns 429–31.
Mansfield, N. (2019). *Soldiers as Citizens: Popular Politics and the Nineteenth Century British Military*. Liverpool University Press.
Mather, F. (1959). *Public Order in the Age of the Chartists*. Manchester University Press.
Melbourne, Vt. W. (1839) speech in the House of Lords 20 August. HL Debs, Vol. 50, columns 431 and 432.
Minutes of the City of Manchester Watch Committee. (1869), 23 September. Unpublished.
Municipal Corporations (England and Wales) Report. (1835). *Report of the Royal Commission on Municipal Corporations*. HMSO, House of Commons, Paper 116.
Neocleous, M. (2000). Social Police and the Mechanisms of Prevention. Patrick Colquhoun and the Condition of Poverty. *British Journal of Criminology, 40*, 710–726.
Palmer, S. (1978). Calling out the Troops. The Military, The Law and Public Order in England, 1650–1850. *Journal of the Society for Historical Army Research., 56*(228), 198–214.
Police Service of Northern Ireland. (n.d.). A History of Policing in Ireland. *Police Service of Northern Ireland* [Online]. https://www.psni.police.uk/inside-psni/our-history/a-history-of-policing-in-ireland/. Accessed 18 Jan 2022.
Rawlings, P. (2008). Policing before the Police. In T. Newburn (ed.), *Handbook of Policing* (2nd ed.). Willan Publishing.
Report of the Select Committee on Police. (1853). *Parliamentary Papers* XXXVI (Police), Session 1852–3.
Steedman, C. (1984). *Policing the Victorian Community: The Formation of English Provincial Forces, 1856–80*. Routledge and Kegan Paul.
Storch, R. (1975). The Plague of Blue Locusts: Police Reform and Popular Resistance in Northern England 1840–1857. *International Review of Social History, 20*(1), 61–90.

Taylor, D. (1998). Crime, Policing and Punishment in England, 1750–1914. Palgrave/Macmillan.

Webb, S., & Webb, B. (1906). *English Local Government*, Vol. 1. Longmans Green & CO, re-printed in 1963 by Frank Cass and Co Ltd.

Part IV

Crime and Punishment 1850–1920

10

Issues Affecting Policing 1850–1920

Introduction

This chapter will discuss a range of developments that affected policing 1850–1920. It will evaluate what was it like to be a police officer in the period after 1850 by considering issues such as pay and conditions of work and how these impacted on staff turnover during the latter decades of the nineteenth century.

The chapter will then examine issues that affected the way in which police work was performed. These issues include allegations of corruption and abuse of power and events that resulted in police strikes in 1918 and 1919, the culmination of which was the 1919 Police Act which made it henceforth illegal for police officers to strike. The chapter also considers the small advances that were made regarding the involvement of women in policing in the late nineteenth and early years of the twentieth century.

The chapter discusses the governance of policing and changes that occurred during the late nineteenth century which resulted in the emergence of a tripartite division of responsibilities that involved the Home Office, Chief Constables and local government (in the form of Watch Committees in urban areas and Standing Joint Committees in the counties). The chapter will also analyse the extent to which police-public consent was achieved by the end of the nineteenth century and compare and contrast the different views of orthodox and revisionist police historians on this topic.

P. Joyce and W. Laverick, *History of Policing, Crime, Disorder, Punishment*,
https://doi.org/10.1007/978-3-031-36892-9_10

Policing in the Middle Decades of the Nineteenth Century

This section will especially draw upon the City of Manchester in order to evaluate what life as a police officer was like 1850–1920. Manchester was not, however, an untypical force in relation to issues that are considered in this chapter and references to other police forces will also be made where appropriate.

Recruitment and Retention

Few qualifications were required of police officers in the early years of the City of Manchester's jurisdiction. Initially an age qualification of 40 years and a height qualification of 5′8″ (1.7 metres) was needed to gain entry into the force, qualifications which altered as the century progressed. In 1866, the chief constable of Manchester, Henry Palin, wrote that

> to make a really good and useful police officer a man must possess respectability of character, which has to be ascertained by careful inquiry. He must be strong, healthy and active; tolerably proficient in reading and writing. He ought to have above the average intelligence of a working man, and it is essential that he should have a good temper (Palin, 1866, cited in Joyce, 1991: 141).

Detailed records for the Manchester force exist for the period 1859–1900 that provide details of the background of police officers in the Manchester force. Out of an intake of almost 7500 officers in that period, unskilled workers constituted over 50% of the recruits, the majority of whom described their past employment as 'labourers'. Those who listed skilled or semi-skilled former employments were especially drawn from the textile industry which comprised around 10% of the intake between 1859 and 1900 (Joyce, 1991: 142).

Training in Manchester was limited at the outset. Initially new recruits to the force were employed as 'supernumeraries' who stood in for permanent officers who were unavailable for duty for reasons such as sickness. Supernumeraries would join the force when vacancies occurred. This situation also gave the force the opportunity to assess the suitability of would-be recruits as a supernumerary could be 'struck off' if they were deemed unsuitable for subsequent full-time employment. In 1859, the system of supernumeraries was replaced by 'probationary constables' which operated in a similar manner save that probationary constables were sworn in for the period of their apprenticeship.

What training that was provided initially took the form of drill and it was not until 1864 in Manchester that a training book was issued on which 'a systematic course of instruction and examination' was provided for officers by the end of the nineteenth century (Minutes of the City of Manchester Watch Committee 3 February 1898, cited in Joyce, 1991: 141). This was an important development in which policing moved from the status of a 'job' to that of a 'trade'. It also implied that police officers were able to read to a relatively good standard.

Recruitment and retention proved to be thorny issues in Manchester for much of the century. It was especially governed by economic factors, Chief Constable Palin informing his Watch Committee that

> the police service has few attractions for young men of the class from which its ranks and chiefly recruited. They seldom enter with the intention of remaining, and it is only when the trade of the country is dull that a significant supply can be perceived; whilst, on the other hand, a prosperous season subjects the service to the loss of its most promising hands (Palin, 1861, cited in Joyce, 1991: 143).

This quotation suggests that retention was a problem for the Manchester force and it was not solely confined to Manchester. Poor discipline of those recruited was an issue in the early decades of professional policing elsewhere. In Liverpool, it was stated that

> in 1838, 73 officers resigned, and 101 dismissed. Some of those dismissed were for offences of drunk on duty (25), for being the worse for liquor and being in public houses when on duty (19), for being asleep on their beats (3), for being absent from their beats and neglect of duty (15), for being the worse for drink when off duty (3) and 23 for other offences (Hellier, 2023: [Online]).

Additionally,

> 60 officers were fined or reduced in rank for being drunk on duty, 396 for being in a public house or being the worse for drink whilst on duty, 550 for being absent from beats and 107 for being asleep on duty (Hellier, 2023: [Online]).

The following year, however, it was reported that matters had 'progressively improved' as in that year only 639 cases of drunkenness and 1592 other disciplinary offences had been recorded in a police force whose strength amounted to 574 men (Hellier, 2023: [Online]).

Rapid staff turnover was an important issue later in the century, even when the main cause was resignation rather than dismissal. In the Manchester force, the first decade (1859–1868) for which detailed records survive indicate that the establishment figure for the force rose from 594 officers to 748. In this period, 2930 men joined: 1051 of these (35.9%) did not proceed beyond the grade of probationer constable and 540 (18.4%) served in the police force for less than one month. Those who served over 20 years numbered a mere 141 officers (4.8% of the total intake in this decade). Here, resignation was the main reason for the rapid staff turnover—between 1859 and 1868, 80% of entrants resigned whereas only 12% were dismissed: in the entire period 1859–1900 dismissals were 15% of the intake figure.

Retention was a problem for forces outside of Manchester. In Liverpool it was stated that below 10% of constables served two years in the job. The situation was so serious in the mid-nineteenth century that in 1857, interviews for entry were held every week, on a Thursday (Hellier, 2023: [Online]).

Retention had a serious impact of police force efficiency. Manchester Chief Constable Palin bemoaned this situation when he stated that

> when it is remembered that it takes at least twelve months to make a constable tolerably efficient, and two or three years before he can become thoroughly acquainted with the important duties of his situation, it will be admitted that so large a percentage of young hands must have a very injurious effect on the character and efficiency of the force (Palin, 1861, cited in Joyce, 1991: 142).

In addition to the impact of slumps and booms on recruitment (in which a trade slump would encourage those out of work to join the police, only to re-join their former employment when a trade boom reappeared), other factors also contributed to this situation. One of these was pay.

The perceived need by Watch Committees to exercise strict economy in order to reduce the financial demands imposed on local ratepayers had a detrimental impact on the number of officers employed and the pay they were given. In Manchester, initially (in 1842) a constable earned 17 shillings a week, which did not rise for ten years although in 1845 a small merit bonus of one shilling a week was paid to the well behaved and more intelligent and efficient members of the force. What amounted to a strike secured a pay increase of two shillings a week in 1853 and differential pay scales were introduced in 1860 whereby pay reflected length of service.

Another issue affecting retention was promotion.

Although it was Watch Committee policy in Manchester to fill vacancies in all but the most senior posts from the ranks of its own men, promotion (which carried with it higher wages and status) was a rare occurrence, further suggesting that for most entrants, policing was not an avenue of social mobility: as Chief Constable Palin admitted

> the number of prizes by way of promotion is comparatively small … and vacancies are of such a rare occurrence that a constable may have to wait for years without having the opportunity of being advanced to a superior grade (Palin, 1865: cited in Joyce, 1991: 144).

Accordingly, many suitable men became disillusioned, and left the force.

The conditions of employment were also not conducive to retention. The shifts worked by officers in Liverpool were dubbed 'heavy and oppressive' —

> A police officer would parade for Night duty at 8.45 pm and continued on duty until either 5 am or 6 am as the season may be: The next night he paraded again at 8.45 pm and again worked as before: He then paraded again at 3 pm and worked until 9 pm, the next day he paraded at 6 am and worked until 10 am. He then re-paraded at 8.45 pm that night and his shift pattern started all over again (Hellier, 2023: [Online]).

A further factor that explains the high turnover of staff was the nature of the job. A constable was expected to perform a wide range of functions which in mid-nineteenth century Liverpool included

> Ensuring that pubs closed on time: removal of street obstructions: ensuring that cellar grids are secure: no chimneys set on fire to save the cost of a sweep: visiting lodging houses: ensuring that no excavations were left without protection or proper signal of danger (ropes and lamps): reporting of water leaks: ensuring street lighting was lit and in good order: anything such as defective flagging on pavements likely to cause an accident had to be reported: ensuring no cruelty to animals particularly working horses: ensuring that maids etc. cleaning windows did not sit outside the windows and ensuring that 'no dogs run at large in the month when, according to the old popular superstition, the canine race are more likely than at any other period to go mad.' Police officers had to take into care lost children, assist at fires, suppress vagrancy whilst at the same time ensuring none died from destitution, ensuring prompt medical attention was received at any accident (Hellier, 2023: [Online]).

Manchester Chief Constable Palin further explained that there was

> a tedium and monotony inseparable from the life of a policeman from which other employments are exempt. It is absolutely necessary that he should be reported for any irregularity or infringement of the regulations … He is at the beck and call of everybody, and his temper is frequently tried by the remarks passed on him by the lower orders of the people (Palin, 1861, cited in Joyce, 1991: 145).

It might thus be concluded that poor pay coupled to lack of bargaining power to do much about it, the physical (often confrontational) nature of the job, the dull and monotonous nature of 'pounding the beat' (which was the backbone of police work in those days) and restrictions on social life all served to make policing unattractive as a long-term career in the early-middle decades of the nineteenth century.

Emsley reinforced arguments of this nature that affected forces other than those cited in this section. He stated that the size of the beats walked by constables could be large—in London in 1870, the average day-time beat was 7 miles and 2 miles at night while in rural areas the beat often covered a larger geographic area (Emsley, 1986: 81). Severe restrictions were placed on a policeman's social life—in rural forces, his wife was forbidden to keep a cow, in urban forces his wife was not allowed to run a shop and police officers were denied the right to vote until 1887 (Emsley, 1986: 83).

A final issue that influenced day-to-day conditions related to physical opposition that police officers faced in this middle decades—and beyond—of the nineteenth century. Storch's study of police reform and popular resistance in northern England, 1840–1857 examines anti-police sentiment in detail, arguing that in this period 'the police came as unwelcome spectators into the very nexus of urban neighbourhood life' (Storch, 1975: 84). This often led to violent confrontations between police and public in the form of anti-police riots or physical attacks on individual or small groups of officers. Although it was argued that the nature of violence directed against the police in working-class communities altered in character after the 1850s, assuming a more restricted shape and pursuing objectives that were more limited than early violence that aimed to drive the police out of such communities, violence against the police did remain, for example, to protect members of the community that the police sought to arrest (Storch, 1975: 89–90).

Joyce's study of the City of Manchester revealed that in 1890, a petition to the Watch Committee stated that police officers were exposed to dangers 'by day and by night' and that they were

> Harassed and often assaulted by members of the classes with which he has to deal (Minutes of the City of Manchester Watch Committee, 18 September 1890, cited in Joyce, 1991: 150).

The Chief Constable subsequently submitted to the Watch Committee a list of 26 officers who had been on the Force Sick List between January and September 1890 because of injuries received while on duty which equated to the loss of 403 days (Minutes of the City of Manchester Watch Committee, cited in Joyce, 1991: 150).

It might thus be concluded that resistance to the presence of the police in urban communities was a factor that continued to exert influence over the recruitment and retention of police officers late into the nineteenth century. This issue suggests that policing by consent was not universal by the end of the nineteenth century: this issue will be further considered in more detail later in this chapter.

Changes to Police Governance in the Nineteenth and Early Twentieth Century

Late Nineteenth-Century Legislation

Chapters 8 and 9 discuss the legislation that was concerned with the creation of professional police forces across England and Wales in the early decades of the nineteenth century, culminating in the 1856 County and Borough Police Act which required professional policing to expand throughout England and Wales.

The subsequent development of policing was affected by two Acts enacted in the latter decades of the nineteenth century.

The 1877 Municipal Corporations (New Charters) Act provided that newly incorporated boroughs could only have their own police forces if they had a population in excess of 20,000. However, progress in securing the objective of this legislation which was to reduce the number of police forces through the process of consolidation was slow (Houghton, 2001: 87) since it did not apply to existing Boroughs (Critchley, 1967: 130). Accordingly, a subsequent measure, the 1888 Local Government Act, abolished police forces in towns with populations below 10,000 which resulted in the reduction of Borough forces to the figure of 127 (Houghton, 2001: 87). However, the number rose to 197 in 1900 arising from the incorporation of new boroughs (Critchley, 1967: 133).

Additionally, the 1888 Local Government Act amended the governance arrangements for rural forces. The Act created elected County Councils and provided that control over county police forces would be discharged by a Standing Joint Committee consisting of 50% elected councillors and 50% Magistrates, the latter elected from the County Quarter Sessions (Jefferson & Grimshaw, 1984: 34). An amendment made in the House of Lords inserted the requirement that police officers were required to obey the awful orders of the Magistrates. The Standing Joint Committee was independent from the County Council but received the police budget from the County Council thus providing for an element of local accountability.

The Role of Central Government

As was argued in Chapter 9, the 1856 County and Borough Police Act expanded the role of the state by introducing an element of central government involvement in policing. In return for being required to set up professional police forces, localities of over 5000 people were provided with a central government contribution towards the cost of policing (initially one-quarter of the costs of pay and clothing) provided that the force was deemed to being conducted in an efficient manner. The device whereby this requirement was measured was the newly formed Inspectorate of Constabulary.

There were initially three Inspectors whose role was to visit each police force in England and Wales and provide a certificate to certify efficiency if this was demonstrated.

The certificate would then authorise the payment of the government grant which was raised to one-half of the costs of pay and clothing in 1874. An Act of 1890 altered the conditions under which the Exchequer grant was paid to police forces by including the tests of management and efficiency alongside the existing criteria of numbers and discipline (Jefferson & Grimshaw, 1984: 35).

Although it was suggested in the Preface that inspection when applied to the operations of the private sector did not always succeed in effectively translating the wishes of the central state into positive actions, when applied to a public sector organisation such as policing which was in part dependent on public money, it possessed the potential to considerably influence key actions. It was thus argued that inspection provided the Home Office with a considerable degree of clout over the administration of local police forces which could be reinforced by Home Office officials who

> were most eloquent on the bureaucratic organisation of forces. They would rule and direct on matters of pay and clothing, on the physical provision for police effectiveness—the number of lock-ups and police stations a police authority needed .... The Home Office was not at all a remote authority (Steedman, 1984: 28).

Neither was the Home Office unwilling to use the sanction of denying the grant to a Watch Committee whose police force, in its eyes, was not conducted efficiently. In 1880, for example, the Inspectorate declined—initially—to pay the City of Manchester its grant on the grounds that the expansion of the city had resulted in some areas being under-policed in terms of the number of officers which worked within them. The Watch Committee viewed this action as 'sudden and wholly unexpected' and forced them to take remedial measures which included rearranging the deployment of officers and considering whether an increase in overall police numbers was also required (Minutes of the City of Manchester Watch Committee, 1880a). The grant for that year was paid, but in order to assert the authority of the Treasury, a deduction was made because the Watch Committee had raised the salary of a Superintendent without the Home Secretary's approval (Minutes of the City of Manchester Watch Committee, 1880b).

The payment of the central government grant also imposed severe administrative burdens on Watch Committees. The requirement to submit detailed accounts to the Treasury in order to establish their accuracy in fulfilling the conditions established in the 1856 legislation regarding eligibility for claiming the grant was articulated by the City of Manchester, whose Watch Committee expressed concern regarding the inconvenience and annoyance arising from the Treasury's audit of all of the accounts relating to its police force. It argued that this procedure produced the impression

> that the discretion absolutely vested in the Watch Committee was being unjustifiably interfered with or called into question by those acting on behalf of the Treasury (Minutes of the City of Manchester Watch Committee, 1869).

The role of the Home Office to influence how local police forces operated was also exerted by the mechanism of Home Office Circulars which provided instructions, for example, as to how legislation was required to be implemented. These were important instruments for extending the control that the Home Office exerted over policing in London to the remainder of England and Wales.

This led to the conclusion that

> As the 1880s approached, more and more central legislation came to define local police forces as agencies of central government without any mediation by Magistrates or Watch Committees. Local police forces became, in administrative terms, an agency of central government (Steedman, 1984: 8).

The Role of Chief Constables

The inspection process provided chief constables with the ability to exert additional influence over the administration of local police affairs. As Critchley (1967: 126) noted, the reports submitted by the Inspectors to the Home Office could act as a spur to the reform of individual forces which provided enterprising chief constables with the means to secure their own ends.

There were also attempts made in the later decades of the nineteenth century for chief constables to meet together, posing the possibility of chief officers being more assertive in their conduct of police affairs and perhaps, ultimately, bringing to bear a common voice on police-related issues or, as Critchley (1967: 126) stated, 'a developing sense of common purpose'. In 1858 the County Chief Constables' Club was formed. The 'essentially small and fragmented state of borough forces' (Jefferson & Grimshaw, 1984: 37) stymied a similar development of chief constable power in urban areas in England and Wales until 1896 when the Chief Constables' Association of England and Wales was formed to represent the chief officers of urban forces.

Although such bodies did little more than facilitate social contact between members in the nineteenth century (Joyce & Wain, 2010: 184), they formed the basis of organisation which could develop into a more formidable body to influence police affairs and policing policy overall. This development occurred in 1948 when the two existing Chief Constables' organisations merged to form the Association of Chief Police Officers (ACPO) (which was replaced by the National Police Chiefs' Council in 2015).

Both of these developments posed the potential for altering the balance of power between chief constables and the authorities that administered policing. This was especially so because there was no exact demarcation of responsibilities between these two parties.

Chief Constables and Watch Committees

During the nineteenth century, occasional disputes occurred between urban police authorities (Watch Committees) and chief constables regarding which had the power to determine police policies. This problem was not apparent in rural areas. Critchley (1967: 124) described a county chief constable as 'an autocrat over whom the justices had no power other than the ultimate sanction of dismissal' who fulfilled many of the functions discharged by Watch Committees in Boroughs. This situation resulted in the

> independence of county chief constables in matters of law enforcement—independence which is regarded as a consequence of the tendency of justices and the standing joint committees to allow chief constables to run their forces in the ways they wished and of the powers of chief constables with respect to the appointment, discipline and dismissal of their constables (Jefferson & Grimshaw, 1984: 45).

However, in urban areas, the situation was different. Critchley (1967: 125–6) observed that up until around 1860 'the control of the Watch Committee was absolute' and that this could lead to abuses, especially in smaller towns: 'where the interests of publicans and brewers predominated, a watch committee would insist that no proceedings be taken against a 'licensee' without their express authority' and, 'mischievous' town councils could exert 'improper pressure on its police' and use them 'to support groups of local tradespeople, sectional interests or political parties'.

Jefferson and Grimshaw (1984: 39–46) referred to case studies that illustrated friction between chief constables and Watch Committees later in the nineteenth century. These occurred in Birmingham (1880), Liverpool (1890) (and also Nottingham [1958] which is outside the scope of this book) and asserted that these reflected the ambiguity of the relationship between these two actors in determining police policy in urban areas. The resolution of such disputes, they argue, was determined by 'the political will of the rival authorities' (Jefferson & Grimshaw, 1984: 44), which was characterised by features that included the assertiveness and willingness to compromise by the key actors.

Subsequently, the principle of constabulary independence (or police autonomy) was put forward as a solution to friction between police authorities and chief officers.

Box 10.1: Constabulary Independence

Constabulary independence refers to the concept that police officers should be immune from external control (in particular external political control) in respect of their law enforcement responsibilities.

> This concept is based upon the common law derivation of the office [of constable] whose holders are required to uphold the law using the powers granted to them by law. It follows from this that constables exercise 'original' jurisdiction derived from the office and in performing their duties are accountable only to the law which defines their powers. Legal accountability and constabulary independence are thus closely related doctrines (Joyce & Wain, 2010: 32).

However, this was not a concept used during the nineteenth century to solve disputes of this nature, Marshall (1965: 21) noting that before 1900 there was no justification for an argument that 'equates the position of constables with independence of action and freedom of control'.

The principle of constabulary independence developed during the nineteenth century to define the relationship between police constables and police authorities. It was fully enunciated in the case of *Fisher v Oldham* [1930] in which the

> centrepiece of the judge's ruling was that in executing the office of constable according to law the decisions of a police officer could not be overruled by the watch committee, and moreover that such interference would be illegal (Jefferson & Grimshaw, 1984: 52).

However, it would also be inaccurate to depict the existence of a confrontational relationship between watch committees and chief constables in the latter decades of the nineteenth century as characteristic of the way in which police affairs were conducted. The enhanced responsibilities placed on policing in that period often meant that Watch Committees could not exercise direct supervision over the day-to-day conduct of police affairs and were willing—as was the case in rural areas—to let chief constables get on with the job.

In conclusion, it can be safely asserted that by the early decades of the twentieth century, there were three key parties which had a degree of involvement in exercising responsibility for the conduct of police affairs—the Home Office, Police Authorities (either Watch Committees in the towns or Standing Joint Committees in the counties) and Chief Constables. Thus the tripartite system of police governance was a reality by the early years of the twentieth century.

However, there was a considerable grey area regarding the relationship between these key actors which was frequently shaped by local custom and practice or power relationships determined by politics (defined as 'the behaviour of individuals within a group context') (Joyce, 2020: 1). Ultimately, the 1964 Police Act, which formalised the tripartite division of responsibility for police affairs, aimed to provide for a system of control and accountability which would define the relationships between these three bodies.

Key Issues Affecting Policing in the Late Nineteenth and Early Twentieth Century

Corrupt Behaviour in Policing

It has been observed that 'corruption and suspect behaviour was often a part of the popular image of the policeman, particularly among the working class' (Emsley, 2009: 9). Perceptions of police brutality could occasion outbreaks of violence directed at the police (Storch, 1975: 72).

Periodic accusations of police misconduct and of corrupt behaviour by police officers began to be made in the latter decades of the nineteenth century. These highlighted instances of unethical behaviour on the part of the police which in the contemporary period would be catered for in the Police Code of Ethics. The Code's Standards for professional behaviour highlight the need for officers to act with honesty and integrity, to treat members of the public with respect and courtesy, to behave in a manner that does not bring discredit on or undermine public confidence in policing and to challenge and report improper behaviour and to challenge or take action against the conduct of colleagues which has fallen below the standards of professional behaviour (College of Policing, 2014: 4).

There was, however, no detailed Code in the period 1850–1920 although, as Chapter 8 has argued, Peel's 3rd Principle of Policing emphasised the need for the police to secure and maintain the respect and approval of the public, and the 7th Principle enjoined officers 'to maintain at all times a relationship with the public that gives reality to the historic tradition that the police are the public and that the public are the police' (Peel, 1829, cited in Reith, 1956: 140).

In the Metropolitan Police Force area, S14 of the 1839 Metropolitan Police Act criminalised police misconduct, but this procedure fell into disuse during the nineteenth century (Smith, 2020, Vol. 1: 29). By mid-century, it was argued that criminal prosecution services offered by the police to the public did not fully extend to cases where the suspected offender was a police officer, one consequence of this being that 98.5% of prosecutions for the unlawful use of violence by Metropolitan Police officers were brought as private prosecutions (Smith, 2020, Vol. 1: 42). It was alleged that the standard police managerial response to allegations of police malpractice in London was 'individual error'—a response whereby police managers limited the risk of further scrutiny into police practices by asserting that having discovered the problem, they dealt with it and there was thus no need to investigate the matter any further (Johansen, 2011: 65).

In London, public concerns regarding the investigation of complaints of police misconduct resulted in the formation of The Police and Public Vigilance Society in 1903 (Smith, 2020, Vol. 1: 65). Subsequent allegations of widespread corruption in the Met led to the appointment of a Royal Commission into the Duties of the Metropolitan Police. Its report in 1908 revealed many dubious or overtly illegal practices and also highlighted the inadequacy of the police complaints mechanisms. However, the overall conclusion was that the problem was not institutional but was caused by the actions of a few individual constables (Johansen, 2011: 63).

Box 10.2: Police Misconduct and Corruption

Examples include the following:

Robert Moore, Birkenhead, 1877

As recounted by Watson (2022: [Online]), on 26 May, three young girls were stopped by a police officer, Robert Moore, near Birkenhead Docks for alleged trespass. He told them to accompany him across a field. They refused but he grabbed hold of one of the girls, forced her into a hut that he used for shelter while on duty and proceeded to rape her. However, he was interrupted by her parents whom Moore assaulted.

In an attempt to get away, the girl's father, James Henderson, fell onto iron rails, hit his head and never recovered consciousness, dying on 6 June 1877. Although witnesses contended that Moore was drunk, a fellow officer, PC Alfred Brown, claimed that Henderson had pulled a knife which resulted in the fracas.

A trial took place at Cheshire Assizes in 1872 and Moore was found guilty of manslaughter for which he received a sentence of 20 years penal servitude. The trial judge further urged the Chief Constable to inquire into the conduct of PC Brown since it appeared he had fabricated his evidence regarding a knife in Henderson's possession to protect Moore.

The Turf Fraud Scandal (1877)

In 1877, four senior detectives were charged with perverting the course of justice in connection with the Turf Fraud scandal (or the Madame de Goncourt case). This related to two persons, Harry Benson and William Kerr, swindling gamblers out of large sums of money in relation to horse race betting. One of the victims was a Madame de Goncourt who had been swindled out of a sum of £10,000.

The scandal entailed individuals being provided with a tip as to which horse would win a race. These individuals then sent the winnings to the tipster who was meant to reimburse them. However, the cheques that the tipster sent, bounced.

An investigation revealed that Kerr had bribed Inspector John Meiklejohn, Chief Inspector Nathaniel Druscovich and Chief Inspector William Palmer for information regarding the police investigations into these frauds and in particular to warn them if any arrests were anticipated. A fourth officer, Chief Inspector George Clarke, also became associated with this episode of police corrupt behaviour.

All four police officers along with Benson, Kurr and a solicitor named Edward Froggatt were tried at the Old Bailey in October 1877, charged with unlawfully conspiring to obstruct, defeat and pervert the course of justice. At the trial it emerged that Meiklejohn had been taking payments from a range of bookmakers and swindlers over the course of many years (Emsley, 2009: 166).

Meiklejohn, Druscovich and Palmer received prison sentences of two years although Clarke was acquitted. A subsequent Departmental Commission set up by the Home Secretary resulted in the Metropolitan Police detective branch being reorganised into the Criminal Investigation Department in 1878.

The William Bannister Scandal (1890s)

A scandal occurred in Manchester in the 1890s when, against the chief constable's advice, one William Bannister was promoted to Superintendent. He was a man who

> was connected with brothels and brothel keepers, and used his powers as superintendent to facilitate their operations, and to transfer to the more respectable and remote parts of the district those officers who showed an inconvenient activity (Dugdale, 1897: 4).

This situation highlighted the possibility of police corrupt behaviour being abetted by members of the Watch Committee, it being argued in relation to this case that 'the belief, well or ill-founded, that their superior officer has powerful friends on the Watch Committee' acted as a deterrent to honest police officers to report their concerns to the police authority (Dugdale, 1897: 8).

This episode led an inquiry to argue that situations of this nature could be avoided if the system used in County constabularies were adopted in Borough forces whereby promotions were in the hands of the chief constable since the origin of the problem relating to Superintendent Bannister lay in his appointment against the advice of the chief constable (Dugdale, 1897: 19).

Police Industrial Action

As the nineteenth century wore on, many of those who joined police forces viewed policing as a long-term career as opposed to a short-term measure to provide work when trade was depressed. Scholars endorsed this view by arguing that

> by the late nineteenth century there had been a fundamental change. Turnover rates were much lower and attitudes towards policing had changed. Instead of being viewed simply as a stop-gap measure, or as a short term stepping-stone to a better job, policing was increasingly seen as a job in its own right. There was a growing body of disciplined men who had made a career of policing (Taylor, 1998: 88–89).

A further explanation for this was the statutory right to a pension that was granted in 1890 meaning that policing provided an element of economic security. Prior to 1890, officers were required to pay into local force superannuation funds but received only a small one-off payment (a gratuity) when they retired.

When other members of the working class had a gripe about pay and conditions, they had the option to withdraw their labour—to undertake strike action which was likely to be organised by the trade union to which the workers belonged. However, the police did not have this option. Striking was illegal.

Sporadic outbreaks of dissent by police officers occurred in the latter decades of the nineteenth century usually over pay and conditions. In Liverpool, for example, it was stated that even before the strains imposed on policing by the war there had already been manifested 'the beginning of an articulated and ongoing demand for a union organisation to act as a vehicle form the rectification of felt grievances' (Bean, 1980: 636).

Such sentiments ultimately led the creation of a union (secret and unlawful) called the Metropolitan Police Union which was formed in 1913 (and renamed the National Union of Police and Prison Officers [NUPPO] in 1916). This organisation called a strike on 29 August 1918 which was fairly solid in London with an estimated 12,000 of the force's 18,000 members walking out. This action led Prime Minister Lloyd George to remark that 'this country was nearer to Bolshevism that day than at any time since' (Rosenberg, 1994: 22).

The context within which this strike occurred was important to the government's thinking. Not only was the country still at war with Germany (the First World War ending in November 1918) but a key to the success of the Russian (Bolshevik) Revolution in 1917 had been the defection of state personnel such as police officers who sided with the revolutionaries against the government of the Tsar, Nicholas II. In a time of industrial militancy in the United Kingdom, the government did not want the police to side with fellow members of the working class since this could have revolutionary consequences in the United Kingdom (Jones, 2007: [Online]).

In the wake of an inquiry headed by Lord Desborough in 1919, the government enacted the 1919 Police Act which gave effect to his recommendations. Police pay was both increased and also standardised along with conditions of employment across the country (having previously been subject to local variation). Although the government had initially tolerated NUPPO, the 1919 Police Act reiterated the ban on police officers joining a trade union. Instead, the legislation provided official machinery to represent the interests of all officers up to the rank of chief inspector and to act as a channel through which grievances could be articulated. This was known as the Police Federation which remains today as an influential voice within policing.

A subsequent police strike against the 1919 Police Act mainly affected London and Liverpool. It was estimated that about 10% of officers in London went on strike, joined by about half the force in Liverpool and Birkenhead and ¾ of the Bootle force (Bean, 1980: 633) which was put down forcibly. It was argued that a prime motive of this was for the survival of the NUPPO (Bean, 1980: 645) but was treated by the authorities 'not so much as a labour dispute but rather as an abdication by the police of their allegiance to the state and a challenge to publicly constituted authority' (Bean, 1980: 644). In Liverpool, all strikers were dismissed with total loss of pension rights and 2000 Special Constables were enrolled to maintain law and order in the city (Bean, 1980: 645).

It was observed that by 1924, constables on maximum pay earned around 55–60% more than average male workers in industry and this situation persisted for around the next 15 years. Other benefits included improved leave provisions, and a universal rent allowance. Additionally, high levels of unemployment in policing made police work attractive—in Liverpool in 1926, it was reported that 8000 men had applied for below 200 vacancies in the force (Bean, 1980: 648). Police recruitment also reflected a desire to ensure the allegiance of the police service to the state: in Liverpool many of those who were dismissed for their involvement in the 1919 strike were replaced by former military men (including those who had held officer rank). Such recruits 'were felt to be especially suitable for a disciplined organisation since they were already socialized into the paramilitary mentality of obedience' (Bean, 1980: 648).

Women and Policing

Throughout the nineteenth century, policing was considered 'man's work'. This situation reflected the ideology of the Separate Spheres whereby

> Women were considered physically weaker yet morally superior to men, which meant that they were best suited to the domestic sphere. Not only was it their job to counterbalance the moral taint of the public sphere in which their husbands laboured all day, they were also preparing the next generation to carry on this way of life (Hughes, 2014: [Online]).

Levine (1994: 34–78) stated that the use of plain clothes male police to track women suspected of prostitution under the controversial Contagious Diseases Acts between the mid-1860s and the mid-1880s convinced many activists that a female presence in the intimidating institutions of law enforcement would ensure fairer and more equitable treatment for women. In keeping with a common strand of separatist feminism at this time, the social purity movement also argued that it was more appropriate for women to minister to other women in this capacity. It was in this context that the National Vigilance Association (NVA) urged the government and police authorities in London to engage female officers for the care of female prisoners in the late 1880s.

By 1893, most major towns in England, Scotland and Wales employed a small number of women matrons, warders and searchers in police stations, cells and courthouses. Yet success was limited. The first such appointee in Britain was the lone female visitor authorised in May 1883 by the Metropolitan Police to visit female convicts on licence and women under Police supervision. In 1888, fourteen women were employed by the

Metropolitan Police to superintend female prisoners at the Metropolitan Police Courts.

In the early twentieth century, women became involved in policing through a number of voluntary organisations. These organisations initially comprised the Women Volunteer Police (WVP)—or Women's Police Volunteers—and the Women Police Service (WPS) (Joyce & Laverick, 2020: [Online]).

The Voluntary Women Patrols—which were affiliated to the National Union of Women Workers (NUWW, later becoming the National Council for Women)—were created under Mrs Louise Creighton and set up in 1914 in London. They subsequently operated nationwide and became the largest patrol movement in Britain.

They constituted non-waged and non-uniformed volunteer patrols and tended to be socially privileged and often well educated. In contrast to other more militant feminist movements of this period, these patrols were largely concerned with restraining the behaviour of women and girls, a concern that was prompted by concerns regarding illegitimacy and immorality, prostitution and disease. This accorded to the function that Storch attributed to the police (that of inculcating social and moral discipline on the working class) (Storch, 1975: 63) but also enforcing what would later be described within feminist criminologies as 'double deviance' which suggested that women offenders were judged in accordance with the severity of the offence they had committed and also by the extent to which they have deviated from conformity to stereotypical female roles. The combination of rule breaking and role breaking resulted in harsher treatment (Carlen, 1983; Heidensohn, 1985).

The main concern of the WPS was welfare issues. WPS duties included helping and protecting children, befriending young women, responding to child labour, drunkenness and troops suffering from shell shock, in addition to assisting battered women and protecting girls from what was termed the 'brutal and licentious soldiery'. However, women who undertook such work experienced resistance and hostility from both within the service and externally. They experienced opposition to their presence in court, to their giving evidence, wearing a uniform and acting as witnesses in charges of indecency. However, in 1915, Edith Smith of the WPS was sworn in and given powers of arrest, becoming the first official policewoman in the British Isles (Joyce & Laverick, 2020: [Online]).

Formation of the Women Police

Female inclusion in policing in the sense of women being officially incorporated into police forces rather than operating alongside them was facilitated by the passing of the 1916 Police, Factories & c (Miscellaneous Provisions) Act, which authorised the Home Office contribution towards the costs of policing to include the pay of any women who were employed full time to perform the duties of the police.

In 1918, Major Stanley Clarke, Chief Constable of Gloucestershire, recruited two women who were sworn in under the Special Constables Act of 1831 (legislation that referred to persons as opposed to men, thereby circumventing an earlier barrier to the recruitment of women). His actions paved the way to appoint women as full members of the regular force.

Following the police strike on 31 August 1918 and the appointment of General Sir Nevil Macready as Metropolitan Police Commissioner, a force of women was created for London. On 23 December, Macready issued a Police Order officially inaugurating the Metropolitan Women Police Patrols. Accordingly, on 17 February 1919, the first 25 women patrols left Peel House Training establishment for duty, under the leadership of Woman Superintendent Mrs Sophia Stanley. Many of Macready's recruits were drawn from the ranks of the Voluntary Women Patrols.

The new Metropolitan Women Police Patrols were neither sworn in, nor were they given the power of arrest and if allowed on patrol they did so in pairs and were accompanied by male constables. Their duties were characterised by a gender-specific specialisation of tasks, focusing predominantly upon prostitution, indecency and the protection of women and girls.

However, the motives of Macready in forming his own Women Police Patrols were not designed to promote the cause of female police officers. Rather, his intentions were to side-line the activities of the WPS, towards whom he adopted an aggressive stance by prosecuting the organisation's leadership for impersonating police officers (Joyce & Laverick, 2020: [Online]).

Policing by Consent

Chapter 8 considered the way in which the principle of policing by consent was designed to be translated into action. The chapter examined how it was constructed and pointed to its importance in ensuring the legitimacy of policing in civil society.

But establishing methods on which policing by consent was constructed (the 'pillars' that were referred to) does not necessarily mean that it succeeded in actually creating public consent. This issue is examined here—the extent to which was policing by consent became a reality by the end of the nineteenth/beginning of the twentieth centuries—an issue about which there is considerable debate.

Orthodox Police Historians

There are two broad schools of thought regarding the extent to which consent had been achieved by the police by the end of the twentieth century—the orthodox and revisionists perspectives. Each will be considered in turn.

Academics dubbed 'orthodox' police historians include Charles Reith (whose key works include *British Police and the Democratic Idea* [1943] and *A New Study of Police History* [1956]) and Thomas Critchley (who wrote *A History of Police in England and Wales* [revised edition, 1978]).

The view of orthodox police historians was that after some initial opposition in the 1830s, the success of the police had secured the consent of most sections of society (Critchley, 1964: 55–6; Reith, 1943: 3) by the end of the nineteenth/early twentieth century. Reith argues that this was because of several factors in the way in which the police operated—he refers to issues such as impartiality (the 'complete independence of government policy and Party or class politics' [Reith, 1943: 208]), the use of minimum force and what Reith refers to as 'un-stinted personal service and sacrifice' (Reith, 1943: 207–8). These factors served to produce a high level of cooperation between the police and public which in turn produced 'a new and hitherto-unimagined standard of public order' which led people to realise 'the personal and communal benefits which could be derived' from policing (Reith, 1943: 208). Reith uses the measure of police-public cooperation as the yardstick by which to assess the level of consent.

Revisionist Police Historians

Orthodox historians argued that consent had been largely achieved by the end of the nineteenth century. But not all police historians agree that consent was largely achieved by the end of the century. A different point of view is put forward by what are described as 'revisionist' police historians.

Revisionists emphasised that the motive for police reform was 'the maintenance of order required by the capitalist class' (Reiner, 1985: 25), whose control over policing (exercised by local urban elites through the mechanism of the Watch Committee) enabled them to ensure that the attention of the police was directed at all criminal and deviant actions that threatened to undermine it, namely 'crime, riot, political dissidence and public morality' (Reiner, 1985: 25).

The intention of professional policing was therefore not to serve the interests of all members of society impartially but, rather, to regulate the habits of the working classes in order to serve the interests of industrial capitalism (Storch, 1976).

This meant that the role of the police extended beyond combating crime to that of seeking to curb deviancy. The term 'deviancy' includes behaviour that is socially disapproved of but is not necessarily criminal. It may, however, pose a threat to the existing social order and for this reason is often viewed as dangerous to those whose position and status depend on maintaining the social status quo. This view reflects the political function served by law enforcement (Sheptycki, 2000).

For such reasons, working-class consent was not readily accorded to the police who resented their intrusions into the lives and everyday leisure pursuits of the working class—all phases of working-class life were monitored (Storch, 1975: 66). Storch also points out that working-class communities tended to view the police as 'unproductive parasites' (Storch, 1975: 71) in the sense they were paid from the public purse even though they were not engaged in productive labour.

This led to a conclusion that consent towards the police was not universal but that it was heavily determined by a person's position on the social ladder. It was thus asserted that

> The "public" (meaning the middle and upper classes) ... held their "bobby" in patronising "affection and esteem", which he repaid with due respectfulness, but these sentiments were never shared by the undermass, nor in fact by the working class generally (Roberts, 1971: 76–7).

In addition to resentment towards the intrusions of the police into working-class life, there were additional reasons why consent may not have been universally accorded to the police. These included police corruption and malpractice (which has been considered above) as explanations of mistrust by the working class towards the police, coupled with a complaints process that was unlikely to offer any effective solution to the problem. To this might be added

> the long-standing system of wheeling and dealing between police and underworld that had its own unwritten rules and at which command officers had no choice but to connive. Blind eyes were turned, favours exacted and reciprocated, informers employed, bribes exchanged and some brutality was standard practice (Brown, 2011: [Online]).

This was not a situation to provide for trust and confidence and policing and contributed towards a feeling of hostility towards the police by the working class who felt impotent in the face of police misbehaviour that was often directed towards them.

The level of consent was greatest from propertyowners whereas those at the lower end of the social hierarchy granted tolerance to the police which was, at best, 'passive acquiescence, broken by frequent outbreaks of conflict throughout the nineteenth century' (Brogden, 1982: 202–28). Scholarship such as that by Archer's study of Liverpool also suggests that policing was largely unpopular with the nineteenth-century working class in that city although open hostility reduced to an extent during the 1890s (Archer, 2011).

However, it has been argued that it is hard to generalise concerning police-public relations in the latter decades of the nineteenth century since encounters between the police and public were variable—sometimes good, sometimes bad. Emsley (1986: 85) argued that members of the working class were able to call on the police when victims of crime such as theft in the same way that middle-class persons did. The claim has also been made that much of the opposition was directed at specific aspects of police-public encounters (the nature of the encounter and/or dislike of specific officers) as opposed to being fuelled by a more general anti-police sentiment. This means that, however, grudging, policing by consent was 'a reality' in the late nineteenth century (Taylor, 1997: 137–8). A further view suggests that

> It would be wrong to conceive of the relationship between the working class and the police in the second half of the 19th century as entirely one of mutual hostility. Many members of the working class also sought respectability and desired orderliness and decorum. It is probable that … the appearance of the police on the streets increasingly led members of the working class to believe that they too had the right to freedom from the annoyance of crime and public disorder (Emsley, 1996: 80).

One local study suggested that there was a generally improved relationship between police and public in the early years of the twentieth century which could be mainly explained by social changes which occurred after the First

World War (Cohen, 1979, quoted in Fitzgerald et al., 1981: 119). Subsequent developments such as the greater level of workingclass affluence after the Second World War helped to create a society that was more socially integrated. These changes gave rise to 'the golden age of policing' that was 'marked by popular respect and obedience for authority' (Fielding, 1991: 36) and was characterised by the television programme *Dixon of Dock Green* which exemplified the virtues of home beat policing.

Police Property

In the above section, the word 'respectability' was used. 'Respectability' refers to a situation in which by the late nineteenth century, workers who were skilled and in regular employment tended to look down on those members of the working class who were unskilled and/or unemployed: an important aspect of this respectability was that hard work and employment meant male workers could look after their families. Additionally, violence that was frequently associated with the working class and excessive alcohol consumption were viewed as the very opposite of behaviour associated with respectability (Taylor, 1998: 82).

Thus the working class was not a unified body but contained divisions which had importance for police-working-class relationships.

The concept of police property (Lee, 1981) has been applied to social groups possessing few or no rights in society and thus were not in a position to formally object to their treatment by the police. The elites who controlled nineteenth-century policing were willing to give the police a relatively free hand to control the behaviour of lower social orders (which in nineteenth century Liverpool constituted 'participants in the street economy' (Brogden, 1982: 232), thereby considerably enhancing the level of discretion exercised by police officers in both a supervisory and an on-the-streets role.

These people were effectively 'owned' by the police who could do what they wanted to them. Firm action undertaken by the police towards these socially marginalised groups helped secure consent towards professional policing by the other members of society, including the 'respectable' working class. However, those on the receiving end would resent their treatment by the police, hence the absence of universal consent to the police and occasional episodes of resistance to their work and to their presence in the communities.

Conclusion

This chapter has considered a number of issues that relate to the development of policing in the wake of the 1856 County and Borough Police Act which has been considered in Chapter 9. In particular it has considered the conditions of work that affected recruitment and retention of staff into police forces in the period after c 1850 and has also discussed issues that include police abuse of power and corruption that impact on the consent that the police secured in this period. The chapter has evaluated changes affecting police governance which led to the emergence of a de facto tripartite system of police governance by the end of the nineteenth century and has also discussed the debate concerning the extent to which policing by consent was attained by the end of the nineteenth century. The following chapter will discuss the nature of crime in the period 1850–1920 and the way in which the criminal justice system responded to it.

? Summary Question

To what extent had the principle of policing by consent been achieved by the early decades of the twentieth century?

References

Archer, J. E. (2011). *The Monster Evil: Policing and Violence in Victorian Liverpool*. Liverpool University Press.

Bean, R. (1980). Police Unrest, Unionization and the 1919 Strike in Liverpool. *Journal of Contemporary History, 15*(4), 633–653.

Brogden, M. (1982). The Police: Autonomy and Consent. Academic Press.

Brown, R. (2011). "*Being a Policeman*". *Richardjohnbr.* [Online] https://richardjohnbr.blogspot.com/2011/04/being-policeman.html?m=0. Accessed 25 January 2022.

Carlen, P. (1983). *Women's Imprisonment*. Routledge & Kegan Paul.

Cohen, P. (1979). Capitalism and the Rule of Law. In*National Deviancy Conference/Conference of Socialist Economists*, London: Hutchinson, quoted in M. Fitzgerald, G. McLennan and J. Pawson. (1981). *Crime and Society: Readings in History and Theory*. Routledge.

College of Policing. (2014). *Code of Ethics A Code of Practice for the Principles and Standards of Professional Behaviour for the Policing Profession of England and Wales*. College of Policing Ltd.

Critchley, T. (1967). *A History of Police in England and Wales*. Constable.

Dugdale, J. (1897). *City of Manchester. Police Inquiry. A Report to the Secretary of State, Home Department.* Unpublished, contained in Minutes of the City of Manchester Watch Committee, 22 July 1897.

Emsley, C. (1986). Detection and Prevention: The Old English Police and the New 1750–1900. *Historical Social Research, 37*, 69–88.

Emsley, C. (1996). *The English Police. A Political and Social History* (2nd ed.). Routledge.

Emsley, C. (2009). *The Great British Bobby. A History of British Policing from the 18th Century to the Present*. Quercus.

Fielding, N. (1991). *The Police and Social Conflict: Rhetoric and Reality*. Athlone Press.

Heidensohn, F. (1985). *Women and Crime*. Macmillan.

Hellier, J. (2023). "Policing Nineteenth Century Liverpool". *Liverpool City Police*. [Online] https://www.liverpoolcitypolice.co.uk/articles/19th-century-policing/. Accessed 19 January 2022.

Houghton, J. (2001). *Policing and Local Government in England*. Unpublished PhD thesis, Manchester Metropolitan University.

Hughes, K. (2014). "Gender Roles in the Nineteenth Century". *British Library*. [Online] https://www.bl.uk/romantics-and-victorians/articles/gender-roles-in-the-19th-century. Accessed 15 January 2023.

Jefferson, T., & Grimshaw, R. (1984). *Controlling the Constable: Police Accountability in England and Wales*. Cobden Trust.

Johansen, A. (2011). Keeping Up Appearances: Police Rhetoric, Public Trust and 'Police Scandal' in London and Berlin 1880–1914. *Crime, History and Societies, 15*(1), 59–83.

Jones, O. (2007). "The 'Spirit of Petrograd' ? The 1918 and 1919 Police Strikes". *Whatnextjournal*. [Online] http://www.whatnextjournal.org.uk/Pages/Latest/Police.html. Accessed 25 January 2022.

Joyce, P. (1991). Recruitment Patterns and Conditions of Work in a Nineteenth Century Urban Police Force: A Case Study of Manchester 1842–1900. *Police Journal, LXIV*(2), 140–150.

Joyce, P. (2020). *Politics. A Complete Introduction*. John Murray Press.

Joyce, P., & Laverick, W. (2020). "Celebrating A Century: The Baird Report and 100 Years of Women in Policing". *Policing Insight*, 3 October. [Online] https://policinginsight.com/features/analysis/celebrating-a-century-the-baird-report-and-100-years-of-women-in-policing/. Accessed 25 January 2022.

Joyce, P., & Wain, N. (2010). *A Dictionary of Criminal Justice*. Routledge.

Lee, J. (1981). Some Structural Aspects of Police Deviance in Relation to Minority Groups. In C. Shearing (Ed.), *Organisational Police Deviance.* Butterworths.

Levine, P. (1994). "Walking the Streets in a Way No Decent Woman Should": Women Police in World War I. *The Journal of Modern History, 66*(1), 34–78.

Marshall, G. (1965). *Police and Governance*. Methuen.

Minutes of the City of Manchester Watch Committee. (1869). 23 September. Unpublished.
Minutes of the City of Manchester Watch Committee. (1880a). 18 March. Unpublished.
Minutes of the City of Manchester Watch Committee (1880b). 25 March. Unpublished.
Reiner, R. (1985). *The Politics of the Police*. Wheatsheaf Books.
Reith, C. (1943). Preventive Principle of Policing. *Journal of Law and Criminology, 34*(3), 206–209.
Reith, C. (1956). *A New Study of Police History*. Oliver and Boyd.
Roberts, R. (1971). *The Classic Slum. Salford Life in the First Quarter of the Century*. Manchester University Press.
Rosenberg, C. (1994). Revolution in the Air. *Socialist Review, September*(178), 21–22.
Sheptycki, J. (Ed.). (2000). *Issues in Transnational Policing*. Routledge.
Smith, G. (2020). *On the Wrong Side of the Law. Complaints Against the Metropolitan Police 1829–1964*, Vol. 1. Palgrave/Macmillan, Critical Policing Studies.
Steedman, C. (1984). *Policing the Victorian Community. The Formation of English Provincial Police Forces, 1856–1880*. Routledge and Kegan Paul.
Storch, R. (1975). The Plague of Blue Locusts: Police Reform and Popular Resistance in Northern England 1840–1857. *International Review of Social History, 20*(1), 61–90.
Storch, R. (1976). The Policeman as Domestic Missionary. *Journal of Social History, 4*, 481–509.
Taylor, D. (1997). *The New Police in Nineteenth-Century England: Crime, Conflict and Control*. Manchester University Press.
Taylor, D. (1998). *Crime, Policing and Punishment in England, 1750–1914*. Palgrave/Macmillan.
Watson, C. (2022). "The Dark Side of Victorian Policing". *Legal History Miscellany*. [Online] https://legalhistorymiscellany.com/2022/03/31/the-dark-side-of-victorian-policing/#_ftn21. Accessed 3 December 2022.

11

Policing Politically Motivated Activities 1850–1920

Introduction

This chapter focuses on political activities that posed a threats to public disorder, some of which further challenged the legitimacy of the central state. Initially the chapter will consider a number of key examples of activities of this nature, examining the background to these events and the way in which the state responded to them, particularly the circumstances in which the military was used in civilian affairs.

In the middle decades of the nineteenth century, the issues considered include the Murphy riots (1866–1871) and agitation in connection with the 1867 Reform Act (the 1866 Hyde Park Riot).

The chapter will also consider the political background that affected the conduct of working-class politics in the late nineteenth and early decades of the twentieth century. This period saw the rise of socialist societies (that ultimately resulted in the creation of the Labour Party) and also of militant trade unionism that was characterised by the 'new unions' (comprised of unskilled workers) and whose actions were inspired by the philosophy of syndicalism.

Accordingly, this period witnessed episodes of public disorder (such as Black Monday in 1886 and Bloody Sunday in 1887) and a number of industrial disputes (such as the 1889 London Dock Strike) which served as preludes to a wide range of industrial unrest (such as the South Wales Miners' dispute 1910–1911, the 1911 Transport workers' strike and the 1912 National Coal strike) in the early years of the twentieth century.

P. Joyce and W. Laverick, *History of Policing, Crime, Disorder, Punishment*,
https://doi.org/10.1007/978-3-031-36892-9_11

The chapter will also consider other forms of political action conducted outside of Parliament (including the suffragette campaign for the right of women to vote).

Ireland was part of the United Kingdom in this period and the chapter will analyse the nature and response to politically motivated violence that was associated with the cause of Irish independence as well as revolutionary violence that included the 1916 Easter Rising and the Irish war of Independence 1919–1921.

Within the context of a discussion of 'high policing', this chapter will illustrate how the role of the state (via the police service and a range of related agencies that included MI5 and MI6) expanded into the policing of political ideas and opinions rather than focusing solely on crime and disorder.

Disorders in the Middle Decades of the Nineteenth Century

Severe outbreaks of public disorder occurred after 1850. The following section will consider two of these events in relation to what issues they were concerned with and how the state responded to them.

The Murphy Riots (1866–1871)

The Murphy riots owed their name to an anti-Catholic agitator, William Murphy, who provoked 25 riots (or anticipated riots) from 1866 to 1871, mainly in urban areas. These riots which often followed a lecture delivered by Murphy usually occurred in the open streets and 'drew on violently felt community antagonisms that were not created by, but were used by, Murphy' (Steedman, 1984: 34). They resulted in violent attacks being made on Catholic people and communities and their property. Most property that was damaged, however, belonged to that of the 'poorer classes' and the public buildings that were attacked were usually churches (Steedman, 1984: 37).

These events occurred between 1866 and 1871, reaching a peak in the Summer and autumn of 1868 (Steedman, 1984: 33–34). Troops were summoned to deal with these disturbances on 10 occasions (Fielding, 1991: 58), although they were not necessarily deployed (Steedman, 1984: 34). Police from outside the affected area were called upon on 11 occasions, the Volunteers were used twice and the militia and yeomanry were used each on one occasion in conjunction with the military. Special Constables were enrolled on 11 occasions, primarily in defence of their own property.

Fourteen riots were handled by local police forces without other forms of assistance. The Riot Act was read on several occasions but only once (at Blackburn in 1868) was this a prelude to the deployment of troops to disperse the crowd. On other occasions when it was read, force was used by bodies that included the local police, the country constabulary or Special Constables (Steedman, 1984: 37).

Steedman (1984: 37) drew attention to the differing philosophies governing the operations of borough and county police forces. Fielding (1991: 58) explained that this translated into a situation whereby public order policing was an accustomed role for county forces but this was not so in the Boroughs where defence of property from theft and related offences was—under the direction of Watch Committees—of prime importance.

Police public order tactics to prevent disorder during the Murphy riots included isolating and then arresting persons (in particular ringleaders) possessing weaponry that could be used to instigate rioting and keeping the streets clear (Steedman, 1984: 35). Baton charges were also used to disperse crowds or to isolate members it contained and on some occasions the police were issued with cutlasses. Cordoning off property that was likely to be attacked was also used as a tactic of riot control and it was noted that while no police operation had the capacity to quell the kind of disturbance that Murphy brought about, 'by acting in a body, by providing a well-disciplined human wall around a lecture theatre or a church under threat, a police force could avert an attack'. However, 'once a disturbance had moved from the vicinity of a building, or a well-defined, enclosed space (a square, an Irish ghetto, a cul-de-sac) the police were generally powerless' (Steedman, 1984: 35).

Steedman (1984: 36) observed that the disorders were usually ended only when Murphy left the town and thus one further tactic used by local authorities was to prevent Murphy from lecturing or even being able to visit their locality (Steedman, 1984: 37).

The 1866 Hyde Park Riot

By the mid-1800s, Hyde Park and Trafalgar Square were the only two large open spaces in central London and were periodically used for public meetings which sometimes became disorderly. An early example of this occurred on 24 June 1855 when a crowd of initially around 50,000 people (swelling to over 200,000) (Harrison, 1965: 223) gathered in the park to express opposition to Lord Grosvenor's Sunday Trading Bill which would have prohibited all buying and selling in London on a Sunday (with the exception of meat and fish sold before 9 a.m. and newspapers and cooked food sold before 10.00 a.m. (Harrison, 1965: 221). A further disorder occurred in Hyde Park in 1867.

The 1867 Representation of the People Act provided for the enfranchisement of many members of the male working class, increasing the electorate by 938,427 (Herrick, 1934: 220), thus raising the number of adult males who could vote from around 1 million to 2 million. The legislation also abolished the practice of compounding so that all male householders who paid rates in person were eligible to vote. Graduates, professionals and persons with over £50 in savings were given additional votes—inclusions that became known as the 'fancy franchises'. The county franchise was slightly expanded to include an increased number of renters which meant that around three-quarters of the total number of new voters resided in the Boroughs (Herrick, 1934: 220).

The measure was introduced by a Conservative government, headed by Lord Derby and in which Benjamin Disraeli played a leading role as Chancellor of the Exchequer. It followed an attempt by Gladstone's Liberal government to introduce a modest measure of reform that would have given the vote to 'respectable' working men (while excluding unskilled labourers and the poor). A split in the Liberal Party (in which the anti-reform Adullamites, around 40 MPs in number, led by Robert Lowe) led to the measure's defeat and the government's downfall.

However, although the Conservatives opposed the Liberal reform measure, they went on to introduce their own legislation in the belief that this would aid their Party's electoral fortunes. It was also put forward because the mood of the country seemed to favour electoral reform, whose cause had been advanced by the Reform League (which cooperated with the middle-class and moderate Reform League) and which used mass public meetings and demonstrations to put their case for an enhanced level of male suffrage across. This led to the conclusion that the measure did not emanate from one source but was the product of several impulses—

> public opinion as stirred up partly by economic conditions and social conditions, partly by the Reform League, partly by John Bright, partly by trade unions (Park, 1920: 133–134).

And that, 'one section of the House was merely trying to outbid, for popular favor, the other' (Park, 1920: 232).

In the wake of the defeat of the Liberal Party's reform measure, several meetings were held which attracted crowds that often comprised hundreds of thousands of people. Major events took place at Trafalgar Square, London, in June 1866 which was followed by processions that would end up in Hyde Park on 23 July. This event was significant for illustrating the police and state's response to protest in the middle decades of the nineteenth century.

The government banned the Hyde Park event and locked the Park gates but the numbers who turned up made it impossible for the police to enforce the ban, even though large numbers (including 1600 who intended to halt the procession at Marble Arch) were present. The pressure of the crowd caused the Park failings to collapse and an estimated 200,000 entered the Park. The police called upon the military (in the form of the Royal Horse Guards) for support. They attended but did not intervene even though the crowd stoned the Metropolitan Police Commissioner, Richard Mayne. The meeting was thus allowed to proceed without police or military intervention. The police present in the Park were attacked (thus providing further support for the arguments presented by Storch (1975) regarding the degree of anti-police sentiment that existed in areas other than those in Northern England that his article surveyed) in contrast to the friendly reception accorded to the military, indicating that 'the police had now replaced soldiers as the perceived enemies of English liberties' (Taylor, 1995: 391–392). A meeting the following day was held at Trafalgar Square, also without police or military involvement.

Support for the Reform League grew in the subsequent months of 1866 and major meetings were held in Birmingham (August), Manchester (September), Leeds and Glasgow (October) and Dublin (November). This pressure was maintained when the Conservative government produced its reform proposals in February 1867. A major meeting was subsequently held in May 1867 at Hyde Park, London. The government banned the event and mobilised thousands of troops, police and Special Constables to enforce the ban. But the size of the crowd made it impossible to deploy force against them and the meeting was able to go ahead, resulting in the resignation of Home Secretary Spencer Walpole.

The force of the agitation propelled the government into making concessions that increased the size of the electorate more substantially than they had initially proposed. However, the overall extent to which extra-parliamentary political agitation was a key cause of reform has been debated.

Particular attention was drawn to July 1866 meeting in Hyde Park, one source declaring that 'the fall of the Park railings did for England in July 1866 what the fall of the Bastille did for France in July 1789' (Wilson, 1957: xxvi). A contemporary source stated that although little damage had been done inside the park on the day of the meeting, the following day witnessed a considerable degree of destruction that had been caused by 'bands of idle vagabonds armed with big sticks and pieces of broken railings' and whose mood became aggravated by the presence of police officers who were forced to run away for their own protection. The article's author noted that 'the sight of a policeman has as irritating an effect on Londoners as a red rag on a bull'. Order was restored in the evening by the deployment of Horse and Foot Guards in support of foot and mounted police who entered the park in advance of the military 'using their batons very freely'. Sir Richard Mayne was present at the scene, accompanied by Horse Guards (*Manchester Guardian* Correspondent, 1866).

However, not all scholars agree that the Hyde Park event in 1866 had a major impact on promoting political reform. One source downplayed the impact of the 1866 Hyde Park meeting ('which only damaged an old fence and some shubbery') (Herrick, 1934: 223) on the cause of reform while another source argued that the 1866 event 'was more an assertion of the right of assembly … than of the right to vote' (Himmelfarb, 1966: 104). This position was underpinned by legal ambiguity as to whether the government had to right to ban an event at this location (Taylor, 1995: 388–389).

Moral Panic Theory (which is considered in the following chapter) may also have exaggerated the magnitude of disorder in 1866, perhaps to deter 'respectable' people joining forces with the lower social orders. Taylor commented (1995: 394) that this event 'awakened long-standing fears of "the Mob" amongst middle class reformers. A cartoon in the magazine *Punch* on 30 November 1867 depicted the passage of the Reform Act as 'a check to King Mob', in the sense that there was no longer any justification for large numbers of unruly people appearing on the streets to agitate for political reform since this had now been granted.

If it was intended to neuter protest by driving a wedge between the various classes who had taken to the streets, the Reform Act achieved this purpose in the short term. The concessions contained in the 1867 measure led to the demise of the Reform League which was formally dissolved in March 1869.

Late Nineteenth-Century Politics and Public Disorder

In order to provide a context within which extra-parliamentary political methods (including strike action) occurred in the latter decades of the nineteenth century, it is first necessary to very briefly chart the political ideas that underpinned these activities, namely the growth of socialist organisations and developments affecting trade unionism that occurred in that period.

These were influential forces that sought an expanded role for the state, for promoting collectivism at the expense of individualism and, in some cases, for challenging the legitimacy of the capitalist state.

Socialist Societies and Organisations

The latter decades of the nineteenth century witnessed disorders associated with the conduct of working-class politics, in particular the emergence of socialist societies. These argued that inequalities in the distribution of wealth and political power were responsible for social injustices such as unemployment and poverty that were revealed by the investigations of by social scientists that included Charles Booth, William Preston and Seebohm Rowntree. They demonstrated through social scientific investigation that a significant number of working-class people lived in the verge of starvation and squalor (Duffy, 1961: 311).

British socialism drew its inspiration from a number of separate sources. These included the economic theories of David Ricardo (which argued that the interests of capital and labour were opposed) and the reforming endeavours of Robert Owen who suggested that the means of production should be owned by small groups of producers that were organised into societies based on the spirit of cooperation.

The traditional Christian concern for the poor coupled with the early experience of a society in which property was held in common was voiced by Christian socialists who included Charles Kingsley and by organisations such as the Guild of St. Matthew. The writings of Marx and Engels exerted a further important influence on the development of socialism in Britain towards the end of the century. Marx argued that the exploitive nature of capitalism made a proletarian revolution inevitable. The revolution would involve the overthrow of the capitalist ruling class and the emergence of a new society based upon the dictatorship of the proletariat (Joyce, 1999: 22).

The various sources that inspired British socialism led to the formation of a number of new political organisations in the 1880s. These included the Socialist Democratic Federation (the SDF, formed in 1884 and led by Henry Hyndman), the Socialist League (which was closely identified with William Morrison and formed in 1885 following a split in the SDF), the Fabian Society (set up in 1884 whose initial leading members included Sydney and Beatrice Webb and George Bernard Shaw) and the Scottish Labour Party (formed in 1888). These organisations put forward different methods through which socialism could be achieved, underpinned by the dispute between fundamentalism and social democracy.

Although these socialist organisations differed on key issues such as how society should be reformed, they served to popularise the objective of the creation of an independent working-class political party, culminating in the creation of the Independent Labour Party in 1893 which put forward a programme of reforms to benefit the working class but which could be achieved within the existing framework of capitalism. This spirit of working-class cooperation subsequently resulted in the formation of an umbrella group in 1900 called the Labour Representation Committee. It was composed of organisations that included the Independent Labour Party, the Fabians, some trade unions and—briefly—the Socialist Democratic Federation. Its philosophy was 'Labourism'. This emphasised working-class self-reliance and independence against employers and stressed the importance of trade unions to an independent working-class political organisation. It viewed its role in sectional terms—to advance the 'bread and butter' needs of organised labour: it was 'trade unions politics "pure and simple"' (Foote, 1997: 38). It provided the Labour Party with a broad philosophical framework within which a range of ideologies could be accommodated (Joyce, 1999: 25).

In 1900 the LRC secured the election of two MPs. It fared much better in 1906 (when 29 of its candidates were elected, mainly because of a non-aggression pact between the LRC and Liberal Party that had been formulated in 1903 between Herbert Gladstone and Ramsay MacDonald) after which it adopted the new name of 'Labour Party' and ensured that the Parliamentary route became the chief method through which socialism would be achieved in Britain.

However, many working-class socialists believed that the workplace was the arena to fight capitalism and this view underlaid several labour disputes that occurred in the period before the First World War which are considered later in this chapter.

Demonstrations

Socialist organisations discussed above were responsible for a number of major demonstrations, two of which are discussed below.

'Black Monday'

Events in Trafalgar Square and the West End of London that occurred on 8 February 1886 were dubbed 'Black Monday'. What started off as a meeting and counter demonstration by two political opposed groups—the Conservative Fair Trade League and the Marxist Social Democratic Federation (SDF)—resulted in violence in the form of riots in which property was attacked and looted and people associated with the rich and wealthy were attacked and robbed. These events took place against the backdrop of unemployment and hardship for many working-class people and it was they to whom the SDF pitched its appeal, labelling their counter demonstration as 'Demonstration of Unemployed Workmen'.

Although the police re-routed the SDF counter demonstration, it did not prevent disorders from taking place. Allegations were made regarding extremist sentiments contained in speeches being made and for this reason four leaders of the SDF were put on trial for seditious conspiracy but all were acquitted.

'Bloody Sunday'

'Bloody Sunday' took place on 13 November 1887.

A demonstration to protest against the adoption of coercion in Ireland had been organised by the Metropolitan Federation of Radical Clubs which was supported by the SDF and the Socialist League. A specific demand was the release from prison of William O'Brien MP, whose support for land reform led him to organise a rent strike which resulted in his imprisonment. It also attracted support from the unemployed.

The police were more organised than had been the case a year previously (Awcock, 2014: [Online]). In early November 1887, the Metropolitan Police Commissioner, Sir Charles Warren banned all meetings in Trafalgar Square and mobilised around several thousand police officers (including mounted police) and Special Constables (which if the need arose could be reinforced by 600 troops) to enforce the ban and maintain order. Police intervention also prevented many would-be demonstrators from arriving at the Square.

Those who did manage to reach the Square were subjected to violence from the police who managed to maintain control of the situation. Those in the SDF who felt that a working-class revolution was around the corner at that time had to re-think their strategy as the tactics used by the police seemed more than capable of defeating purposes of this nature.

Consequences of These Events

Two important consequences for the policing of disorder arose from the events referred to above.

First, following 'Bloody Monday', the 1886 Riot (Damages) Act was passed. Under this measure, persons whose property had been damaged, destroyed or stolen by persons who were 'riotously and tumultuously assembled' were eligible from compensation that was paid out of the police fund for the area where the disorder(s) took place. This remained in force until repealed and replaced by the 2016 Riot Compensation Act. This measure made it essential that the police contained disorderly crowds since the force would suffer a financial penalty if they failed to do so.

Following 'Bloody Sunday' in 1887, the 1890 Police Act was passed. One provision of this catered for the ability of one police force to come to the aid of another when the first was facing an event that could lead to severe disorder. This became known as 'mutual aid'. Houghton (2001: 89) stated that this procedure originated in the response to industrial unrest in the 1860s and 1870s whereby ad hoc requests were made by police forces for officers to be supplied to them for a specific event, with the receiving force paying for the services of the 'imported' officers.

The 1890 Act provided for a voluntary form of standing arrangement whereby chief constables could make advance arrangements of this nature with their neighbouring forces if they wished to do so. But there was no compulsion to do so. One advantage of this was to reduce any reliance on the military.

Policing Industrial Unrest in the Late Nineteenth Century

Developments Affecting Working-Class Politics

The Reform Acts of 1867 and 1884 gave the vote to large numbers of the urban and rural working class. The Liberal Party was the recipient of much of the working-class vote. The belief that the interests of employer and employee were compatible appealed to the skilled (or 'respectable') workers who constituted the bulk of the working-class electorate and this sentiment resulted in 'Lib-Labism' whereby the craft unions that were composed of skilled workers dominated the Trades Union Congress. These cooperated with the Liberal Party in return for which they secured legislation that was favourable to their interests (such as the 1871 Trade Union Act) and also the adoption of a small number of working-class candidates by local Liberal associations. If elected, these candidates took the Liberal Whip but articulated working-class concerns in Parliament.

The vitality of an independent working-class political party depended on it securing trade union support. Although, as has been noted above, the existing unions represented skilled trade workers, during the 1880s semi-skilled and unskilled workers began to organise themselves into unions. The resultant new unions (led by men that included Will Thorne of the Gasworkers and General Labourers Union and Ben Tillett of the Dockers Union) became involved in a number of major industrial disputes and also affected the traditional 'Lib-Lab' stance of the TUC (Joyce, 1999: 19).

However, the stance of the TUC and its constituent unions was also affected by changes in the attitude of the craft unions towards an independent working-class political party and industrial militancy. Developments that included the enhanced use of mechanisation whereby machinery replaced skilled labour (thereby making employment more precarious in the longer term) and the adoption of increasingly hostile attitudes by employers towards trade unions were the causes of this shift in position which was heavily influenced by court judgements that included Lyons v. Wilkins (1896/9) and Taff Vale (1901). The first of these judgements, arising from a case heard in the Court of Appeal, suggested that virtually any form of picketing, peaceful or not, was unlawful. The latter judgement (arising from a case brought by the Taff Vale Railway Company against the Amalgamated Society of Railway Servants) held that a union could be sued for damages caused by the actions of its officials in industrial disputes.

Actions of this nature made members (although not necessarily, at the outset, the leaders) (Duffy, 1961: 314) of the older craft unions more receptive towards cooperating with other sections of the working class in political activity that included industrial action. It was observed that by 1900 trade union membership rose to over two million and striking became the recognised method by workers seeking improved pay and conditions of work (Manwaring-White, 1983: 9). Between 1900 and 1914, mainly because of the growth of the new unions of semi-skilled and unskilled workers, trade union membership had reached 4,145,000 (Peak, 1984: 27). However, as Davis (undated: [Online]) noted by 1914, 90% of all trade unionists were men and over 90% of women workers remained unorganised, most of those who were being employed in the textile industry.

Box 11.1: Syndicalism

Socialism can be achieved in many ways, one of which entails strike action (and other forms of direct action that included sabotage) being undertaken by workers organised into unions based upon their industries. Actions of this nature helped to create a sense of class consciousness among workers. The growing intensity of strikes was seen as a prelude to a general strike which was seen as the chief revolutionary weapon of the class war whereby workers would seize control of the means of production and overthrow capitalism and the capitalist state that was viewed as the tool of oppression. A post-capitalist society would then be established, based on workers organised in production units, termed *syndicat*.

Syndicalism was advanced by labour unions in France towards the end of the nineteenth century. It views the interests of the bourgeoisie and proletariat as incompatible and trade union militancy was seen as the mechanism through which the class struggle should be waged.

The Grand Northern Consolidated Trade Union that was set up in 1834 (which aimed to replace capitalism with a cooperative system based on workers' control and which sought to achieve this objective through a national strike, termed the 'Grand National Holiday') was a forerunner of syndicalist thought in Great Britain.

Leading trade unionists whose views were influenced by syndicalism included Tom Mann who advocated that trade unionism and socialism were the only means through which socialism could be achieved. His activities included playing a leading role in the 1889 dispute in the London Docks and chairing the strike committee during the 1911 Liverpool general transport strike. Syndicalism was latterly attributed to inspiring labour protests in Great Britain in the period 1910–1914 (Darlington, 2008: 38–39).

Syndicalism was also influential in Ireland where it inspired the Irish Transport and General Workers' Union (ITGWU) which fused trade union activity with socialist republicanism, an approach labelled 'Larkinism' after the ITGWU founder, James Larkin. The union membership included both skilled and unskilled workers. An attempt by the union to unionise workers on the Dublin United Tramway Company Dublin's trams resulted in a strike.

Employers across the city then threatened to lock out workers unless they disavowed any intention to join the ITGWU, thus transforming a single dispute into a city-wide confrontation. This event was known as The Dublin Lockout which took place between 26 August 1913 and 18 January 1914. It involved 20,000 workers and around 300 employers, a key demand being the workers' right to unionise.

The use of blackleg labour by the employers during this period resulted in disorder arising from strikers and locked out workers using the tactic of mass picketing and the Dublin Metropolitan Police and Royal Irish Constabulary took firm action against events such as workers' rallies that included a baton charge at a meeting on 31 August 1913 which had been banned, an episode termed 'Bloody Sunday'. This intervention left two dead and around 300 injured. Additionally, the army was sometimes deployed to aid strike-breaking operations (Yeates, 2001: [Online]).

The refusal of the TUC to engage in a sympathetic strike in support of the ITGWU resulted in workers returning to work in January 1914.

Examples of Late Nineteenth-Century Industrial Militancy

The following section examines the 1889 London Dock Strike as an example of industrial unrest associated with new unionism that occurred in the latter decades of the nineteenth century.

The London Dock Strike (1889)

The London dock strike of 1889 followed other developments that suggested a new mood of militancy by unskilled workers. These included a strike in 1888 by 1400 women and girls employed at the Bryant and May factory match making factory at Bow, East London and the successful organisation in 1889 of London gas workers into the National Union of Gas Workers and General Labourers by Will Thorne which succeeded in securing a pay increase for workers employed at the gas works at Beckton, East London. These events indicated that the unskilled and semi-skilled were becoming unwilling to any more accept the poor pay, unsafe working conditions and poor living standards that they and their families were being forced to endure.

Although the strike occurred in a period of relative affluence (Duffy, 1961: 306), dock wages were low—on average 3–7 shillings [15–35 new pence] a week compared to the 13 shillings [65 new pence] (Sweeney-Lynch, 2022: [Online]). Additionally, employment at the docks was an irregular form of work. Most dockers were employed on a casual basis based upon a 'call on' system whereby workers would congregate at each dock at certain times of the day and a foreman would decide which of them to employ based on the requirements of work—namely the arrival of ships requiring to be unloaded.

A localised dispute in the South West India Dock in the Port of London occurred in August 1889 in connection with the unloading of a cargo ship, the *Lady Armstrong*. The dispute arose from a decision by the general manager of the East and West India docks company to cut dockers' 'plus' rates (which were financial incentives to unload ships speedily) in order to attract ships to this dock by virtue of charging lower unloading rates. Led by Ben Tillett, the dockers at West India Quay walked out.

This dispute escalated to involve a wide range of employees who worked at the docks due to the activities of organisers that included Tom Mann, Ben Tillett, John Burns, Ben Cooper, Will Thorne and the leader of the seamen's union, Havelock Wilson. It resulted in the formation of the Dock, Wharf, Riverside and General Labourers' union (whose General Secretary elected after the strike had ended was Tillett).

From 20 August 1889, the entire Port of London was closed with 100,000 workers joining the strike. Their demands included that dockers' pay should be raised to six [old] pence [2.5 new pence] an hour—hence the name given to the strike of 'the Dockers' Tanner'—the slang word for the old sixpence. A key feature of the strike was large demonstrations in favour of the dock workers which were peaceful and helped create sympathy of the dockers' cause especially from the middle classes. Although these events were attended by a strong police presence, it was not required to maintain order.

Money subscribed to the strike fund in Britain was augmented by money raised from dockers in Australia which ensured the indefinite continuance of the strike (Sweeney-Lynch, 2022: [Online]). The employers sought negotiations in early September, the chief mediator being the Catholic Archbishop of Westminster, Cardinal Manning. Agreement on the 'tanner' and other demands (in particular that shifts should last no more than 4 hours) was reached on 10 September and the dockers returned to work on 16 September, preceded on 15 September by a large demonstration in London's Hyde Park.

The success of the strike action helped inspire the creation of other new unions of largely unskilled workers and also helped boost the numbers enrolled in existing craft unions. However, as Duffy (1961: 307–308) argued, while the dock strike gave impetus to the organisation of the unskilled, this was a development whose origins pre-dated 1889. It was aided by the removal of legal obstructions to trade union membership in the mid-1870s and in the 1880s developments associated with new unionism included, for example, the formation of the National Labour Federation in 1886 on Tyneside which was described by Duffy (1961: 313) as the first of the new unions. Its chief policy was the institution of an 8-hour day as a means to combat unemployment. Subsequently, the National Amalgamated Labour Union began organising dock labourers in Swansea in 1888 and became established in Cardiff the following year. The distinguishing feature of these unions that contrasted with the older unions was militancy, a disposition to take action to further their members' interests rather than to look to sympathetic governments to provide solutions (Duffy, 1961: 308 and 317).

Nonetheless, the development and successes enjoyed by the new unions were not consistently sustained following the Dock Strike. Issues that included the employers' offensive and the consolidation of the power of the older unions in the TUC in the late nineteenth and early years of the twentieth century served to act as a brake on the influence that they wielded (Davis, undated: [Online]).

Disorder in the Early Decades of the Twentieth Century

Dangerfield (1935) drew attention to a wide range of difficulties that faced the Liberal government after the 1906 general election. These included industrial militancy, the suffragette campaign and the Home Rule dispute in Ireland, which are discussed in this chapter.

Policing Industrial Unrest 1909–1914

The period that led up to the First World War was known as 'The Great Unrest'. It has been argued that between 1910 and 1914, working people 'were in a more rebellious mood than at any time since the 1840s, as real wages declined while prices and employers' profits were on the increase' (Peak, 1984: 27). This resulted in a period of 'open class antagonism' (Peak, 1984: 27).

In 1911, Sir Edward Troup at the Home Office expressed concern regarding the consequences of national strikes for an urbanised society vulnerable to the interruption of its food supply. He suggested that emergency powers and administrative centralisation were required to counter the threat (cited in Fielding, 1991: 61) whereby the police would be under the control of central government (cited in Fielding, 1991: 61).

In 1912, a total of 1,233,016 workers were involved in 857 strikes in which a total of 38,142,101 working days were lost (Dangerfield, 1935: 307). The formation of the 'triple alliance' of dockers, railway and transport workers in 1913 suggested the potential for industrial unrest to escalate. There were over 1000 strikes in 1913 alone (Manwaring-White, 1983: 10). This section discusses a small number of key episodes that occurred in this period.

The South Wales Miners' Dispute 1910–1911

The South Wales coal strike of 1910–1911 arose over a dispute regarding the price to be paid for mining a new seam at the Ely pit of the Naval Colliery Company (a subsidiary of Cambrian Collieries Ltd.) in which miners demanded more than the owners offered. Although relatively few of the miners employed at the pit were to work this seam, in order to force the issue, all 800 miners employed at the Ely pit were locked out on 1 September 1910. In response, the South Wales Miners' Federation called a strike involving all 12,000 miners employed by the Cambrian Combine. The lock out was thus transformed into a strike on 1 November 1910 which escalated so that around 30,000 miners were either on strike or were locked out in the South Wales coalfield by mid-winter.

The coal owners intended to use imported (or 'blackleg') labour to break the strike and aware that clashes between strikers and imported labour was likely, took steps to obtain police assistance to protect the latter. This prompted the chief constable of Gloucester to reinforce his police with officers drawn from Cardiff and Bristol.

On 6 November the intention to use imported labour at the Glamorgan colliery at Llwynpia resulted in clashes between striking miners and the police who were present there. Although the police successfully beat back the miners using baton charge (which probably resulted in the death of one miner) (Geary, 1985: 47), their actions caused resentment in the Valley and damage to property and looting at occurred Tonypandy, about a mile from the Llwynpia colliery on 8 November. This was very much an isolated incident arising when striking miners found the town devoid of a police presence. Thus they resorted to violence, perhaps borne of frustration at the failure of their attempts to close the colliery or possibly in an attempt to force police at the colliery to leave the site in order to protect the town (Geary, 1985: 29–30).

This prompted the chief constable to make requests for military aid, perhaps in the knowledge that the government would send Metropolitan Police officers instead or maybe because local authorities did not have to pay for their services unlike the payment they would have to foot when Metropolitan officers were sent to their area (Geary, 1985: 35–36). Following a conference chaired by Home Secretary Winston Churchill, the troops requested by the chief constable were halted *en route* and instead mounted police and 200 foot police were sent to restore order. However, General Macready was placed in charge of the cavalry that had been stopped at Cardiff with instructions to go into the troubled areas if the police reinforcements were unable to restore order. The involvement of the Home Secretary has been described as 'very surprising' since the legal responsibility for maintaining law and order rested with the local Magistrates (Geary, 1985: 35) and was possibly, therefore, unconstitutional or even illegal (Peak, 1984: 26). Additionally, central control was evidenced with the control that General Macready exercised over both the Metropolitan Police and the military: he, in turn, reported to the Home Secretary (Geary, 1985: 36). Local control was exerted only over the local police.

While the Metropolitan Police were travelling to their destination at Pontypridd, reports of a deteriorating situation led to a decision to send a further 200 Metropolitan Police officers to the area. In the meantime, General Macready advanced to Pontypridd with one squadron of the 18th Hussars. Although on his arrival the situation seemed to have calmed down, discussions between Churchill, Macready and the Chief Constable of Glamorgan, Capt. Lindsay, resulted in a third contingent of 300 Metropolitan Police officers being sent to the area. In total, therefore, 1400 police officers (comprising local officers and Metropolitan Police officers, of whom 120 were mounted) were present in the area together with 300 infantrymen who were moved to Newport and a further 200 to Pontypridd (Geary, 1985: 27–28). A 'representative' from the Home Office, Mr. Moylan, was also sent to relay back to the Home Office any information from General Macready or Capt. Lindsay.

Moylan, together with employers, the local police, Magistrates and General Macready acted as conduits of information to the Home Office regarding the progress of the strike and supplying central government with intelligence. It was reported that Moylan and General Macready contacted the Home Office on 31 occasions in November 1910, employers on 5 occasions, the chief constable on eight occasions and Magistrates twice (Geary, 1985: 38). General Macready also made use military personnel who were despatched to the area by the War Office, in particular regarding the disposition of troops and also of two Welsh-speaking CID officers sent from Scotland Yard who attended strike meetings and reported to the General (Geary, 1985: 39).

On the evening of 9 November, following discussions held between Churchill, Macready and Lindsay, Churchill ordered Lindsay to send the third contingent of 300 Metropolitan Police officers to Tonypandy where it was felt disturbances were most likely to occur. An additional force of 300 infantry and 200 cavalry were placed on standby to move into the area if the situations justified their presence. Such arrangements seemed unnecessary since disorder more or less petered out by the end of 1911. In August 1911 the Cambrian miners returned to work, the Miners' Federation having accepted a settlement earlier in June.

The tactics used by the strikers were primarily designed to enforce the strike by using cordons to prevent non-strikers from entering working collieries and taking direct action to immobilise pit machinery. The violence that resulted in the destruction of property at Featherstone Colliery in 1893 was largely absent from this dispute (Geary, 1985: 28–29). Clashes between strikers and the police took the form of stone throwing but was frequently associated with police attempts to prevent attacks on houses of the 'blacklegs'. There was a reluctance to actually use the troops against the strikers and they came into contact on just one occasion when troops used a bayonet charge to disperse stone-throwing strikers (Geary, 1985: 35). However, police baton charges against strikers (which was the standard crowd control tactic used by the police at that time) were a more common occurrence (Geary, 1985: 40–41) and on one occasion on 8 November a miner died from head wounds inflicted by a police baton charge.

The 1911 Transport Strikes

The miners' strike in South Wales was accompanied by a series of widespread labour disputes in the Summer of 1911. These strikes also witnessed a continuation of the policy of central government to prefer the use of Metropolitan Police officers rather than soldiers who would be used only as a last resort. Again, both Metropolitan Police and soldiers were under the control of General Macready.

In June 1911 a seamen's strike for higher wages occurred in Liverpool which the spread to Hull, Cardiff, Manchester, Bristol and Southampton. Dockers and transport workers struck in sympathy with the seamen and traffic through the docks of Britain virtually ground to a halt. The employers responded to the strike through the use of imported labour which included Chinese and Finns to which the strikers responded by attempting to prevent the blackleg labour from working, actions that were perhaps also influenced by racial prejudice in an era (as is argued in this chapter) when such sentiments were often articulated. The police were used to maintain law and order and some violent incidents took place, sometimes in response to police actions that aimed to prevent strikers from seeking to persuade blackleg labour from working, a right granted by the 1906 Trade Disputes Act (Geary, 1985: 31–32). In Hull, serious disorders in which the police were stoned led to the local police being reinforced from neighbouring forces and 500 members of the Metropolitan Police. Soldiers from the South Staffordshire Regiment were placed on standby to attend either Liverpool or Hull but in the event were not needed. In both of these cities, the disputes were settled on 3 July and the imported police were withdrawn.

Disorders, however, continued elsewhere. On 5 July General Macready and 200 Metropolitan Police officers were sent to Salford and the following day were joined by the military consisting of two squadrons of Scots Greys and a battalion of infantry. A local settlement led to the police and military being withdrawn but it continued elsewhere and on 18 July 300 Metropolitan Police officers were sent to Cardiff. A week later a further 100 Metropolitan Police officers were sent to the city.

A strike by dockers employed at the Port of London in August led Churchill to request the deployment of 25,000 troops to ensure essential supplies (in particular food) could be moved through the port. The unloading of a ship by soldiers threatened to escalate the level of violence and by 10 August, 80,000 workers were on strike (Peak, 1984: 29). However, other leading politicians, including Chancellor David Lloyd George urged him to moderate his stance in case this action resulted in widespread violence. Instead the government exerted pressure on the Port of London Authority and the strike was settled on the terms demanded by the strikers on 11 August.

Railwaymen were involved in a series of localised disputes in August which arose over expressions of solidarity with the dockers but also because employers were refusing to recognise their unions. Riots occurred in Liverpool where both a railway strike and dock lockout took place. Police reinforcements were sent from Birmingham and Leeds and Churchill reinforced them with two squadrons of Scots Greys, three battalions of infantry, a regiment of cavalry and a warship, the cruiser HMS *Antrim*. During the disturbances, troops fired over the heads of one crowd and bayonet charged another. On 15 August an attempt to free convicted rioters brought the crowd into contact with a prison van's escort of Hussars and Scots Greys which opened fire, killing two people (Peak, 1984: 29). Further violence in the form of clashes between rioters and the imported police and military occurred in which looting took place and the troops used bayonet charges.

On 16 August local railway strikes became transformed in the first ever national rail strike in which 200,000 railway workers went on strike and rioting occurred in many areas of the country. Some 58,000 troops were mobilised in 35 cities and towns, mainly in Yorkshire, Lancashire, the Midlands and Wales (Peak, 1984: 30) to ensure that the railway system remained able to operate (as opposed to the more usual practice of using the military to maintain public order).

This action by Churchill constituted a departure from the usual practice of troops being involved only when a request was made by a local civil authority and instead responsibility for handling the strike was handed over to a joint organisation that involved the War Office and Home Office and in which the military dominated (Peak, 1984: 30). Troops were deployed in seven Strike Areas placed under the charge of a senior military officer who reported to the War Office (Peak, 1984: 30) whether or not local authorities wanted them (Geary, 1985: 37; Peak, 1984: 30), perhaps reflecting a fear on the part of the government of the revolutionary potential of a national strike (Geary, 1985: 46).

On one occasion, at Llanelli station, strikers stopped a train carrying blackleg workers. The army (following the reading of the Riot Act by a magistrate), responded to being stoned by first advancing towards the crowd with fixed bayonets and then opening fire on the strikers, killing two of them including persons in their own gardens overlooking the scene of the confrontation (Geary, 1985: 45–46). Subsequent violence resulted in the deaths of four more people. Pressure from central government also urged the police to adopt a robust attitude towards the strikers and a circular was sent to chief constables urging a more repressive interpretation of the law on picketing (cited in Geary, 1985: 44). Pressure on the railway companies by Lloyd George again resulted in the strike being settled.

The National Coal Strike 1912

In early 1912, the Miners' Federation of Great Britain called Britain's first ever national strike. By 1 March, over 1 million miners stopped work across England, Scotland and Wales and coal production ground to a halt. This constituted 'the most extensive stoppage in the history of the industrialised world' (Geary, 1985: 33) and parallels were drawn with the 1905 strike in Russia. The widespread nature of the strike meant that disorder was minimal and also prevented the widespread use of non-unionised blackleg labour. Where such labour was used, isolated violence took place in the last two weeks of March.

The government responded by sending troops to the strike areas but no clashes occurred. Instead the government took legal action against union leaders (including Tom Mann) under the 1797 Incitement to Mutiny Act. However, public outcry against the prosecutions forced the Home Secretary to use the royal prerogative to reduce the sentences of 5 persons who had been convicted. The strike ended in early April when the Miners' Conference decided on a return to work and all troops were withdrawn.

Britain's involvement in the First World War saw a cessation of industrial militancy. Some small-scale disputes occurred in 1916 on Clydeside and in Lancashire but it was not until 1918 that a wave of industrial unrest occurred involving munitions workers in Coventry, cotton workers in Lancashire and the police in London. These were settled with little public disorder but more serious disturbances arose in connection with a general strike in Glasgow in 1919 and in connection with demobilisation where serious rioting that included race riots taking place in South Wales, London's East End and Liverpool. The July 'Peace Day' celebrations also witnessed riots taking place in Wolverhampton, Salisbury, Epsom, Luton, Essex, Coventry and Swindon (Fielding, 1993: 51). Localised miners' disputes also took place and in August the police went on strike which led to looting and rioting in Liverpool to which troops and a battleship were despatched to deal with. A national railway strike towards the end of the year also occurred but, again, with minimal disorder and the troops that were deployed were not involved in confrontations with the strikers. A national coal strike in 1920 also saw very little disorder.

In 1920 the Emergency Powers Act provided the government with powers, including the deployment of troops, to deal with certain types of national emergencies, including strikes, having first declared a State of Emergency.

Policing the Suffragette Campaign

The suffragette campaign aimed to secure the right of women to vote in political elections. A number of organisations were associated with achieving this objective including the National Union of Women's Suffrage Societies that was led by Millicent Fawcett. This body sought to achieve this objective through the use of non-violent methods which contrasted with the more militant methods associated with the Women's Social and Political Union which was founded by Emmeline Pankhurst in 1903.

Initially the WSPU's tactics entailed the use of disruption and forms of civil disobedience, such as interrupting political meetings. An important example of which was the 'rush' on Parliament in October 1908 when the public were encouraged to join them in an attempt to invade the House of Commons. 60,000 people gathered but the police cordon proved effective. It also used demonstrations (the first 'monster meeting' taking the form of a number of processions through central London in June 1908 and which attracted a large crowd) and a weekly newspaper, *Votes for Women*, to put its case across.

The lack of Government action led the WSPU to undertake more violent acts—especially after 1911—which included attacks on property, usually in the form of window breaking, arson (which included setting fire to pillar boxes), planting bombs and other forms of law-breaking such as chaining themselves to government buildings and attacking pictures in art galleries. In June 1913 a suffragette, Emily Davison, died of her wounds after throwing herself in front of the King's horse at the Epsom Derby. This militancy caused divisions in the WPSU which resulted in the organisation losing control of Votes for Women which they replaced with a new publication, *The Suffragette*.

The government resorted to imprisoning suffragette campaigners. Around 1000 suffragettes were imprisoned (Purvis, 1995: 103). Many went of hunger strike which resulted in them being force fed using a nostril or stomach tube or a stomach pump (Miller, 2009: 361). When this policy failed, the government enacted the 1913 Prisoners (Temporary Discharge for Ill-Health) Act (usually referred to as the Cat and Mouse Act) whereby hunger striking suffragette were released from prison when they became weak but would subsequently be re-arrested and returned to once their health had improved. This approach was summarised by the composer and supporter of women's rights, Ethel Smyth

> The authorities dared not let the women die, so would release them, sometimes half-dead, to be rearrested as soon as they were judged fit to serve the remainder of their sentence. Whereupon the whole hideous business would begin again, the idea being that by degrees bodies and wills would be broken past mending. How a group of civilized Christian men could lend themselves to this proceeding rather than perform a simple act of justice already fifty years overdue is inconceivable (Smyth, 1933: 212).

The militant campaign died out when the First World War broke out in 1914 and suffragette prisoners were also released. The 1918 Representation of the People Act gave the vote to a restricted category of women aged 30 and above. This prompted the disbandment of the organisation in 1918.

Irish Home Rule

This section considers political activities associated with the politics of Ireland that were conducted in the latter decades of the nineteenth century. In that period, all of Ireland was part of the United Kingdom the activities of those who wished to break up the UK state by securing the independence of Ireland from the United Kingdom form the focus of this discussion.

Those who sought the independence of Ireland (otherwise known as home rule) were termed nationalists. One way through which home rule might be achieved was through the use of violence. Those who supported this course of action were termed 'Fenians' in the nineteenth century, the word 'Fenian' being taken from the Fenian Brotherhood—a secret organisation set up in New York in 1858 to fight for Irish home rule. The term 'Fenian' is used in connection with this organisation and also the Irish Republican Brotherhood that was set up in Ireland, also in 1858, to advance the cause of the creation of an independent Irish Republic by force of arms.

The violence that was associated with Fenianism in the latter decades of the nineteenth century occurred both in Ireland and also in England. One episode of this was the 1867 Fenian Rising which entailed actions taking place in Ireland and also England. The use of spies and informants very much neutered its impact in Ireland.

Box 11.2: The Fenian Rising on Mainland Britain 1867

Key events that occurred on mainland Britain included an attempt to rescue imprisoned Fenian leader Richard O'Sullivan Burke from Clerkenwell Prison, London. Gunpowder was used to blow up the wall that surrounded the prison which resulted in the deaths of 6 people and injuring over 100 others. Michael Barrett was the only person convicted of carrying out the Clerkenwell attack and was hanged on 26 May 1868, the last public execution to take place in England (Moss & Skinner, 2013: 36).

In Manchester, England in 1867, a van containing Fenian prisoners who were being transported from court to Belle Vue Gaol was attacked by Fenians and in the process a Manchester police sergeant, Charles Brett, was shot dead. Three persons, members of the Irish Republican Brotherhood,—William Philip Allen, Michael Larkin, and Michael O'Brien—were subsequently hung in public outside Salford Gaol for this murder. A grateful Queen Victoria renamed the Irish Constabulary as the Royal Irish Constabulary.

From the state's point of view, a public execution of this nature was designed to deter further acts of this nature from being carried out. However, from the point of view of those who supported violence—and the broader community from which they came—state violence of this nature both served to justify violence to secure home rule and also encouraged others to pursue a similar path of action by following in the footsteps of those who were subsequently known to history as 'the Manchester Martyrs'.

Violence associated with Fenianism occurred throughout the remainder of the nineteenth century, one important episode being what was termed the 'dynamite campaign' waged on mainland Britain in 1883–1885. This was a bombing campaign (around 20 attacks in total, mainly in London) that targeted soldiers, police officers, politicians and infrastructure that included the London underground system and gasworks. In excess of 80 people were injured in these attacks, 70 of these at a bombing attack at Praed Street (Paddington) underground station: one young boy was killed as were three of the bombers in an attack on London Bridge in 1884.

This was carried out in conjunction with activities conducted in Ireland, perhaps the most infamous being the assassinations of the British Chief Secretary for Ireland Lord Frederick Cavendish and Permanent Under Secretary at the Irish Office Thomas Henry Burke on 6 May 1882. They were killed with surgical knives in Phoenix Park, Dublin, on their way to the residence of the Lord Lieutenant of Ireland at the Vice-Regal Lodge. A previously unknown group called the Irish National Invincibles, members of a Fenian assassination squad, claimed responsibility.

Violence of this nature prompted the creation in London of a political policing unit known as the Fenian Office in 1881. Subsequently a small unit known as the Special Irish Branch was set up within the Metropolitan Police's CID in 1883 which replaced the Fenian Office (Sloan, 2013: 334). The latter was composed of 4 CID officers and 8 uniformed policemen, all of Irish birth save its head, Inspector Littechild who was Scottish (Bunyan, 1977: 104). Its work has been considered in more detail above.

A different model of political policing had been adopted in Ireland following the Phoenix Park assassinations. A permanent Irish secret service was created in the Office of the Under Secretary for Police and Crime which sought to counter further episodes of violence through the gathering of intelligence. It made use of spies, informants and agents provocateurs to secure such information and was headed by Edward George Jenkinson.

Although this unit had some successes, concern regarding the un-British nature of its operations resulted in it being disbanded in 1887 with counter-terrorism work becoming the sole preserve of the Special Irish Branch (whose role is discussed below). The collection of political intelligence in Ireland then became the responsibility of the RIC's 'Crimes Special' Branch (which was responsible for gathering political intelligence from all of Ireland's 32 counties, with the exception of Dublin where the Dublin Metropolitan Police possessed its 'G-Division' whose role included monitoring political extremists in the city (Sloan, 2013: 335–336).

Revolt to Revolution—Disorder in Ireland

The rise of the Irish Parliamentary Party (IPP) (which was led by Charles Stewart Parnell between 1882 and 1891) in the latter decades of the nineteenth century justified advocating the constitutional route to independence rather than a resort to violence. The agreement reached between Herbert Gladstone and Parnell in 1885 whereby the Liberal Party agreed to put forward legislation to provide for Irish Home Rule in return for the IPP's support for other measures of its programme underpinned this strategy. However, it took decades to secure this objective, the House of Commons rejecting a Liberal Home Rule Bill in 1886 and the House of Lords rejecting a similar measure in 1893 after the Commons had passed it. Further delays were caused by the Liberal Government's dispute with the House of Lords which rejected David Lloyd George's budget in 1909.

Finally, a third Home Rule Bill was introduced in 1912. It was twice rejected by the House of Lords but when re-introduced for a third time became enacted as the 1914 Government of Ireland Act, the House of Lords' veto being overridden under the provisions of the 1911 Parliament Act. However, the outbreak of the First World War resulted in the implementation of the measure being delayed under the terms of the 1914 Suspensory Act. It was never implemented and was later superseded by a fourth Home Rule Measure, the 1920 Government of Ireland Act.

The grant of independence to Ireland was fiercely opposed by Unionists: these were Protestant in religion and wished for Ireland to remain within the United Kingdom. They were concentrated in the NE of Ireland, in six of the counties that comprised the historic province of Ulster. As it became clear that the Liberal government was minded to grant independence to Ireland, they began to organise themselves to resist its imposition on them. This opposition took the form of the Ulster Covenant, whereby Unionist opponents of Irish independence pledged themselves to oppose Home Rule and formed in 1912 a paramilitary organisation, the Irish Volunteer Force, as their vehicle for doing so. An additional concern for the British government was the 1914 Curragh 'Mutiny' (in which senior officers voiced their disapproval should orders be given by the British government to take the offensive against the Unionist Ulster Volunteers). This suggested that the loyalty of the British army in countering this Unionist threat could not be taken for granted.

Box 11.3: The 1916 Easter Rising

Nationalists and Unionists committed themselves to fight for the British cause against Germany in the First World War.

However, concerns arose in nationalist quarters that Unionist opposition to Home Rule might induce the British government to renege on the grant of home rule in favour of the partition of Ireland.

This fear was legitimised by the British government having put forward a Bill in 1914 that would have allowed Ulster to be excluded from Home Rule, although the Suspensory Act was the course of action that was ultimately adopted.

Accordingly, the more extreme nationalists (spearheaded by the military council of the Irish Republican Brotherhood, the Irish Volunteers, the Irish Citizen Army and around 200 women of *Cumann na mBan*, or Irishwomen's Council) attempted to seize this Home Rule by force in an event in 1916 known as the Easter Rising. Several buildings in Dublin were seized by the revolutionaries whose actions also included proclaiming a Proclamation of the Irish Republic on 24 April 1916. The rising was short lived and put down mercilessly.

Initially the Rising was not viewed favourably by many nationalists but government actions (spearheaded by the army that was commanded by General Maxwell and comprising of mass arrests and executions) smacked of overreaction. Around 3500 prisoners were taken (Townshend, 2006: 263–264) of which 1800 were sent to internment camps in Britain. Trial by courts-martial resulted in the execution of 16 leaders of the Rising.

As the end of the First World War approached, there were concerns that home rule in the form provided for in the 1914 legislation would not be secured as Lloyd George's government sought to compromise the grant of independence with the opposition of Unionists who opposed it through the mechanism of partition. These factors shifted Irish public opinion in favour of a more radical form of nationalism. Bowden (1974: 221) referred to the emergence of 'an amazing renaissance of 'Irishness' and a complete change of allegiance on the part of the main body of Irish opinion. He attributed this to the negative response of Irish people to the aftermath of the 1916 Rising and to the influence of the Christian Brothers in regenerating Irish political will (Bowden, 1974: 221–224).

The new sign of the times was evidenced in the 1918 general election held after the First World War had ended. The IPP was virtually wiped out, replaced by a new Party, Sinn Fein, which won 85 seats. This Party set up its own revolutionary legislature, the *Dáil Éirann* and declared Ireland to be an independent republic. This action (which was immediately outlawed by the British government) (Mitchell, 1995: 245) made armed conflict inevitable. This took the form of the Irish War of Independence which was waged between 1919 and 1921.

Learning from the failure of the Easter Rising, republican military tactics changed. Instead of seeking to conduct a stand-up fight with the British army, the revolutionaries (organised into a body known as the Irish Republican Army) waged guerrilla warfare tactics through the tactic of 'flying columns'. The Royal Irish Constabulary were very much in the firing line of this campaign which took the forms of boycott and vilification which was designed to 'degrade the police in the eyes of the Irish people' and which was actively supported by the Catholic Church (Bowden, 1978: 179–180). The ability to deploy such tactics illustrates the weaknesses of policing based on the Roman Law model (as described in Chapter 8) which did not operate with the consent of the public. Vilification and boycott were the precursors to campaigns involving assassination and the general use of terror tactics against the RIC (Bowden, 1974: 226). The manner in which they were organised in small detachments scattered across the length and breadth of Ireland made them especially susceptible to this form of warfare and very soon the police were forced back into the towns and became an ineffective guardian of British rule.

From 1 January 1919 to 2 October 1920, 109 RIC officers were assassinated, 174 injured and 484 unoccupied barracks were destroyed and 2861 raids for arms were made, mainly on police stations (Bowden, 1974: 226). Bowden commented that the RIC had effectively 'collapsed in the face of terror and boycott. With their demise, English civil law and order ceased to exist' (Bowden, 1974: 225).

The violence of the revolutionaries was met with violence by the police in the form of reprisals. The RIC adopted what amounted to terror tactics of its own in response to the violence it faced (Bowden, 1978: 181). The government adopted this policy of police reprisals as 'the official, if covert, policy' since it seemed to work, it being observed that 'where reprisals have taken place, the whole atmosphere of the surrounding district is changed from one of hostility to one of cringing submission' (Bowden, 1978: 181).

Thus mercenaries enrolled in two organisations—the Black and Tans and the Auxiliaries were despatched to carry out a policy of counter-terror—'to make Ireland a hell to live in' (Bowden, 1978: 182). These were ex-soldiers who volunteered for service in Ireland whose role was to meet terror with violence of their own. They arrived in Ireland in the Spring of 1920. The culmination of this violence occurred in an event known as 'bloody Sunday' on 21 November 1920: the assassinations of 12 undercover British intelligence officers (termed the 'Cairo Gang') was countered by an attack made by British forces that comprised of the Black and Tans, Auxiliaries and Army on spectators at a Gaelic football match being held in Croke Park, Dublin. Sixteen civilians were killed and over 60 were wounded (Foley, 2014: 202, 204–206). This event also perhaps suggested to the leaders of both the British government and the IRA that neither side could win this conflict and a compromise was the best course of action.

Accordingly, a truce was signed between the British government and the IRA in 1921. Subsequently, the 1921 Anglo-Irish Treaty was concluded which created the Irish Free State. The six counties that comprised Northern Ireland were to be included in this state unless their devolved administration presented an Address to the Monarch requesting that they be allowed to opt out—a course of action that they adopted on 7 December 1922.

The Physical Response to Political Actions: The Role of the Military

Examples cited above have indicated that on occasions, the military was used in an attempt to combat disorder. This section will focus on the use of the military in civil affairs on mainland Britain since their use in Ireland was compatible with their traditional role as fighting those (seen as 'enemies') whose views and activities constituted a threat to national interests.

The procedure that was adopted by a local authority seeking military aid in the face of anticipated disorder in the middle decades of the nineteenth century derived from the requisitioning procedure that had been introduced around 1720) (Peak, 1984: 23). Magistrates constituted the 'civil authority' or 'civil power' and performed the key role regarding the use of the military in civil disturbances: they determined when to summon military aid, where it should be deployed and also authorised the use of lethal force (Geary, 1985: 23). This situation reflected the centuries-old British hostility to the existence of a standing army controlled by the government or the monarch (Peak, 1984: 21). In the early twentieth century, the Home Secretary began to perform a more prominent role.

Requests by the civil authority for the use of troops were made to the Home Office. In cases where it deemed that the local police force deemed insufficient to contain disorder, Home Office advice usually took the form of swearing in as many Special Constables as possible, call on the county constabulary and then the yeomanry (if possible swearing their members in a Special constables). The deployment of troops (if only for the purposes of being stationed in a locality) was officially frowned upon in favour of the use of local police forces. Steedman (1984: 33) argued that during the 1860s a distinction began to be made between an insurrection/rebellion (for which the use of arms could be justified) and riot which unarmed local police forces were expected to handle.

Continued reliance was placed on the military to maintain public order in the period 1850–1920. Between 1869 and 1893 they were deployed on 18 occasions and on 6 occasions between 1893 and 1908 (Geary, 1985: 16). This situation arose for several reasons—professional police forces were often too small to be effective in combating pubic disorder (in 1893, the West Riding Police consisted of 1042 officers who were pitted against 80,000 miners engaged in the industrial unrest then taking place in the local coalfields), the Home Office was increasingly reluctant to despatch Metropolitan Police Officers as the nineteenth century wore on and the mutual aid arrangements of the 1890 Police Act were not widely adopted—by 1908 only 57 of the 192 police forces in England and Wales had made such arrangements (Geary, 1985: 16). A Select Committee in 1908 (cited in Peak, 1984: 24) urged the strengthening of these mutual support arrangements but they only became more generally adopted after 1925 following a recommendation of the Desborough Committee and this made military involvement less likely to be required henceforth.

In the wake of the deaths at Featherstone colliery in 1893, changes derived from a Departmental Committee were introduced in 1895 regarding the procedures to be used to summon military aid in civil situations, the aim being to stop unnecessary requests being made by Magistrates. Subsequently, requisitions for the deployment of troops would be made through the Mayor of a Borough (the Mayor being the chief magistrate) while in the counties the request would have to come via the Chief Constable who thus became the de facto civil authority. Magistrates remained expected to attend disturbances where military aid had been dispatched but the order to open fire would be made by the troops' commanding officer rather than the Magistrate.

Box 11.4: Crowd Behaviour: Theoretical Perspectives

Gustave Le Bon (1895) provided the late nineteenth and early years of the twentieth century with an academic context within which crowd behaviour could be viewed.

His work (which was first translated into English in 1896) constituted a study in-group psychology in which he argued that when

> A certain number of … individuals are gathered together in a crowd for purposes of action, observation proves that, from the mere fact of their being assembled, there result certain new psychological characteristics (Le Bon, 1895: v).

In other words, Le Bon asserted that people acted differently when they were in crowd situations. The anonymity associated with being part of a crowd resulted in a loss of self restraint and was the precursor to contagion.

Le Bon described as this as the 'mind of the crowd', a situation in which personal concerns and values became subordinated to the collective interest of all who were gathered together. He suggested that individuals in crowds became 'de-individualised' and displayed a lower standard of behaviour than that exhibited by individuals—

> the individual forming part of a crowd acquires, solely from numerical considerations, a sentiment of invincible power which allows him to yield to instincts which, had he been alone, he would perforce have kept under restraint (Le Bon, 1895: 6).

Views of this nature suggested that crowds were to be feared by the authorities who would be justified in adopting a robust stance to neuter the articulation of their demands. Subsequently, group think theory had relevance to the actions undertaken by people in the setting of a crowd. This idea referred to a mode of thinking that people engaged in when they were deeply involved in a cohesive in-group, when the motivation of participants to realistically appraise alternative courses of action was overridden by their desire for unanimity (Janis, 1982: 9).

The Intelligence-Gathering Response to Political Actions

High Policing

This section will consider the policing of activities associated with political aims and objectives. This has been termed 'political policing' (Bunyan, 1977) which embraces the official scrutiny of ideas and opinions. More recently, the concept of 'political policing' has been put forward as a core feature of what is termed 'high policing' (Brodeur, 1983: 507). This term has already been referred to in earlier chapters.

It was originated by Chapman (1970) in connection with the utilisation of secret means to safeguard state security in a manner that was associated with 'Continental' or 'Bourbon' system of policing in France in the late eighteenth and early nineteenth centuries. In a more recent period, it entails activities such as 'surveillance, tracking, and keeping secret files on everyday activity' and whose purpose is to reach out 'for potential threats in a systematic attempt to preserve the distribution of power in a given society' (Brodeur, 1983: 513).

A key aspect of high policing is that it is based on the collection and assessment of intelligence. Before the age of technology that embraced activities such as telephone tapping, bugging and internet monitoring, informants played an important role in enabling the state to keep tabs on individuals and organisations who threatened to secure political reform that in the early nineteenth century was viewed as revolutionary.

'High Policing'—The Formation of Special Branch

As has been argued in Chapter 4, the state's involvement in intelligence gathering directed against organisations and individuals suspected of involvement in subversive activities can be traced back many centuries.

However, in response to the campaign of violence waged on mainland Britain between 1883 and 1885 (which is discussed below), the Special Irish Branch was set up whose role was to keep observations on Irish militants, to make inquiries on behalf of the government of Ireland and to supervise guarding the Queen and her Ministers (Bunyan, 1977: 104).

Its tactics regarding the first of these functions were described thus

> Rather than employing agents, it sought to prevent Fenian attacks by using a strategy peculiar to Victorian Britain: picketing. This involved identifying individuals as threats to national security (History Extra, 2019: [Online]).
>
> Once identified, plain-clothes policemen would maintain a brief surveillance of the suspect, with no attempt to incubate informers. After monitoring a suspect's movements, the officers would follow their observations with an arrest and questioning of those believed to be 'dynamitards'. If the evidence was solid against a prisoner, and he could not account for himself, he was charged. Foremost in this strategy was a preference for openly recorded arrests and clear evidence (History Extra, 2019: [Online]).

It was not totally effective and in 1884 its headquarters were blown up by a Fenian bomb.

Following the end of the dynamite campaign, the Special Irish Branch was retained, operating as a separate squad within the Met's CID. In 1888, mirroring the broadening of its functions beyond Ireland, it was renamed Special Branch.

In the late nineteenth century, foreign immigrant groups, especially anarchists (who drew their inspiration from Proudhoun and Russian thinkers that included Bakunin and Kropotkin), came under the radar of Special Branch on the pretext that they intended to achieve their political aims through acts of violence (Bunyan, 1977: 105–106). Many of these groups were based in the East End of London. Organisations that secured anarchist support and involvement (such as the Legitimation League which was formed in 1895, seeking the granting of full rights to illegitimate children but which also served as a platform for ideas such as free love which were considered obscene and deviant in late Victorian Britain) also came under Special Branch scrutiny using tactics that included infiltration by Special Branch officers and the use of agent-provocateurs (Bunyan, 1977: 105–106).

It was observed that between 1907 and 1909, the activities of the anarchists diminished but those of the Bolsheviks increased, although there was often an overlap in the activities of both of these sets of revolutionaries (Deacon, 1980: 198). In the early twentieth century, Special Branch attention was directed at the suffragette campaign and also to industrial disputes in the 'Great Unrest' between 1911 and 1914, where a key issue was the ideology that underpinned these events which entailed direct action by the working class.

However, the impact of Special Branch to counter both of these events was limited: the tactics of infiltration were hampered by the absence of any female police officers (regarding the suffragettes) and the non-hierarchical organisation adopted by groups associated with industrial unrest (including the syndicalists, the shop steward's movement and the communists) which made infiltration difficult (Bunyan, 1977: 110–111). As was the case in the late nineteenth century, the focus of Special Branch was London, the monitoring of political and industrial groups elsewhere in Britain being conducted by local police forces Bunyan (1977: 110).

During the First World War, Special Branch and the CID in London operated as 'one unit' (Bunyan, 1977: 112), with Special Branch activity becoming expanded to cover national security (including detecting spies and saboteurs, a task shared with MI5), and exercising surveillance over the socialist movement as a whole, for although the Labour Party and TUC endorsed the war, many socialists opposed it from both a pacifist perspective and in opposition to conducting an 'imperialist' war (Bunyan, 1977: 112).

Its remit regarding monitoring socialist groups was further extended when Prime Minister David Lloyd George used Special Branch to monitor and report on industrial unrest and subversion in the arms-production industry—a task which has previously been performed by a separate directorate of intelligence. It was argued that this task effectively extended surveillance to a wide range of individuals and organisations engaged in anti-war activity (such as pacifism and opposition to conscription when this was introduced in 1917) and industrial action—'in short, everyone who was ideologically to the left of the Tory Party became a potential subversive' (Bunyan, 1977: 114)—a situation aided by the term 'subversive' being nebulous in nature.

Special Branch was involved in countering industrial unrest in 1917 and in infiltrating the militants who were involved in the 1918 police strike (Bunyan, 1977: 114–115). Concerns regarding the motives of industrial unrest were exacerbated by the 1917 Bolshevik revolution and strike action intensified in 1918 and 1919, requiring Special Branch to conduct surveillance operations at meetings identified as being subversive all over the country (Bunyan, 1977: 117). Special Branch also received reports from provincial forces regarding matters of this nature (Bunyan, 1977: 118). However, during the 1920s (as is stated below), MI5 assumed the role of the key agency to combat subversion, with Special Branch playing a more limited role in this activity, although acting as arresting officers for MI5 (Bunyan, 1977: 118).

'High Policing'—The Formation of the Security Service

The Security Service (MI5) was set up in 1909, assuming responsibilities for work related to internal security, censorship and the protection of British ports and harbours that had been conducted by a sub-committee of the Committee for Imperial Defence (Bunyan, 1977: 154). It was initially headed by Captain Vernon Kell who reported to the Director of Military Operations.

Its initial role was to foil the spying activities performed by foreign governments that were conducted on British soil by German agents and the spy rings within which they operated in Britain (especially in connection with foiling sabotage). In order to monitor such activities, MI5 intercepted mail and became the 'pioneer of mail opening' (Bunyan, 1977: 155). It was also the policy of MI5 that once a spy or suspected spy had been identified, a permanent watch would be kept on him (Deacon, 1980: 213).

The use of mail interception by MI5 was aided by a decision made by Home Secretary Winston Churchill whereby the requirement to obtain a warrant to intercept a specific individual's mail was replaced with MI5 being given a general warrant to intercept and open all letters sent or received by persons who were listed by Kell as being of interest to MI5 (Deacon, 1980: 214). The activities of MI5 in this context enabled over 20 German spies to be rounded up the day after war was declared in 1914. This ensured that the British Expedition Force was able to cross the Channel without its movements being reported back to Berlin and deprived Germany of an effective spy network operating in the United Kingdom for the best part of a year (Deacon, 1980: 214–215).

The term 'Special Intelligence Department' was used in this period to cover the counter-espionage work that was engaged upon by Special Branch, MI5 and the Naval Intelligence Department (Deacon, 1980: 217).

Following the end of the First World War in 1918 its remit was extended so that it became an agency whose role was to counter subversion within the United Kingdom by monitoring political ideas and opinions and the persons and organisations that were associated with articulating them (Joyce & Wain, 2010: 223). This function was initially triggered by the 1917 Bolshevik Revolution in Russia arising from 'general fears of the ruling class that communism would sweep through Europe' (Bunyan, 1977: 155). It led MI5 to monitor a wide range of socialist organisations, thus extending the role of the state into what has been termed 'political policing' which, as has been argued above, is a key aspect of 'high policing'.

Bunyan (1977: 156–157) documented the rivalry that existed between the Metropolitan Police Special Branch and MI5 in connection with counter-espionage which was resolved in 1921 in favour of MI5 which henceforth became the key player in this work which was conducted by 'secretive and wholly undercover methods of operation' (Bunyan, 1977: 157). During the 1920s this was directed at both socialist organisations—including the communist party that was set up in 1920—and working-class industrial organisations and took the form of infiltration into such bodies and performing 'dirty tricks' in the form of various 'Red Scares' (Bunyan, 1977: 157–158). This included involvement in the Zinoviev letter in 1924, a hoax purporting to urge the creation of a revolutionary insurrection in the United Kingdom and which 'enabled the Conservative Party to paint [Labour Prime Minister] MacDonald as the dupe and abettor of Bolshevism's subversive aims' (Chester et al., 1967: 33) which contributed to Labour's defeat in the 1924 General election.

Conclusion

This chapter has discussed the extent and nature of politically motivated crime in the period 1850–1920. It has considered the extent of public disorder after 1850 which took numerous forms that included industrial unrest, and political reform, in particular the suffragette campaign to secure the vote for women. It has evaluated the concept of 'high policing' and discussed the agencies that were created in this period to conduct it. The following chapter will evaluate crimes other than those which were politically motivated and assess the response by the state to these activities.

? Summary Question

Evaluate the rationale for, and significance of, developments associated with 'high policing' that took place between 1850 and 1920.

References

Awcock, H. (2014). On This Day: Bloody Sunday, 13 November 1887. *Turbulentlondon.com* [Online]. https://turbulentlondon.com/2014/11/13/on-this-day-bloody-sunday-13th-november-1887/. Accessed 27 Jan 2022.

Bowden, T. (1974). "Ireland Decay of Control" and "Ireland: the Impact of Terror". In M. Elliott-Bateman, J. Ellis, and T. Bowden (Eds.), *Revolt to Revolution.* Manchester University Press.

Bowden, T. (1978). *Beyond the Limits of the Law.* Penguin Books.

Brodeur, J.-P. (1983). High Policing and Low Policing: Remarks About the Policing of Political Activities. *Social Problems, 30*(5), 507–520.

Bunyan, T. (1977). *The History and Practice of the Political Police in Britain.* Quartet Books.

Chapman, B. (1970). *Police State*. Pall Mall.

Chester, L., Fay, S., & Fay, S. (1967). *The Zinoviev Letter*. Heinemann.

Dangerfield, G. (1935). *The Strange Death of Liberal England, 1910–1914.* Constable and Company.

Darlington, R. (2008). *Syndicalism and the Transition to Communism: An International Comparative Analysis.* Ashgate Publishing.

Davies, M. (undated). The Union Makes Us Strong. *TUC History Online* [Online]. http://www.unionhistory.info/timeline/1880_1914.php. Accessed 1 Dec 2022.

Deacon, R. (1980). *A History of British Secret Service.* Granada Publishing Ltd.

Duffy, A. (1961). New Unionism in Britain, 1889–1890: A Reappraisal. *The Economic History Review, 14*(2), 306–319.
Fielding, N. (1991). *The Police and Social Conflict: Rhetoric and Reality*. Athlone Press.
Fielding, N. (1993). *The Police and Social Control: Rhetoric and Reality*. The Athlone Press.
Foley, M. (2014). *The Bloodied Field: Croke Park. Sunday 21 November 1920*. The O'Brien Press.
Foote, G. (1997). *The Labour Party's Political Thought: A History* (3rd ed.). Palgrave Macmillan.
Geary, R. (1985). *Policing Industrial Disputes 1893–1985*. Methuen.
Harrison, B. (1965). The Sunday Trading Riots of 1865. *The Historical Journal, 8*(2), 219–245.
Herrick, F. (1934). The Reform Bill of 1867 and the British Party System. *Pacific Historical Review, 3*(2), 216–233.
Himmelfarb, G. (1966). The Politics of Democracy: The English Reform Act of 1867. *Journal of British Studies, 6*(1), 97–138.
History Extra. (2019). The Victorian War on Terror. *History Extra* [Online]. https://www.historyextra.com/period/victorian/the-victorian-war-on-terror/. Accessed 29 Jan 2022.
Houghton, J. (2001). *Policing and Local Government in England*. Unpublished PhD thesis, Manchester Metropolitan University.
Janis, I. (1982). *Groupthink* (2nd ed.). Houghton Mifflin.
Joyce, P. (1999). *Realignment of the Left? A History of the Relationship Between the Liberal Democrats and Labour Parties*. Basingstoke: Palgrave Macmillan.
Joyce, P., & Wain, N. (2010). *A Dictionary of Criminal Justice*. Routledge.
Le Bon, G. (1895, July 26). *The Crowd: A Study of the Popular Mind*. Félix Alcan. Published in *Manchester Guardian* Correspondent (1866) "The Disturbances in Hyde Park". *Manchester Guardian.*
Manwaring-White, S. (1983). *The Policing Revolution: Police Technology, Democracy and Liberty in Britain.* The Harvester Press Ltd.
Miller, I. (2009). Necessary Torture? Vivisection, Suffragette Force-Feeding, and Responses to Scientific Medicine in Britain c. 1870–1920. *Journal of the History of Medicine and Allied Sciences, 64*(3), 333–337.
Mitchell, A. (1995). *Revolutionary Government in Ireland*. Gill & Macmillan.
Moss, A., & Skinner, K. (2013). *The Victorian Detective*. Shire Publications.
Park, J. (1920). *The English Reform Bill of 1867*. University of Columbia.
Peak, S. (1984). *Troops in Strikes: Military Intervention in Industrial Disputes*. The Cobden Trust.
Purvis, J. (1995). The Prison Experiences of the Suffragettes in Edwardian Britain. *Women's History Review, 4*(1), 103–133.
Sloan, G. (2013). The British State and the Irish Rebellion of 1916: An Intelligence Failure or a Failure of Response? *Journal of Strategic Security, 6*(3), 328–357.
Smyth, E. (1933). *Female Pipings in Eden*. P. Davies Ltd.

Steedman, C. (1984). *Policing the Victorian Community. The Formation of English Provincial Police Forces, 1856–1880*. Routledge and Kegan Paul.

Storch, R. (1975). The Plague of Blue Locusts: Police Reform and Popular Resistance in Northern England 1840–57. *International Review of Social History, 20*, 61–90.

Sweeney-Lynch, Z. (2022). The Great Dock Strike. *Poplar London* [Online]. https://poplarlondon.co.uk/great-dock-strike-london/. Accessed 1 Dec 2022.

Taylor, A. (1995). "Commons-Stealers", "Land-Grabbers" and "Jerry-Builders": Space, Popular Radicalism and the Politics of Public Access in London, 1848–1880. *International Review of Social History, 40*(3), 383–407.

Townshend, C. (2006). *Easter 1916: The Irish Rebellion*. Ivan R. Dee Inc.

Wilson, J. D. (1957). Introduction. M. Arnold. (1869). *Culture and Anarchy* (J. D. Wilson, Eds.). Cambridge University Press.

Yeates, P. (2001). The Dublin 1913 Lockout. *History Ireland, 9*(2) [Online]. https://www.historyireland.com/the-dublin-1913-lockout/#:~:text=15%2C000%20workers%20locked%20out,TUC%20food%20fund%20for%20survival. Accessed 30 Nov 2022.

12

Responses to Crime

Introduction

This chapter will examine arguments related to 'ordinary crime' and will evaluate debates related to the existence of a distinct 'criminal class'. It will also discuss some of the more serious crimes in the late nineteenth and early twentieth century, referring to the garrotting panic of 1862, the Ripper murders of 1888–1891 and the emergence of disorderly youths (as manifested in scuttling gangs). An examination of these issues will be conducted within the criminological theories of moral panics, sub cultural theory and opportunity theory. The chapter will also evaluate the emergence of hate crime in the form of the articulation of anti-immigrant sentiments.

The chapter will then focus on responses to crime after 1850. It will discuss developments that affected the detection of crime in this period (such as those derived from the application of forensic science). It will further examine the nature of punishment, how this influenced the prison regime and why changes to the role and environment of prisons were put forward at the end of the nineteenth century so that an emphasis on punishment (epitomised by the sentence of penal servitude) conducted through a harsh prison regime (which made use of the crank and treadmill) was—especially at the behest of Herbert Gladstone', 1895 report—reformed to emphasise the role of prisons in the reform and rehabilitation of offenders.

P. Joyce and W. Laverick, *History of Policing, Crime, Disorder, Punishment*, https://doi.org/10.1007/978-3-031-36892-9_12

The chapter will also consider developments associated with the introduction of a bespoke system to deal with young offenders that stemmed from the pioneering endeavours of reformers such as Carpenter, Mary and which bore legislative fruit in the form of the 1908 Children Act and the 1908 Crime Prevention Act. It will also evaluate the prison regime for female offenders within the context of arguments related to the cause of female criminality.

Crime and the Working Class

It has been argued that 'figures of the number of offences known to have been committed were not kept before 1857, and one cannot therefore estimate at all accurately the amount of crime during this period' (Hart, 1955: 412—'this period' being the period that the article discussed, 1835–1856).

Much crime in the early years of new policing consisted of 'low level' crime—pick pocketing, theft from homes, warehouses and factories and damage to property that included that owned by the railway companies. Emsley stated that what was understood by crime in the middle decades of the nineteenth century was 'theft and, to a lesser extent, assault' (Emsley, 1986: 85). He further observed that the delivery of preventive policing through the beat system was of questionable effectiveness in combating crime of this nature since in urban areas since most crimes took place behind closed doors or closed windows: a burglar could thus wait for a policeman to pass by on his beat and then enter the premises, especially if the householder or factory-owner was absent. Officers walking the beat would rarely be in a position to arrest a thief (Emsley, 1986: 81–82) although they may act in the capacity of 'capable guardians' as outlined in routine activities theory (Cohen & Felson, 1979) and prevent crimes of this nature from occurring.

What is clear regarding policing, is that much of it was directed at the working class and directed at those aspects of their behaviour that was regarded as deviant. This accords with the role of the police as outlined by Storch (1975, 1976) which has been discussed earlier in this book, in particular the previous chapter.

As was argued previously in this book, controlling vagrancy received a high level of police priority in the nineteenth century whose purpose was to enforce the system of waged labour on the lower classes—a purpose that could be subverted if forms of income other than that of legitimate employment were available (Neocleous, 2000: 724). The role of the police was thus to close off these alternative avenues and the Vagrancy Act was a key means at their disposal to achieve this purpose.

Vagrancy was often associated by the police with other forms of crime and there was considerable discretion available to a police officer in determining if someone was a vagrant and then to arrest him or her for a range of actions. Those sleeping rough often fell foul of the Vagrancy Act which could also be used against pick pockets and forms of street gambling that included pitch and toss (a gambling game in which the player who manages to throw a coin closest to a mark gets to toss all the coins, winning those that land with the head up). The role of the police with regard to vagrancy was added to when they undertook the role of relieving officers—a task that was ended in the counties in 1881.

Disorderly conduct also justified police intervention. This was sometimes directed against disorderly youths who loitered on street corners and was also often associated with drunkenness. These tasks have been associated with viewing the role of the police as that of enforcing social discipline on the urban working classes, a role that depicted the new police as domestic missionaries—

> monitoring and control of the streets, pubs, … was a daily function of the "new police" … a direct complement to the attempts of urban middle class elites… to mold a labouring class amenable to new disciplines of both work and leisure (Storch, 1976: 481).

In other words, if reforms in areas that included education, public health and housing failed to alter their behaviour, it could be achieved in a more coercive fashion through the law enforcement functions of the new police. And to secure this objective, the size of police forces grew so that in England and Wales, the 20,500 officers that were employed in 1861 had risen to 54,300 by 1911 (Taylor, 1998: 88).

The 'Criminal Class'

Victorians tended to believe that crime was on the decrease by the middle of the century, a situation that lasted until the early years of the twentieth. Factors that included rising living standards, lower food prices, political stability and reduced levels of interpersonal violence, seemed to have produced more law-abiding subjects and a new consensus on public order (Gattrell, 1990). Improvements in policing, which were discussed in the previous chapter, also played their part in crime reduction.

However, while older forms of crime such as highway robbery declined, other forms appeared. Most offenders were young males and the bulk of crime (estimated at half-three-quarters) (Emsley, 2018: 31–32) consisted of petty offences (such as small-scale theft and street-based offences such as drunkenness, assault and vagrancy). Pickpocketing became common, particularly among children. Crimes committed by women were frequently linked to prostitution and consisted of 'victimless' crimes such as soliciting, drunkenness, disorderly conduct and vagrancy. Despite the falling rates of crime, rates of housebreaking and burglary remained fairly consistent (Emsley, 2018: 31).

By contrast, serious crime was relatively rare and it has been estimated that between the 1850s and 1890s, the number of homicides (that is, both murder and manslaughter involving actions whereby one person killed another) reported to the police averaged below 400 per year (Emsley, 2005: 42).

Nonetheless, this idyllic situation was not universal. As will shortly be discussed, there were episodes of serious violence. Additionally, attention was drawn to the existence of criminal districts where the inhabitants were depicted as deviant. An important Victorian source on this issue was Henry Mayhew who wrote between 1851 and 1862 a 4-volume work, *London Labour and London Poor: A Cyclopaedia of the Conditions and Earnings of Those that Cannot Work, and those that Will not Work.*

Although Henry Mayhew did not originate arguments relating to the existence of a 'criminal class', he was nonetheless an important contributor to the claim of its existence (in fact, of several criminal classes). They resided in criminal areas of cities known as rookeries, the most notorious rookery of which was that of St. Giles off of Oxford Street, which was characterised by narrow alleyways and over-crowded housing and was dubbed 'Little Ireland' (King, 2013: 391).

Those who lived there would not work, which was usually attributed to a moral defect. They were depicted as the marginal people within the urban poor, a subset of the working class, overwhelmingly male, consisting of vagrants, beggars, thieves, prostitutes and cheats together with those who were dependant on them and their activities. These have been defined as 'products of the urban environment, born and bred into the immorality and vice in deprived and densely populated areas of the expanding cities and towns' (Johnston, 2015: 12)—'not casual offenders but those who were believed to be living by crime' and to whom the term 'habitual offender' became to be applied by the late 1860s (Johnston, 2015: 27).

It was also in areas such as these ('bad places') 'that persons were to be found indulging in the boisterous popular culture which so offended Victorian sensibilities and which the police were directed to control'—

> in the same places, and from the same groups were to be found the street traders who were "moved on", the men on the tramp and the seasonal workers suspected of being criminals because they were on the roads .... and in garrison towns from the mid-1860s until the mid-1880s, it was young women from the working class who were stopped and questioned on suspicion of being prostitutes under the Contagious Diseases Acts (Emsley, 1986: 84).

Expressing sentiments that would be later put forward by the biological positivist criminologist, Cesare Lombroso (whose views are considered in more detail in this chapter), Mayhew argued that they were different physically from non-criminals from whom they also differed in their habits and social conduct—

> There is a greater development of the animal than of the intellectual and moral nature of man.... They are more or less distinguished for their high cheek-bones and protruding jaws - for their use of a slang language - for their lax ideas of property - for their general improvidence - their repugnance to continuous labour - their disregard of female honour - their love of cruelty - their pugnacity - and their utter want of religion (Mayhew, 1851: Vol. I:3).

However, unlike Lombroso, Mayhew did not argue that criminality was a biological inheritance and believed it to be caused by factors that included poverty and poor parenting. He also distinguished between professional criminals who made their living from crime and casual criminals who sometimes committed crime, usually because of the 'pressure of circumstances'. But, nonetheless, this view of the criminal class depicted them as the criminal 'other' a class apart from other, 'civilised' members of society.

The existence of a criminal class or classes is not now supported by many scholars, one issue being whether those engaged in petty offences could be legitimately categorised as a 'class'. Additionally, this concept has been depicted as a construction by the 'respectable' whose 'perceptions stereotyped and exaggerated the gravity of the threat' (Beier, 2005: 501). However, whether actual or not 'the effects of the construction were no less "real" to those who created it and to those who felt the brunt of the criminal justice system' (Beier, 2005: 501).

The enactment of the 1869 Habitual Criminals Act and the 1871 Prevention of Crimes Act—which created the category of 'habitual criminal' and provided the police with considerable regulatory powers over those they suspected of obtaining a living by dishonest means—is testament to the reality which many in late Victorian England accorded to the existence of a criminal class and also echoes the differentiation between the deserving and undeserving poor which had been made in the reform of the Poor Law in 1834.

Emsley further argued that labelling individuals as criminals and the districts where they lived as criminal served to enhance the professionalism of the police 'by giving them an identifiable enemy to observe, catalogue, and, when appropriate, to arrest for the good of society' (Emsley, 1986: 84). However, this could also result in self-fulfilling prophecies 'by propelling first-time offenders into further crime since they were now stigmatized, and by urging any "respectable" families to do their best to move out of a stigmatized neighbourhood' (Emsley, 1986: 83).

Crime Detection

Professional policing was perceived as a preventive organisation when it was developed in the early decades of the nineteenth century. One reason for this, and a factor that considerably hindered the development of detective work within policing, was the concern that equated detective work with spying on the population, thus undermining their traditional rights and liberties. It has thus been argued that

> When the "new police" came into being in 1829, resistance resulting in part from prejudice and partly from fear and suspicion [...] inhibited the formation of a detective unit or plain-clothes branch. The principal aims of the police at the time were the prevention of crime and the maintenance of order, as opposed to investigation and detection (Matassa & Newburn, 2007: 43).

This situation ensured that detective specialisms within the professional police forces in the early decades of the nineteenth century were either small in terms of the personal or were slow to develop. Reliance was often placed on regular officers to perform detective work in serious criminal cases such as murder. A small number of detectives (eight in total) were employed in the Metropolitan Police in 1842 following an unsuccessful attempt on Queen Victoria's life (Moss & Skinner, 2013: 5, 17) but it was only after the 1867 Fenian outrages that full-time detectives were appointed at divisional level in 1869. The Metropolitan Police did not set up a centralised detective department—the Criminal Investigation or CID—until 1878, headed by Howard Vincent. By the mid-1880s, the Met's CID numbered around 800 officers (Emsley, 1986: 82). The City of London introduced their own detectives in 1857 (Moss & Skinner, 2013: 7).

Detective work in the latter decades of the nineteenth century was glamourised by the fictional detective, Sherlock Holmes, who was a character invented by the author Sir Arthur Conan Doyle. He made his first appearance in 1887 and his work as a detective was characterised by his skills in making observations and using his brilliant deductive mind to get to the bottom of a case and discover who had carried out the crime.

Although making careful observations and inspired deductions could play an important part in detective work in the latter decades of the nineteenth century, there were other techniques at their disposal to solve crimes, even though these resources were limited. Scenes of crime work were difficult for although cameras were available in the 1830s, they were of a cumbersome nature and were not widely used in crime detection work. Portable cameras—Kodaks—did not become available until 1888 in America which subsequently made it possible to consistently and accurately record scenes of crime information.

The most reliable way to detect a criminal was to catch them in the act of actually carrying out the crime or take evidence from a person who had seen the crime occur. If a suspect was found through either of these two ways, securing a confession from them was likely to be the best form of evidence that could be presented in a court.

However, if these circumstances were not met, there were other ways to try and detect crime, but they were not always reliable. These are considered below.

Forensic Science

Forensic science entails material at the scene of a crime being gathered which is then scientifically analysed in an attempt to detect the offender. In the latter decades of the nineteenth century, evidence such as footprints or blood stains often formed the basis of evidence available to detectives in this period which could be evaluated in a manner which might help identify suspects—for example, a footprint would—obviously—provide insights into the size of a person's foot and a series of them would indicate the length of stride which in turn might help to identify a person's height or weight or even age (since an older person would make a different type of imprint to that of a younger person). If a suspect were identified, surveillance methods could be used in an attempt to gather more information.

However, in the late nineteenth century, forensic science was very much in its infancy—for example, it was difficult to distinguish between a human blood stain and that of an animal. It was argued that deficiencies in detective work considerably hindered the police quest to apprehend the person responsible for the Whitechapel murders (Gray, 2015: 62). Nonetheless, some methods relevant to forensic science were available in the later part of the nineteenth century, one of which was fingerprint analysis.

The study or use of fingerprints is known as dactylography. The use of fingerprints to identify criminals was a nineteenth-century development, and the earliest recorded case of their use was in connection with a burglary committed in Tokyo in 1879 (Moss & Skinner, 2013: 52).

The use of fingerprints became widely adopted following the publication of the book *Finger Prints* by the British anthropologist Francis Galton in 1892. This work proved that each individual's fingerprints were unique. However, the classification system that he devised was difficult to operate in practice until improvements were made by Sir Edward Henry whose work, *Classification and Use of Fingerprints*, was first published in 1900. This development prompted the establishment of the fingerprint department of New Scotland Yard in 1901. The convictions of Alfred and Albert Stratton for robbery and murder in 1905 was the first time fingerprinting had secured a conviction and prompted its subsequent wider use in police work (Gray, 2015: 65).

In cases of murder a dead body may in itself contain important types of evidence that could be revealed by an autopsy being carried out. This was especially the case in connection with murder by poisoning—arsenic being the favoured poison in the nineteenth century. There were 98 criminal poisoning trials in England and Wales between 1840 and 1850. Although a reliable test known as the Marsh Test had been devised in 1838 by the English chemist James Marsh to detect arsenic, if this poison was administered over a lengthy period of time it could cause death from a range of symptoms that included abdominal pain, vomiting, diarrhoea or jaundice which were frequently confused with cholera. These symptoms were sufficiently common that a doctor may not investigate further, believing that death arose from natural causes (McDermid, 2014).

Poisoning was a method of murder favoured by female criminals: it has been concluded that

> More than 90% of convicted spouse murderers in 19th-century Britain were men. But men were far more likely to stab or strangle their wives; twice as many wives as husbands stood trial for poisoning (McDermid, 2014).

In 1860 the National Crime Records was set up. This entailed new technology being used in policing, with telegraph communications being used to allow police forces to communicate with each other quickly and effectively. However, although forces might keep records of criminals who had been convicted, this information often had little practical value since the methods of identification available at that time were primitive—at best a picture (perhaps accompanied with a name and address). But a person who used a different name, moved to a different address and made a few changes to his or her physical appearance, might escape the prying eyes of a detective and this be able to carry out further crimes.

In order to solve problems of this nature, a new form of forensic science known as anthropometry was developed in which detailed records of the body (and also other physical features such as tattoos or scars) were applied to police record keeping in order for previous offenders to be more easily identified. For then, as now, much crime was committed by persons who had offended previously and who would immediately 'enter the frame' when a crime with which they were associated was committed.

Anthropometry was pioneered by the French police officer, Alphonse Bertillon during the 1880s, whereby features of a person's body which included the head, face and limbs were recorded in a standardised way which made future recognition of that person an easier task than had previously been the case, especially in cases where a suspect had given a false name. Bertillon used this method in connection with identifying repeat offenders, or recidivists. There were weaknesses with this approach, in particular that unlike fingerprints, physical characteristics could be shared by several people. Bertillon used this approach in conjunction with another that he pioneered during the 1880s—the criminal mugshot—incorporating a full face shot and a profile view that was designed to make identification of a persons suspected of committing a crime easier. Both of these techniques were used in connection with the detection of crime within British policing at the end of the century.

Serious Crime in the Latter Decades of the Nineteenth Century

It has been argued above that much of the crime that was associated with the latter decades of the nineteenth century was of a low-level type, especially consisting of petty theft. Increasingly after 1850, there was a move towards increasing the number of offences that could be tried summarily through legislation that included the 1855 and 1879 Criminal Justice Acts and the 1847 and 1850 Juvenile Offenders Acts.

There were, however, exceptions to the normal low-level nature of crime and this section will explore four examples of the more serious crime that occurred in this period. These illustrate how criminal behaviour helped to shape the operations of the criminal justice system.

Gang-Related Crime and the Formation of the Metropolitan Police Flying Squad

The turn of the century witnessed episodes of gang-related crime in London. There were several of these documented by Morton (2003: 1–13) which included the Bessarabian Tigers, consisting of Russian Jews who operated in the Whitechapel area of East London and who operated protection rackets on the Russian Jewish shopkeepers who lived in that area. In addition to exhorting money from such persons they also engaged in gang warfare against their rivals which in the case of the Bessarabian Tigers was the Odessians.

Other examples of organised crime included the pickpocketing of the Blind Beggar Gang (named after a public house of the same name in Mile End Road, East London, although much of their activity was carried out in London's West End) and the Strutton Ground Mob from Westminster who ran protection rackets. However, Morton (2003: 5) concluded that following the crack down on the Bessarabian Tigers and Odessians properly organised crime in the East End died away' at least for a short time and most of the gangs that continued to operate consisted of 'informal associations' (Morton, 2003: 6).

Post-war I, gang-related crime was especially associated with Alfie Solomon (who was born in the East End but operated in Camden) and the activities of the Sabini gang which operated protection rackets, initially at race courses. One of the leading detectives engaged in tackling pre-war I organised crime in London was Detective Chief Inspector Frederick Wensley.

Wensley's methods included the use of undercover officers and his willingness to ignore divisional boundaries to apprehend criminals.

Box 12.1: The Flying Squad

In 1919, the Metropolitan Police set up a specialist squad (eventually known as the Flying Squad) to respond to a post-war crime wave.

The spur to the formation of the Flying Squad was post-war I crime and lawlessness. It was stated that

> Armed hold-ups became an almost daily occurrence, the number of house-and shop-breakings soared, pick pockets were an infestation and gang warfare, which had previously been confined to the race tracks … now flooded the streets and pitched battles were fought (Kirby, 2019: 6).

The reorganisation of the Met's CID in 1919 enabled Wensley (who was one of the detective Superintendents in charge of the 4 divisions which covered London) to organise a Squad to combat crime of this nature. It was known as the Mobile Patrol Experiment and consisted of 12 detectives. Their main role was to conduct target known burglars, robbers and pickpockets which they did using horse drawn canvas-covered carriages with holes cut into the side. They would leap out and make arrests if circumstances required it.

The unit also involved itself in combating organised crime which was viewed as being linked to overseas orchestration (Walker, 2020: [Online]). It conducted surveillance operations on known criminals which included them attending venues where such people were known to visit such as public houses and clubs (Metropolitan Police Service, undated: [Online]). The Squad was also willing to use methods that included cultivating participating informants from within criminal gangs who supplied information and were not then arrested for their part in a crime which was considered unorthodox police work at that time (Kirby, 2019: 12–13).

The unit was constantly reorganised and enlarged in the 1920s and the name 'Flying Squad' was adopted around 1921 perhaps as the remit of the officers covered all of London as opposed to being confined to specific police divisions. Its role became that of responding to serious and armed crime that was taking place in London at that time.

Examples of Serious Crime in the Late Nineteenth Century

The London Garrotting Panic 1862

Garrotting entailed robbery that was conducted by grabbing a person from behind, holding them around the neck in a choke hold and then strangling them using the arm or implements such as wire or cloth. This action was designed to incapacitate the victim while the robbery occurred rather than to intentionally kill them. Johnston (2015: 31) noted that the press had identified this as a problem during the 1850s when the perpetrators were identified as prisoners who had been released on a 'ticket of leave'. Concerns related to garrotting became an important source of concern in London in 1862.

However, subsequent discussions have suggested that this was an example of a moral panic. Those responsible for the production of a moral panic are usually moral entrepreneurs or the mass media (Scott, 2014: 492). This is not to deny that garrotting actually happened but, rather, suggests that it was not the serious problem it was made out to be. It was the scale of the crime that was artificial, designed to serve the financial and political values of those that owned key sections of the mass media.

Box 12.2: Moral Panic Theory

Moral panics describe a situation whereby 'a condition, episode, person or group of persons emerges to become defined as a threat to societal values and interests' (Cohen, 1980: 9).

The media was accorded a crucial role in the production of a moral panic. It was initially responsible for making people feel uneasy concerning the direction which society was taking. An important way of achieving this objective was to report incidents suggesting a decay in traditional moral values.

Having created an underlying cause of concern, the media then focused attention on an action that epitomised the perversion of traditional social values. This entailed focusing on an issue that was then amplified out of all proportion to its real importance through sensationalised treatment and the provision of selective information.

The media associated the issue with a specific group of people (termed 'folk devils') who become scapegoated. A moral panic arose as the consequence of an adverse social reaction to the activities that had been associated with the scapegoated group whereby public opinion demanded that the state should act robustly in order to curb their activities. This objective could be accomplished by legislation giving the police additional powers or by the more vigorous use of existing ones.

Moral panics generally occur in periods of rapid social change and can be said to locate and crystallise wider social anxieties about risk (Jewkes, 2011: 77). Problems such as recession, unemployment or the growth of monopoly capitalism lead many members of the general public to become disquieted concerning the direction society is taking, especially those whose interests or values seemed directly threatened by these changes. Those affected by feelings of social anxiety were especially receptive to the simplistic solutions provided by scapegoating a segment of the population, depicting them as the physical embodiment of all that was wrong with society and institutionalising prejudice towards them, thereby diverting attention away from economic and/or political issues and/or the policies and practices of government.

The behaviour of young people (often, but not exclusively, of working-class origin) is frequently the subject on which moral panics are based. Industrialised society's tendency to direct moral panics at the actions of the working class indicated a fear that the key threat to dominant social values was presented from this segment of society.

Panics rooted in middleclass fears of a threat to their social position have allegedly surfaced on a regular basis (approximately every 20 years): it has been asserted that these have sought to resurrect the social values of what was seen as a previous 'golden age' but which in reality was based upon a blinkered and over-romanticised view of the past (Pearson, 1983).

The panic over garrotting crystallised popular concerns over crime and disorder in the 1860s. Transportation had ended and the removal of this sanction was viewed by people of this period as the end of an important deterrent to committing crime. This form of crime was also viewed as barbaric and un-British, the product of foreign influences let loose in London which, however, was far from the truth since this crime that had a long historic pedigree in England (Pearson, 1983: 130 and Bibby, undated: [Online]).

The saturation coverage given to this form of criminality by the some sections of the popular press made it appear to be a huge problem in London in the 1860s that greatly increased the fear of crime in the capital. It was thus the reaction to crime of this nature by the media, public, police and the government that was the key issue rather than the crime itself. The attack on a Member of Parliament, Hugh Pilkington, as he made his way home from the House of Commons, helped sensationalise media coverage of this type of crime.

The aim of a moral panic is to produce an increased element of social control and discipline as a means to deter this form of offending. This aim was achieved through the enactment of the 1863 Security from Violence Act (the 'Garrotter's Act) which required anyone caught for this crime to be given up to 50 lashes of the whip as well as a lengthy prison sentence. It also helped create a climate in which prison conditions grew far harsher, emphasising the retributive aspects of the responses to crime in the latter half of the nineteenth century.

Then the crime suddenly appeared to die out. This was so for various reasons, one of which was the use of what would now be called 'saturation' policing methods in London in which plain clothes officers provided a large police presence both to deter and apprehend criminals of this nature. But an important explanation for the apparent end of garrotting was that the media grew tired of it. The story had served its purpose, it had sold copies of newspapers but the story had reached saturation point and it was now time to move on to something else.

The Ripper Murders

Murders associated to Jack the Ripper are an important example of serious crime that took place in the latter decades of the nineteenth century. These will be considered within the context of serial killing.

A serial killer is defined as someone who commits a string of murders that take place intermittently over a period of time and who frequently uses a similar method of killing, a *modus operandi*. There may also be a similarity in the targets that are selected to become a serial killer's victims.

There is no minimum or maximum number attached to the number of murders that have to be carried out in order for the offender to be labelled a 'serial killer', although three or more murders is sometimes used as a criterion and those who carry out a large number of killings are sometimes described as 'prolific' serial killers. Nor is there any limit set to the period of time over which the offences take place—it may be months, years or even decades. It is important, however, to the definition of a serial killer that there is a gap (sometimes referred to as a 'cooling off period') between each episode of murder. Persons who commit two or more murders without this cooling off period are termed 'spree killers'.

Eleven murders took place between 1888 and 1891 in the impoverished, run-down and violent Whitechapel area of East London, which was noted for violence and crime. The victims were all women, most of whom (and possibly all) were prostitutes.

At least five of the murders carried out in 1888 were attributed to a serial killer known to history as 'Jack the Ripper'. This name appeared in a letter that was claimed to have been written by the murderer, although doubt was subsequently cast on its authenticity. Two of these deaths occurred on one night in September 1888. These were set apart from the other murders that occurred in Whitechapel by the extremely violent, brutal and grotesque nature of the killings. The victims had their throats cut and in most cases the lower abdomen of their bodies had been savagely mutilated. In some cases organs had also been removed.

Box 12.3: The Ripper Murders
The *modus operandi* of the killer has been summarised as follows:

> A number of females, commonly recognized as 11 victims, were murdered in separate events in Whitechapel, London between 1888 and 1891. An evaluation of the murders revealed that six of those murders were linked by a number of distinct, personal signature characteristics, including picquerism, overkill, incapacitation, domination and control, open and displayed, unusual body position, sexual degradation, mutilation, organ harvesting, specific areas of attack, preplanning and organization, and a combination of signature features (Keppel et al., 2005: 1).

[Picquerism refers to stabbing or penetrating the skin of the victims.]

There is no certain explanation as to why the murders ceased in 1891. The Metropolitan Police, the City of London Police and a private organisation, the Whitechapel Vigilance Committee, were involved in the search for the killer but the murderer was never caught. The nature of the wounds inflicted on the women gave rise to suggestions that the murderer had anatomical knowledge and may have been medically trained.

Disorderly Youths and Scuttling Gangs

A contemporary of the period defined a scuttler as 'a lad, usually between the ages of 14 and 18, or even 19', and explained that 'scuttling consists of the fighting of two opposed bands of youths, who are armed with various weapons' (Devine, 1890: 2).

Scuttling gangs consisted of neighbourhood-based youth gangs that were formed in working-class areas of East Manchester and Salford in the latter decades of the nineteenth century, commencing in the early 1870 and reaching a peak in the early 1890s. These areas were not unique to such forms of activity and similar groups also existed in London. In South and East London in the 1890s, for example, street gangs (to which the name 'hooligan' was applied following disorders that occurred on the August Bank Holiday of 1898) (Pearson, 1983: 74–76) vented their anger and hostility towards immigrants, especially Jewish communities as well as conducting pitched battles among themselves.

Box 12.4: Sub Cultural and Opportunity Theory

The phenomenon of late nineteenth-century scuttling gangs was relevant to later discussions within criminology regarding sub cultural theory and opportunity theory.

Subcultural theorists combined Merton's strain theory (which explained individual deviancy) with the Chicago School's ecological theory (which was concerned with collective deviancy). Whereas Merton argued that delinquency arose from a mismatch between goals and the means to achieve them, subculturalists focused on group responses to goal blockage and asserted that this situation resulted in the emergence of deviant values that constituted a delinquent subculture.

Albert Cohen was a leading exponent of subcultural theory. He argued that workingclass boys experienced inner tensions in a society that was dominated by middleclass values. The school was seen as an important forum in which this 'status frustration' occurred. They could choose to conform to these values (either by seeking to achieve middle-class success goals or by exploiting the limited opportunities with which they were presented as fully as they could—characteristics which Cohen identified with the college boy and corner boy respectively) or they could rebel against middleclass norms of behaviour and engage in delinquent actions.

Cohen labelled this latter reaction as the response of the delinquent corner boy. This situation resulted in the emergence of a delinquent subculture in which society's values were rejected and new ones were substituted in their place. These new values formed the basis of a delinquent subculture—'a system of values that represented an inversion of the values held by respectable, lawabiding society' and it was in this sense that it was asserted 'the world of the delinquent is the world of the lawabiding turned upside down' (Sykes & Matza, 1957: 664).

The delinquent actions which arose from the deviant subculture were not necessarily designed to advance material goals but were especially concerned with achieving status and prestige among the delinquent's peers which resulted in him acquiring selfesteem which mainstream society denied them (Cohen, 1955).

Strain and subcultural theories were developed by 'opportunity theory' (Cloward & Ohlin, 1960). This drew on Merton's strain theory and Sutherland's concept of differential association and was concerned with the legitimate and illegitimate ways of achieving success in society.

According to this theory, the legitimate opportunity structure was mainly available to upper- and middle-class youths whereas working-class juveniles, finding the legitimate route to success blocked, were more likely to rely on illegitimate ways to achieve it. Unlike Cohen, opportunity theory did not involve any psychological explanations for delinquent behaviour. Instead, this behaviour was viewed as arising from an objective/quasi-rational assessment that it was impossible to achieve success through legitimate means. This strain resulted in lower-class youths banding together with others in a similar position.

However, opportunity theory also attempted to explain why varying forms of delinquent subculture were evidenced in different areas. The explanation centred on the balance struck in particular communities between the legitimate and illegitimate ways to achieve success in society.

It was asserted that lower-class juveniles who were denied the possibility of achieving success through legitimate means would form gangs whose behaviour was dependent on the kind of illegitimate opportunities that were available to them.

Three scenarios were identified:

- *The crime-oriented gang*: this consisted of a juvenile gang whose main activity was stealing. It was associated with an area in which there was a high degree of tolerance towards crime, thus existing alongside (and perhaps orchestrated by) more hardened adult criminals who served as role models for disaffected youths and could arrange for the disposal of goods that had been stolen by them. In these areas, juvenile crime was characterised by a relatively high level of organisation.
- *The conflict gang*: this gang was especially characteristic of socially disorganised neighbourhoods. The absence of effective restraints on the behaviour of young people (including the lack of criminal opportunity structures which were found in areas in which juvenile criminal gangs operated) resulted in violence that might take the form of warfare in which rival gangs vied with each other for control of an area (and the status which derived from this). As is discussed below, this response is especially appropriate to a criminological explanation of scuttling gangs.

- *Retreatism*: those who failed to achieve success in society through legitimate or illegitimate means might embrace a more passive rejection of society and its values which was characterised by drug-taking. This activity was more loosely structured than the delinquency of crime and conflict gangs, and could entail individual as opposed to group responses to the inability to achieve society's success goals.

The conflicts that arose between scuttling gangs were of a territorial nature. Territoriality formed 'the basis of allegiance to the gangs' (Davies, 1998: 352). Gangs vied with each other in adjacent neighbourhoods but might also pool their resources to defeat intrusions by scuttling gangs from other parts of Manchester or Salford.

Gang members wore distinctive clothes that distinguished them from other young men in the areas where they operated and they carried weapons including belts with large buckles which were used as offensive weapons in a fight. Some of the disorders that occurred were large scale, involving several hundred people.

The phenomenon of scuttling was attributed to factors such as lack of parental control, boredom, the lack of discipline in schools and 'base literature'. The latter consisted of what were termed the 'penny dreadfuls' which were seen to encourage young people to imitate crime which was favourably portrayed in these publications. However, it has also been argued that in this time, parental control was harsh, involving fathers beating their sons—actions which served to educate boys that 'violence was a customary means by which men vented their anger' (Davies, 1998: 354).

A more recent scholar drew attention to the manner in which gang conflicts of this nature 'provided a systematic means for young men to prove themselves against their peers' and for those involved to demonstrate their '"hardness", or toughness' which was considered 'a quintessential masculine virtue. Considerable kudos was derived from displays of fighting prowess and the ability to withstand pain, and boys and youths continually tested each other's mettle in order to prove themselves, and thus their masculinity, in the eyes of their peers' (Davies, 1998: 350). Public displays of aggression and acts of violence in affrays between rival gangs 'allowed those on the brink of adulthood to derive considerable status, and to imagine themselves as "hard" men' (Davies, 1998: 356).

It was thus 'toughness' and 'manliness' that underpinned violence of this nature as opposed to economic conditions or ethnic tensions (Davies, 1998:

350–351). To justify this assertion, it is argued that violence reached a peak in 1889/90 when economic conditions were good (Davies, 1998: 352).

The judicial system was relatively impotent to offer a remedy to the problem. The police force was not organised in a way that easily defeat widespread and organised public disorder and while the courts could pass severe sentences (including that of penal servitude) these had no lasting impact on the crime as gang members returned to their past activities upon release.

A number of factors led to the demise of scuttling gangs by the end of the century. This included slum clearance programmes, but especially to the creation of charities to try and stop youths falling in with the wrong crowds and providing ventures to provide for alternative outlets for working-class youths, such as working lads' clubs. Activities such as sporting rivalries could replace street fighting. One example of these ventures in was St. Marks (West Gorton) Football Club, set up by the Church Rector, Arthur Connell and his wife Anna. It is now more familiar with its modern name—Manchester City Football Club. Another of these initiatives was the creation of the Boys' Brigade which was formed in Glasgow by Sir William Alexander Smith in 1883. Initiatives such as these justify Foucault's (1977) concept of the 'disciplinary society', characterised by the dispersal of power and constructed upon methods of surveillance which blurred the difference between punitive and non-punitive institutions thus presenting 'a view of society that is a mesh of disciplinary relations' (Marsh, 2004: 53).

Box 12.5: Female Gangs

Although the material discussed above in this chapter locates males as a major source of crime and delinquency, female gangs also existed in the late nineteenth century. One of these was The Forty Elephants, also known as the Forty Thieves who were dubbed 'the most profitable and fearsome gang in the history of the UK' (Chard, 2018: [Online]).

The Forty Elephants was an all-female crime organisation which was based in the Elephant and Castle area of South London. It was recorded that 'though the first traceable news about this criminal organization appeared in 1873, it's believed that this group of women had operated in London since the late eighteenth century' (Chard, 2018: [Online]). They specialised in shoplifting but also conducted smash and grab raids.

The Forty Elephants worked alongside the Elephant and Castle gang, a group of male criminals who dominated the South London underworld.

Policing Hate Crime

Introduction

Hate crime (or bias-motivated crime) refers to actions whereby a perpetrator targets a victim because of his or her perceived or actual membership of a social group. The perpetrator is motivated by prejudice towards the group to which the victim is presumed to belong. The concept of hate crime extends the criminal justice agenda into a consideration of the motives that led to a person breaking the law.

Ideas regarding the impact of population growth and increased interaction between different groups of people (described as 'dynamic density') comprised a key element of modernisation approaches. Associated with the work of Émile Durkheim (1893), scholars examined the impact of processes of rapid social change upon social and political order. Societal transformation was regarded as potentially undermining traditional mechanisms of social control, creating social strain and pathological conditions within society (including the loss of social cohesion and increase in crime) (Ritzer, 1996).

These ideas were later picked up by theorists of late-modernity, post-modernism and more recently within globalisation scholarship, examining the impact of social transformations and globalising processes (including the increased mobility of people, money, goods and ideas) upon society, culture, structures of governance, security, crime and crime control. Thus, immigrant populations, migrant workers and refugees have become conceptualised as economic, political and ideological security threats within both state and regional political discourse and policy.

This section will examine early manifestations of hate crime as an aspect of turbulence that commenced in the Edwardian period (1901–1910) and continued in the years leading to the First World War and following the cessation of hostilities.

Racism Directed at Early Black and Asian Immigrants

Negative sentiments towards Black and Asian people have a long historical pedigree in the United Kingdom.

The Slave Trade

The slave trade was an important aspect of the perception of black people as inferior beings. The slave trade that existed in eighteenth and early nineteenth-century Britain drew upon 'a reservoir of popular racist ideas' to justify commerce of this nature (Law & Henfrey, 1981: 5), an important aspect of which was the dehumanisation of Black slaves who became viewed as goods and commodities rather than human beings (Law & Henfrey, 1981: 5–6).

Fryer discussed how black slave labour on sugar plantations in the West Indies comprised British industry's springboard. Thus, racism was regarded as not only justifying 'plantation slavery and, later, colonialism' but was also implicated in 'poison[ing] the lives of black people in Britain' (Fryer, 2010: xiii–xiv).

The Colonial Heritage

The abolition of the slave trade (which commenced with Lord Mansfield's judgement in 1772 and was formally terminated by the 1807 Abolition of the Slave Trade Act, and the subsequent abolition of slavery in British colonies in 1833), resulted in racism taking on 'a new and...deeper form as it became fused with the image of empire and British domination especially during the Victorian period' (Law & Henfrey, 1981: 10). It was in this sense that it was argued that racism evolved and became 'a principal handmaiden to empire' (Fryer, 2010: 165). A key aspect of this racist thinking was to reinforce the idea mentioned above that depicted Black people as members of a naturally inferior class (Law & Henfrey, 1981: 22).

As was argued by Fryer, 'English racism was born of greed', with racist narratives used to justify the purchase of, kidnapping, trafficking, branding, coercion and violence distributed to slaves (Fryer, 2010: 6–8). The subsequent teaching of history in schools that glorified the Empire further reinforced negative images of black people which was reinforced by patronising literature directed at children that included Helen Bannerman's *The Story of Little Black Sambo* (initially published in 1899). From the nineteenth to the twentieth centuries, pseudo-scientific racism and empire developed side by side, with racism underpinning notions of 'imperial trusteeship' and British 'native policy' from the 1840s to the 1940s (Fryer, 2010: 165).

Competition for Scarce Resources and Political Threat

Britain's racial history is also intimately entwined with anxieties related to public order. Concern was raised during the late eighteenth century regarding the prospect of political reform and societal disorder driven by black slaves, the poor white working classes and their supporters. During the nineteenth century, negative sentiments towards resident black people were articulated (Fryer, 2010: 230–231). In addition to efforts to reduce the numbers of black and Indian residents already settled within Britain, action towards immigration and population control occurred.

As discussed by Fryer (2010: 169–170), by the 1860s working people in Britain seemed intent upon challenging the political and economic power of those who ruled and employed them. Thus, Fryer suggested that there was evidence of cooperation and/or at least sympathy between Irish patriots and Chartists, with Indians and Africans also gaining confidence in their political activities resulting in 'Lesser breeds' and 'lower orders', including the Irish, non-European native peoples, discontented natives in the colonies and labour agitators in the mills having 'much in common, not at least in the threat they presented to law and order' (Fryer, 2010: 169–170).

The nineteenth century therefore witnessed significant legislative provisions and repeated efforts to introduce access controls, and sanctions to deter further immigration to Britain, in addition to efforts to expel undesirable, politically inflammatory and/or destitute Black and Asians, through methods of deportation and transportation.

Anti-immigrant Sentiment in the Early Twentieth Century

In the late nineteenth and early twentieth centuries, anxiety and hostility against immigrants was articulated. Jewish people were one target of this sentiment. The British Brothers League was created in 1902 (Rubin, 2010: 372). It gained a significant following in urban areas, seeking to limit Jewish immigration from Eastern Europe (see also Law & Henfrey, 1981: 372).

In order to restrict population numbers, and in response to the problem of Jewish emigration and the intrusion of East European Jews on labour markets, the 1905 Alien Act placed restrictions upon the entry of 'undesirable immigrants', including those lacking the means of 'decently' supporting themselves and their dependents, lunatics and idiots (arising from infirmity or disease) and those 'likely to become a charge on rates or otherwise a detriment to the public' in addition to those subject to extradition for a non-political offence.

The twentieth century also witnessed trade union agitation against Chinese and Indian Labour. Concerns were expressed regarding the use of Chinese labour within shipping, which, the unions believed, lowered the standard of life for white men and were also regarded as posing considerable safety issues. These sentiments were further illustrated by seaman strikes against Chinese and Indian Labour in 1911 and 1914.

Racial Unrest 1914–1920

In 1914, the circumstances of Black and Asian people in Britain changed temporarily. Domestically, black and Indian labour was required during the war effort within factories, the merchant service and within the military, with large numbers finding employment during that time.

However, although the involvement of Black soldiers and workers during the First World War was generally welcomed in Britain, attitudes towards Black people reverted to antagonism when hostilities ended in 1918 (Law & Henfrey, 1981: 30). Black and Asian seamen and factory workers faced discrimination and violence including stabbings, beatings, and attacks against hostels and lodging houses.

The year 1919 was marked by severe social and racial disorder, both within Britain and abroad. Such disturbances arose against the background of a labour surplus following demobilisation after the end of the First World War in which persons of foreign descent were made scapegoats for post-war economic problems and accused of taking jobs (and also houses in areas where sailors settled in the United Kingdom) from the indigenous white community.

Within Britain, rioting occurred between January and August 1919, directed at minority ethnic workers from a variety of backgrounds that included African, African-Caribbeans and South Asians. Anti-black, anti-Arab and anti-Chinese racial disturbances and riots took place within several ports including Tyneside, London, Liverpool, Glasgow, Cardiff, Hull and Newport.

In race riots in Liverpool, 'white rioters numbering up to 10,000 at times, attacked Black people in the streets, in their homes and in lodging houses' and the police were accused of pursuing initiatives in response to the violence that were 'distinctly racialist involving…arbitrary and induced repatriation' (Law & Henfrey, 1981: 31). This violence claimed the life of Charles Wooton who was chased into Liverpool Docks by a white mob and drowned attempting to escape from his attackers (Cook, 1993: 167).

The government response to manifestations of hate crime involved encouraging Black seamen to return to their country of origin and legislative action to restrict immigration.

The Prosecution of Crime in the Late Nineteenth Century

Although Jeremy Bentham in 1790 had criticised the manner in which prosecutions were bought in England and Wales (Journal of Criminal Law, 1984: 302), the creation of a Director of Public Prosecutions was not officially recommended until a report of the Criminal Law Commission in 1845, which argued that private prosecutions facilitated 'bribery, collusion and illegal compromises'. It was further argued that 'the duty of prosecution is usually irksome, inconvenient and burthensome; the injured party would often rather forgo the prosecution than incur expense of time, labour and money. When, therefore, the party injured is compelled by the magistrate to act as prosecutor, the duty is frequently performed unwillingly and carelessly' (Criminal Law Commissioners, 1845, cited in Wooler, 2014: [Online]). The solution that was put forward was the appointment of public prosecutors.

However, over a further decade elapsed before the Select Committee on Public Prosecutors was established in 1856. This suggested that District Agents should be appointed by the Home Secretary whose role would be to bring before the magistrates those persons suspected of having carried out a criminal offence where this course of action had not already been performed (Journal of Criminal Law, 1984: 302). However, nothing of any substance was introduced to implement this proposal: the County and Borough Police Act 1856 allowed the Home Office to ask the Treasury Solicitor's Department to take on cases of particular importance, but this meant that most cases fell outside of this system.

Ultimately, the office of Director of Public Prosecutions (DPP) was created in 1880, following the enactment of the 1879 Prosecution of Offences Act. It was initially part of the Home Office, superintended by the Attorney General, being given its own department in 1908. The DPP was initially responsible for the prosecution of a small number of major cases, the remainder being prosecuted by the police service.

Punishments in Late Nineteenth Century

Several important developments were introduced after 1850 as responses to crime.

Whipping

Whipping conducted in private (usually a prison) continued, usually as a punishment for male offenders and its use was increased following the enactment of the 1863 Security from Violence Act connection with theft with violence. It was not formally abolished as a punishment until 1948.

Penal Servitude

New forms of punishment which were based on imprisonment were developed during the nineteenth century. One of these was penal servitude in which a person convicted of a crime would be required to perform hard labour while serving his or her prison sentence which was carried out in a convict prison placed under the control of the Home Office. This reflected a belief that the aim of punishment was retributivist in intention.

The sentence of penal servitude was initially authorised by the 1853 and 1857 Penal Servitude Acts. A sentence of penal servitude initially lasted for a minimum of three years (increased to five following the enactment of the 1864 Penal Servitude Act and which could be extended to 7 if the convicted person had previously been convicted of another felony). Following the end of transportation (which formally occurred in 1868 although the use of it declined after the 1840s), penal servitude became the only long-term punishment available to the state and incorporated a system (similar to parole) of release on licence or what was termed a 'ticket of leave'.

Penal servitude sought to break the spirit of offenders. Its aim was purely that of punishing offenders. Initially prisoners would be sent to a state-run prison such as Millbank or Pentonville where they would endure the separate system. They would then be transferred to a convict (or public works) prison where they would perform some form of public works outside of the prison (or sometimes forced to work for private contractors) that was supervised by the Board of Directors of Convict Prisons. Three public works prisons were built between 1848 and 1856, and more were constructed following the abolition of transportation. The aim of this aspect of punishment was for prisoners to repay their debt to society (May, 2006: 21).

Penal servitude has been described as 'ferocious sentences' (Emsley, 2018: 292). It was often inflicted on persons who had not committed particularly serious crimes by the standards of the late nineteenth century and was often directed at repeat petty offenders. Under the provisions of the 1908 Prevention of Crime Act, persons over the age of 16 and who had three previous convictions, and were leading a 'dishonest life' and who were serving a period of penal servitude were categorised as 'habitual criminals'. This meant they could be sentenced to an additional period of imprisonment of between 5–10 years for the protection of the public.

This sentence was abolished in 1948. Penal servitude was distinct from a sentence of hard labour which was inflicted on persons serving a period of imprisonment of up to two years and who were required to perform industrial work within the prison. This included picking oakum and using a treadmill. Prisoners sentenced to hard labour spent the first two weeks of their sentence sleeping on a bed made from a plank of wood—a penalty that remained in place until 1945 (May, 2006: 23). The sentence of hard labour was abolished in 1948.

Prison Regimes and the Philosophy of Prisons After 1850

Imprisonment had become the most widely used punishment for crime from the end of the eighteenth century. One explanation for this is that inserting the power to punish 'more deeply into the social body' (Foucault, 1977: 82) was a more effective means of exercising social control over the population through the related processes of individual and general deterrence than could be achieved through one-off public executions.

The size of the prison population peaked during the 1860s with around 20,000 men, women and children confined in local prisons and around 10,000 in convict prisons at any one time (Crone et al., 2018: 21). Between 1837 and 1901 there were estimated to have been more than 15 million receptions into prisons: four out of five sentences were for less than one calendar month, indicating that the chief purpose of prisons had become that of retributivism in the form of punishment and deterrence rather than reductivism, seeking the reform and rehabilitation of those convicted of crime (May, 2006: 17).

Prison Regimes

The silent system (which has been discussed earlier in this work) was promoted following the enactment of the 1865 Prison Act which was based upon the Caernarvon Committee's examination of prison discipline (1863). Conditions were made unpleasant in order to deter offenders from returning, Caernarvon's Committee (1863: para III) noting that the 'strictly penal element' of prison discipline was 'the chief means of exercising a deterrent influence'. The 1865 Act was introduced following the garrotting crisis of 1862 and aimed to increase the deterrent intention of punishment. The rule of silence was not relaxed until 1920 and was formally abandoned in 1950 (May, 2006: 16).

Accordingly, after 1865 the view of the role of prisons moved away from reform and rehabilitation and towards deterrence and retribution. Thus, the 'hard labour, hard board, hard fare' regime with which the silent regime was associated (Johnston, 2015: 96) increasingly became hard, long and pointless, consisting of tasks that included turning the crank, being confined to a treadmill or shot drill (which entailed prisoners either standing in a line and passing cannon balls to each other or performing a walking exercise in which at regular intervals they would pick up and put down cannon balls). Initially, the intention of this was to instil the work ethic into prisoners. However, views that providing prisoners with skills through work experience and education rewarded them for committing crime (Emsley, 2018: 285–286) resulted in the orientation of the prison regime being that of the retributivist strategy of punishing offenders.

The level of re-offending in this period further influenced the purpose of prisons as being that of exacting retribution on those who had offended and also underpinned the disciplinary regime in prisons: in 1911 there were 313 published rules affecting local prisons and a further 1441 unpublished standing orders to regulate 'the minutiae of prison life' (May, 2006: 27).

Fluctuations in the purpose of prisons and the nature of the prison regime also questioned assumptions associated with Durkheim who (as is argued in Chapter 6) had suggested that the transition from a mechanical to an organic society resulted in methods of punishment becoming more lenient. By contrast, Marxist penology suggested that society's response to crime was subject to fluctuations based upon changes effecting the labour market whereby a shortage of labour resulted in lenient punishments whereas an abundance of labour resulted in a more severe response to crime.

Mid-Victorian Prison Conditions

See Figs. 12.1 and 12.2

THE PENAL ESTABLISHMENT AT PENTRIDGE.—THE SILENT SYSTEM.—SEE PAGE 6.

Fig. 12.1 The Whipping Post Lawford's Gate Prison

Fig. 12.2 An illustration of the silent system

Women in Prisons

As has been stated in Chapter 2, while women accounted for around 40% of the defendants at London's Old Bailey from the 1690s to the 1740s, the proportion subsequently declined significantly, so that by the early nineteenth century only 22% of defendants were women and by the early twentieth century the proportion had declined to 9%. By this point in time serious crime had come to be perceived as essentially a masculine problem (The Proceedings of the Old Bailey, 2018: [Online]).

In connection with custodial sentences, it has been estimated that in the second half of the nineteenth century, women constituted 17% of the prison population and constituted about 20% of those convicted of crime. In the late Victorian period, 90% of female prisoners received short custodial sentences that were served in local prisons where they constituted around 25% of all inmates (May, 2006: 34). Far fewer women received sentences of penal servitude to be served in a convict prison, Johnston (2015: 130) estimating that the figure fell from a high of 1050 committals in 1860 to below 100 in 1890.

The crimes which women committed were mainly 'low-level or minor offences', although many women were repeat offenders and in the latter part of the nineteenth century outnumbered men in this respect (Johnston, 2015: 122). It was also observed that overall, women tended to commit offences that were financially motivated, thus challenging the 'widely held notion of female criminals as sexually motivated or driven by impulse to commit irrational, behavioural offences' (Zedner, 1994: 40).

The concept of differential socialisation refers to children being treated differently because of beliefs within society concerning the roles they will later hold in adult society. This is achieved by utilising mechanisms to ensure that children fulfil these social expectations. The main instruments that are responsible for achieving this purpose are the family, the education system and the media. This served to explain the differences in the volume of crime committed by females and males and also of society's reaction to male and female criminality.

Male offending was attributed to a perversion of acceptable masculine traits whereby boys are encouraged to be 'aggressive, ambitious and outwardgoing' (Smart, 1977: 66). Factors which include competitiveness, the demonstration of physical strength, aggressiveness and the importance of achieving (in particular in connection with supporting the family) were key aspects developed during the process of male socialisation which may also serve to underpin criminal behaviour (Oakley, 1982). Alternatively, females were depicted as 'housemakers; their domestic role was to care for the family' (Johnston, 2015: 123). According to the social construction of femininity, female criminality was seen as unnatural a perversion of socially expected traits that included passivity, domesticity, caring and nurturing. This implied that women who committed crime were psychologically disordered and were thus often treated as lunatics while in prison.

Explanations of female crime were rooted in theories derived from late nineteenth-century biological positivism initially put forward by Lombroso and amplified, with specific regard to female offending, in a work by Lombroso and Ferrero in 1895. Female crime was primarily attributed to 'impulsive or irrational behaviour caused by a reaction to factors which included hormonal changes occasioned by biological processes of menstruation, pregnancy and childbirth'. Sexual immorality was also put forward as an explanation of female crime (The Proceedings of the Old Bailey, 2018: [Online]). View of this nature insisted that women could not be held responsible for their criminal actions that additionally were virtually devoid of meaning for those who carried them out (Smart, 1995: 25) and for which the woman had no regard or awareness of the consequences of her actions (Johnston, 2015: 129).

By the end of the nineteenth-century crackdowns on female crime were initiated, triggered by a debate about 'national deterioration' which embraced eugenics as a means of preserving the national 'stock'. This resulted in criminal women being treated more firmly, an example being the 1898 Inebriates Act which authorised preventive detention for a period of up to 3 years of habitual drunkards and those who had committed serious offences while under the influence of alcohol.

The regime in women's prisons was influenced by the belief that female criminals were capable of being reformed while in prison if subjected to reforming influences and go on to lead useful lives in, for example, domestic service or shop work. These were provided both by female prison wardens and also by middle-class Lady Visitors. For much of the nineteenth century, the 'typical' female prisoner was uneducated and drawn from the lower end of the social ladder, which tended to enhance the closed nature of female prison life. However, the imprisonment of suffragettes (which is discussed in the previous chapter) did serve to enable abuses in the prison regime to become publicised.

Women's prisons developed alongside other institutions that included reformatories and refuges that supported women who manifested various aspects of deviant behaviour (Johnston, 2015: 138–139). It was estimated that between 1898 and 1914, women made up around 80% of admissions into inebriate reformatories, although successful treatment of inebriate women at this stage was rare (May, 2006: 35).

The Gladstone Report and the Role of Prisons

In 1830 there were around 300 prisons but this number had been reduced by the 1865 Prison Act to 126 local prisons and 9 convict prisons (Crone et al., 2018: 25). Local prisons were controlled by the relevant local authority and for much of the nineteenth century (until the distinctions were ended by the 1865 Prison Act which introduced the term 'local prisons') comprised of a range of institutions that included goals, bridewells, houses of correction and lock ups (Crone et al., 2018: 25) where offenders served short sentences, typically below 3 months. Convict prisons were under Home Office control.

The 1877 Prison Act ended the distinction between local and convict prisons. Under the 1877 Act, all prisons were placed under central control, administered by the Prison Commission, based on the concern for uniformity in prison regimes, Caernarvon's Committee noting in 1863 the absence of a uniform system of labour, diet and treatment across the prison estate (Caernarvon, 1863: para II).

Following the enactment of this legislation, the number of institutions formerly designated as local prisons dropped to 62 and the number of convict prisons rose to 13 although by the end of the century this figure was reduced to 5 (figures derived from Crone et al., 2018: 25).

The main purpose of prisons was viewed as that of deterring offending behaviour. On the face of it, this approach was working. One scholar observed that

> Between 1879 and 1894, the daily average population in convict prisons fell by over half, from 10,880 prisoners to 4,770, and the population of local prisons fell by one-third, from 20,833 prisoners to 13,850 (Bailey, 1997: 287).

However, he went on to argue that

> The drop in the prison population was probably less a function of prison discipline, however, than of the fall in recorded crime, a reduction in the minimum duration of penal servitude (from 7 years to 3 years), and an increasing resort by courts to noncustodial penalties. For every 1,000 offenders sentenced at higher and summary courts in 1896 for indictable crimes, 516 were imprisoned, 19 sentenced to penal servitude, 194 fined, 120 bound over in their recognizances, and 34 sent to reformatory and industrial schools. As the century of the prison drew to a close, the confidence in deterrent imprisonment was decidedly on the wane (Bailey, 1997: 287).

Towards the end of the nineteenth century a new approach, that of rehabilitation, emerged as a key function of prisons. The Gladstone Report of 1895 was a key development in promoting the role of prisons as rehabilitative institutions (see Hudson, 1987: 3–11).

The report of Herbert Gladstone sought a move away from the harsh conditions that had existed in Britain's prisons since the middle of the nineteenth century. It identified the main fault of prison as being that 'it treats prisoners too much as irreclaimable criminals, rather than reclaimable men and women' (Gladstone, 1895: 16). The report was based upon the belief that prisoners were sent to these institutions *as* punishment rather than *for* punishment and it ultimately resulted in changes to prison conditions.

Although the deterrent role of prisons was not abandoned, it was balanced by placing a similar emphasis on the objective of the reform of convicted offenders. The report argued that prison discipline and treatment should be designed to maintain, stimulate or awaken the higher susceptibilities of prisoners, to develop their moral instincts, to train them in orderly and industrial habits, and whenever possible to turn them out of prison better men and women, both physically and morally, than when they came in (Gladstone, 1895: 7–8). Its key provisions were incorporated into the 1898 Prison Act.

This legislation emphasised the importance of reforming prisoners as a key role of prisons and led to changes in prison conditions affecting the separate system and hard labour. Prisoners were to be allowed to associate while performing work where this was practicable and the crank and treadmill were phased out, both being formally abolished in 1902. Isolation was permitted for a period of up to one month. It was responsible for ensuring that work performed in prisons would be productive and of a nature that would enable prisoners to secure employment upon their release: oakum picking was now allowed only if no other work was available. Those who were given prison sentences without hard labour would henceforth be categorised by the courts into one of three divisions which affected the treatment they received while in prison.

Significance of the Gladstone Report

It has been argued that the Report was of considerable significance to penal reform—

> it is the Report's attitude to three matters in particular which make it a landmark in the history of English penal reform. These matters are the regard paid to the possibility that prison conditions might be so contrived as to have a positive reformative effect, the recognition of the need to ameliorate the lot of the prisoner, and the recognition of the problem of recidivism (Cross, 1971: 4–5).

Nonetheless, the extent to which the report was responsible for advocating a change in the philosophy of prisons whereby rehabilitation rather than punishment was regarded as their main role is not universally accepted. The type of work performed in these institutions (such as sewing mailbags) indicated that retribution had not been entirely eliminated from the prison regime.

It has been argued that

> The importance of the Gladstone Committee is disputed, with some seeing it as a radical departure, heralding the approach of the 'rehabilitative ideal', while others see it as a continuation of a penal system primarily concerned

> with deterrence and retribution, which by reforming the system made it more acceptable. In our opinion, the Gladstone Committee was not itself a major contributor to the rehabilitative ideal, but did lay down some foundations on which others could build (Robinson & Crow, 2009: 20).

Additionally, as was argued by Johnston (2015: 2–3), the motives behind criminal justice reform and reformers are the subject of debate. The opinions of what she terms 'traditional or Whig accounts' (which view reforms such as the decline in bodily punishments and the increased use of imprisonment as a vehicle to reform the habits of a criminal) are contrasted with 'revisionist accounts'. The latter have examined the 'class interests and motives of the police and criminal justice reformers' (Johnston, 2015: 3). These highlight concerns regarding the exercise of power and social control, depicting the penitentiary as operating 'in the interests of capitalist society' and in which 'the inmates were taught and have instilled in them the habits and discipline of labour' (Johnston, 2015: 4).

The Punishment of Young Offenders

Initially the English criminal justice system failed to draw any distinction between juvenile and adult offenders. There was no formal age of criminal responsibility (this was introduced by the 1933 Children and Young Persons Act which set this age at 8). Children were viewed as 'small adults', and treated and punished in a similar way to them. This could mean that very young child law-breakers were dealt with in a very harsh manner in Victorian Britain. Sentences of hard labour and transportation were meted out to offenders, especially to repeat offenders, guilty of 'larceny (theft).' In extreme cases, children who broke the law could be hung.

The legal position regarding how the law treated young people was founded on Blackstone's *Commentaries on the Laws of England* (1765–1769) which were regarded as the main authority on of English Law. This held that an infant aged 0–7 could not be held responsible for his or her criminal actions but a child aged 7–13 could be: the presumption of *doli incapax* applied unless the court felt otherwise and believed the child did know right from wrong in which case he or she could be imprisoned or even executed (Magarey, 1978: 18). However, during the second quarter of the nineteenth century, the concept of *doli incapax* effectively fell in disuse so that children and young people were committed 'trifling delinquencies' were treated as if they had, in fact, carried out 'grave offences' for which they were often punished by imprisonment.

Changes in the law, and in particular the enactment of the 1824 Vagrancy Act, the 1827 Malicious Trespass Act and the 1829 Metropolitan Police Act broadened the scope of the criminal law and facilitated a punitive response to young delinquents (Magarey, 1978: 20–21). It was argued that the 1829 measure, supplemented by the 1839 Metropolitan Police Act made London's street children 'particularly susceptible to arrest' (Magarey, 1978: 21). Subsequent legislation that included the 1847 Juvenile Offenders Act directed that those under 14 (raised to 16 by the 1850 Juvenile Offenders Act) charged with simple larceny up to the value of five Shillings should be tried in the Petty Sessions court served to increase the number of juveniles who came before the courts (Johnston, 2015: 139–140).

Magarey referred to anxieties by property owners concerning juvenile delinquency in the second quarter of the nineteenth century for which, she accepted, 'there was some justification' (Magarey, 1978: 13). She stated that

> The shifts in the labour market, the poverty, the overcrowded housing and disease which dominated the lives of the poor and labouring classes in this period made city streets, for some of the nation's rapidly increasing number of children, their principal means of survival (Magarey, 1978: 13–14).

Such developments justified placing young offenders within the broader notion of 'the criminal class' by around the 1840s (Johnston, 2015: 140).

As was noted by Pinchbeck and Hewitt (1978: 431), the first systematic investigation into the contemporary causes of juvenile delinquency occurred under the auspices of the Society for Investigating the Causes of the Alarming Increase of Juvenile Delinquency in the Metropolis in 1815. The Committee's comments, together with similar statements from a variety of other sources, were regarded as important in influencing contemporary attitudes to the problem of juvenile delinquency, encouraging voluntary effort in providing institutions whose aim was to reform, not merely punish, delinquent youth, and to push for legislative reform regarding juvenile crime.

Quoting from Howard's original Report on the Condition of Prisons, the Committee argued 'if it were the aim and wish of the magistrates to effect the destruction present and future, of young delinquents, they could not devise a more effectual method than to confine them so long in our prisons, those seats and seminaries, as they have been properly called, of idleness and vice' (Report of the Society for Investigating the Causes of the Alarming Increase of Juvenile Delinquency in the Metropolis, 1816: 24).

In May 1818 Peter Bedford and his friends founded the Society for the Improvement of Prison Discipline and for the Reformation of Juvenile Offenders. This was underpinned by the belief that a separate prison system for young offenders, with a system adapted to the reformation of youth, combining education, classification and employment, could substantially reduce juvenile delinquency.

Debates concerning the solution to juvenile offending revealed a tension between those who wished to punish young people for the crimes they had committed and who made out a case for separate juvenile prisons to be set up and those who wished to reform the habits of the child criminal and sought to achieve this purpose by setting up reformatories which would provide education and work experience.

Concerns during the early decades of the nineteenth century by the middle classes that juvenile delinquency was a growing problem (which was mirrored by the increase in the number of persons committed to prison in England and Wales, rising from 9696 in 1839 to 11,720 in 1843 and, in regard to persons under 17 years, of age, from 13,900 in 1843 to 11,360 in 1853) (Magarey, 1978: 16–17) served to popularise the notion of punishment and the creation of separate juvenile prisons which was embodied in the 1838 Parkhurst Act which set up the first separate prison for juvenile offenders.

An important pioneer who advocated the alternative approach to juvenile delinquency was Carpenter, Mary, who advocated the need for reformatory schools for young offenders. She put her ideas into practice by establishing a privately run reformatory in her home town of Bristol in 1852. This was initially for both boys and girls but subsequently, two establishments were created along the lines of single sex institutions, the one for girls situated at the Red Lodge Museum in Bristol and opened in 1854, being the first reformatory school for girls in England.

Her work inspired the enactment of the 1854 Reformatory Schools (Youthful Offenders) Act. This legislation authorised voluntary societies to establish reformatory schools which were to be given powers of compulsory detention for children committed to their care by the courts. The period of detention lasted between two to five years. Each school was governed by 'managers', the body of subscribers who drew up their school rules. The Home Secretary was provided with powers to certify the schools as satisfactory and was also given the right to veto any rules he thought undesirable. Wherever possible, parents were required to make some financial contribution to the upkeep of their children while at the school.

By 1857, 45 of reformatory schools had been set up either by private individuals or local authorities. The Home Office took over responsibility for these institutions in 1860. Additionally, the 1857 Reformatory Schools Act created industrial schools which catered for children aged between 7 and 14 years of age who had been convicted of vagrancy. Magistrates were also empowered to place children who had not been convicted but who were deemed to be in 'moral danger' in industrial schools which were registered with the Home Office. The Local Government Board (which was set up in 1871) later took over the role of the Home Office in registering both reformatory and industrial schools.

By 1873, there were 65 reformatory schools and 104 industrial schools in England and Wales that jointly held around 17,500 children (Cayoun, 2018: [Online]). It was noted that the distinction between these two different institutions remained blurred, both using punitive regimes that included the use of corporal punishment (Cayoun, 2018: [Online]).

Box 12.6: Carpenter, Mary

In 1856, Carpenter, Mary published a book *Juvenile Delinquents, their Conditions and Treatment* (1856) in which she outlined the principles that guided her work.

These emphasised the need to reform and rehabilitate young offenders rather than to exact retribution on them for the crimes they had committed.

In this book, she expressed compassion for what she described as the poor 'pariah children' who, by virtue of their upbringing 'have at twelve, perchance even at eight or nine years of age, the determined will, the violent passions, even the knowledge, in crime, of a man' (Carpenter, 1856: 6) and to which society responded 'by a desire of self-protection, and too often also a spirit of revenge' even though it was known that such a response would harden and probably corrupt the child (Carpenter, 1856: 7).

Her solution was that Christian men and women should become the mothers and fathers of these 'moral orphans'—they must 'restore them to the true condition of childhood, give them a home, open their souls to good and holy influences, if need be correct them, but with a loving severity, and so under God's blessing restore them to society, prepared to fill well their station within it, and to pass honourably through this life, always striving to attain to a better' (Carpenter, 1856: 7–8).

The Origins of the Early Twentieth-Century Juvenile Justice System

The latter decades of the nineteenth century witnessed a move away from imprisoning juvenile offenders. The Summary Jurisdiction Act of 1879 provided that a juvenile could, for petty offences of which he was undoubtably guilty, be let off with an 'admonition' instead of a formal conviction. Subsequently, the 1887 Probation of First Offenders Act gave magistrates discretionary powers to release any delinquent convicted of an offence punishable by not more than two years' imprisonment. However, both measures suffered from an implementation deficit, with magistrates preferring to send offenders to industrial schools. This problem resulted in the Home Secretary issuing a Home Office circular to the draw attention of sentencers to these measures (Matthews, 1892: column 9).

The origins of the contemporary system for dealing with juvenile offenders separately from adults lie in the 1908 Children Act. This measure abolished imprisonment for offenders below 14 and permitted imprisonment for those aged 14 and 15 only in exceptional cases (for which the court had to issue an 'unruly' certificate). The legislation formally abolished the death penalty for a child or young person below the age of 16 and established a separate system of juvenile courts to deal with offenders aged 15 years and younger. The concept of separate youth courts was pioneered in Chicago in 1899 and their role was to manage a new category of transgressor, the juvenile delinquent. Initially these courts also had powers to intervene in cases of child neglect.

Those who came before juvenile courts might be 'advised, assisted and befriended' by the Probation Service (which, newly established by the 1907 Probation of Offenders Act, had specific responsibilities for juvenile offenders) or, if they were aged between 16 and 21, they might be sent to borstal, an institution that was formalised by the 1908 Crime Prevention Act (being based on an experiment whereby a separate youth custodial establishment had been set up in Borstal, Kent).

Borstals were designed to provide education and training for juvenile criminals (initially aged 16–20, but the upper age limit was raised to 21 in 1936) in a craft or trade within the environment of a strict regime that was based around physical training; the object was to enable trainees to secure employment and be more adequately equipped for life outside the institution. A semideterminate sentence of between one and three years was served in these institutions, and on release this was followed by supervision by the Probation Service for a minimum period of six months.

Box 12.7: Positivist Criminology and Responses to Crime

Classicist criminology asserted that criminals possessed free will but that their ability to make the right choices had been subverted by factors that included poor or bad parenting, the absence of moral guidance and the environment in which they had been brought up. It was thus possible to use the criminal justice system to reboot the offender's character in order to enable him or her to make the 'right' moral decisions in the future.

However, in the late nineteenth and early years of the twentieth century, alternative views regarding the causes of crime to those put forward by classicist criminology began to emerge, termed positivism. These views suggested that criminals possessed different characteristics that separated them from other members of society. Cesare Lombroso developed the belief that it was possible to identify criminals by their biological make-up.

In the first edition of his book *L'Uomo Delinquente* (Lombroso, 1876), he came to two main conclusions:

- *Criminals were those individuals who had failed to evolve*: in keeping with the Darwinian background to his work he perceived criminals to be primitive biological freaks who possessed characteristics appropriate to earlier, primitive man. This view is commonly referred to as the concept of atavism.
- *Criminals could be identified by their physical features*: his studies of executed criminals led him to assert that the 'criminal type' could be identified by distinguishing physical features (such as the shape of the skull or facial characteristics) which he referred to as 'stigmata'. Many of these were inherited, reflecting biological inferiority which indicated that the person had a propensity for committing crime. These physical traits included non-hereditary features such as tattoos.

These views were compatible with the view that criminals were 'born bad' and were influential regarding the purposes of punishment. The classicist view of punishment being guided by the idea of deterrence, underpinned by a view that human beings made rational choices, became challenged by the determinist assumption of what became known as the Italian School of Positivist Criminology—individuals could not be held responsible for their actions and their behaviour was controlled by forces over which they were unable to exert control.

Lombroso's ideas were subsequently modified by Ferri. He asserted that there were three categories of criminals—those who were born bad, those who were insane and those whose actions were the consequence of a particular set of social circumstances in which they found themselves (Ferri, 1917). In his later writings Lombroso modified his 'born bad' stance by including factors extraneous to the individual (such as climate or education) as explanations of criminal behaviour.

Lombroso's ideas were significant in shaping attitudes in the twentieth century towards why people committed crime and how society should respond to it.

He shifted attention away from the criminal law by making individual offenders the focus of his studies. He rejected the classicist view that punishment should fit the crime by asserting that the rationale of state intervention should be that of protecting society.

The aim of the criminological enterprise was thus to identify those exhibiting criminal features and remove them from society where their shortcomings could be treated (as opposed to being punished).

This approach, however, also rejected the idea that criminals could be reformed and returned to society as rehabilitated persons.

Conclusion

This chapter has discussed the nature and extent of crime in the period 1850–1920, drawing attention to the academic debates regarding the existence of criminal class. It has also, through the use of selected examples, discussed a number of more serious crimes that occurred in this period and has also discussed the emerging phenomenon of hate crime during the early years of the twentieth century.

The chapter has discussed improvements to the way in which crime was detected and has also evaluated changes affecting the punishment of crime, drawing attention to the shift from harsh responses based on a retributivist philosophy to a reductivist approach that sought to reform and rehabilitate offenders.

The chapter has also considered the way in which women and children were published during the period 1850–1920, emphasising similar trends affecting the philosophy of punishment. Finally, the chapter considered the emergence of positivist criminology in explaining why people committed crime and the implications of this for the response by society towards their actions.

? Summary Question

Based on your reading of this chapter, identify the major challenges for the crime and criminal justice agenda that were likely to arise in the first half of the twentieth century.

References

Bailey, V. (1997). English Prisons, Penal Culture and the Abatement of Imprisonment, 1895–1922. *Journal of British Studies, 36*(3), 285–324.

Bannerman, H. (1899). *The Story of Little Black Sambo.* Grant Richards

Beier, L. (2005). Identity, Language and Resistance in the Making of the Victorian "Criminal Class": Mayhew's Convict Revisited. *Journal of British Studies, 44*(3), 499–515.

Bibby, M. (undated). *The 19th Century Garroting Panic.* HistoricUK.com [Online]. https://www.historic-uk.com/HistoryUK/HistoryofBritain/Garotting-Panic/. Accessed 27 Jan 2022.

Blackstone, W. (1765–1769) *Commentaries on the Laws of England* (4 Vols.). Clarendon Press.

Caernarvon, L. H. (1863). *Report from the Select Committee of the House of Lords on the Present State of Discipline in Gaols and Houses of Correction.* House of Lords, Paper 37.

Carpenter, M. (1856). *Juvenile Delinquents, Their Condition and Treatment.* W. and F. G. Cash.

Cayoun, M. (2018). A Brief History of the Law and Policy on the State's Provision of Care for Children in England and Wales 1800–2017. *National Archives* [Online]. https://webarchive.nationalarchives.gov.uk/ukgwa/20221028230433/https://www.iicsa.org.uk/key-documents/7854/view/INQ002472.pdf. Accessed 17 Jan 2023.

Chard, M. (2018). The Wicked Female Gang That Terrorized London During the Nineteenth Century. *Culturacolectiva* [Online]. https://culturacolectiva.com/history/the-forty-elephants-gang/. Accessed 16 Jan 2023.

Cloward, R., & Ohlin, L. (1960). *Delinquency and Opportunity.* Free Press.

Cohen, A. (1955). *Delinquent Boys: The Culture of the Gang*. Chicago Free Press.

Cohen, S. (1980). *Folk Devils and Moral Panics.* Martin Robertson, first published in 1972.

Cohen, L., & Felson, M. (1979). Social Change and Crime Rate Trends: A Routine Activity Approach. *American Sociological Review, 44*(4), 588–608.

Committee for Investigating the Causes of the Alarming Increase of Juvenile Delinquency in the Metropolis. (1816). *Report of the Committee for Investigating the Causes of the Alarming Increase of Juvenile Delinquency in the Metropolis.* J.F. Dove.

Cook, D. (1993). Racism, Citizenship and Exclusion. In D. Cook & B. Hudson (Eds.), *Racism and Criminology* (pp. 136–157). Sage.

Crone, A., with Hoskins, L., & Preston, R. (2018). *Guide to the Criminal Prisons of Nineteenth Century England.* Prisonhistory.org [Online]. https://www.prisonhistory.org/wp-content/uploads/2018/06/Guide-to-the-Criminal-Prisons-of-Nineteenth-Century-England-R1.pdf. Accessed 12 Apr 2022.

Cross, R. (1971). *Punishment, Prison and the Public: An Assessment of Penal Reform in Twentieth Century England by an Armchair Penologist.* Steven and Sons.

Davies, A. (1998). Youth Gangs, Masculinity and Violence in Late Victorian Manchester and Salford. *Journal of Social History, 32*(2), 349–369.

Devine, A. (1890) *Scuttlers and Scuttling: Their Prevention and Cure.* Manchester Guardian.

Durkheim, E. (1893/1964). *The Division of Labor in Society.* Free Press cited in Ritzer, G. (1996). *Sociological Theory* (4th ed.). McGraw-Hill International Editions.

Emsley, C. (1986). Detection and Prevention: The Old English Police and the New 1750–1900. *Historical Social Research, 37*, 69–88.

Emsley, C. (2005). *Hard Men: The English and Violence Since 1750.* Hambledon Continuum.

Emsley, C. (2018). *Crime and Society in England 1750–1900* (5th ed.). Routledge.

Ferri, E. (1917). *Criminal Sociology.* Little, Brown.

Foucault, M. (1977). *Discipline and Punish: The Birth of the Prison.* Vintage.

Fryer, P. (2010). *Staying Power. The History of Black People in Britain.* Pluto Press.

Gattrell, V. (1990). Crime, Authority and the Policeman State. In F. Thompson (Ed.), *Cambridge Social History of Britain, 1750–1950* (Vol. 3.). Cambridge University Press.

Gladstone, H. (1895). *Report from the Departmental Committee on Prisons,* Sessional Paper 1895, c. 7702. HMSO.

Gray, D. (2015). *Crime, Policing and Punishment in England, 1660–1914.* Bloomsbury Academic.

Hart, J. (1955). Reform of the Borough Police 1835–1856. *English Historical Review, 70*(276), 411–427.

Hudson, B. (1987). *Justice Through Punishment: A Critique of the 'Justice Model' of Corrections.* Macmillan.

Jewkes, Y. (2011). *Media and Crime* (2nd ed.). Sage.

Johnston, H. (2015). *Crime In England 1815–1880: Experiencing the Criminal Justice System.* Routledge.

Journal of Criminal Law. (1984). Proposed Independent Prosecution Service: The Prosecutor's Viewpoint. *Journal of Criminal Law, 48*(3), 302–311.

Keppel, R., Weis, J., Brown, K., & Welch, K. (2005). The Ripper Murders: A *Modus Operandi* and Signature Analysis of the 1888–1891 Whitechapel Murders. *Journal of Investigate Psychology and Offender Profiling, 2*, 1–21.

King, P. (2013). Ethnicity, Prejudice and Justice: The Treatment f the Irish at the Old Bailey 1750–1825. *Journal of British Studies, 52*(2), 390–414.

Kirby, D. (2019). *Scotland Yard's Flying Squad: 100 Years of Crime Fighting.* Barnsley, Yorkshire: Pen and Sword Books Ltd.

Law, I., & Henfrey, J. (Ed.). (1981). *A History of Race and Racism in Liverpool, 1660–1950.* Merseyside Community Relations Council.

Lombroso, C. (1876). *L'uomo delinquente.* Hoepl. Translated into English in 1896 T. Fisher Unwin.

Lombroso, C., & Ferrero, W. (1895). *The Female Offender.* Fisher Unwin.

Magarey, S. (1978). The Invention of Juvenile Delinquency in Early Nineteenth-Century England. *Labour History, 34*, 11–27.

Marsh, I. (2004). *Criminal Justice: An Introduction to Philosophies, Theories and Practice*. Routledge.

Matassa, M., & Newburn, T. (2007). Social Context of Criminal Investigation. In T. Newburn, T. Williamson, & A. Wright (Eds.), *Handbook of Criminal Investigation*. Willan Publishing.

Matthews, S. H. (1892). Statement in the House of Commons 28 March. HC Debs, Vol. 3, Column 9.

May, T. (2006). *Victorian and Edwardian Prisons*. Shire Publications.

Mayhew, H. (1851). *London Labour and the London Poor: The Condition and Earnings of Those That Will Work, Cannot Work, and Will Not Work*. G. Woodfall and Son.

McDermid, V. (2014). The Grisly History of Forensics—By Crime Writer Val McDermid. *Guardian*, September 26.

Metropolitan Police Service. (undated). "Flying Squad". www.metpolice.uk [Online]. https://web.archive.org/web/20090417233856/http://www.met.police.uk/history/flying_squad.htm. Accessed 11 Oct 2022.

Morton, J. (2003). *Gangland* (Vol. 1). Time Warner Paperbacks.

Moss, A., & Skinner, K. (2013). *The Victorian Detective*. Shire Publications.

Neocleous, M. (2000). Social Police and the Mechanisms of Prevention: Patrick Colquhoun and the Condition of Poverty. *British Journal of Criminology, 40*, 710–726.

Oakley, A. (1982). Conventional Families. In R. Rapoport, R. N. Rapoport, & R. Fogart (Eds.), *Families in Britain*. Routledge & Kegan Paul.

Pearson, G. (1983). *Hooligan: A History of Respectable Fears*. Macmillan.

Pinchbeck, I., & Hewitt, M. (1978). *Children in English Society from the Eighteenth Century to the Children Act 1948* (Vol. II). Routledge and Kegan Paul.

Ritzer, G. (1996). *Sociological Theory* (4th ed.). McGraw-Hill International Editions.

Robinson, G., & Crow, I. (2009). *Offender Rehabilitation: Theory, Research and Practice*. Sage.

Rubin, B. (2010). The Rise and Fall of British Fascism: Sir Oswald Mosley and the British Union of Fascists. *InterSections, 11*(2), 323–380.

Scott, J. (2014). Moral Panic. In J. Scott & G. Marshall (Eds.), *A Dictionary of Sociology* (4 ed.). Oxford University Press.

Smart, C. (1977). *Women, Crime and Criminology: A Feminist Critique*. Routledge & Kegan Paul.

Smart, C. (1995). *Law, Crime and Sexuality*. Sage.

Storch, R. (1975). The Plague of Blue Locusts: Police Reform and Popular Resistance in Northern England 1840–1857. *International Review of Social History, 20*(1), 61–90.

Storch, R. (1976). The Policeman as Domestic Missionary. *Journal of Social History, 9*(4), 481–509.

Sykes, G., & Matza, D. (1957). Techniques of Neutralisation: A Theory of Delinquency. *American Sociological Review, 22*, 664–670.

Taylor, D. (1998). *Crime, Policing and Punishment in England, 1750–1914*. Palgrave/Macmillan.

The Proceedings of the Old Bailey. (2018). Gender in the Proceedings. *Old Bailey Proceedings Online* [Online]. https://www.oldbaileyonline.org/static/Gender.jsp. Accessed 13 Jan 2023.

Walker, A. (2020). Flying Squad: Sweeney's Changing Face. BBC News, November 10 [Online]. http://news.bbc.co.uk/1/hi/uk/1016855.stm. Accessed 11 Oct 2022.

Wooler, S. (2014). The Independent Review of the Prosecution Activity of the Royal Society for the Prevention of Cruelty to Animals. Rspca.org [Online]. https://www.rspca.org.uk/webContent/staticImages/Downloads/WoolerReviewFinalSept2014.pdf. Accessed 12 Apr 2023.

Zedner, L. (1994). Wayward Sisters: The Prison for Women. In N. Norris & D. Rothman (Eds.), *The Oxford History of the Prison: The Practice of Punishment in Western Society.* Oxford University Press.

Additional Resources

As was noted in the preface, a text book of this nature is designed to provide readers with a basic introduction to the very wide range of issues that affected policing, crime, disorder and punishment between 1689 and 1920.

More detailed information can be obtained from sources that are listed below. These include video resources which help to bring the subject to life.

Key Texts

Beattie, J. (2001). *Policing and Punishment in London 1660–1750. Urban Crime and the Limits of Terror.* Oxford University Press.

Beattie, J. (2012). *The First English Detectives: The Bow Street Runners and the Policing of London, 1750–1840.* Oxford University Press.

Critchley, T. (1967). *A History of Police in England and Wales.* Constable.

Davey, B. (1983). *Lawless and Immoral: Policing a Country Town 1838–1857.* Leicester University Press.

Emsley, C. (1983). *Policing and Its Context 1750–1850.* Macmillan.

Emsley, C. (1996). *The English Police: A Political and Social History* (2nd ed.). Routledge.

Emsley, C. (2005). *Hard Men. The English and Violence Since 1750.* Hambledon Continuum.

Emsley, C. (2009). *The Great British Bobby: A History of British Policing from the 18th Century to the Present.* Quercus.

Emsley, C. (2018). *Crime and Society in England 1750–1900* (5th ed.). Routledge.

Foucault, M. (1977). *Discipline and Punish: The Birth of the Prison.* Vintage.

P. Joyce and W. Laverick, *History of Policing, Crime, Disorder, Punishment,* https://doi.org/10.1007/978-3-031-36892-9

Gatrell, V. (1996). *The Hanging Tree: Execution and the English People 1770–1868*. Oxford University Press.
Geary, R. (1985). *Policing Industrial Disputes 1893–1985*. Methuen.
Gray, D. (2015). *Crime, Policing and Punishment in England, 1660–1914*. Bloomsbury Academic.
Haliday, G. (2017). *Victorian Policing*. Pen and Sword History.
Hay, D., Linebaugh, P., Rule, J., Thompson, E. P., & Winslow, C. (2011). *Albion's Fatal Tree: Crime and Society in Eighteenth Century England* (Rev. ed.). Verso, originally published in 1975.
Hobsbawm, E., & Rudé, G. (2001). *Captain Swing*. Phoenix Press, originally published in 1969.
Levine, P. (1994). "Walking the Streets in a Way No Decent Woman Should": Women Police in World War I. *The Journal of Modern History, 66*(1), 34–78.
Ignatieff, M. (1978). *A Just Measure of Pain: The Penitentiary in the Industrial Revolution 1750–1850*. Pantheon Books.
Johnston, H. (2015). *Crime in England 1815–1880: Experiencing the Criminal Justice System*. London: Routledge.
Mather, F. (1959). *Public Order in the Age of the Chartists*. Manchester University Press.
McLynn, F. (1989). *Crime and Punishment in Eighteenth Century England*. Oxford University Press.
Palmer, S. (1988). *Police and Protest in England and Ireland 1780–1850*. Cambridge University Press.
Pearson, G. (1983). *Hooligan: A History of Respectable Fears*. Macmillan.
Quinault, R., & Stevenson, J. (1974). *Food Riots in England 1792–1818*. Routledge.
Reith, C. (1956). *A New Study of Police History*. Oliver and Boyd.
Reynolds, E. (1998). *Before the Bobbie: The Night Watch and Police Reform in Metropolitan London 1720–1830*. Macmillan.
Rudé, G. (1964). *The Crowd in History: A Study of Popular Disturbances in France and England, 1730–1848*. Wiley.
Rudé, G. (1970). *Paris and London in the Eighteenth Century: Studies in Popular Protest*. Fontana.
Steedman, C. (1984). *Policing the Victorian Community: The Formation of English Provincial Forces, 1856–80*. Routledge and Kegan Paul.
Taylor, D. (1998). *Crime, Policing and Punishment in England, 1750–1914*. Palgrave Macmillan.
Thompson, E. P. (1963). *The Making of the English Working Class*. Victor Gollancz.
Tobias, J. (1972). *Nineteenth Century Crime. Prevention and Punishment*. David and Charles.

Journal Articles

Beattie, J. (1975). The Criminality of Women in Eighteenth Century England. *Journal of Social History, 8*(4), 80–116.

Beier, L. (2005). Identity, Language and Resistance in the Making of the Victorian "Criminal Class": Mayhew's Convict Revisited. *Journal of British Studies., 44*(3), 499–515.

Booth, A. (1977). Food Riots in the North West of England 1790–1801. *Past and Present, 77*(1), 84–107.

Brodeur, J.-P. (1983). High Policing and Low Policing: Remarks About the Policing of Political Activities. *Social Problems, 30*(5), 507–520.

Dodsworth, F. (2008). The Idea of Police in Eighteenth Century England: Discipline, Reformation, Superintendence, c 1780–1800. *Journal of the History of Ideas, 69*(4), 583–604.

Emsley, C. (1986). Detection and Prevention: The Old English Police and the New 1750–1900. *Historical Social Research, 37*, 69–88.

Hart, J. (1955). Reform of the Borough Police 1835–1856. *English Historical Review, 70*(276), 411–427.

Hobsbawm, E. (1952). The Machine Breakers. *Past & Present, 1*(1), 57–70.

Holmes, G. (1976). The Sacheverall Riots: The Crowd and the Church in Early Eighteenth Century London. *Past and Present, 72*, 55–85.

Joyce, P. (1991). Recruitment Patterns and Conditions of Work in a Nineteenth Century Urban Police Force: A Case Study of Manchester 1842–1900. *Police Journal, LXIV*(2), 140–150.

Joyce, P. (1993). The Transition from "Old" to "New" Policing in Early Nineteenth-Century Manchester. *Police Journal, LXVI*(2), 197–210.

Lindley, K. (1983). Riot Prevention and Control in Early Stuart London. *Transactions of the Royal Historical Society, 33*, 109–136.

Lyman, J. (1964). The Metropolitan Police Act of 1829. *Journal of Criminal Law and Criminology, 55*(1), 141–154.

Magarey, S. (1978). The Invention of Juvenile Delinquency in Early Nineteenth-Century England. *Labour History, 34*, 11–27.

Neocleous, M. (2000). Social Police and the Mechanisms of Prevention: Patrick Colquhoun and the Condition of Poverty. *British Journal of Criminology, 40*, 710–726.

Palmer, S. (1978). Calling Out the Troops: The Military, the Law and Public Order in England, 1650–1850. *Journal of the Society for Historical Army Research, 56*(228), 198–214.

Shoemaker, R. (1987). The London "Mob" in the Early Eighteenth Century. *Journal of British Studies, 26*(3), 273–304.

Storch, R. (1975). The Plague of Blue Locusts: Police Reform and Popular Resistance in Northern England 1840–1857. *International Review of Social History, 20*(1), 61–90.

Storch, R. (1976). The Policeman as Domestic Missionary. *Journal of Social History, 4*, 481–509.

Talbot, P. (2001). The English Yeomanry In The Nineteenth Century and the Great Boer War. *Journal of the Society for Historical Army Research, 79*(317), 45–62.

Thompson, E. P. (1971). The Moral Economy of the English Crowd in the Eighteenth Century. *Past and Present, 50*(1), 76–136.

Video Material

"Bill of Rights 1689" available at the link
• https://www.lawteacher.net/acts/bill-of-rights-1689.php
"Glorious Revolution and the Bill of Rights" available at the link
• https://www.youtube.com/watch?v=WqAA0hgSBtQ
"Drawn and Quartered—Worst Punishments in History" available at the link
• https://www.youtube.com/watch?v=crcFImOwiJg
"Transportation of British Criminals to Australia" available at the link
• https://www.bbc.co.uk/programmes/p00w67x1
"Peter Ackroyd on Newgate and Tyburn" available at the link
• http://www.executedtoday.com/tag/1750s/page/2/
"What Is a Pillory ?" available at the link
• https://www.youtube.com/watch?v=VHyByZBYFuc
"Highway Robbery" available at the link
• https://www.youtube.com/watch?v=oiMfEwTQOVA
"The True Story of the Golden Age of Piracy" available at the link
• https://www.youtube.com/watch?v=sKNW1J6i0Rg
"The History of Smuggling and Smugglers on the Kent Coast" available at the link
• https://www.youtube.com/watch?v=5Xjwsu4MG40
"Poaching 1500–1750" available at the link
• https://www.youtube.com/watch?v=-N4et01_9R0
"Night Watchmen and Town Constables 1500–1700" available at the link
• https://www.youtube.com/watch?v=A0echbTvbe4
"Thief Taker. Jonathan Thief Taker General" available at the link
• https://www.youtube.com/watch?v=DAkpzWaOpsc
"Tolpuddle Martyrs" available at the link
• https://sites.google.com/site/foxfordhistory/home/crime-and-punishment/1700-1900-crime-and-punishment
"18th March 1834: Tolpuddle Martyrs Sentenced to Transportation to Australia" available at the link
• https://www.youtube.com/watch?v=W3G22nNRw94
"Letter from J. Norris to Lord Sidmouth" at the link:
• https://media.nationalarchives.gov.uk/index.php/letter-j-norris-lord-sidmouth-manchester-6-october-1819/
"Christian Changemaker John Howard" available at the link

• https://alchetron.com/John-Howard-(prison-reformer)

"Elizabeth Fry and the Reform of the Prisons" (6 minutes) available at the link

• https://www.youtube.com/watch?v=_pU7mCdRh2Y

"Bentham's Panopticon" available at the link

• https://criminologyweb.com/jeremy-bentham-panopticon/

"Pentonville Prison: Mr. Prior History" available at the link

• https://www.youtube.com/watch?v=uVJ3nK4KTlc

"Brutal Victorian Prisons—Lincoln Castle Prison" available at the link

• https://www.youtube.com/watch?v=3EdZoIhAtXs

"Sir William Garrow—His Life, Times and Fight for Justice" available at the link

• https://www.youtube.com/watch?v=hL9LJIPxIJQ

"The Fieldings and the Bow Street Runners" available at the link

• http://www.youtube.com/watch?v=2rZfckouVKc

"Policing London—The Bow Street Runners" available at the link

• https://www.youtube.com/watch?v=H5l75BSJZo8

"The Thames River Force, Forefathers of Modern Policing" available at the link

• https://westindiacommittee.org/historyheritageculture/projects/thamesriverpolice/

"How Did Ideas of an Idle Poor Shape the New Poor Law ?" available at the link

• https://www.youtube.com/watch?v=WB_zFLF_CCg

"29th September 1829: The Metropolitan Police Begins Operating in London" available at the link

• https://www.youtube.com/watch?v=X-827WQ00lw

"Who Created the Metropolitan Police? Bobbies, Peelers or Blue Devils ?" Which is available at the link

• https://www.youtube.com/watch?v=WMGmPvMzaSc

"Why Are the City of London Police Separate to the Met?" available at the link

• https://www.youtube.com/watch?v=rZGD2PSHSZ8

"What Is High Policing?" available at the link

• https://www.youtube.com/watch?v=v8_gU-WR7J0

"The London Garrotting Panic" available at the link

• https://www.youtube.com/watch?v=KBXgEwRgSno

"Jack the Ripper—The Whitechapel Murders" available at the link

• https://www.youtube.com/watch?v=CH-u8ZKtiwc6

"Scuttlers of Manchester 1/2" available at the link

• https://www.youtube.com/watch?v=3hetQrocFFg&t=0s&list=PLyoIeZGzlHf2zxwPEaOcZ_9gxuKQ5nU9U&index=4&app=desktop

"Scuttlers of Manchester 2/2" available at the link

• https://www.youtube.com/watch?v=8YG9yCWTtNU&feature=emb_rel_end

A discussion of some of this material can be located in Joyce, P., & Laverick, W. (2022). Bringing History to Life—From 'Old' to 'New' Policing 1689–1839. *Journal of the Police History Society, 36*, 118–125.

Further Resources

Video "29 September 1829: The Metropolitan Police Begins Operating in London", available at the link. https://www.youtube.com/watch?v=X-827WQ00lw

Video "Who Created the Metropolitan Police ? Bobbies, Peelers or Blue Devils ?" which is available at the link. https://www.youtube.com/watch?v=WMGmPvMzaSc

Video (which consists of a powerPoint slide presentation with a voice over) entitled "Why are the City of London Police Separate to the Met ?", available at the link https://www.youtube.com/watch?v=rZGD2PSHSZ8

Index

P. Joyce and W. Laverick, *History of Policing, Crime, Disorder, Punishment*,
https://doi.org/10.1007/978-3-031-36892-9

P

Made in the USA
Monee, IL
13 September 2026

62973717R00225